SECOND EDITION
Masterworks
A Musical Discovery

D. Kern Holoman
University of California, Davis

Prentice
Hall

Upper Saddle River, New Jersey 07458

Library of Congress Cataloging-in-Publication Data

Holoman, D. Kern (date)
   Masterworks : a musical discovery / D. Kern Holoman—2nd ed.
     p.   cm.
   Discography: p.
   Includes index.
   ISBN 0-13-020543-5
   1. Music appreciation.   I. Title
  MT6.H574M37 2001
781.1'7—dc21   00-037359
                                          CIP

Editorial Director: Charlyce Jones Owen
Senior Acquisitions Editor: Christopher Johnson
Director of Production and Manufacturing: Barbara Kittle
Senior Production Editor: Barbara DeVries
Marketing Manager: Sheryl Adams
Manufacturing Manager: Nick Sklitsis
Prepress and Manufacturing Buyer: Ben Smith
Creative Design Director: Leslie Osher
Art Director: Anne Bonanno Nieglos
Interior and Cover Design: Kenny Beck

Package Design: Kenny Beck, Laura Gardner,
  and James Bruce Killmer
Photo Director: Melinda Reo
Photo Researcher: Abby Reip
Image Permissions Coordinator: Nancy Seise
Editorial Assistant: Evette Dickerson
Cover Art: Michael Gosbee/Image Bank
Media Editor: Deborah O'Connell
Web/Media Production Manager: Mike D'Angelo

This book was set in 9/12.5 Caxton Light by Stratford Publishing Services
and was printed and bound by Banta Company.
The cover was printed by Banta Company.

© 2001, 1998 by Prentice-Hall
A Unit of Pearson Education
Upper Saddle River, New Jersey 07458

Printed in the United States of America
10 9 8 7 6 5 4 3 2 1

ISBN 0-13-020543-5

Prentice-Hall International (UK) Limited, London
Prentice-Hall of Australia Pty. Limited, Sydney
Prentice-Hall Canada, Inc. Toronto
Prentice-Hall Hispanoamericana, S.A., Mexico
Prentice-Hall of India Private Limited, New Delhi
Prentice-Hall of Japan, Inc. Tokyo
Pearson Education Pte. Ltd., Singapore
Editoria Prentice-Hall do Brasil, Ltda., Rio de Janeiro

Contents

Preface   vii

Introduction
Hearing the Music   1

Grammar   2
Chronology   2
Geography   3
Languages   5

Composers and Performers   7
The Public   10

Interactive Learning   10
The Repertoire   11

Part 1
Fundamentals of Music Study   13

Chapter 1
What's Happening?   15

■ Listening Chart   *Gershwin: "Summertime,"*
from Porgy and Bess *(1935)   17*

Pitch and Its Notation   17
Pitch   19
Staff Notation   20
The Keyboard   22

**Rhythm, Melody, Harmony, Texture,
Nuance   22**
Rhythm   22
Melody and Harmony   25
Texture   27
Nuance   30

Voices and Instruments   30
Musical Instruments   31
Keyboard Instruments   34
Electronic Instruments   34
Ethnic Instruments   35

Tonality   35
Scales   35

Function, Key   36
Cadence, Modulation   38

Chapter 2
On Periods, Genres, Title, Forms,
& Schools   41

Periods of Music History   41
Genre   44
Instrumental Music   44
Vocal Music   47
Opera, Music Theater   50

Titles   52

Form   54
Sonata Form   55
Two-Part Forms   57

Schools   58

Part 2
History of Musical Style   61

Chapter 3
The Middle Ages & Renaissance   63

The Middle Ages   63
Plainchant   64

■ Listening Chart   *Plainchant:* Kyrie eleison
(Kyrie Cunctipotens genitor)   *68*

■ Listening Chart   *Hildegard of Bingen:* Kyrie
eleison *(c. 1150)   71*

■ Listening Chart   *Plainchant Hymn:* Pange
lingua *(c. 1264)   72*

Secular Medieval Music   74
Polyphony   75

■ Listening Chart   *Anonymous:* Sumer is icumen
in *(c. 1240)   80*

The Renaissance   81
Mass, Motet, Madrigal   83

- Listening Chart *Josquin Desprez:* Déploration sur la mort de Johannes Ockeghem *(c. 1497) 88*
- Listening Chart *Byrd:* Agnus Dei, *from Mass in 4 Parts (1592–93) 92*
- Listening Chart *Martinez:* Agnus Dei, *from* "Zapotec" Mass *(1636) 94*
- Listening Chart *Monteverdi:* Io mi son giovinetta *(1603) 98*
- Listening Chart *Dowland:* Flow My Tears *(1600) 102*

Chapter 4
The Baroque 105

Venice: Monteverdi and the Opera 106
Opera 108

Basso Continuo; the Ritornello Principle 111
- Listening Chart *Purcell:* "When I Am Laid in Earth" (Dido's Lament), *from* Dido and Aeneas *(1689) 114*
Baroque Instruments 116

Vivaldi, Bach, Handel 118
Antonio Vivaldi (1678–1741) 118
Johann Sebastian Bach (1685–1750) 119
George Frideric Handel (1685–1759) 121

The Baroque Concerto 122
- Listening Chart *Bach: from Double Concerto in D Minor, BWV 1043 (c. 1720), movt. I: Vivace 126*

Fugue 127
- Listening Chart *Bach: Fugue in C Minor from* The Well-Tempered Clavier *book I, (1722) 131*

The Suite of Dances 132
- Listening Chart *Bach:* "Badinerie," *from Orchestral Suite No. 2 in B Minor, BWV 1067 (c. 1735) 133*

Chorale, Cantata, Oratorio 133
- Listening Chart *Bach: from Cantata 80:* Ein' feste Burg *(c. 1734) 137*
- Listening Chart *Handel: excerpt from* Messiah, *part I (1741) 141*

Chapter 5
The Classical Style 143

Precursors of the Classical Style 145

Vienna 146
The New Style 147

The Viennese Sonata 151
- Listening Charts *Mozart: from* Eine kleine Nachtmusik, *K. 525 (1787), movts. I, III 155, 156*

Mozart and Haydn 157
Franz Joseph Haydn (1732–1809) 157
Wolfgang Amadeus Mozart (1756–91) 159

Classical Genres 161
The String Quartet 161
- Listening Chart *Haydn: from String Quartet in C Major, op. 76, no. 3* ("Emperor," 1797), *movt. II: Poco adagio; cantabile 163*
The Piano Sonata 164
- Listening Chart *Haydn: from Piano Sonata No. 59 in E♭ Major (1790), movt. I: Allegro 165*
The Solo Concerto 166
- Listening Chart *Mozart: from Piano Concerto in C Major, K. 503 (1786), movt. I: Allegro maestoso 171*
The Symphony 172
- Listening Chart *Mozart: from Symphony No. 40 in G Minor, K. 550 (1788), movt. I: Allegro non troppo 173*

Mozart Operas 174
Haydn after Mozart 175

Chapter 6
Romanticism 179

The French Revolution; Napoleon 179

Beethoven 181
The Heroic Period (1803–14) 182
- Listening Charts *Beethoven: Symphony No. 5 in C Minor, op. 67 (1808) 188–91*
Late Beethoven (1817–25) 188

Schubert 192

■ Listening Chart   *Schubert:* Gretchen am Spinnrade *(1814)   194*

Romanticism   195

■ Listening Chart   *Schumann: from* Carnaval *(1835): Arlequin—Valse noble; Chiarina—Chopin   198*

Europe After Napoleon   199

Paris: Berlioz, Liszt, Chopin   202

■ Listening Chart   *Berlioz: from* Symphonie fantastique *(1830), movt. V: Dream of a Witches' Sabbath   208*

Franz Liszt (1811–86)   209
Fryderyk Chopin (1810–49)   213

■ Listening Chart   *Chopin: Mazurka in A Minor, op. 17, no. 4 (1834)   215*

Leipzig: Schumann and Mendelssohn   216

Robert Schumann (1810–56)   216
Felix Mendelssohn (1809–47)   218

Romanticism, Again   219

Romantic Opera   220

■ Listening Chart   *Bellini: "Casta Diva," from* Norma *(1831)   223*

**Chapter 7
Götterdämmerung   227**

Verdi and Wagner   228

Giuseppe Verdi (1813–1901)   228

■ Listening Chart   *Verdi: from* Otello *(1887): Love Duet (Otello, Desdemona, Act I): "Quando narravi"   232*

Richard Wagner (1813–83)   233

■ Listening Chart   *Wagner: Brunnhilde's Immolation (Final Scene), from* Götterdämmerung *(1876)   239*

Brahms, Mahler, and Strauss   243

Johannes Brahms (1833–97)   243

■ Listening Chart   *Brahms: from* Variations on a Theme by Haydn, op. 56a *(1873): Theme, Variations I–III, Finale   246*

Gustav Mahler (1860–1911)   247

The Nationalists   250

Bedřich Smetana (1824–84)   250

■ Listening Chart   *Smetana: "Furiant," from* The Bartered Bride *(1887)   252*

Russian Nationalism: The Mighty Handful   254

Tchaikovsky, Puccini   256

■ Listening Chart   *Tchaikovsky:* Romeo and Juliet *Overture-Fantasy (1869)   257*

Paris, Again: Debussy, Ravel, the Ballets Russes, Stravinsky   259

Claude Debussy (1862–1918)   260

■ Listening Chart   *Debussy:* La Soirée dans Grenade *(1903)   263*

Sergei Diaghilev and the Ballets Russes   263
Igor Stravinsky (1882–1971)   265

■ Listening Chart   *Stravinsky: from* Le Sacre du printemps *("The Rite of Spring," 1913): Introduction–Les Augures printinières: Danses des Adolescentes   268*

■ Listening Chart   *Boulanger: Psalm 24 (1916)   271*

Part 3
Music Here and Now   273

**Chapter 8
Music in the Land of Plenty   275**

Congregational Singing   275

William Billings (1746–1800)   277

■ Listening Chart   *Billings:* David's Lamentation *(1778)   278*

■ Listening Chart   *Billings:* David's Lamentation *(recorded 1959)   280*

Music of the Slaves   281

Parlor Songs and Quicksteps   283

John Philip Sousa (1854–1932)   284

■ Listening Chart   *Sousa:* Semper Fidelis *(1888)   286*

Scott Joplin (1868–1917)   288

■ Listening Chart   *Joplin:* Maple Leaf Rag *(1899)   289*

Jazz 290

The Blues 290

■ Listening Chart   *Handy:* St. Louis Blues *(1914) 294*

New Orleans 294
The Big Bands 295

■ Listening Chart   *Ellington:* New East St. Louis Toodle-O *(1937) 298*

Bebop 298

■ Listening Chart   *Parker:* Lady Be Good *(1946) 300*

American Classical Music 301

■ Listening Chart   *Beach: from Violin Sonata in A Minor, op. 34 (1896), movt. II: Scherzo 303*

Ives, Gershwin, Copland 305

■ Listening Chart   *Ives: "Putnam's Camp," from* Three Places in New England *(1912) 306*

■ Listening Chart   *Gershwin: "Summertime," from* Porgy and Bess *(1935) 309*

Broadway 311

■ Listening Chart   *Rodgers & Hammerstein: "Some Enchanted Evening," from* South Pacific *(1949) 313*

Leonard Bernstein (1918–90) 314

■ Listening Chart   *Bernstein: "Somewhere," from* West Side Story *(1957) 316*

Searching for Our Identity 317

**Chapter 9
Getting Hip & Staying That Way 319**

Schoenberg, Berg, Webern 319

■ Listening Chart   *Schoenberg: from* Pierrot lunaire *(1912):* Mondestrunken—Valse de Chopin *323*

■ Listening Chart   *Webern: from Symphony, op. 21 (1928), movt. II: Theme and Variations 326*

Serial Music 326

The Emigration 331

The Avant-Garde 334

The Electronic Age 335

Electronic Composition 336
Synthesized Sound 337

■ Listening Chart   *Babbitt: from* Philomel *(1964) 340*

Rock and Pop 343
The Beatles (1961–70) 344

Fusing the Elements 346

■ Listening Chart   *Shulamit Ran:* Private Game *(1979) 349*

Minimalism 350
Serious Music Today 353

■ Listening Chart   *Tan: "Opera in Temple Street," from* Symphony 1997 *(1997) 356*

**Epilogue
What Next? 359**

Glossary 363

Anthology of Musical Scores 372

Recommended Listening 392

Credits 395

Index 397

Preface

*I*n the Introduction that follows, you will find the central features of *Masterworks* described: how it investigates the possibilities of integrated multimedia for the study of art music at the introductory level, and how it proposes a coordinated training of the ear, eye, memory, and mind for participatory listening. The objective is for students to achieve control of the materials of good music—from its sociocultural contexts through its languages and notation—in short order, to invest them with both the skills and commitment that encourage active citizenship in an acculturated public. My best advice, here at the beginning, is "Read on."

The second edition of *Masterworks* has been corrected, revised, and updated to account for the changes in our world since the first edition was readied for publication in 1997. Chief of these has been the rapid advance of Internet technologies, including the pretty well universal use of web browsers and, now, useful approaches to streaming audio. Accordingly, we have unified the appearance and operation of the *Masterworks* CD-ROM and Website to be virtually identical; take your pick. The success of the first edition made it possible to add a fourth CD's worth of repertoire this time out. I took this as the opportunity to include not only standard repertoire that simply didn't fit before (Hildegard of Bingen's *Kyrie,* a movement of Mozart's G-Minor Symphony, Tchaikovsky's *Romeo and Juliet,* music by Amy Beach and Charles Ives) but also some less familiar material that for one reason or another I just happen to like (a bit of the "Zapotec" mass, a psalm by Lili Boulanger, Tan Dun's Bianzhong bells).

The repertoire chosen for study is published on four Sony Music Special Products compact discs, which may be used either with conventional CD players or with multimedia computers. In addition, the program features a companion Website and off-line CD-ROM that work in tandem with the music CDs to help students learn the fundamentals of music. Chief among the electronic features are listening charts with clickable real-time cues, where users have essentially instant access to the corresponding cue point in the recorded music. (Real-time cue points are also given beneath the clef sign in relevant musical examples in the text.) This new ease of finding musical events on one's own affords a significant improvement in the environment for learning musical strategies: the ability, for example, to compare material in the second group of an exposition and corresponding recapitulation in order to hear the difference of key area—or, for that matter, the chance to practice well for listening quizzes. The technology also lends itself readily to classroom use, where the instructor can lecture and control playback from the podium while simultaneously projecting any screen from the Web or CD-ROM.

A principal objective of the CD-ROM/Website tutorials is to achieve some degree of parity among the students, during the early weeks of the class, in their mastery of the rudiments of musical discourse. Thus they can share common preparation for the historical survey that begins in Chapter 3. Students enroll in introductory music courses with every level of preparation and experience, from none at all to years of lessons and live performance; growing numbers arrive with the feeling that art music somehow belongs to the ones who've already had music lessons. *Masterworks* contends that disparities in background can be addressed most efficiently in self-paced autotutorial instruction, rather than in class or countless hours of one-on-one staff time devoted to remedial measures. The autotutorial units thus summarize the rudiments of music: staff notation, major and minor scales, a little harmony, and the instruments of the orchestra. They can be completed in a few hours—a weekend, perhaps—at one's own convenience, and our field experience suggests that the retention level is on the whole quite high. Throughout the course, students can test themselves, by chapter, using the genial quiz bank found on the Website/CD-ROM. Questions are designed to reinforce key concepts and attitudes as well as factual content found in the textbook.

For the rest, the focus of *Masterworks* is on the narrative treatment of the music and the cultures from which it comes: on serious reading for the pleasure of discovery. The listening charts and a few other materials included in the text duplicate the content of the electronic media in order to accommodate those who lack easy access to the required equipment; illustrations and pages of musical score have been included in sufficient number to evoke the appropriate visual surrounding. But in general we have made a systematic attempt to break away from the traditional textbook "look," where the author's companionship with the reader too often gets sidetracked in a page-by-page layout of sidebars and graphics. The text part of *Masterworks* is meant instead for linear reading, left to right, beginning to end. An early admonition is to read the book under a tree, or in your favorite quiet place, and a full chapter at a time.

Among the threads and motives that run through *Masterworks* is an attempt to identify the present generation of students as the focus of an age-old tradition of elders passing art and culture on to their posterity. Hence the choice of Josquin's *Déploration* on the death of his *bon père* Johannes Ockeghem, the illustrations of teachers with their students (notably the famous photograph of Schoenberg and his pupils), the selections by such noteworthy composer/teachers as Milton Babbitt and Shulamit Ran. In keeping with the technological orientation of the work is the suggestion that a new style period for music begins in the 1950s with the stereo recording and eventually digital systems that so altered how we make and receive music and how we think about it today. We focus on song as a particular identifier of American culture, lying as it does at the root of jazz, Broadway musicals, and the pop idioms. And nowadays, to be sure, there must be emphasis on the student listener's centrality to the very survival of art music, for it is a given that the future rests with the young and the young at heart.

The repertoire selected for study is mostly familiar fare, with one complete multimovement work (Beethoven's Fifth Symphony) and, where possible, self-contained shorter works. The point is not so much to venerate the canon as to touch the necessary bases in a reasonably comprehensive survey. Here, too, there are motives and threads, for example, the revisiting of passacaglia treatment in the finale of Brahms's Haydn Variations, and of theme-and-variations approaches in both the Brahms excerpt and the movement from Webern's Symphony opus 21. Fitting the material to four CDs and six survey chapters is meant to accommodate the 10- to 15-week academic term with relative comfort. But the text also provides entrée, under the rubric Recommended Listening, for the instructor to tailor the course to specific institutional needs and to vary its content in successive offerings. Updates, corrections, enhancements, and ancillaries are to be found on the Website:

http://www.prenhall.com/masterworks

We mean to keep *Masterworks* bright and shiny, to which end the author and publisher welcome the participation of the adopters, faculty and students alike, in contributing to its accuracy, look, and feel.

CKNOWLEDGMENTS

As for the previous edition, my thanks, admiration, and enduring love go first of all to my family—Elizabeth, Kate, and Michael—for the hundreds of ways they helped see the undertaking through.

My thanks, also, to my collaborators at Prentice Hall and the academic reviewers who offered such useful observations on the strengths and weaknesses of the first edition. These were: Katharine Boyes, Wake Forest University; Helen E. Campbell, Bishop State Community College; William Andrew Cottle, University of Delaware; David E. Feller, Weber State University; and Jerry H. Ulrich, Hofstra University

Masterworks was developed, and continues to be reshaped, in successive offerings of the popular Music 10 course at the University of California, Davis. Always there is substantial participation of the students in the class, majors and graduate students in music, and students in computer science. I am especially grateful to Donald Meyer and Mark Brill, who were lead teaching assistants for the course when the project was piloted and now teach it themselves at their own institutions. Brill, who wrote the *Instructor's Manual,* drafted the discussion of the "Zapotec" Mass in this edition.

I am grateful to Paul Hillier and The Theatre of Voices for fitting the two Gregorian chants into an already cramped studio recording session, and to Suzanne Elder-Wallace and InQuire for recording other medieval and Renaissance material for this edition.

At Prentice Hall, Senior Acquisitions Editor Chris Johnson coordinated corporate complexities, while Barbara DeVries managed production of the book. Media Editor Deborah O'Connell developed the Website/CD-ROM and Mike D'Angelo, Web/Media Production Manager, coordinated its production. At Sony Special Productions, Tom Laskey translated my ideals for the recordings into practical solutions. To all of them go lasting thanks.

Last of all, and perhaps most of all, both the publisher and I thank the many undergraduate students at the University of California, Davis who participated in the project with unfailing enthusiasm, eagle eyes and ears, and imaginative thought. Successive classes learned the material over three manuscript editions of the book and ancillaries, watched the unfinished charts and images emerge, and waited patiently as the computer elements were made workable. This is, and always has been, their project, and their book. We all had fun getting there.

D. Kern Holoman
Davis, California

Introduction

Hearing the Music

$\mathcal{G}$o read this book under a tree somewhere, or in your favorite quiet place. Leave the necessities of modern college life—your headphones and your highlighting pen, for instance—in your backpack. Read, and reflect for a time on art and on life. (In this particular book the best strategy is to read long stretches at a sitting.) Begin, as you formulate your attitude toward taking a music course, by pondering the components of the Good Life—not a two-car garage, I mean, or even foie gras and a good Bordeaux, but a voyage toward enhanced wisdom. A life surrounded by books and newspapers and magazines, doing good works for civilized reasons, rich conversations, intimacies of the spirit, museums and the theater. And, to be sure, concerts and recordings of serious music.

The central goal of a music appreciation course is simply to train the mind to hear the music: to participate in a work of musical art by following its discourse and reflecting on its meaning. You work at coordinating the ear, the eye, and the brain—left and right: knowledge, instinct, feelings—into a network of musical understanding. In our civilization, I am pleased to say, music is all around you. And whether your previous schooling in music is comprehensive or altogether nil, you can always condition yourself to listen a little more closely, a little more analytically, to the palette of sounds you hear everywhere, every day. The significant step to take, here at the beginning, is to commit now to a daily regimen of concentrated listening. With a little luck this will become a lifetime habit; in any event, the techniques you'll acquire will always serve your powers of observation well.

You can dive into the world of arts and letters anywhere you like, then follow your instincts and passions to the next step—always taking care to plug the gaps and fill in the blanks. Your interest in Leonardo da Vinci might lead you naturally to Michelangelo and Raphael, one step at a time, until you've begun to master the Italian Renaissance; a fondness for the novels of Anne Tyler might invite you toward those, perhaps, of John Updike, Scott Fitzgerald, and so on, until for some reason you find yourself one day roaring with pleasure at the stage comedies of Oscar Wilde. Similarly, you can begin your study of music anywhere, with Beethoven or Debussy or Scott Joplin. The important thing is to listen attentively and in detail, and at length to begin to remember the tunes.

Remembering how, say, Beethoven's Fifth *goes* is not so difficult, once you determine to do it. You merely sing the music back to yourself over and over again, adding a little more each time, until you know it. Singing to oneself is the key to musical literacy.

"Under a tree." The American composer Steven Mackey as an undergraduate student.

Nearly everybody, after all, has a voice. Sing to yourself all the time: in the shower, cycling to school, walking from class to class. Driving a car, with the windows up, you can sing as loud as you like—"*and,*" says one of my students, "no one *cares!*" Little by little the sounds of great music should become part of your inner experience.

GRAMMAR.   Obviously, there's a grammar and vocabulary of music to be learned, and the matter of its notation: the way music is written down. You'll definitely want to learn to read music notation well enough to follow a score, because only the score can reveal to you certain aspects of how things work. But this is easier to manage than received wisdom might have you believe, and you can master these things step by step as the course unfolds. We begin to treat basic music terminology in Chapter 1: What's Happening?

CHRONOLOGY.   It is equally necessary to develop the knack of placing musical compositions in their appropriate historical context, for those associations reveal even more of what the music is about. It makes good sense, at this juncture, to think through and consolidate in your mind at least a rudimentary chronology of modern Western civilization. A handful of dates could form the scaffolding:

www.prenhall.com/masterworks
timelines

800	Charlemagne crowned Holy Roman Emperor
1066	Norman conquest of England
1492	Columbus and the New World

1611	King James Bible
1776	Declaration of Independence
1789	French Revolution begins
1812	Napoleon retreats from Moscow (Waterloo: 1815); United States at war with Britain
1848–49	Revolutions in Europe; Gold Rush in California
1914–18	World War I
1939–45	World War II
1963	John F. Kennedy assassinated
1984	The Macintosh computer

You'll expand on this almost immediately and with specific reference to music, beginning probably with J. S. Bach, 1685–1750, or the dates for whichever composer is being commemorated in the year you take the course. The year 1998, for instance, commemorated the great medieval composer and prophetess Hildegard of Bingen on the 900th anniversary of her death. The 200th anniversary of the birth of the French composer Hector Berlioz in December 1803 is being recognized in festival seasons beginning in 2000 and stretching over four concert seasons.

www.prenhall.com/masterworks
introduction
geography

GEOGRAPHY. Consider carefully, too, the map of Europe (page 4), fixing in your mind once and for all time the location of its musical capitals, notably Vienna, Paris, and London. Figure out the difference between north Germany (Berlin, Leipzig, Dresden) and Bavaria (Munich) and the Rhineland (Bonn, Cologne). Note the central European axis of Budapest-Vienna-Prague and the route north from Berlin through Poland to Russia. The main trade routes of Europe, reflecting the geography of its mountain ranges and rivers, were established centuries ago, many of them used and improved by the Romans. Whether one traveled by foot, beast, carriage, or boat, or in later years profited from the steamship or the railroads that sprang up alongside the avenues themselves were age old. Now they are the autoroutes, autostradas, and Autobahnen.

Musicians, like missionaries of all sorts, are a migratory species. Imagine what it meant to the spread of musical repertoire for a Renaissance composer trained in the Low Countries to take employment, as many did, with the pope in Rome; or for the nineteenth-century pianist Chopin to come from Warsaw to Paris, or Liszt to visit St. Petersburg and Ottoman Turkey. Imagine the excitement, in the sixteenth century, of a book of music printed in Italy arriving in England. Maps help tell the story of how thought moves from its birthplace into the world at large.

Take a close look at the eastern seaboard of North and South America (page 5): Here lay the meccas for European performers in search of new publics—and, it must be said, of new income in what they often pictured, like everybody else, as El Dorado. They would begin in Boston or New York, go south to Philadelphia, Baltimore, Richmond, Charleston, New Orleans, sometimes Havana; then perhaps to Shreveport, El Paso, and as far as San Francisco, Sacramento, and Salt Lake City; and finally back through St. Louis and Chicago. In South America, Buenos Aires was an important point of call,

Western
Europe

particularly for the Spaniards and French. Here, too, are the ports of embarkation from which the American musical experience, notably jazz, went east and from which any number of gifted young Americans left our shores to perfect their art abroad: Edward MacDowell to study in Paris, Wiesbaden, and Frankfurt, for example, or Aaron Copland to study with Nadia Boulanger in Paris, and countless hundreds of singers and instrumentalists and conductors in pursuit of the virtuosity only Europe could teach them. And think with a shiver of satisfaction of the role the United States had as a haven for serious musicians when, in this century, Europe collapsed, and of the immense contribution those artists—Bartók, Hindemith, Stravinsky, Szell, and Solti, to name only a tiny fraction of them—went on to make to our lives.

North and South America

CANADA

UNITED STATES

Boston
New York
Baltimore
Washington
Philadelphia
Richmond
Charleston
Savannah
New Orleans

ATLANTIC OCEAN

Havana
CUBA
PUERTO RICO

MEXICO

VENEZUELA

COLOMBIA

ECUADOR

PERU

BRAZIL

BOLIVIA

PARAGUAY

Rio de Janeiro

PACIFIC OCEAN

URUGUAY
Montevideo
Buenos Aires

CHILE

ARGENTINA

LANGUAGES.   It is true, of course, that music is an international language, and thus the tongues that go with it are numerous indeed. For most of the Middle Ages and Renaissance, Latin was the common language of educated people; for most of the eighteenth and nineteenth centuries, it was French. Since father Bach, however, so much serious music making went on in Germany and Austria (and so much commentary to go with it) that it became essential to know German. Even in places like Boston and New York in comparatively recent times, German was the common language of music and musicians. Not until this century did English gradually emerge as a daily language of music; before then the only musicians to know much English were those who had worked in London. Handel's English was only passable; Haydn and Mendelssohn

Languages: poster for the first performance of Schoenberg's *Pierrot lunaire* (1912), treated in Chapter 9.

and Berlioz (whose first wife was Irish) spoke a few words of English. But that was about all.

And from the Renaissance forward, Italian—a relatively easy language, by the way—has been *the* language of music. It's from Italian that we get words like *piano* and *forte* and *sonata.* Italian still serves as the primary language for specifying the attributes of music: speed (*allegro, adagio*), nuance (*staccato, legato*), attitude (*passionato, furioso*), and instrumental effect (*pizzicato,* "pluck the string"; *con sordino,* "with a mute").

The bottom line here is that any kind of meaningful study of music requires you to commit to a certain polyglottism. The American habit of simply skipping over foreign words and phrases is inexcusable in any event and suicidal in music study. How difficult can it be to figure out what *Le Carnaval des animaux* means, or *Das Lied von der Erde*—especially if you have some paperback dictionaries at hand?[1]

Now a word of encouragement. You've been led by the culture in which you've been born, I fear, to consider art music a forest of mysteries and (worse) the exclusive domain of the gifted or prodigious. Nothing could be further from the truth. Music is for everybody; its vocabulary and notation are no more rigorous than that of many other dis-

---

[1] Answer: *The Carnival of the Animals* and *The Song of the Earth.* The word *Lied* will become second nature to you; don't be embarrassed if you had to look up *Erde.*

ciplines you will encounter in your college career. Just begin and be patient. The rewards are limitless.

*C*OMPOSERS AND PERFORMERS

www.prenhall.com/masterworks
composer profiles

What, then, does a composer do? Generally speaking, good composers of art music imag ine themselves to be ordering the universe of sounds around them into coherent, convincing expressions of beauty. Their craft rests on a technique acquired through years of disciplined study; their art springs from the tireless pursuit of invention and discovery. Art, too, is a matter of expressing oneself—one's dreams and joys, longings and secrets, inner view of cosmic order—and of forging personal links with the universal human experience. Composers don't follow rules so much as they adhere to their inbred sense of what is beautiful, a sense always conditioned by the society in which they live.

Artists, when they are students, most often begin by imitating distinguished predecessors. Gradually they break away from convention into a personal style, making their own unique contributions and achieving a stride. At this juncture, if they are both good and lucky, they garner a reputation with the public at large, and sometimes a measure of financial security. Composers who live long enough may evolve as the years pass into a period of relatively confident mastery of musical language as they perceive it, sometimes becoming obsessed with leaving behind them some magificent summary of their art (Bach's *Art of Fugue,* for example, or Wagner's *Parsifal*). All this yields for most composers early, middle, and late style periods—but of course there are any number of cases where that generality doesn't apply.

Shostakovich

A composer's working methods are unique to his personality. Some composers are fluent and fast. Rossini, it is said, preferred rewriting a page to picking up a leaf of manuscript fallen to the floor, and Mozart appears to have been able to keep the totality of a work in his mind's ear at every turning point. Beethoven worked with great difficulty, and Mahler revised compulsively, forever tinkering with bass drum strokes and cymbal crashes. Particular composers get absorbed by particular issues, say, text painting (how to reflect the words in musical terms: Think, for instance, about the phrase "all we like sheep have gone astray") or a search for "the long line." And, always, they live by setting themselves greater and greater challenges.

For every composer of exceptional genius there are, in every era, dozens of lesser contemporaries who labored honestly and well in their pursuit of musical beauty and who died respected by all for what they had accomplished. (I will pass quickly over the inevitable hacks, thieves, prostitutes, and opportunists of music history.) It follows that for every masterwork there are a couple of hundred humdrum compositions. In music courses such as this one, you encounter only the masterpieces. Each piece represents something of great value, and it's up to you to try to work out a definition of beauty that includes all, or virtually all, of it. The passage of time has a way of winnowing out the boring and the ephemeral, although you should keep a lookout for works that historical circumstance has unfairly allowed to fall from public view.

In fact, it's not always easy to say what distinguishes good music from bad and great music from good. Pleasing formal strategies, good technique, pretty sounds, tunes, and rhythms—all these are necessary, perhaps, but clearly insufficient for greatness. Greatness has something to do with daring, inspiration, and discovering one's unique voice. You can see it, for example, when you encounter the most gifted composers solving problems. Purcell triumphed over a silly libretto in his opera *Dido and Aeneas,* and in *The Magic Flute* Mozart makes of an impossible plot something of timeless wonder. Composers after Beethoven wrestled with the issue of how to go about writing symphonies after Beethoven's Ninth seemed to have cornered the market on genius. No two works could be more different than Berlioz's *Symphonie fantastique* of 1830 and Brahms's First Symphony of 1876, but each presents a distinguished solution to precisely that dilemma. Greatness, too, has something to do with engaging the universals—love, death, ecstasy, and tragedy—with our search for meaning in life.

Financial success, or the lack of it, is no sure measure of anything. Art music is, and so far as I can tell always has been, a money-losing proposition. A composer is lucky to find a post—with a church, a royal enterprise, or nowadays a university—that can provide a living wage, and luckier still to sell a composition for enough money to cover the cost of having it copied and first performed. The patronage of monied individuals committed to the arts has always helped. Patrons commission works from composers and see to the expenses of the first performance. Some examples, chosen from the twentieth century, would be Mr. and Mrs. Robert Woods Bliss of Washington, D.C., who commissioned works of Stravinsky; Elizabeth Sprague Coolidge, whose foundation paid for Copland's ballet *Appalachian Spring;* and Serge and Natalie Koussevitzky, the conductor and his wife (it was her family's money), whose ongoing foundation has commissioned hundreds of significant works, among them Bartók's famous Concerto for Orchestra. But while the inherited image of the poor starving composer is probably a little overdone, it's also true that few composers have ever made a fortune at it. Performers make more money.

Performers, that most captivating subdivision of the musical establishment, are the conduit by which the composer's creation reaches the ears of the public. Each generation has its idols and stars, musicians who have reached the pinnacle of success and captured the public fancy by virtue of their exceptional talent and very hard work—and who thoroughly merit their fees. Artists of this caliber come from every corner of the globe and every stratum of society and are measured by unrelenting critical scrutiny and by the inevitable comparison with the legends who preceded them. Today's phenomena, for example, include Luciano Pavarotti and Jessye Norman, both of

Stars: Seiji Ozawa, conductor

whom have risen up from the most modest family circumstances; the distinguished conductor Seiji Ozawa, born in Manchuria of Japanese parents at a time you would have guessed he hadn't a chance; and small-town Americans like Van Cliburn (Shreveport, Louisiana) and Kathleen Battle (Portsmouth, Ohio). Equally essential to music's good health are the thousands of working musicians the world over, prepared to give you their all so the great masterpieces might live in your own mind as vividly as they do in theirs.

Stars: Yo-Yo Ma, cellist

This cast of characters is always changing and bears careful attention. One of the thrills of being involved in music is to know that a prodigious talent might blossom in one's own community and to discover the work of the brilliant newcomer. Not so long ago audiences first listened with delight to Charles Dutoit and the Montreal Symphony in their ravishing recordings of the French repertoire, and to the Hilliard Ensemble in vocal works of the Franco-Flemish Renaissance. Names like Michael Tilson Thomas and Dawn Upshaw entered the vocabulary. Then audiences were introduced to Roger Norrington's performances of Beethoven on old instruments with what appear to be Beethovenian tempos; the work of Esa-Pekka Salonen, now the conductor in Los Angeles; and a wave of young violinists: Nigel Kennedy, Joshua Bell, Midori, Anne-Sophie Mutter. Their careers are living proof that classical music is alive and well.

One revels in the ambitious prowess of youth; one venerates the patricians of the art. Art music is life-giving, and great conductors or instrumental soloists at 60 may just be entering their prime. At 80 they can embody the spirit of their century and serve as windows to the past that molded them. The French composer Saint-Saëns, at the age of 81, embarked by steamer to give concerts in South America—a child of Romanticism playing before live audiences during World War I. Marvel at the violinist Yehudi Menuhin (1916–99), a celebrity from age 11, who was still conducting young people's orchestras in the 1990s with all the fire of a teenager. Or watch the video of Leonard Bernstein conducting his operetta *Candide,* recorded in 1989 a few months before his death at 72 and released afterward. It is such experiences as these that give all of us a sense of our place in the living history of art and culture.

Stars: Jessye Norman, soprano

Curious performers join composers in an ongoing commitment to expanding the repertoire, in turn expanding everyone's horizons. Nowhere is this clearer than in the thousands of hours of compact disc recordings made in the last decade, which now offer a range of listening opportunities it would take a lifetime to absorb. Of particular note is the early music "movement," where works from the beginning of notated music through much of the nineteenth century have been reexamined and recorded using performance techniques and instruments appropriate to their era. This has affected forever, probably positively, our attitude toward many of the most venerable masterworks. Where once we would have played Handel's *Messiah* with the biggest forces we could muster (a tradition extending well back into the nineteenth century), we now favor smaller performance halls, far fewer musicians, faster tempos, and crisper playing all around. Just how authentic a rendition of the past these efforts represent is a subject of heated debate, but one can hardly complain that the world of performers and performance has gone sterile.

THE PUBLIC. The public, too, is essential to art music. You are not merely consumers of a product but active participants without whom art can have little meaning. Too often the public is prone to whims and vogues, and it can be cruelly impatient with the unfamiliar. But to the extent that the listener can avoid the hard sell of marketing strategists who sometimes don't care what they sell, or to whom, and recognize changing tastes for what they are, the best interests of serious music will be served. The Vivaldi craze and Pachelbel Canon fever were on the whole a good thing; it doesn't matter if you developed your passion for Mozart piano concertos or Richard Strauss tone poems from the movies or even television commercials.

Go to every concert your time and purse will allow. Listen widely, and listen well. Devour good music. Above all, abandon the notion that music is a subdivision of entertainment, or constitutes passive leisure activity. Instead it demands your full participation. The rewards are well worth the effort.

INTERACTIVE LEARNING

The *Masterworks* package investigates the promise that ongoing developments in electronics can make a music appreciation course more exciting and more efficient than ever before. The study of music has always been a multimedia affair, involving lectures, reading of text, listening to live and recorded performances, and examining notated music. Nowadays with digital media, however, the conjunction of the personal computer and the laser-read compact disc—not to mention the exploding possibilities of the Internet—makes it possible for your listening to be guided at the computer, particularly where it involves cuing up specific musical events. There's no rewinding of tapes or wondering if you're in the right spot, and you can return again and again to the passages in question until you're certain you understand the point.

www.prenhall.com/masterworks

In this course you'll go to lectures and discussion sections as usual. You should read this book one full chapter at a time for a narrative overview of the course material, then return to it for reference and test preparation. (It's a good deal shorter than music appreciation texts often are.) Beware of simply memorizing the text's characterizations of how the music functions. Speak, instead, from your own experience of the work, gained through repeated listening to the CDs.

The computer program is a hypermedia application, which means the screens are interlinked so you can navigate through them in hundreds of different ways at the click of a mouse. The content of the Masterworks companion Website and CD-ROM has been reorganized so that both mirror the textbook's chapter organization. All material on the Website is also contained on the CD-ROM.

Please note marginal icons in the book that alert you to related learning opportunities on the Website and CD-ROM. There are tutorial presentations that can teach you the rudiments of musical notation and tonality and introduce you to musical instruments at your own pace. Summaries of background information you need to know about the repertoire chosen for study are available. The program also sends you to listening charts where you can jump to specific musical events by clicking with the mouse on real-time cues. Enjoy, for example, the interactive timelines that link to dozens of the great masterpieces of visual imagery. There are self-paced quizzes for every chapter and a variety of supporting materials for your reference, and, I hope, amusement.

The package comes with four CDs that contain the essential listening for the course; these can also be played on an ordinary CD player. To make full use of the package, you'll need a Macintosh computer or a PC with Windows 95 or later; both versions require 16 megabytes of RAM and an internet browser to function efficiently. The multimedia features require a CD-ROM drive attached to your computer, or you can use the multimedia stations at your school.

The point is to spend a great deal of time in this course listening to the CDs with the listening charts in front of you. You'll be enclosed in your own little world, which is the most efficient place for your brain and ear to come to an understanding.

If you don't have any access to a computer at all, you can use the listening charts in the textbook, which are virtually the same as those in the software package.

www.prenhall.com/masterworks
listening charts

THE REPERTOIRE. For the orchestral literature from Bach to Stravinsky, we most often chose from a repertoire recorded by Columbia and marketed as Columbia (and CBS Records) Masterworks, Great Performances, and (more recently) Sony Essential Classics. Columbia Records was the powerhouse of American classical music in the 1960s and early 1970s, having established exclusive contracts with three of the nation's best orchestras and conductors: the Cleveland Orchestra under George Szell, the New York Philharmonic with Leonard Bernstein, and the Philadelphia Orchestra with Eugene Ormandy. Their roster of virtuoso soloists was no less distinguished, featuring most prominently violinist Isaac Stern, pianists Rudolf Serkin and Glenn Gould, and cellist Pablo Casals. Szell's performances of Mozart, Beethoven, Brahms, and Dvořák express such intelligence, precision, and warmth that after they were made no self-respecting orchestra could ignore them. They have permanently affected the way we play and hear these great works. Much the same can be said of Bernstein's recordings with the New York Philharmonic, which burn with the tempestuousness of his middle years. You realize how much Bernstein is missed if you have the opportunity to hear him narrating Prokofiev's *Peter and the Wolf* and Saint-Saëns's *Carnival of the Animals* (featuring the young flutist Paula Robison and the bassist Gary Karr, both of whom became stars).

From the same archive of recorded performances we chose, too, some of the discoveries of the generation just afterward: the sensational reading of Stravinsky's *Rite of Spring* by Pierre Boulez, Bernstein's successor at the New York Philharmonic, and the lovely Mozart of the pianist Murray Perahia. Columbia Records became a division of the Sony Corporation in 1989, during the period of multinational conglomeration in the media industries. A major corporate objective of such operations as Sony and Time/Warner was to acquire precious libraries of tapes, films, and video with the multimedia revolution in mind. What you see and hear before you is a step in that process.

We selected from other lists as well, relying, for the Gregorian chants, on recordings made for us by the Theatre of Voices, as directed by Paul Hillier, and InQuire, led by Suzanne Elder-Wallace. For jazz we chose from the prestigious Smithsonian Collection of Classic Jazz. Finally, in addition to the music contained on the three included CDs, the text also refers to numerous other works for recommended listening. Narrative commentary and listening charts cued to specific recordings can be accessed from the Prentice Hall Masterworks website on the World Wide Web:

http://www.prenhall.com/masterworks

In general, our preference was for recordings born and bred in the United States, since these artifacts of the age of electronics represent a significant American contribution to our culture.

The young
Leonard Bernstein

Bernstein late in his
career

Part 1

Fundamentals
of
Music
Study

Chapter 1

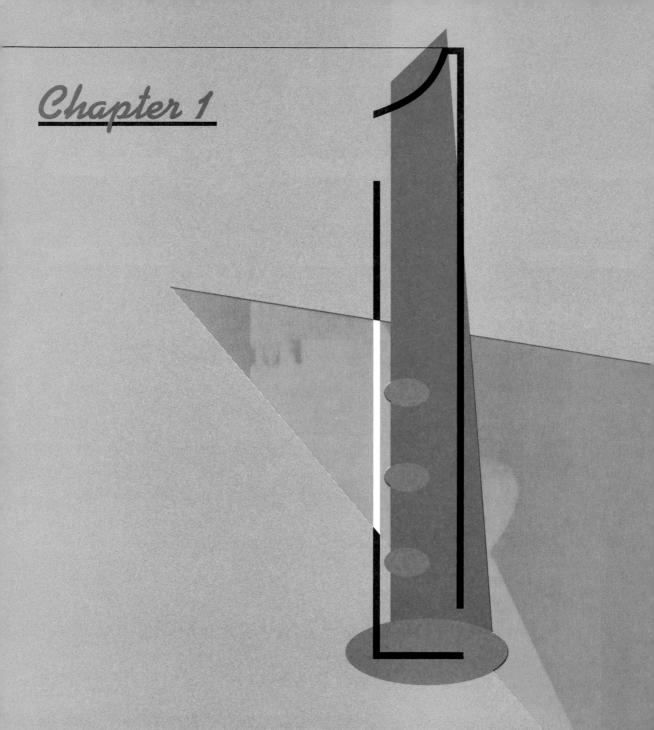

*W*hat passion cannot Music raise and quell?

—John Dryden (1631–1700),
in "A Song for St. Cecilia's Day" (1687)

What's Happening?

*B*efore you begin this chapter, listen to "Summertime," a famous number sung at the beginning of the opera *Porgy and Bess* by the American composer George Gershwin. Listen until you've memorized the song well enough that you can hear the details mentioned in the following text in your mind's ear, until, that is, you retain the music well enough to experience it for yourself without the recording at hand.

 GERSHWIN: "SUMMERTIME," FROM *PORGY AND BESS* (1935)

A woman named Clara sings to her baby from a room in a tenement house in Catfish Row, a shanty street of Charleston, South Carolina. As you think attentively about this wonderful lullaby, begin to ponder (that is, *analyze*) what's happening. First register in your mind the performing force, in this case a female singer and instruments—or, more formally, soprano and orchestra. Try to recall the bell-like twinkles from the orchestral introduction and the soulful interludes between the singer's lines. (The nasal instrument playing these you will learn to recognize as the English horn.) At about the halfway point comes the entry of additional voices in the background; this is the chorus making its presence felt.

"Summertime"

At the same time, listen to the text and begin to sense the rudiments of the formal organization. This number has a clear midpoint, where the orchestra restates its opening material; then the soprano begins again and a wordless chorus joins in the dreamy accompaniment. The words are different, but the music stays much the same. In short, she's singing the second of two verses, or *stanzas*, or *strophes*. Repeating forms like this one are called *strophic*. And at the end there's a lovely concluding touch where the soprano lifts to a very high pitch and fades longingly away. We call this kind of improvisation toward the end of a piece a *cadenza*.

An initial assessment of "Summertime," then, might look like this:

Introduction	Orchestra
Strophe 1	
Interlude	Orchestra
Strophe 2	Chorus enters
Cadenza	

One might extend such a chart further to account for the similarity of phrases that make up a stanza. You recognize, for example, that the music for "Summertime, and the livin' is easy" is the same as that for "Oh yo' daddy's rich and yo' ma is good lookin'":

a	Summertime, an' the livin' is easy
b	Fish are jumpin' an' the cotton is high.
a	Oh yo' daddy's rich, and yo' ma is good lookin'
c	So hush, little baby, don' yo' cry.

Or, a + b is stated, then answered by a + c. Now is as good a time as any to get used to representing musical events with letters of the alphabet. You are beginning to account for structure in music, and this way of thinking will become second nature to you. Structure is a substantial component of what's happening.

Noting the phrase structure and the performing force is well and good, and indeed essential, but it doesn't quite get to the root of why this sultry lullaby is so moving. The breaking down into parts is necessary, you might say, but insufficient to explaining its power.

If you already know that the setting is Catfish Row and the lullaby interrupts a crap game of sweaty dockhands in their undershirts, you also sense that it is composed, purposefully, to evoke an indolent moment of a sticky southern evening. I think the composer does this, first and most significantly, by the way the harmonies move; the undulation of chords suggests relaxation (as do all proper lullabies) and may well suggest rocking. Having gotten that far, you might observe that these undulations halve in speed just near the beginning, where you hear the bell sounds. Then there's the matter of those English horn breaks that so exquisitely elide the sung phrases, merging one into the other with a kind of tender determination.

These are the sorts of things you think about, and ask yourself, when wondering how a piece of music works. There are some hard-and-fast answers here (x form, key of y, meter of z). All the rest of how you hear it you must work out for yourself.

One might, for example, muse on the many associations this famous song brings to mind. It seems an elegant example of the riches African Americans have given our music, yet it was composed by a first-generation American Jew born of immigrant parents, who became a Roaring Twenties idol by virtue of his genius and diligence. It absorbs, too, the traditions of European opera and the Broadway stage and glistens with Gershwin's mastery of orchestral sound. I hope you will come to feel your brain exploding with the magic of it all, but also that you have begun to describe for yourself, in English words, *how it works.*

Listening Chart

 CD 1, TR 1

George Gershwin (1898–1937)
Porgy and Bess **(1935)**
 "Summertime"

For: Clara (sopr.), chorus, orchestra

Text: By Ira Gershwin (1896–1983), after a novel by DuBose Heyward
 (1885–1940)

Type: Opera aria,
 strophic
Meter: ¢
Key: B minor
Duration: 02:17

Catfish Row, Charleston, South Carolina. A woman named Clara sings her baby a lullaby. Two strophes, with dreamy orchestral introduction, interlude, and closure; the wordless chorus enters for the second strophe.

00:00	Introduction	Horn and bassoon, then languid clarinet.
00:05		Undulating figure begins in clarinet, then halves in speed (bells).
	Strophe 1	
00:14	a	Rocking motion continues in accompaniment.
00:27	b	. . . Elision in English horn, strings.
00:41	a	Same as before + English horn elision.
00:53	c	Reaches closure, with flute solo to conclude.
01:07	Interlude	Like the introduction.
	Strophe 2	
01:11	a	Adds chorus "oohs" and violin countermelody.
01:24	b	Richer accompaniment continues; note that the
01:37	a	melody is now doubled in woodwinds.
01:49	c	
02:00	Cadenza	Singer lifts to a high point, then floats downward.
02:11	Orch. close	Reminiscence of melody in low strings. (The scene continues.)

The listening charts summarize what happens in a particular selection by giving real-time (minutes-and-seconds) cues for musical events in column one, a simple formal outline in column two, and brief descriptive commentary in column three. For "Summertime," the listening chart is shown above.

There are charts of this sort for every selection treated in this package, both in the book and on the CD-ROM/Website. You can use the computer to go directly to each of the events described by clicking on its real-time cue.

ITCH AND ITS NOTATION

Note: People come to college-level study of music, like any other subject, from all sorts of backgrounds. Yet students in music appreciation courses tend to assume from the start that they're at a competitive disadvantage because they didn't take as many music lessons as the person in the next seat. This chapter summarizes the rudiments of music notation and technical parlance so that at the end of it everyone in the class can be at a common starting point. The first two autotutorial segments on the CD-ROM/Website, Notation and Tonality, cover the same material more leisurely and in greater detail. Nobody is likely to know already everything presented here, so read this chapter and at least skim through the autotutorials, if only to refresh your memory. Beginners will need a little more time but should not find the basic vocabulary more daunting than that of any other introductory course.

Back up now and consider the properties of some particular musical sound around you. *Volume,* for example, is an easily discernable element—whether something is loud or soft. Your ear might likewise be drawn to the time patterns of ambient sounds, for example, the cadence of a Xerox machine churning out copies. In this case you are noticing characteristics of *rhythm* and *meter.* Or you might sense intuitively that it's your telephone ringing, and not somebody else's, by a subtle differentiation in the *pitch* or *tone quality* of the bell.

Test your own voice for a moment, from the lowest note to the highest—gently: no need for heroism here. Or sing a verse of "The Star-Spangled Banner," noting its lows ("O, *say*") and highs ("rockets' *red glare,*" "land of the *free*")—a queer tune for group singing, by virtue of its very wide range. When you sing "The Star-Spangled Banner," assuming you at least try to manage the tune, you experience in the first person some extremes of the world of pitch.

Notation: Table from *The Continental Harmony* (Boston, 1794)

PITCH. A discrete sound known as a *pitch* is emitted when a string, a column of air, or some similar medium is set vibrating. The vibrations oscillate as waves measured in cycles per second, or *frequency.* If you shorten the string or the wind column, the pitch goes up; the pitch goes down when you lengthen it. A violin or guitar player shortens the string by stopping it short of full length with the finger; the flute player opens holes and thus shortens the tube; the trumpet player alters the length of the air column by opening and closing valves. On instruments with hammers—piano, xylophone, and so on—the player simply strikes the sound source of the right length. In each case, a pitch is generated.

www.prenhall.com/masterworks
fundamentals
pitch

In common usage, a "pitch" and a "note" are the same thing. Working musicians also use the term *pitch* to describe justness of tuning (intonation), or the lack thereof, as in "We're having problems with pitch tonight."

Analyzing the mathematical and physical properties of sound waves is part of the fascinating study of acoustics. If you shorten the string or wind column by exactly half, for example, the resulting vibrations will be twice as fast, the pitch thus twice as high. The interval separating these two pitches is called an *octave* (pronounced "*oc*-tive"); it is as perfectly concordant as two different pitches can be.

By dividing a string or wind column into other fractional proportions, a process ancient mathematicians were fond of demonstrating, you can generate smaller intervals and thus other pitches. The pitches so produced came to have the names of the first seven letters of the alphabet. At the eighth pitch (or *octa*ve), perfect concord is reached, so the series begins again.

> A B C D E F G a b c, . . .

Arithmetical theory and common practice among musicians are not, however, always the same. In real-life situations, because it sounded better, singers and players would sometimes round a pitch upward (*sharp* it) or down (*flat* it). Later theorists recognized that common practice divided the octave into 12 equal degrees, called half steps, that incorporated these sharps (♯s) and flats (♭s):

> Upward: → A A♯ B C C♯ D D♯ E F F♯ G G♯ A →
> Downward: ← A B♭ B C D♭ D E♭ E F G♭ G A♭ A ←

These 12 pitches, in all their octave *transpositions* (from as low to as high as the ear can hear), are in essence the musical alphabet.

Of course a particular pitch has other properties besides frequency: *duration* (or length), *intensity* (or volume), *timbre* (for example, the difference between a violin and a clarinet playing the same pitch), and *nuance* of attack, release, and decay. All these figure into compositional thought and your own response to the music.

Composing a piece of music, to be reductive and rudimentary about it, arranges pitches in time to create some artful or craftsmanlike sound structure. One can improvise a piece of music on the spot and pass it down for generations simply by singing it or playing it to one's offspring and disciples, as is the case with the Halloween song "Five Jolly Fat Pumpkins," composed (it is said) by Uncle Chreston Holoman and sung now, with the embellishments of successive generations, by his great grand-nieces and grand-nephews. In fact, that is how, over the ages, most music has been transmitted.

A more efficient mode of transmission, and certainly one destined to preserve the music more accurately, is to write it down.

STAFF NOTATION. The invention of medieval thinkers, staff notation identifies pitches according to where they sit in the lines or spaces of a staff relative to the pitch specified by the *clef.* (The word *clef* is from the Latin word for "key," as in key to a lock.) Ordinary staves have five lines. The treble clef spirals around the second line from the bottom to indicate it is G; the bass clef around the fourth line from the bottom to indicate F. Both are ornamented, highly stylized versions of letters that might be fashioned with a quill pen. We use the terms *treble clef* and *G clef* interchangeably, likewise *bass clef* and *F clef.* The advantage of these two clefs, in particular, is that they intersect at a pitch called "middle C."

www.prenhall.com/masterworks
fundamentals
staff, notation

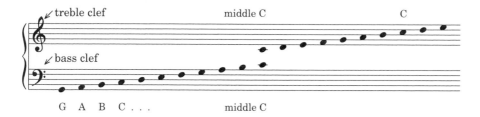

Staff notation

In addition to intersecting at middle C, the overall span of the pitches on a bass-treble pair of staves covers roughly the range of the human voice, that is, from the men's low G to the women's high E, F, and G. Indeed, the pitches from bass low G to treble high E were thought to encompass the very possibilities of musical pitch, the *gamut.* ("Running the gamut" thus means covering all the possibilities.)

Moreover, the combination of one bass staff and one treble staff works very nicely for keyboard music, where the assumption is that the left hand begins at the bass staff and the right hand at the treble. (In the Anthology at the end of the book, see the music for Bach's Fugue in C Minor, the Chopin Mazurka in A Minor, and Scott Joplin's *Maple Leaf Rag.*)

Notation that allocates a staff to each instrumental or voice part is called a *score.* The first page of Mozart's little serenade, *Eine kleine Nachtmusik,* first movement, appears on the next page. You'll see several different kinds of scores in the Anthology, all of them ordinary and representative. (Staves need not always have five lines, as you'll note from the examples of Gregorian chant in the Anthology on page 372; and you can devise notations that show finger position instead of pitch, called *tablature,* as in the lute part

Mozart, Eine kleine Nachtmusik, Movement I: Allegro (CD 1, TR 18).

of Dowland's *Flow My Tears* on page 101.) Whatever its notational conventions, the score is the primary written source for a musical work.

Staff notation, as it mutated and developed over the centuries, is a triumph of the human imagination. Even the most rudimentary music notation system must solve the complex but basic problem of notating both pitch and duration simultaneously; a usefully advanced system needs to show a myriad of other intricacies as well. Composition and notation are inextricably linked. Good notation makes certain kinds of music possible; other kinds of music require new notation altogether. The process is ongoing.

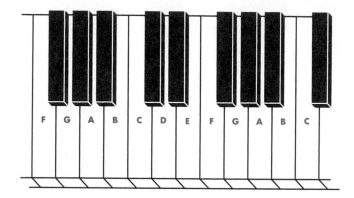

F G A B C D E F G A B C

THE KEYBOARD.   Over the centuries the universal standard for playing a score has become the keyboard, where each octave is separated into twelve subdivisions, or *half steps* (also called *semitones*). All modern keyboards—pianos, organs, Korg 01Ws—have the same configuration of black and white keys.

www.prenhall.com/masterworks
fundamentals
keyboard

Due to the whims of history (and the intersecting bass and treble clefs described earlier), the central pitch on a keyboard is not A but C. From one C to the next C on the white notes of a keyboard is a *major scale;* A to A on the white notes produces a version of the *minor scale;* using all the white and black keys in order makes a *chromatic scale.* We'll return to scales later on. For the moment the important thing is to get to a keyboard and acclimate yourself as to what it looks and sounds like. You can also practice with the sample keyboard in the autotutorial.

One thing to keep in mind as you begin to use a keyboard. When you play the pitch C at the piano, you may assume that, if the piano has been properly tuned, a somehow "true" pitch C comes out, and if you're a little more experienced you've probably heard that a proper A is a sound wave that cycles 440 times per second. (This is A = 440, the tuning pitch an oboist plays before a symphony concert begins.) But pitch as played and sung by human beings is seldom so set in its ways; it migrates up and down, and principles of tuning have changed a good deal over the ages. The important thing is that everybody agrees to a set pitch standard, that they "tune up" before beginning.

So much for pitch in the abstract. To organize pitch into music requires controlling rhythm, melody, and harmony.

 HYTHM, MELODY, HARMONY, TEXTURE, NUANCE

RHYTHM.   *Rhythm,* like pitch, is anthropological, an all-pervasive aspect of life. In its most general use, rhythm describes what the French composer Berlioz called the "vast and fertile" world of time and motion in music. Rhythm proceeds from the notion of *beat,* the pulse that divides the passage of time into set increments. You fix the speed of the beat with a clock tick or the pat of a foot or a visual gesture like the conductor's stroke or the nod of a violinist's head.

www.prenhall.com/masterworks
fundamentals
rhythm and meter

With a beat established, one can describe the lengths of sounds, their *duration* or *rhythmic value,* in terms of the number of beats they last. A particular sound lasts a beat, for example, or two beats, or a beat and a half.

Rhythm is notated according to a system of changing note heads and flags or beams, where each successive note value is twice as long as the one before it. (A complete treatment of rhythmic values, with notated examples, appears in a tutorial presentation on your CD-ROM/Website.) Dots add half a note value; triplets, and similar note fractions force the given number of values into a space generally occupied by another number, for instance, three into the space of two.

The speed of the beat is its *tempo.* You can establish this using clock time, say 120 beats per minute, or with some vaguer verbal description. In music terminology we use the Italian language for these general descriptions. *Allegro* is a fast beat, *adagio* a slow beat. A tempo of 120 beats per minute represents an ordinary sort of allegro. This is about the speed at which American military units parade (120 paces per minute) and thus the speed of a Sousa march. A football band, at that rate, can cover 75 yards of the field in one minute of play. We use a *metronome* to set tempo exactly: M.M. ♩ = 120 calls for 120 quarter note beats per minute, and if you set your metronome to 120 you would hear it tick at that speed. M.M. stands for "Metronome de Maelzel," Monsieur Maelzel having been the reputed inventor of the machine.

www.prenhall.com/masterworks
fundamentals
rhythm and meter

Meter organizes the passage of these beats into regularly recurring units marked by a strong pulse at the beginning of each unit. The simplest possibilities are *duple* and *triple:*

ONE two ONE two ONE two ONE two
ONE two three ONE two three ONE two three

Meter is thus a simple matter of establishing hierarchy in the beats. Once meter is established, you can talk of strong beats and weak beats, *downbeats* and *upbeats,* or even crusis and anacrusis; all are ways of distinguishing between the strong pulse at the beginning of the metric unit and the other, lesser pulses. We separate the units with bar lines and call each unit a *measure* (colloquially, *bar*).

Meters are identified by fraction-like symbols showing, on top, *how many beats* there are in the measure and, on the bottom, the rhythmic value of the beat; the c and ¢ (for $\frac{4}{4}$ and $\frac{2}{2}$, respectively) are vestiges of medieval notational practice. The *meter signature* comes at the front of the score just after the clef. Just as pitch symbols mean little without a clef to show what pitches they are, the passage of time means little without an established meter.

Simple duple and triple meters can be combined in *compound meters,* which have the usual strong downbeat as well as internal hierarchies of beat. The easiest is $\frac{4}{4}$, two groups of two, with heavy downbeat and semistressed third beat; $\frac{6}{8}$ consists of two groups of three; $\frac{9}{8}$, three groups of three; and so on. Note that $\frac{6}{8}$ and $\frac{3}{4}$ both have six eighth-note beats per measure, but the effect is quite different: $\frac{6}{8}$ is two groups of three with *two* beats to the bar; $\frac{3}{4}$ is three groups of two with *three* beats to the bar.

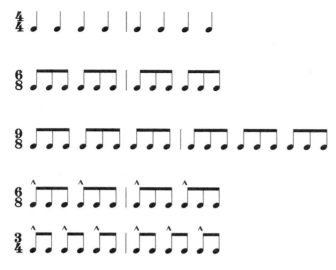

Sample meters

A meter need not be regular. In modern works you might see $\frac{5}{8}$, $\frac{7}{16}$, and the like. Tchaikovsky composed a lovely movement in $\frac{5}{4}$, where each measure consists of unequal halves of two beats plus three beats.

Tchaikovsky: Symphony No. 6 ("Pathétique"), movt. II.

Meter can even change every bar or so, and compositions occasionally try to survive without any meter at all.

The ebb and flow of time in music intrigues musicians of all periods and all cultures. Medieval composers dealt in overlapping rhythmic and melodic loops and in mathematical puzzles with rhythm and meter. African and Polynesian drum bands deal in metric effects of immense technical complexity. Modern multitracking and sequencing allows rhythmic patterns that would be impossible for live performers to accomplish. Train your ear to notice rhythmic device as acutely as it notices melody or form, for therein lies one of the secrets of expectation and fulfillment.

Now that you know pitch notation and the elements of rhythm and meter, you can read and perhaps write simple tunes, like the two below, without too much difficulty. Note that "Row, Row, Row," as a round, requires three lines to notate properly, one for each *voice*.

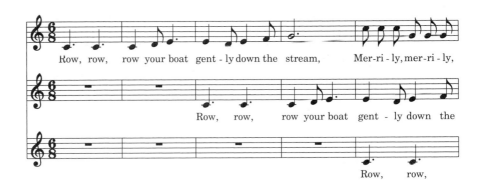

www.prenhall.com/masterworks
fundamentals
melody and harmony

MELODY AND HARMONY. The concepts of *melody* and *harmony* are probably second nature to you. Melody is the horizontal component of a piece of music, and harmony the vertical. Melody is the tune and harmony the chords. Melody concerns the left-to-right progress of a musical line; harmony, that which sounds simultaneously at any given musical moment.

Composers tell us of the thrill of discovering the melodic germ of a new piece, how it dominates their thoughts and haunts their dreams, how they sense it taking shape and growing outward in multiple directions. Their palpable excitement at having come up with a good new melody is something you may have felt if you've ever tried to compose a song.

Melodies come in all sorts of shapes and sizes, but whatever their structure, they survive best if well proportioned and singable. Some of the most memorable melodies simply follow scales and outline simple chords, fashioning a coherent whole from almost naive successions of subphrases and phrases. "Twinkle, Twinkle," for example, consists of three elementary phrases arranged in the scheme a-b-a. The famous melody from Haydn's "Surprise" Symphony, of similar contour and pulse, seems to propose an idea and then respond to it, in the scheme a-a'.

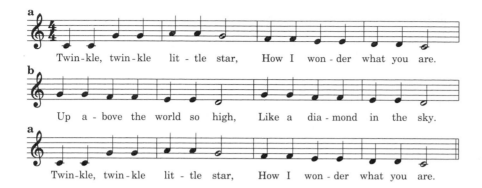

Haydn: "Surprise" Symphony, movt. II

We call the principal melodies in a larger work its *themes.*

Harmony supports and enriches melody in a succession of chords, which lend weight and meaning to the structure of the melody. Most chords are three-part sonorities called *triads,* built on the various scale degrees. The triads, properly ordered, contribute to the progress of a work of music by establishing sensations of repose and tension at appropriate places. Put another way, a melody properly harmonized can have a much more exciting musical effect than the same melody standing alone.

We call intervals and chords that sound pleasing to the ear (octaves, for example) *consonant* and those that are jarring or disruptive *dissonant.* It is the interplay between consonance and dissonance that makes harmony function the way it does and *tonality* happen.

www.prenhall.com/masterworks
fundamentals
melody and harmony

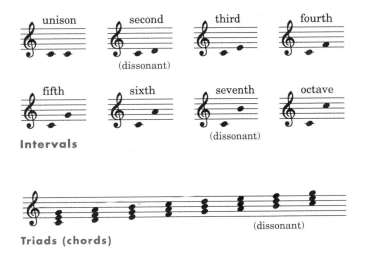

Intervals

Triads (chords)

www.prenhall.com/masterworks
fundamentals
texture

TEXTURE. Only the simplest kinds of music consist merely of a tune and supporting chords. "Silent Night" with its original guitar accompaniment is an example. More common is music of many constituent parts, relying for some of its effect on the various levels of interplay among the lines, or *voices.* Vocabulary describing how the voices work together is that of musical *texture.*

Start by distinguishing between *monophonic* and *polyphonic,* that is, between single and multiple voices. "Twinkle, Twinkle" without any accompaniment is monophonic, as is the old Gregorian chant of the Catholic church. "Row, Row, Row Your Boat" is monophonic when you sing it by yourself, polyphonic when others join you in a round. The term *homophonic* suggests textures where all the voice parts change pitches simultaneously, as in the first part of "Angels We Have Heard on High." Anything much more complex by way of polyphony gets into the realm of *counterpoint,* the technique of combining multiple voice lines in a manner pleasing to the ear.

Angels We Have Heard on High

Old French Carol

1. An - gels we have heard on high, Sweet-ly sing - ing o'er the plains.
2. Shep - herds, why this ju - bi - lee? Why your joy - ous strains pro - long?

And the moun - tains in re - ply, Ech - o - ing their joy - ous strains.
What the glad - some ti - dings be Which in - spire your heav'n - ly song?

Glo - - - - - - - - ri - a __ in ex - cel - sis De - o!

Glo - - - - - - - - ri - a __ in ex - cel - sis De - o!

"Angels We Have Heard on High," a strophic carol, is thus *homophonic* through the verse, then turns highly *contrapuntal* at the Glorias. The interplay of the horizontal lines is complex both at the two-voice and at the four-voice level. In the two upper parts, for example, it fills in beautifully everywhere you look.

Glo - - - - - - - - - - - ri - a

"Angels We Have Heard on High"—good counterpoint.

Writing good counterpoint is a skill sought after by all fine composers. The subgroupings of counterpoint are many and sophisticated. One of these is *imitative polyphony,* where one voice imitates another that went before it, often duplicating the first several intervals at a different pitch level.

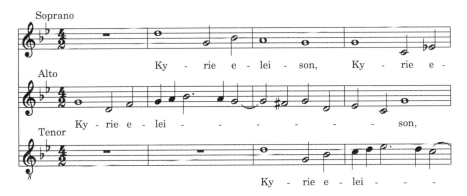

Kyrie eleison.   Lord, have mercy upon us.

William Byrd: *Kyrie eleison,* from Mass in 4 Parts

A *canon* is a stricter kind of imitative polyphony where one voice leads and the other follows exactly. Rounds like "Row, Row, Row" and "Three Blind Mice" are more subtle structures still, for they can cycle on and on indefinitely. We'll learn about the *fugue,* with its subjects and answers, as we go along.

Imitative polyphony is at the root of much music of the Renaissance, whereas fugal writing is a major preoccupation of Baroque composers, and of most later composers whenever they wish to prove their mastery of the great musical traditions. But good counterpoint is a requirement of all multivoiced music. In a Bach chorale, for example, you can hear how each individual voice part works pleasingly against the others, although the prevailing texture is homophonic.

NUANCE. Melody, harmony, and rhythm, then, are the essentials of notated music. Until relatively recently in the musical past, most of the rest—changes in volume, manner of attack, ornamentation, and even instrumentation—was supplied by the performers. What the composer specifies in a work varies by individual, era, and genre, although generally the closer to the present you get, the more the composer tries to specify every detail with precision.

www.prenhall.com/masterworks
fundamentals
nuance

Dynamic level is specified by abbreviations based on the Italian words *piano* ("soft") and *forte* ("loud"). The manner of attack is indicated by markings attached to the note or by Italian words that describe the effect, for example, *staccato* (short, detached), *legato* (smooth), or *marcato* (marked). Various kinds of *ornamentation,* the wiggles and curlicues that indicate the decoration of a pitch, can be specified by the composer, supplied by the performer, or a combination of both.

One of the most common indications of musical nuance is the curved line, or *slur.* Slurs are used for a variety of related purposes, such as to mark a phrase (a musical idea that belongs altogether), to show a player to connect all the slurred notes in a single breath uninterrupted by the tongue, or to imply changes of direction in the bow stroke to a strings player. You determine the precise meaning by the context of the slur.

OICES AND INSTRUMENTS

Probably the most natural and certainly the most familiar performance medium is the human voice. Voices are joined, as everybody knows, in *chorus.* For several centuries from the beginning of notated music in the West, the majority of art music was composed for an unaccompanied church chorus of men and boys.

www.prenhall.com/masterworks
fundamentals
voices and instruments

By the eighteenth century the typical chorus was divided into the four parts that are now customary: women (or boys) and men, high and low:

Soprano	women, high
Alto	women, low
Tenor	men, high
Bass	men, low

This is, for example, the distribution of the "Hallelujah Chorus" from Handel's *Messiah.* It is also the usual division for congregational singing, as for example in "Angels We Have Heard on High."

Any number of chorus parts is possible, and six- and eight-part choruses are not uncommon. These are usually simple divided parts (sopranos I and II, for example, i.e., "first and second" sopranos), although you may encounter the specialized terminology for the intermediate voices like *mezzo-soprano* (a "half," or low soprano), *contralto* (a low alto), or *baritone* (a low tenor/high bass).

Professional soloists classify themselves even further, according to the particularities and color of their voices and their chosen repertoire: lyric soprano, coloratura soprano, dramatic soprano, lyric tenor, heroic tenor, bass-baritone, basso profundo, and so on. Such terminology is part useful, part narcissistic, and part public relations; it need not concern you too much here. Whatever the qualifier, in the world of opera, the leading soprano and tenor are the stars. Heroines are nearly always sopranos; heroes, tenors. Villains and laughingstocks are often basses; the alto is a sister, or the trusted servant.

MUSICAL INSTRUMENTS. Familiarize yourself with what the principal musical instruments look and (much more importantly) what they sound like. The piano is an easy one, and you're likely to hear a good deal of it in class. Equally important is to know the instruments of the *orchestra,* that regal assemblage of players for which so much of the greatest music has been composed. Its instruments are classified by families:

www.prenhall.com/masterworks
fundamentals
musical instruments

Woodwinds	Brass	Percussion	Strings
Flute	French horn	Timpani	Violin I
Oboe	Trumpet	Bass drum	Violin II
Clarinet	Trombone	Cymbal	Viola
Bassoon	Tuba	Snare drum	Cello (violoncello)
		Other (e.g., triangle, xylophone)	Double bass
		Harp and keyboards	

Orchestras come in different sizes and instrumentation, again depending on their time, place, and purpose. But whether large or small, the orchestra offers composers inexhaustible colors and opportunities. Composers delight in showing their imagination and skill at deploying it; some—Berlioz, Richard Strauss, Rimsky-Korsakov—earned repute for exceptional *orchestration* long before their excellence as composers was universally acknowledged. (In general, though, you have to be a good composer to be a good orchestrator.) Whether they think of orchestration as deploying soldiers on a battlefield or simply the finishing touch to a work conceived primarily at the keyboard, composers know that without idiomatic treatment of the performing force, their best ideas will be for naught.

Two excellent works to introduce students of all ages to the orchestral instruments are *Peter and the Wolf,* by the Russian composer Sergei Prokofiev, and Benjamin Britten's *Young Person's Guide to the Orchestra.* In the *Young Person's Guide,* Britten takes a theme

Woodwinds

of the Baroque master Henry Purcell and composes a different setting for each family of instruments and then a variation for each individual instrument; for a finale he writes a *fugue,* one of the most complicated of all the contrapuntal modes of composition, where each instrument has its solo entry, or *subject,* as the intricate texture builds toward a grand final statement of Purcell's theme.

Brass

Prokofiev's shorter and simpler fairy tale assigns each character in the story a particular theme on a particular instrument. It's such a successful, clever, and memorable tactic that people ever since have thought of the clarinet as catlike and the bassoon as grandfatherly in a gruff sort of way. Purists, however, consider the Walt Disney cartoon version a curiosity, for it abbreviates Prokofiev's score, reorders some of the music, and gussies up the story.

RECOMMENDED LISTENING:

Prokofiev: Peter and the Wolf *(1936)*
Britten: The Young Person's Guide to the Orchestra *(1948)*

www.prenhall.com/masterworks
recommended listening

Composers learn orchestration not so much from books as by hearing live artists at work. This you can and should do as well, inasmuch as you're doubtless a member of a college or university community with a music department and student performing groups. Go to rehearsals, get close to the players, and keep your eyes and ears open.

Musical instruments are intriguing artifacts of their civilizations and cultures. The viols, crumhorns, and sackbuts of the Renaissance testify to that era's artistic tastes and objectives, as well as to the engineering prowess of its craftsmen. Violins, harpsichords, and lutes make a similar commentary on the character of the Baroque age. Some instruments go out of style or are made obsolete by technological advances. By and large, however, each of the orchestral instruments represents generation after generation of craftsmanship and imaginative effort to bring a good basic idea to perfection. Even for comparatively recent instruments like the tuba or concert harp, the saga is one of 150 years or more; the trombone achieved its basic structure 500 years ago—five centuries, half a millennium.

From one perspective, indeed, today's orchestral instruments are hopelessly anachronistic. Imagine dragging horsehair across catgut for a living, or blowing along a piece of grass into a cylinder with cranks and levers on it. People complain that the orchestra risks becoming a museum. But that is its very thrill: There is no more ravishing example of the past living in the present than the modern symphony orchestra.

You can, of course, form an orchestra (or band) out of anything you like: jungle drums, Hawaiian ukeleles, accordions. The thing that distinguishes an orchestra is its size—let's say some dozen players or more. The modern orchestra began to take recognizable shape toward the beginning of the Baroque period (c. 1600), when the violin

family began to achieve popularity, and when the ideal of variety of sounds, with mixed strings, winds, and keyboard, replaced the Renaissance notion of purer matched groupings called *consorts*. You'll find the orchestra for an early opera like Monteverdi's *Orfeo* (1607) to be a weird and wonderful assemblage of the old and new. Bach's orchestra of schoolboys numbered about 18 on a good day; Beethoven's orchestra, in the low dozens.

A Viennese orchestra around 1812 featured pairs of flutes, oboes, clarinets, bassoons, horns, and trumpets (and three trombones in

Percussion

situations requiring clamor or solemnity); timpani; violins I and II, violas, cellos with double basses following along at the octave below. Beethoven's orchestras add the occasional piccolo and contrabassoon, a second pair of horns, and from time to time military percussion. Composers later in the nineteenth century, following Beethoven, thought bigger and added more and more instruments: English horns, E♭ and bass clarinets, more brass, more percussion, and lots more strings.

Thus the full philharmonic or symphony orchestra, capable of playing everything from Bach in 1720 to Mahler in 1910 (and more), emerged. At its full complement it numbers around a hundred players. Of the three or four members of each woodwind section, one and sometimes two may need to play the auxiliary instruments like piccolo or English horn. There are four to six horn players, three or four trumpets, three trombones, a tuba, and a minimum of three percussion players. Of the strings there are a dozen each of violins I, violins II, violas, and cellos, and a minimum of six double basses.

Needless to say, an orchestra contracts as well for all sorts of extras (*ringers* they're called) for particular gigs. A performance of Gustav Holst's *The Planets* (1916) takes all the above plus alto flute, bass oboe, tenor tuba, pipe organ, celesta, and a full female chorus, kept offstage. Yet more than half the orchestral repertoire requires only three or four dozen players—hence all the goings and comings on stage between the selections at an orchestra

Strings: the celebrated Pablo Casals (1876–1973), cellist

concert.

KEYBOARD INSTRUMENTS. The most significant keyboard instrument is the piano, or *pianoforte,* an instrument developed at the beginning of the eighteenth century and admired for its ability to play loud and soft according to the player's touch. This was the result of a very ingenious mechanism, still in use, that allows hammers to strike against strings with more or less the same force the player uses on the keys. The predecessor of the piano was the *harpsichord,* which achieved prominence during the seventeenth and early eighteenth centuries. It looks similar to the piano in that the strings are strung across a harp-shaped lyre, but sounds very different because they are plucked by quills (called plectra). The resulting sound is sharp and metallic; it can change volume only by plucking more strings at once and tone quality only by using a different keyboard activating different kinds of plectra.

www.prenhall.com/masterworks
fundamentals
keyboard instruments

The *pipe organ,* the roots of which extend back to the Middle Ages and possibly as far as ancient Alexandria, has a bellows that pushes wind through series (or *ranks*) of pipes of varying construction and thus varying tone quality. In modern times, the bellows has been replaced by an electric fan. Both harpsichords and organs can use multiple keyboards to control the ranks of strings or pipes. Those played with the hands are called *manuals;* the feet play a pedal board.

Pipe organ

ELECTRONIC INSTRUMENTS. These synthesize sound by setting speakers in motion instead of strings and air columns. The first generation of electronic instruments (Hammond organs, for example) accomplished this with oscillators and vacuum tubes. The second generation of *analog synthesizers* used FM (frequency modulation) technology with transistors and printed circuits. The third, most recent, generation uses digital sampling technology. The revolution in musical thought brought forth by the "Age of Electronics" is every bit the equivalent of that which accompanied the discovery of staff notation.

www.prenhall.com/masterworks
fundamentals
electronic instruments

Synthesizer

www.prenhall.com/masterworks
fundamentals
ethnic instruments

ETHNIC INSTRUMENTS. Violins and clarinets and timpani are upscale versions of instruments found in just about every culture. Ethnologists have devised a system that classifies all instruments by vibrating medium: *chordophones* (string instruments), *aerophones* (winds), *membranophones* (drums), and *idiophones* (where the whole instrument is the vibrating medium, as in rattles, cymbals, and wind chimes). One finds lutes, for example, in cultures the world over, and double-reed instruments akin to the oboe are common through the Middle East and Africa. Even the instruments frozen in time on the vases of ancient Greece (see p. 59) are recognizable variants of a relatively few basic types.

Ravi Shankar, sitarist

ONALITY

www.prenhall.com/masterworks
fundamentals
tonality

The Western art music you will be studying is based for the most part on a system called *tonality.* Reputable theorists from medieval academicians to Leonard Bernstein have argued that tonality is rooted in natural acoustic laws and is thus a kind of normal process in musical discourse.

Tonality is based on the notion that certain kinds of sounds function in certain ways when set out over a span of time; specifically, chords and sonorities embodying *dissonance* pull toward resolution in *consonance.*

Once again, don't panic at the fairly rapid-fire presentation of material over the next several pages. Go back and read the note on p. 17. This same material is covered with more leisure on the CD-ROM/Website. The main purpose of covering it here is to have the musical examples set out for you to follow in case your instructor wants to cover these concepts in class.

www.prenhall.com/masterworks
fundamentals
scales

SCALES. The building blocks of tonality are the major and minor scales. Both major and minor scales subdivide the octave (see page 19) into seven scale degrees, one for each letter-named pitch in the scale. What is different between major and minor is the pattern of half and whole steps used to construct the scales. In the major scale, the half steps come between scale degrees 3 and 4, and 7 and 8. In the minor scale, the half steps come between 2 and 3, and 5 and 6 (with the 7 often raised as well).

*Minor scales show optional raised 7th.

That tiny difference in whether the half step is at 3–4 or 2–3 makes for a substantial and quite audible distinction between the quality of major and minor scales. The major mode is the brighter, more forthright, and on the whole simpler mode; minor is the more colorful, more complex, somewhat more complicated mode.

Street wisdom calls major happy and minor sad, and it's OK to adopt this orientation if you like. Kings are indeed crowned in C major, and funeral marches are typically minor. Only make sure you note the exceptions to this rule of thumb. ("When Johnny Comes Marching Home," for example, is in the minor mode; but perhaps Johnny *won't* come marching home, and going off to war is a melancholy event in any case.)

Scales composed of these combinations of steps and half steps, one letter name per step, are called *diatonic.* A scale where all the half steps in an octave are used is a *chromatic* scale. You're more likely to hear shorter chromatic passages used for color or to slide from one place to someplace else. The chromatic scale is of use mainly to instrumentalists, who run up and down it to perfect their finger technique.

FUNCTION, KEY.   The scale degrees themselves have strong functions. The degrees of most concern are the *tonic* pitch, or first note of the scale, and the *leading tone,* the seventh scale degree, which pulls strongly upward to the tonic. When used in the bass, the fifth scale degree, or *dominant,* pulls strongly downward, toward the tonic.

www.prenhall.com/masterworks
fundamentals
function, key

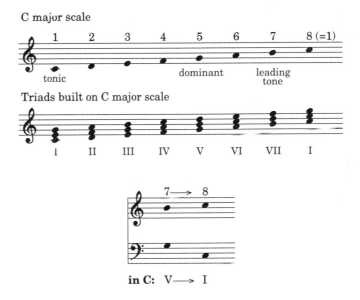

Likewise, the triads one can build on each scale degree have functional, hierarchical relationships with each other. The chord built on the first scale degree is, of course, *tonic.* The chord built on the fifth scale degree is *dominant;* it includes both the dominant pitch pulling downward toward the tonic and the leading tone pulling upward toward the tonic.

A simple cadence

Incidentally, if you combine the triads built on V and VII, you have a four-note chord (and not a triad) called a *seventh chord* (because the top note is seven scale degrees above the bottom one). This particular chord, abbreviated as V^7, has a very strong dominant function because the seventh pulls strongly downward, the leading tone strongly upward, and the dominant pitch is in the bass. The progression V⁷–I constitutes one of the strongest functional pulls of all.

These, then, are the two polarities of tonality: tonic (I) and dominant (V). They are modified by the other chords, of course—those on II and IV are subdominant, leading to dominant—but V and I are the defining functions. It is the motion from dominant to tonic that establishes a particular scale as the *key* of a work. You describe key simply by naming the tonic triad and whether it is major or minor: C major, for example, E♭ major, F# minor, and so forth.

Key is a serious issue in large-scale musical compositions, dictating in some measure the personality of the work, its color, and its possibilities. Composers choose their keys carefully. Mozart in E♭ major is an entirely different personality than Mozart in F# minor. Both C and E♭ majors are the Enlightenment keys of God and kings and triumph and victory, D major is the key of Baroque rejoicing and of the Romantic lullaby, and G♭ major is a good key for love duets. Think on it.

CADENCE, MODULATION.   You establish being in a scale or a key by beginning on the tonic and confirming it with a dominant-tonic progression in its own key. This progress of confirming key is called a *cadence*. Cadencing is the process of coming to rest melodically, rhythmically, and harmonically. The most common cadence is a simple dominant to tonic, V⁷–I, usually embellished with a subdominant (II) sonority:

www.prenhall.com/masterworks
fundamentals
cadence, modulation

If (and only if) you are firmly established in one key, you can then travel to another key through a process called *modulation.* The simplest way of modulating is to begin to introduce whichever pitch is different between the two keys. For example, between the keys of C major and G major only a single pitch is different; to modulate between them, the F in C major becomes an F♯ in G major. It suffices merely to sneak in the pitch that is different, then set the cadence in the new key. Once that process has been accomplished, we can say that a modulation has taken place.

You've already noted the theme of Haydn's "Surprise" Symphony (page 26). Look at the sly F♯ in measure (m.) 7. This begins to carry the melody, which began in C major (no sharps), off toward G major (one sharp). You wouldn't quite call this a full-blown modulation, but if you listen thoughtfully to the tune, you'll sense that it can't be over yet; it yearns to return to C major, where it began.

That's probably enough for now. Try to sense the big picture even if you haven't got all the details down pat. Controlling the grammar of music comes from adding fact onto fact and sound onto sound. Give it time.

What, precisely, you should be able to hear in a couple of weeks is the following:

- the difference between major and minor;
- what a cadence sounds like; and, little by little,
- the process of modulation happening.

Start now to try to recognize repeating elements when you hear them (the grandfather's theme in *Peter and the Wolf,* the phrases of "Twinkle, Twinkle" or "Summertime" that are identical with one another) and, by extension, those that contrast.

Additionally, it's imperative that you follow musical notation. So go through the musical examples in this chapter and the Anthology and do a little listening. Try playing the opening few seconds of *Eine kleine Nachtmusik,* first movement, until the score leaf on page 21 makes sense.

Chapter 2

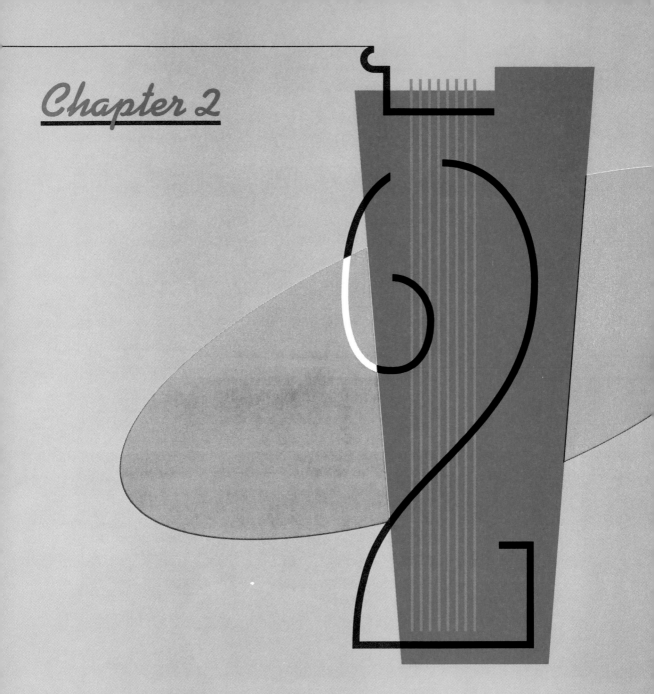

It will be generally admitted that Beethoven's Fifth Symphony is the most sublime noise that has ever penetrated into the ear of man.

—E. M. Forster (1879–1970), in *Howard's End* (1910)

On Periods, Genres, Titles, Forms, & Schools

I wrote earlier that you could dive into the study of musical masterworks wherever you liked. Sooner or later, however, it's useful to organize your knowledge along more or less conventional lines of communication. We classify the musical repertoire in several ways: chronologically, of course, and whether sacred or secular; by *performing force* (opera, symphony, choral music) and form (sonata, concerto grosso, polyphonic mass); and by *nationality* or locality (the Notre Dame School, New Orleans jazz). Cubbyholes such as these help establish connections and similarities from work to work, however individual the particular composition may be. Understanding how art works compare with each other, what *style* they share, is another major component of what's happening. A tidy designation like "funk," for example, says something about all these cubbyholes—time period, performing force, form, and location—at the same time.

What follows is an overview of these terms for you to keep in mind once you begin the chronological narrative. Return to this summary when reviewing for tests and to consolidate your grasp.

*P*ERIODS OF MUSIC HISTORY

Names of the style periods were mostly adopted from general history and art criticism, musicology having been a fairly late arrival on the scene. The names are broad and perhaps excessively general, but educated people know roughly what they mean and thus they have the usefulness of common parlance. Take a moment to register the names of the composers around whom our narrative revolves.

Now a chart like this raises eyebrows the minute you pause to ponder it. It starts so late, in the high Middle Ages, because that's when a useful musical notation was developed in Europe, marking the beginning of a certain kind of recorded music history. A more comprehensive look would go all the way back to the beginning of culture and spread its umbrella over many more civilizations.

Somewhat more troublesome is the matter of the period called Modern, which extends from the First World War to the present. Taking a very long view, that is probably OK. But I think everybody would now agree that the sorts of turning points that generally

Period	Date	Forms and Genres	Composers
Middle Ages *c. 800–1400*	800: Charlemagne crowned 1066: Norman conquest	chant motet	Leonin Perotin Machaut
Renaissance *c. 1400–1600*	1492: Columbus	polyphonic mass motet madrigal	Dufay Ockeghem Josquin Byrd Dowland
Baroque *1600–1750*	1611: King James Bible	opera concerto fugue suite of dances cantata oratorio	Monteverdi Purcell Corelli Vivaldi Bach Handel
Classical *1750–1830*	1776: Declaration of Independence	sonata symphony	Mozart Haydn
			transitional:
	1789: French Revolution 1812: Napoleon at Moscow, U.S. and Great Britain at war	piano concerto opera string quartet	Beethoven Schubert
Romantic *1830–1914*	1848–49: revolutions in Europe, Gold Rush in California	concert overture symphonic poem Romantic opera song cycle plus Classical forms and genres	Schumann Mendelssohn Berlioz Liszt Chopin Wagner Verdi Brahms Tchaikovsky Debussy
Modern *1914–*	1914–18: World War I 1939–45: World War II 1963: Kennedy assassinated 1984: the Macintosh computer	serialism ballet free forms plus Classical and Romantic forms and genres	Stravinsky Schoenberg Webern Babbitt Ran

define the emergence of a new style took place in the 1950s, with the dawn of the age of electronics and technology. The most common solution to this problem is to call the more recent period we live in "postmodernism," but this term clearly won't do for long.

Early music: a lutenist

Probably we will increasingly see the period from 1914 to about 1950 as the period of world wars and the period since 1950 as the electronic age.

Likewise to designate the whole of music from Beethoven's death to World War I—a fertile period in any event, and one connected to our own by all sorts of uninterrupted traditions—as Romantic seems unnecessarily broad. We might do well to do some subdividing here too, separating, around the mid-1850s, the first-generation Romantics from Verdi and Wagner, the two major figures of late Romanticism. (Chapters 6 and 7 reflect this separation.) For that matter, shoving so significant composers as Beethoven and Schubert into a cubbyhole marked "Classical (1750–1830)" won't really work because much of the artistic response to the French Revolution, and certainly the most influential work of both composers, throbs with Romantic qualities. Thus Beethoven and Schubert appear in the table on page 42 as "transitional," and their work is treated at the beginning of Chapter 6: Romanticism.

Note that two terms you encounter all the time, *early music* and *contemporary music,* are primarily chronological in implication, and both, particularly the former, encompass vast repertoires. "Early music," as the term is colloquially used, refers to the music of J. S. Bach and before, notably that which takes a harpsichord. Nowadays this is the domain of highly specialized vocalists and instrumentalists, but the early instrumentalists have edged ever forward in their interests, recently reaching as far as Berlioz's *Symphonie fantastique* and even works by Brahms. Probably it's best simply to enjoy the work of the "performance practice movement" and not worry too much about where "early music" starts and stops.

"Contemporary music" likewise suggests a repertoire that requires performers especially experienced in the sometimes extraordinary demands (rhythmic, metric, and for singers melodic) of twentieth-century music. Yet the term is properly reserved for music by living composers, notably first performances. One would no longer call Stravinsky a

Contemporary
music: the Kronos
Quartet with poet
Allen Ginsberg

contemporary composer; he's been dead longer than most readers of this book have been alive. By the way, it is highly inappropriate to use the term *contemporary music* pejoratively or to dismiss works the public finds harsh or difficult or simply doesn't like. New music, if it survives at all, is immensely successful.

ENRE

Genre simply means "category," and is a very loose concept based primarily on the nature of the performing force or medium, the most audible aspect that distinguishes one composition from another. Three umbrella groupings suggest themselves: instrumental music, vocal music, and theater music.

INSTRUMENTAL MUSIC. *Orchestral music,* and that for similarly large ensembles (bands, for example), is characterized by the size of the force and the fact that at least some of the parts are played by groups of musicians playing the same line. *Chamber music,* by contrast, has one on a part. In the symphony hall you will encounter the following genres.

SYMPHONY. The preeminent instrumental form of the eighteenth and nineteenth centuries, the *symphony* is a multimovement work of serious purpose for full orchestra. Usually there are four *movements* (individual pieces of varying speed and character, with a pause between them, that go to make up the whole). The symphony was the principal art form of Haydn, Beethoven, Brahms, Mahler, Tchaikovsky, Sibelius, Shostakovich, and many more. Symphonies constitute the bulk of the modern orchestral literature.

CONCERT OVERTURE. Composers sometimes write freestanding single-movement works they call *overtures,* which are descended from the orchestral overture for a stage

Instrumental music: the Paris Conservatory Orchestra (c. 1938)

work (i.e., music before the first curtain, intended in part to settle the audience and whet its appetite for what is to follow). Concert overtures often have evocative titles. Mendelssohn's *Fingal's Cave* is a rolling-over-the-sea piece having to do with a voyage to the stony lair of a mythical Celtic poet; Berlioz's *Roman Carnival Overture* evokes the swirling masses in the Piazza Colonna of Rome on Mardi Gras. Quite a few opera overtures are heard more frequently in the concert hall than the theater, the operas that go with them having been essentially forgotten. This is the case with several Rossini overtures: *The Thieving Magpie,* for example.

CONCERTO. This is the oldest of the true orchestral genres, going back to the beginning of the Baroque. What they called in those days concerted music implied the alternate opposition and coming together of contrasting forces, often one or more soloists and the full ensemble. *Concerto* was the generic title of such works. Typically there are three movements: fast-slow-fast.

Mozart, who was attracted to the notions of dialogue and social interaction implied by the solo concerto (and who was himself a virtuoso piano soloist), perfected the sonata-based Classical concerto over the course of his two dozen or so efforts in the form. Beethoven and his followers continued to develop Mozart's precedent.

SUITE (of Dances). Dance music having always been a prime responsibility of instrumental musicians, it was also one of the first instrumental genres, predating even the concerto. In the Baroque era, suites of dances were assembled in a more or less understood order and preceded by a substantial overture. The dances may each have their own national character based on the rhythm and meter of the associated dance step. The overture is often of the sort called a *French overture,* where a pompous opening in regal rhythms is succeeded by a fast, imitative midsection and short return to the opening material at the end.

Central to the genre are Bach's four orchestral suites and Handel's *Water Music* and *Royal Fireworks Music;* additionally, there are hundreds of suites for solo keyboard and chamber ensemble, along with Bach's fine suites for unaccompanied violin and cello.

Suite (of Incidental Music).   The nineteenth-century descendant of the suite of dances is the suite that has as its purpose to draw together the best music from stage works, leaving aside the inevitable dross—music for entries, exits, and so forth. Many such suites are drawn from *incidental music* for stage plays, from the days when every theater had its own orchestra and composers would be invited to write overtures, interludes, and songs and dances for the production of a play. Beethoven composed such music for Goethe's play *Egmont,* Mendelssohn for Shakespeare's *A Midsummer Night's Dream,* Grieg for Ibsen's *Peer Gynt,* and several composers including Fauré for Maurice Maeterlinck's surrealistic play *Pelléas et Mélisande.* Additionally there are famous suites drawn from operas (*Carmen*) and ballets (*The Nutcracker, Swan Lake*), and a few from the movies (*Lieutenant Kije* by Prokofiev).

Tone Poem (Symphonic Poem).   The *tone poem* emerged in the mid-nineteenth century, when composers were experimenting with ways to tell stories in their music. It is by definition a single movement. What distinguishes it from the concert overture is its greater length and the fact that often its subparts are similar to the standard symphonic movements. An early master of the poem was Liszt (*Les Préludes*); Richard Strauss was its most ardent later proponent, having composed tone poems in preference to symphonies (*Till Eulenspiegel's Merry Pranks, Death and Transfiguration*). Other composers excelled at less grandiose conceptions: Smetana (*The Moldau*), Saint-Saëns (*Danse macabre*), and Sibelius (*The Swan of Tuonela*), for example.

Chamber music is that intended for smaller, more intimate performance, originally in the music room of one's palace or the parlor of one's apartment. Any solo work is by definition a chamber piece. Otherwise, the number of players ranges from a pair to a handful, identified by number: duo, trio, quartet, quintet, and, in a few instances, sextet, septet, octet, nonet. The composer calls for whatever group is appropriate to the purpose at hand. A string quintet might have two violins, two violas, and a cello for a rich contralto register, or two violins, viola, cello, and double bass for a prominent lower one. A string trio is for violin, viola, and cello; a piano trio is for violin, cello, and piano.

A *string quartet* is always for two violins, viola, and cello. Quartets are the mainstay of the chamber repertoire, with strong four-movement forms similar to that of the symphony. Haydn, Mozart, and Beethoven brought the genre to prominence in the Classical period, and it has carried into the present, owing not least to the superb series of six quartets by the twentieth-century Hungarian composer Béla Bartók.

The implication of chamber music is that the players and listeners are known to each other and to some extent interchangeable: Frequently the composer would be one of the players. Thus chamber music runs from roll-up-your-sleeves music, like the trios Haydn wrote for himself and his employer to play after luncheon, to some of the most esoteric music that exists, including Beethoven's late quartets. There's a privacy to chamber music that is unmatched in other genres. The insomniac French novelist Marcel Proust summoned a string quartet to play the César Franck quartet for him late into the night,

Chamber Music:
United States Air
Force Band of the
Golden West,
Golden West
Winds Quintet

and more than one last will and testament calls for a string quartet to assemble regularly at an appointed hour to play in the salon, whether or not anyone is there to hear it.

The instrumental *sonata* may be for piano alone or for an orchestral instrument with piano, as is the case with the violin sonata and the cello sonata. For the most part these are three-movement works. The *trio sonata,* for two violins with cello and keyboard, comes from the Baroque period. Its subdivisions are the *sonata da camera* (chamber sonata) and the *sonata da chiesa* (church sonata).

At the other end of the spectrum, chamber music merges with dinner music ("potted-palm music," as it is sometimes called), serenades, diversions, dance music, and music-lesson music (*études*). Until halfway into our century it was thought that all cultivated people should express themselves through their own music making—certainly a precedent worth following. Besides, it made good sense to learn how to play the piano well enough to engage the object of one's affection in a Schubert duet, where the hands deliciously mingle and cross.

VOCAL MUSIC. Singing is the musical activity with which all human beings, from their infancy, are most intimately familiar. People sing unto the Lord and serenade the objects of their affection; they use song to lament the dead, celebrate the rituals of life, and lull babies to sleep. As with instrumental music, we distinguish between *solo* song and that for ensembles, called *choral.*

SOLO SONG. The repertoire of song is limitless in scope. Text and music for solo singing is preserved from the most ancient civilizations forward. The medieval troubadours and trouvères set down hundreds of art songs on the general subject of courtly love, while Bach wrote songs on pipe smoking and coffee. The Americans George Gershwin and Irving Berlin and Cole Porter became wealthy writing songs. And as you know, the musical repertoire of young Americans consists almost exclusively of songs.

In the nineteenth century songs for singer and piano with German Romantic texts are called *Lieder;* a connected series of songs is called a *Liederkreis,* or *song cycle.* An evening devoted to such song, greatly popular among Schubert's friends and acquaintances, was called a *Liederabend,* the forerunner of our modern concept of the voice recital. This repertoire is dominated by Schubert, Schumann, Brahms, Mahler, and Richard Strauss, the latter two of whom excelled at Lieder with orchestral accompaniment.

TEXT. The use of text in music demands that the composer respond to the words. Textual atmosphere can never be ignored. "Summertime, and the livin' is easy" requires a different approach than "Oh, what a beautiful mornin'" or "In vain I seek her footprints in the snow." Schubert sets his song *An die Musik* ("To Music") passionately, almost religiously; his song about a girl standing by a hedge-rose (*Heidenröslein*) is by contrast simple and naive. Nor can the sound, shape, or color of the words themselves be overlooked. In Latin church music the words "Sanctus, Sanctus, Sanctus" suggest something reverent and tripartite, whereas "Rex tremendae majestatis" ("King of awful majesty") calls for something regal and majestic, perhaps even terrifying.

Composers also note individual words that have obvious musical connotations, such as fleeing, sinking, resurrection. The creativity of composers particularly gifted with the ability for text setting—one often called *text painting*—is always to be admired, and very emphatic modes of text setting enjoyed vogues from time to time in music history. One such period is that (around 1600) of the English madrigal and lute song, where lines like "Flow my tears" and images like "Sweet honey-sucking bees" motivate the musical contours. A later master of this text painting was Haydn, who in his oratorio *The Creation* reveled in music for whales, lions, and the lowly worm. Nature music (running water, thunder, birds, not to mention shepherds, pipes, and tinkling bells) can be heard in all sorts of works, both vocal and instrumental. Orchestral accompaniments to arias and art songs also provide not a little serpent music (trombones and tubas) and an occasional snore or sneeze, put there to be enjoyed by the attentive listener.

It is the composer who selects and often revises the text. The words stimulate the composer's imagination and occasionally open his or her mind to formerly unimagined possibilities of design. Just as poetry is better suited than prose to certain conditions of life, your personal response, to the pangs of love or rattle of death, a kiss, or a palpitating heart, once you have encountered the world of song, is likely to be in part musical.

CHAMBER SINGING. An extension of solo song is one-on-a-part chamber singing for the singers' own amusement. The *madrigal* of the sixteenth century in Italy, with its secular, often pastoral (i.e., concerning shepherds and shepherdesses), and sometimes bawdy texts, was hugely successful in its day, spreading like wildfire to France, England,

Chamber singing (with lute and viol, 1635)

and German-speaking lands. These led to all manner of part-songs, sometimes called "catches" or "glees," very often to a low, not high, literary end. The music for "The Star-Spangled Banner," for example, is borrowed from an English drinking song.

Choral music. Through the Renaissance, as long as the Church had a predominant hold on art music, choral music sung in Latin by Catholic chapel choirs was the norm. The chorus was essential to Protestantism, too, so there is a great deal of fine choral music for the Anglican and Lutheran denominations. Classical composers dutifully carried on in that tradition but not with the purity of purpose encountered in earlier periods. In the nineteenth century the chorus (like every other institution) became a political and social instrument. Huge glee clubs and oratorio societies were constituted throughout the world, and these and their descendants still exist today.

Mass. Mass is a public church service of the Roman Catholic church, during which the Last Supper is commemorated in the form of holy communion. The music that composers wrote to these ancient and honorable texts is called the *mass.* If the movement titles—Kyrie, Gloria, Credo, Sanctus, Agnus Dei—are not familiar to you now, they will be soon.

Requiem. The Requiem is the Roman Catholic mass for the dead. Some of the sung texts (Kyrie, Sanctus, Agnus Dei) come from the regular mass; others are particular to the funeral occasion. Of these latter the most important is the *Dies irae,* a text centering on terrifying images of Judgment Day. The words "Requiem aeternam" ("Eternal rest" . . . grant unto them, O Lord) begin the service and recur throughout it.

Motet. One of the oldest terms associated with composed art music, *motet* means different things at different periods. For the moment, think of it as an unaccompanied vocal work, usually in Latin, to a sacred text. Most motets are from the Renaissance.

Cantata. Usually a work with soloists, chorus, and orchestra to a religious text, the *cantata* often includes the singing of well-known hymn tunes (chorales). Bach was the great master of this genre, having been required by his appointment to perform one or more a week; his cantatas are Protestant works for performance in a relatively small church. More generally, a *cantata* is any multimovement sung work with instrumental accompaniment. Handel, in his youth, wrote dozens of solo cantatas with secular Italian texts.

Oratorio.   The *oratorio* is a much larger work for soloists, chorus, and orchestra that recounts a Bible story. Handel developed the modern version, for the English paying public, with such works as *Messiah* and *Israel in Egypt;* his principal successors were Haydn (*The Creation*) and Mendelssohn (*Elijah*). Thus the so-called English oratorio is a curious genre because its major composers were foreigners.

Anthem.   The *anthem,* a one-movement composition for unaccompanied choir, is the Anglican counterpart of the Latin motet from post-Reformation England. Many of the texts are chosen from the Psalms, often with high poetic imagery:

> As the hart panteth after the water brooks,
> So panteth my soul after Thee, O God. (Psalm 42:1)

National anthem is a more specialized term; the tone is solemn, and national anthems often venerate military victory, as does the American one.

OPERA, MUSIC THEATER.   Music is a vital component of most theater, including Greek tragedy and Shakespeare, both of which are full of song texts and cues for music that hasn't come down to us. It was in an effort to imitate the Greeks, in fact, that Italian humanists cultivated opera at the beginning of the Baroque. Since then, opera has become a vital, thriving form of musical expression, especially interesting in the study of the humanities because it represents a blending of literature, theater, and music. Common to virtually all opera is the use of soloists and ensembles, orchestra, dance, and sets and costumes. Most operas are sung from beginning to end, without spoken dialogue. Operas come in both tragic and comic forms as well as various in-between solutions. You will read later of the difference between the speechlike *recitative* and the solo *aria* that follows. The non-solo movements are named for the number of singers participating, as in the love duet, the sextet from *Lucia di Lammermoor,* the Anvil Chorus from *Il Trovatore,* and the Pilgrims' Chorus from *Tannhäuser.* An opera begins with the *overture,* an orchestral curtain-raiser.

For the moment, you can best envisage opera as coming in generations: Baroque opera, mostly in Italian; Mozart opera; early Romantic opera, notably the work of the Italians Rossini, Donizetti, and Bellini; Verdi and Wagner in the mid-nineteenth century; and modern opera.

The text of an opera is called its *libretto* (because it is sold to the public as a "little book"). The text author is the *librettist,* who works in partnership with the composer. With opera there is always the question of whether or not the text should be heard in its original language or translated into the language of the audience. It's a controversy of many nooks and crannies but generally boils down to two contrasting positions. Some say the very essence of opera comes in understanding the words; others hold that only in its original language can the composer's musical treatment of the words have its full power. Since opera began in Italy, Italian has been the lingua franca of the musical stage, such that for two centuries Italian opera companies thrived in the capitals of Europe

Theater music: Martha Graham in Copland's ballet *Appalachian Spring*

whatever their native language. By the nineteenth century, taste and nationalistic sentiment strongly favored the native language and particular customs of the local house.

Careers have been made translating the masterworks of opera into modern, singable English. The San Francisco conductor Donald Pippin, for instance, specializes in exceptionally witty translations for his Pocket Opera. He calls Mozart's *Die Entführung aus dem Serail* "Yanked from the Harem" (and makes the hero a Yankee). The more sober translation is "The Abduction from the Seraglio."

Nowadays there are better alternatives. Opera houses, following the lead of cinema and television, often project translated supertitles over the proscenium, a nice tactic that allows you to ignore them entirely if you like. For the present, try to develop the knack of following both the text and the translation as closely as possible, until the sound and meaning of the composer's language become second nature. A good written translation will put as many critical words in parallel position as possible:

DESDEMONA:

Quando narravi l'esule tua vita	When you recounted the exile of your life
e i fieri eventi e i lunghi tuoi dolor,	and of daring deeds and your long suffering,
ed io t'udia coll'anima rapita	and I listened, with soul ravished
in quei spaventi e coll'estasi nel cor.	by those terrors, and with ecstasy in my heart.

—Verdi: *Otello*

Ballet. A closely related form of music theater is the ballet, which had its roots in the same stage spectacles that led to opera. Dance is a significant component of a great deal of the operatic repertoire, and opera companies keep ballet troupes on the staff. Freestanding ballet achieved a particular vogue in France in the nineteenth century—think of the beautiful Degas paintings—and in Russia just afterward (Tchaikovsky's *Sleeping Beauty, Swan Lake, The Nutcracker*). In the twentieth century, ballet has been one of the major components of modernist art; examples include ballets by Stravinsky (*The Firebird, Petrushka, The Rite of Spring*), Copland (*Rodeo, Billy the Kid, Appalachian Spring*), and Prokofiev (*Romeo and Juliet*). Ballet today is passing through a transitional phase, owing in part to the deaths from old age of central choreographers George Balanchine and Martha Graham and the devastating effect of AIDS on the younger generation

(Robert Joffrey, for instance). Less new music is composed for the ballet today than just a few decades ago. Nevertheless, dance troupes continue to thrive in the United States and abroad.

The term *pas de deux* (*trois, quatre*) refers to a movement for two (three, four) solo dancers.

OTHER MUSIC THEATER. We know the thriving theater of the Middle Ages had a great deal of music associated with it. Music for *mystery plays* and other church dramas illustrating biblical stories has been preserved, as well as a little secular music theater (notably a piece called *The Play of Robin and Marion*). Later centuries, too, had many forms of musico-theatric diversion: masques in Stuart England (costume-and-machinery pieces where at the end all were invited to dance), madrigal-comedies in Italian, and, for the common people, operetta, lower comedy, and stage vulgarities of all sorts.

In the United States in this century, a significant mingling of entertainment and art music developed in New York on the Broadway stage (and later extended in Hollywood films). It's not always easy to formulate a dispassionate critical position on music that makes so much money and is so popular, and thus Rodgers and Hammerstein (*Oklahoma!, The Sound of Music*) and their rivals are sometimes regarded in art-music circles with disdain. A rather less snooty view would recognize the centrality of Broadway show music to America's musical identity, certainly in the case of such distinguished composers as George Gershwin (*Porgy and Bess*) and Leonard Bernstein (*Candide, West Side Story*).

TITLES

Musical works carry either generic titles—Symphony, String Quartet—or more specific ones, often based on the story or text: *The Creation, St. John Passion, Fingal's Cave, Peter and the Wolf.*

Generic titles require something a little more specific if they are to be of much use, traditionally the key and numeric position among works the composer wrote in that genre:

Brahms: Symphony No. 2 in D Major

The *opus number* is usually assigned to a work by the publisher and tends to suggest position of the work in the composer's overall published output:

Beethoven: Symphony No. 5 in C Minor, op. 67

Opus (abbreviated *op.*) simply means "accomplishment" or "work." You can imagine that for prolific composers these systems could make for all sorts of confusions: how to account for an unpublished symphony, for example, or what to do if (as in the case of Haydn) more than a hundred symphonies were numbered one way in one country and another way in the next. Or if the traditional numberings were later shown to be out of historical order, or if Haydn didn't write one of those works after all. Scholars dealing with these issues have assembled complete catalogs of composers' works, and for several of the major composers citations to these catalogs are often given in the title:

> Mozart: Symphony No. 40 in G Minor, K. 550
> Bach: Concerto for Two Violins in D Minor, BWV 1043

The K. refers to a Mozart catalog by Köchel (pronounced "Kersh-el"), the BWV to a *Bach-Werke-Verzeichnis,* an Index of Bach's works by a scholar named Schmieder. More later about these intricacies.

Finally, many works in the central repertoire carry familiar names, usually given in parentheses:

> Mozart: Symphony No. 41 in C Major, K. 551 ("Jupiter")
> Beethoven: Piano Sonata No. 14 in C♯ Minor, op. 27, no. 2 ("Moonlight")
> Beethoven: Symphony No. 3 in E♭ Major, op. 55 ("Eroica")

Works get their nicknames in various ways. Mozart's "Jupiter" Symphony was, apparently, so called by a famous British impresario. "Eroica" ("heroic") was Beethoven's own title, replacing the original dedication to Napoleon, but no one knows for sure why Beethoven's Fifth Piano Concerto is called "Emperor." The Czech composer Antonín Dvořák, after a sojourn in the United States, subtitled his E-Minor Symphony "From the New World," and thus everybody calls it the New World Symphony. Schubert's "Unfinished" Symphony (No. 8) is so called for obvious reasons, but do not imagine that death was the specific cause, for Schubert lived to write a Ninth Symphony, which is safe and sound (and very long).

MOVEMENT. The term *movement,* which crops up before you know it in musical commentary, is used to describe the self-contained, more or less freestanding pieces that make up a longer work. It's so called because one of the things that most characterizes the movement is its tempo marking. A symphony typically has four movements:

Darius Milhaud: Symphony No. 12 ("Rurale")
Pastoral
Vif et gai
Paisible
Lumineux

(Milhaud, pronounced "Mee-*yo,*" was a twentieth-century French composer who in later years commuted between his posts at the Paris Conservatoire and Mills College in California.) More often than not there's a very obvious space between movements. The music comes to a full halt, the tension lessens, the artists and conductor pause to mop brows, latecomers are sometimes seated, there may be some

Milhaud

retuning. Occasionally movements are played in sequence without pause, as you'll discover to thrilling effect when you first encounter Beethoven's Fifth.

Hence, for most purposes, "movement" is equivalent to the more colloquial "number." In serious musical discourse, however, we reserve "number" for a movement in a very long work like an opera or oratorio where the composer or publisher has actually enumerated the movements:

Handel: from *Messiah*

42	Recitative	He that dwelleth in heaven
43	Aria	Thou shalt break them
44	Chorus	Hallelujah!

In the Romantic period we encounter the designation "number opera" for an opera with more or less freestanding movements, as opposed to "continuous-flow" operas like those of the mature Wagner.

 ORM

After examining "Summertime" at the beginning of Chapter 1, we concluded that the movement was strophic with framing orchestral passages and a short cadenza toward the end. Those observations relate to *form,* the strategies of design and structure the composer uses to create a musical work that is intellectually pleasing, both overall and in specific detail.

Any work of art is pieced together by the artist one detail at a time. However clear one's preliminary vision of some great achievement of the mind, it must be built from scratch. In music the fundamental options open to a composer reaching the end of a passage of music are to repeat it, to vary it, or to compose something in contrast to it. Out of such decisions come the internal relationships that provide the structure of the work. Often, of course, the composer is following some sort of prearranged overall plan, much as the poet might begin with the notion of composing a sonnet. But the net result is seldom quite what was first envisaged, owing to the kinds of discoveries one can only make once composing has begun.

Most forms boil down to doing one thing, doing something else, then coming back to reiterate the original idea. (An exception to this is music that goes straight through without major internal repeats, called *through-composed* music.) Form may be no more than a loose set of guidelines or a scaffolding or the mere feeling for frame, balance, and closing off—simply a satisfying way of beginning, continuing, and ending.

Sensitivity to form, particularly to big sectional repeats, is an important skill to develop because it gives you an avenue into the work, a place to begin your analysis. Most commonly we use uppercase letters to denote formal sections, usually A for the first section, new letters for contrasting sections, and prime marks for varied repetitions, perhaps A-B-A' or A-B-A-C-A-B-A. This kind of symbolic representation is of necessity very general and loose. In the second of the examples just given, for example, it would be unlikely for each of the A sections to be note-for-note identical. Nevertheless, schemes such as these can give you a sense of how things work. And it's a relatively easy sort of note to take.

In the Classical period, some compelling and more rigorous forms emerged based on the demands of a system made up of strong contrasts and structural blocks that required clear definition. These are easily recognized. For one thing, elements are repeated again and again, so you get the message; for another, these Classical forms stuck, and thus they lie at the heart of a great deal of the music you will hear. (Remember that I said you could dive in anywhere.)

SONATA FORM.   This is the most important of all the true forms, so important that you can often feel sonata processes at work in forms called by other names.

A sonata movement consists of three mandatory elements: the *exposition,* a presentation of the musical materials for the movement; *development,* a further investigation and exploration of their possibilities; and *recapitulation,* where these materials are restated in modified fashion. Optionally there can be an *introduction* (sometimes slow), although nearly every work begins with some sort of initial gesture, and a *coda,* or distinct conclusion. Much of the drama of the sonata form comes from the contrast between the principal, or tonic, key and the one established to oppose it. Setting up the juxtaposition or conflict of these two keys is the role of the exposition.

The exposition begins with the first theme or group of themes. By definition it is in the tonic key. The theme is usually a strong one with an easily perceived phrase structure; usually it is restated in one way or another. But whether the material in the tonic key is a square-cut theme, a group of themes, or merely the setting forth of a strong motive, the very fact that it is in the tonic key area gives it primacy; hence we sometimes use the terms *primary theme* or *primary theme group* (and, of course, *secondary theme* or *secondary theme group*).

Once the statement and any restatements of the theme are complete, it is necessary for the composer to effect a modulation to the new key. (Sometimes we talk of *tonicizing* the secondary key area.) This is done with a *transition,* or *bridge.* The rule of thumb is that if a movement is in a major key, the secondary key area will be the dominant (built five steps above the tonic: G major for a work in C major); if it is in a minor key, the secondary key area will be in the relative major (the major key built three steps above: E♭ major for a work in C minor). The clear indication of having reached the bridge is when the new sharps, flats, or naturals that define the difference between the two keys begin to take hold. You can usually feel the bridge, as familiar territory is left behind on the journey to something new.

What follows is the material in the secondary key area, the *second theme.* The contrast between the two groups is not simply in key, however. The new thematic material will have a new character as well, perhaps differing in dynamic level, instrumentation, texture, and so forth. The composer takes care to affirm the new key area strongly as the exposition begins to reach its conclusion, usually with an obvious *closing theme.* There is nearly always a repeat sign at the end of the exposition directing the players back to the beginning, helping the listener to reexamine all that has come so far. Alas, that indication is often ignored by the performers.

In the *development,* the composer, no longer constrained by predetermined orders and relationships, begins to work out the implications of the materials in the exposition. (The German term for this section is Durchführung, "working out.") The possibilities are limitless, for the composer can take any theme, or any *motive,* or *fragment,* of a theme, and treat it in whatever way seems appropriate and in any key. You might encounter, for example, a portion of the first theme in dialogue with the second, or a detail from the exposition assuming an unexpected prominence, or the unleashing of some pent-up violence. Anything goes.

The *recapitulation* presents the material from the exposition again, with the notable difference that *the second theme group stays in the tonic key,* thus allowing the work to conclude in its own tonic. This makes the *bridge,* or *transition* passage, between the first and second themes a rather curious moment. Where once the point had been to move dramatically from one key to another, now the point is to mark time and stay in the same key area. To conclude, there is a finishing-up passage called a *coda* (Italian for "tail").

It's critically important that you begin to hear and enjoy sonata form from your earliest days in a course like this. Take an hour to listen to, say, three examples of sonata form, watching the listening charts as you go. To choose from the Top Ten, listen to the following three works:

 BEETHOVEN: SYMPHONY NO. 5 IN C MINOR, OP. 67, MOVT. I (1808)

The clever thing here is that the famous, fateful, thumping motive at the beginning is part and parcel of *all* the components of the form; it can be heard in the bridge, second theme, development, and long coda. Since the movement is in C minor, the second theme is in the key of the relative major, E♭. This is a great introduction to Beethoven, his angry, frowning, surging and surly qualities in particular. (This attitude improves in the later movements, which we will discover, express a victory over Fate.)

You can see the full listening chart for the first movement, identical to what appears on CD-ROM/Website, in Chapter 6, page 188.

 MOZART: SYMPHONY NO. 40 IN G MINOR, K. 550, MOVT. I (1788)

A different sort of turbulence is encountered here, in this next-to-last of Mozart's symphonies. Again, because the movement is in a minor key, the second theme is in major; here there's a measure of rest to set it out and reassure you. Note, too, the extreme suavity of Mozart's closing theme in the exposition and recapitulation. The listening chart is on p. 173.

 TCHAIKOVSKY: *ROMEO AND JULIET* OVERTURE-FANTASY (1869)

Tchaikovsky composed this centerpiece of late Romanticism early in his career, when he was captivated by Shakespeare, much as the 17-year-old Mendelssohn was when he wrote his concert overture for Shakespeare's *A Midsummer Night's Dream.* The Romantic period was a time of storytelling music, and here each of the themes is evocative of Shakespeare's tale of star-crossed lovers. Perhaps you'll also be able to sense the freer handling of the form and some of the other reasons we call music like this Romantic. The listening chart is on p. 257.

We'll come back to look much more closely at sonata form during the chronological survey. For now, assume that much of the music you will hear from Mozart and Haydn forward through the beginning of this century is probably some sort of sonata form, with its contrasting themes and textures and the inevitability of recapitulation somewhere along the line.

TWO-PART FORMS. A rather simpler and extremely common kind of form involves two sections, each repeated ‖: A :‖: B :‖, that is, A A B B. The elegance of this form lies in its simplicity: You do something, reconfirm it by doing it again, then do something else, and do that again. This is also called a *binary* form. Nearly all Baroque dance music, for example, is in some sort of binary form.

 BACH: "BADINERIE" FROM ORCHESTRAL SUITE NO. 2 IN B MINOR, BWV 1067 (C. 1735)

This is the concluding movement of a suite of dances for orchestra, a *badinerie* ("play-thing") for the solo flutist. A single tune predominates, but this A section moves from the tonic B minor to the dominant, F♯ minor, and the B section moves, more leisurely, back again. (The listening chart is on p. 133.)

A somewhat cleverer kind of two-part form, called *rounded binary,* has a B part that embraces a return of the A section. The repeat scheme remains ‖: A :‖: B :‖. But the B has a recapitulation of A built into it (and is thus a good deal longer than the A). Thus the net effect is

    ‖: A :‖: BA :‖

This scheme is of historical importance. It is found in many Baroque dance movements, lies at the heart of the minuet and trio of the Classical period, and probably paved the way for Classical composers' thinking about sonata form. Listen to the minuet from Mozart's *Eine kleine Nachtmusik,* for example; the rounded binary form, occurs in both the minuet and the trio (CD 1, TR 19).

Obviously a good composer can accomplish all manner of things with just the two contrasting musical ideas: A-A-B-B, A-B-A, A-A-B, A-B-A-B, A-B-B-A, and so forth. Various kinds of C sections and D sections can thicken the soup. Much more than that and a single movement risks becoming disjunct and incoherent.

So much, at this moment, for large-scale form. The main idea is that music moves along in sections that repeat, or vary, or are completely different. The ear and the mind sense this kind of sectionality as a basic component of musical organization. Moreover, the listener's expectation that certain procedures ordinarily apply, and the A section will return, is something that every good composer knows how to put to great advantage.

 CHOOLS

It can be quite useful to delimit common artistic enterprise using the term *school,* which refers not so much to a true academy with buildings and a curriculum (although there are cases of precisely this) as a small group of individuals known to one another and following similar goals and each other's leads. Historians usually define schools, then seek to discover forerunners and establish subsequent influence. The concept is a good one for forging coherence out of the many divergent paths that constitute the history of an intellectual pursuit. Yet while composers themselves naturally sense artistic affinities with their companions, they seldom bother to think in these terms. In fact, most artists are such strong individualists that they tend to deny membership in a school.

Schools take the name of their location or, sometimes, their artistic stance (nationalists, minimalists). The *Notre Dame School,* for example, describes the work of composers in and around the cathedral of Notre Dame in Paris of the twelfth and thirteenth centuries, where sacred polyphony was much advanced. The *Franco-Flemish School* describes several generations of master composers of the Renaissance who were trained at the choir school of the Cambrai cathedral, where northern France and Belgium (or Flanders) come together, but who took their music all over Europe. And so on through the *English Madrigalists* of the early seventeenth century, the contemporaneous *School of St. Mark's* in Venice, and into the present. The *Viennese School* is that of Haydn and Mozart and their circle; the *Second Viennese School* represents the confluence of Schoenberg, Berg, and Webern in twentieth-century Vienna.

Cocteau, seated, with Les Six (l. to r.): Milhaud, Auric, Honegger, Tailleferre, Poulenc, and Durey

The Russian critic Vladimir Stasov lumped the Russian nationalist composers (Rimsky-Korsakov, Mussorgsky, and their circle) together as *The Mighty Handful,* or The Five, largely for polemical reasons, but the grouping is altogether apt and has since achieved universal recognition. A couple of decades later, the French film director Jean Cocteau, imitating the precedent, called his inner circle of French modernists (Milhaud, Poulenc, and others) *Les Six.* This appellation, too, caught on, despite the fact that the composers involved held relatively little in common. But the press and the public liked the idea.

Musicians can and do belong to affinity groups both formal and informal. The guilds of the Middle Ages begot unions and societies of all sorts, where composers met to discuss and protect their professional interests. It says much of their intellectual world that both Mozart and Haydn were active Freemasons. However staunchly the Romantics protected their individualism, they also took care to mingle with each other, and with poets, painters, bankers, journalists as well, at the aristocratic salons and cafés of Europe's capitals. Radicals, of course, frequented rowdier spots, notably, toward the turn of the twentieth century, cabarets with picturesque names (Le Chat Noir, Le Bœuf sur le Toit). Ravel belonged to a group of outsiders who called themselves The Apaches.

At issue throughout this chapter has been vocabulary that allows us to describe works of art by what they have in common. For central to our purpose of understanding music is the ability to describe *style* in music—the strategies, values, and goals of a group of works, in short, what they sound like. Style says much about the culture it represents: whether one wears a hat to a wedding, for example, or what material is used to bind books. Criticism in music makes precisely these sorts of observations and goes on to try to account for them.

"The Music Lesson" (c. 460 B.C.E.)

You need to think in stylistic terms when encountering works of art, but always remember that, at the same time, each artwork is individual to itself. Concentrate on this proposition as the concept of style unfolds over the next several weeks.

But take care to allow other parts of your mind to wander freely into less quantifiable realms: sentiment and emotion, color, the feeling of other times and places. Human thought naturally grants this luxury of multiple perceptions. When you look at the Mona Lisa, you think simultaneously of the technique, the play of color, the distant landscape, and the meaning of her mysterious smile. When you read Keats's "Ode on a Grecian Urn," couched in sonnet form and commenting provocatively on truth and beauty, you sense a mix of Greek antiquity and nineteenth-century England and the present. By the same token you can reflect on the touching romance of Clara and Robert Schumann while listening to his *Carnaval* for solo piano, and you can never hear Mozart's Requiem, even knowing it was a commissioned work, without thinking of the master's own death.

Allow yourself, in short, to dream, and your imagination its full capacity for wonder.

Part 2

History of Musical Style

Chapter 3

But let us never cease from digging wells of living water. . . . Let us persevere with the digging of our wells, that to us also it may be said: "Drink waters out of thine own cistern, and running waters out of thine own well"; and so let us dig that not to ourselves alone may the knowledge of the Scriptures suffice, but that we may teach others also.

—Peter Abelard (1079–1142), medieval philosopher and college professor

The Middle Ages & Renaissance

HE MIDDLE AGES

www.prenhall.com/masterworks
timeline

The Middle Ages lasted for a thousand years. Between the fall of the last true emperor of Rome in 476 and the wonders of discovery at the dawn of the sixteenth century—Columbus and his voyage of 1492 come just as the Renaissance is gathering its full force—a recognizable Europe began to take shape. This was Christendom: the domain of the church of Christ, or, more specifically, the Church of Rome.

From roots in a dogged determination to preserve the Christian faith, the Church survived to become a powerful broker of politics, social behavior, learning, and art. Under the Goths and the uncertain government in what remained of the Roman empire in Constantinople, it was primarily the Church that kept knowledge alive in western Europe—the ability to read and write Latin, and with it the lessons of history, but also the music of worship, carefully passed down from teachers to pupils over the centuries.

At the turn of the seventh century a progressive western leader emerged in the person of Gregory the Great, the pope in Rome (r. 590–604). Pope Gregory and his advisers thought it in the best interest of orderly worship to establish standard practices from congregation to congregation throughout the Christian world. To do this they relied on the network of monasteries the Church had established (evangelism having been a cornerstone of the Christian agenda from the start) from Rome through Switzerland to France, Spain, and England. Missionaries traveled from one citadel of Christendom to another with instructions from Rome and records of what they had seen and heard elsewhere. In their baggage they carried handwritten books where the prescribed texts for worship services were set forth along with increasingly sophisticated efforts to approximate in written form the music that went with it. These common sources would be copied for the local monastic libraries before the emissaries resumed their journeys, helping gradually to establish the desired uniformity of worship.

By the eighth century the papacy had thus achieved spiritual and intellectual dominion over much of western Europe, and Rome, as the seat of the Papal States, was once again approaching majesty. The reign of Charlemagne (742–814) consolidated a corresponding political power in these same regions. As king of the Franks (he spoke a German dialect, later French and Latin), Charlemagne inherited the lands where France, Germany, and Belgium converge. These he extended in military campaigns throughout most of France and northern Spain, south to Rome, and east to Bavaria and parts of Austria and Hungary, Christianizing his subjects as he went. From his capital at Aachen, or Aix-la-Chapelle (now in Belgium), he established not only a government of laws but a thriving center of intellectual accomplishment as well.

This was indeed a Christian empire, mingling the political and administrative legacy of ancient Rome with the spiritual power and missionary zeal of the Church. (Each local government was, for example, vested jointly in a count and a bishop.) Accordingly, in 800, Charlemagne took the title Holy Roman Emperor, affirmed in a coronation by Pope Leo III in Rome. This event was later seen by many as the moment when Europe emerged from darkness, for the Holy Roman Empire effectively ended any claim of either political or religious rule from Constantinople; moreover, it established the principle, cultivated by Charlemagne's successors, both French and Germanic, of secular monarchies blessed by the Church. Thus, from this date, marking the beginning of the high Middle Ages, we begin to think of modern European history.

Under such circumstances it is not surprising that the music of Christian worship became the foundation of modern western art music. For centuries it had been jealously protected and systematically organized, and (but for the forgotten notations of antiquity) it was the first music to be written down. The vast majority of professional musicians were employees of the Church. The practice of sacred music thrived in the late Middle Ages as the monasteries came under benevolent civil protection and great metropolitan cathedrals began to be planned by the local bishops. Here is the most instructive place to begin our chronological survey of art music.

PLAINCHANT. The music of the Church, *monophonic chant,* consisted of traditional melodic formulas and newer compositions sung by a single voice or unison choir. Rhythm is not specified, and traditional performance gives the pitches roughly equal note values, say slow eighth notes, with pauses to mark the musical and poetic punctuation. The sources of plainchant are very old indeed, extending back to the melodies of pre-Christian Judaism. Tunes and texts had been passed down through the ages by rote, and a great deal of new music was composed along the way. By the high Middle Ages there was a very large body of monophonic sacred music, filling many dozens of manuscript volumes. This is the music we call *Gregorian chant* (in honor of Pope Gregory's role in codifying the practice), *plainchant,* or *plainsong.* These terms are for all intents and purposes interchangeable.

Pope Gregory, dictating chant to his scribe as the dove of the Lord whispers in his ear

THE LITURGY. Chant is organized according to its function in the prescribed order of worship, called the *liturgy.* The liturgy establishes not just the annual religious calendar but also the order of service and specific texts for virtually every waking hour of every day. Most days of the Christian year commemorate one or more saints, each with a particular liturgy; additionally, there are special services for weddings, funerals, church dedications, visits of the bishop or pope, local commemorations, and the like. The church year begins with Advent and Christmas and reaches its high point in the celebration of Easter.

Much of the liturgy was observed in private by the priesthood alone. Ritual events of the monastic day are called the *Divine Office,* or the *Hours* (Matins, Lauds, Vespers, and so on). The size of this portion of the liturgy is quite extensive, consisting of for example, all the Psalms sung every week. In general, the music of the Office is relatively simple, consisting largely of reciting the scriptures on a single note, or *chanting tone,* surrounded by little flourishes at the beginnings and ends of the verses. The example below shows a bit of Psalm 112 as sung at First Vespers on Christmas Day. Two of the eight verses of text are given along with the text of the Doxology which concludes every psalm. Additionally, each psalm is preceded by a short introductory phrase called an *antiphon* (not given here). Try singing this simple example in class.

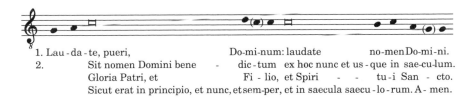

1. Lau-da-te, pueri,   Do-mi-num: laudate   no-men Do-mi-ni.
2.   Sit nomen Domini bene - dic-tum ex hoc nunc et us-que in sae-cu-lum.
      Gloria Patri, et   Fi - lio, et Spiri - - tu-i San - cto.
      Sicut erat in principio, et nunc, et sem-per, et in saecula saecu-lo-rum. A-men.

1. Praise the Lord, ye children of the Lord, praise the name of the Lord.
2. Blessed be the name of the Lord, now and evermore. . . .
    Glory be to the Father, and to the Son, and to the Holy Spirit.
    As it was in the beginning is now and ever shall be, world without end.
        Amen.

The public worship service is called *Mass,* where the Last Supper is commemorated with the Eucharist, or Holy Communion. Texts and music for the Mass are of two categories: those that change with the calendar—for example, those for Christmas, St. Stephen's Day on December 26, or Massacre of the Holy Innocents on December 28—and those common to every Mass. The changing texts are called the *Proper* (or the Proper of the Time); the invariant ones are called the *Ordinary.* It is the portions of the Ordinary sung by the choir (as opposed to portions chanted by the celebrating priest) that are of most interest to composers of art music. These are as follows:

KYRIE ELEISON. This prayer near the beginning of the Mass is noted for its incantational arrangement of three lines each repeated three times (*Kyrie eleison* × 3; *Christe eleison* × 3; *Kyrie eleison* × 3). The 3 × 3 formula almost mystically focuses our attention on the Trinity: God as Father, Son, and Holy Spirit. The text is borrowed from the Greek.

GLORIA. This long text of praise to the Lord begins with the words the angels sang at the Nativity: *Gloria in excelsis Deo, et in terra pax hominibus bonae voluntatis* ("Glory to God in the highest, and on earth peace toward men of good will,"

Luke 2:14). Both in the chanted versions and in later polyphonic settings, a solo cantor intones the opening words, with the choir entering at "Et in terra pax." There are several parallel text lines within the Gloria, for example,

Laudamus te.	We praise thee.
Benedicimus te.	We bless thee.
Adoramus te.	We adore thee.
Glorificamus te.	We glorify thee.

These have the same formulaic, ceremonial quality as the repetitions in the Kyrie—internal symmetries that composers are quick to notice and explore in their music.

The Gloria is omitted in Lent and Advent and for funeral services.

CREDO. The Nicene Creed is essentially identical to the congregational creeds recited in every Christian worship service. The cantor sings the words "Credo in unum Deum," with the choir entering at "Patrem omnipotentem." It reaches the central mystery of the faith just toward the end:

Crucifixus etiam pro nobis	And was crucified also for us
sub Pontio Pilato:	under Pontius Pilate:
Passus, et sepultus est.	Suffered, and was buried.
Et resurrexit tertia die	And the third day He rose again
secundum scripturas.	according to the scriptures.

The Credo is by far the longest text in the Mass Ordinary and is therefore the longest movement (or set of movements) in a composed Mass.

SANCTUS. The incantation "Holy, Holy, Holy" is based on Isaiah 6:3 and concludes with a "Hosanna in excelsis"; it is among the earliest components of the Mass. The Benedictus verse blesses the faithful who come in the name of the Lord, after which the Hosanna is repeated. The Sanctus comes just past the midpoint of the Mass, preceding the Lord's Prayer and Holy Communion.

AGNUS DEI. Another tripartite formulation, this one begs the Lamb of God to have mercy and to grant peace. The image of Christ as redeeming Lamb of God comes from John the Baptist: "Behold the Lamb of God, who takes away the sin of the world!" (John 1:29, see also v. 36). In worship services, the Agnus Dei is associated with the breaking of the communion bread. In unified musical compositions, it comes at the conclusion of the work. Thus the words *Dona nobis pacem* ("Grant us peace") are the last to be heard, and the final *pacem* is nearly always a study in serenity.

The complete text and translations of the choral Mass Ordinary may be found in the CD-ROM/Website program (Texts and Translations). Read the original Latin carefully and try to memorize a few lines. Not only are these some of the most historic and enduring words in any language but also some of the most beautiful. You will encounter Mass movements often enough in the history of music that the longer texts will eventually find a place in your memory, too.

PLAINCHANT: *KYRIE ELEISON (KYRIE CUNCTIPOTENS GENITOR)*

This particular Kyrie (see the Anthology, p. 372) is sung during the Mass for Easter Sunday. The first and second of the four notated phrases serve for the Kyrie I ("Kyrie eleison" × 3) and the Christe ("Christe eleison" × 3). For the Kyrie II there are two phrases ("Kyrie eleison" × 2, plus the last, much longer, phrase), which provide a more ornate conclusion to the work. Much of the melody is without text, sung to the syllable "eh"; these portions are called *melismas.*

The music is elegantly crafted, centered around the pitches A (with which each line begins and where lines 3 and 4 conclude, or *cadence*) and D (on which lines 1 and 2 cadence). Each phrase seems to flow naturally from the one before, in part because they all open with the same musical gesture: A-A-G-A. As the center section (or B part of an ABA form), the Christe gently offsets the Kyries with its more restricted scope and prevailing downward sweep.

With Kyrie II the music begins to lift, abandoning the low Ds on which the previous lines had concluded in order to float around and over the higher partner, A, frequently touching the top C. What makes line 4 longer than line 3 is the extra melisma in the center; otherwise the two are identical but for the turn on the very last syllable.

It's important to sense that this piece is something more than pretty notes in a row: composed music is the thoughtful, artful deployment of the notes. The mounting fervor is achieved carefully, using phrase length, melodic compass, and internal repetition to achieve its desired effect. Note the many details common to the phrases, for example, the cadence pattern shared by the Kyrie I and the Christe. Once you know the piece well enough to hum it to yourself, close your eyes and listen to the cumulative effect as you sing all nine units through, especially the way the recurrent little formulas and cells end up giving the chant its unmistakable identity.

We call this work the *Kyrie Cunctipotens genitor* because an alternative version of the same piece provides a text beginning "Cunctipotens genitor deus," with one syllable of text sung per note of chant.

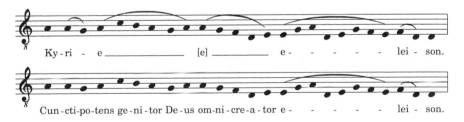

Ky - ri - e _____ [e] _____ e - - - - lei - son.

Cun - cti - po - tens ge - ni - tor De - us om - ni - cre - a - tor e - - - - lei - son.

All-powerful Father, God, creator of all things, have mercy.

Kyrie Cunctipotens genitor: **Untexted and texted versions.**

Thus the Kyrie as sung on your CD is the *melismatic* version, and "Cunctipotens genitor" the *syllabic* version. The text amplifies the sentiments of the Kyrie eleison. Such syllabic texts, perhaps thought to make the music easier to remember, exist for quite a number of Kyries. The interesting thing is that the melismatic and syllabic sources are contemporaneous, and it seems possible that the versions were composed simultaneously.

Listening Chart

 CD 1, TR 2

Kyrie eleison

For: unaccompanied choir, monophonic
Text: from the Catholic liturgy, that for the Mass

Type: Chant (plainchant, plainsong); form follows tripartite text scheme
Meter: Free
Key: Church mode on D
Duration: 02:17

Gregorian chant is *monophonic* and *non-metrical.* This setting of the opening text from the Mass Ordinary consists of elegantly arching phrases with a common opening motive, A-A-G-A.

00:00	**Phrase 1**	Kyrie eleison,	"Lord have mercy on us." The music begins on A, rises
00:15	repeat	Kyrie eleison,	quickly to C, then falls languidly down to cadence on D.
00:31	repeat	Kyrie eleison.	The phrase is sung three times.
00:46	**Phrase 2**	Christe eleison,	The cadential formula ("eleison") is the same as in
01:01	repeat	Christe eleison,	phrase 1. Sung three times.
01:15	repeat	Christe eleison.	
01:29	**Phrase 3**	Kyrie eleison,	The music lifts higher, floating around and over the higher
01:42	repeat	Kyrie eleison,	partner, A, and frequently touching the top C. Sung twice.
01:55	extended	Kyrie eleison.	What makes this phrase longer than the others is the extra melisma in the center; otherwise they are identical.

The musical notation of plainchant as you see it on p. 372 of the Anthology is quite simple, once you know how to read the following two symbols:

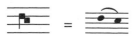 

(stem on left: read down)   (stem on right: read up)

We call these kinds of shapes *neumes,* and this is one form of *neumatic* notation. The unusual neume that appears over each "lei" of "eleison" recognizes the *ei* as a diphthong (a gliding from one vowel to the next).

The staff has only four lines; more are seldom needed owing to the limited range of the music. The clef is more ordinary than you might think, simply indicating the pitch C. The first note of the Kyrie is thus A, and the first note of *Pange lingua* (see below), so E.

What about the rhythm and other instructions for performance, conspicuous in their absence? Probably, as we noted earlier, this sort of chant was sung as a gently flowing succession of equal note values with pauses appropriate to the punctuation—a little yielding at subsidiary points, then full stops at the sentence ends. But no one knows the particulars of how Gregorian chant was performed in the Middle Ages, whether it was gentle or strident, nasal or cultivatedly *bel canto,* rich and rounded in tone quality. It seems likely that metric performances were tried early on and virtually certain that organ accompaniments would have been improvised. In fact, both the style of performance you hear on the CD and the standard notation you see printed are the work of twentieth-century monks and scholars who endeavored to piece together the "true" Gregorian chant from hundreds of manuscript sources and dozens of different methods of notation preserved over six or more centuries.

Onc other thing. If you arrange the pitch content of the Kyrie into its basic scale, bottom to top, you will have the collection D-E F-G-A-B-C. This is neither D major (which requires an F♯ and C♯) nor D minor (which would have a B♭ and added C♯). Instead, it is one of the several so-called white-note scales called the church *modes.* The names are inherited from the music theory of ancient Greece; the medieval theorists referred to the modes by number.

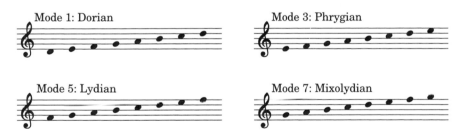

The church modes

Incidentally, the final cadence of *Kyrie Cunctipotens genitor* in mode 1 is on A, not D. The A is a kind of secondary tonic of the Dorian mode.

Modal scales provide the basic pitch collections for the music of the Middle Ages and much of the Renaissance. By 1600 the increasing dependence on added sharps and flats was resulting in the major and minor scales of tonality.

 HILDEGARD OF BINGEN: *KYRIE ELEISON* (C. 1150)

www.prenhall.com/masterworks
composer profiles
Hildegard of Bingen

Hildegard of Bingen (1098–1179), one of the earliest known woman composers and practically the first composer of any for whom we have a real biography, was mother abbess of a convent in the western part of Germany, at Bingen on the Rhine River. The tenth child in her family, she was destined from birth to serve the church, and by the age of eight had been closed away behind the doors of a religious order to lead the strictly regimented life of the recluse. There, for hours each day, she participated in singing Mass and the Divine Office, albeit from a women's cloister that had access to the church only through a window. Music, which she came to regard as humankind's highest form of praise to God, gave her her education: She learned to read both musical notation and the texts that went with it, though never to write without the help of a secretary. She had, nevertheless, much to say.

For Hildegard had visions. These, she later confided to the sisters, had begun in her early childhood. The symptoms she describes are those we now recognize as chronic migraine: perception of dazzling luminous objects, sickness, episodes of blindness and paralysis, euphoria when the illness lifts—and, perhaps above all in her case, moments of great mental clarity. "The heavens opened up," she said of the vision she had in her early 40s, "and a blinding light of exceptional brilliance flowed through my entire brain. It kindled my heart and breast like a flame, not burning but warming, . . . and I understood the meaning of the books." She felt herself called to record her understanding of everything from cosmology to medicine, writings that established her reputation as a seer and prophet, "the Sibyl of the Rhine." People of every description—Germans and Gauls, rich and poor, old and young—visited to profit from her wisdom. She lived through most of the twelfth century.

Aside from a drama-with-music *Play of the Virtues,* Hildegard's 80 or so musical compositions are all short "spiritual songs," monophonic chants using her own lyric poetry. Their purpose is to venerate the Virgin Mary or patriarchs and prophets or, especially, St. Ursula and her Rhineland convent of eleven virgins—mythologized into 11,000 virgins—martyred by the Huns. She had her musical works gathered into a compendium titled *Symphony of the Harmony of Heavenly Revelations.* There is a single movement from the Mass Ordinary, a lovely Kyrie eleison in a church mode on F.

There are many similarities between Hildegard's Kyrie and the Gregorian Kyrie you have on the previous track of the CD, most notably the way the last "Kyrie eleison" (line 9) is extended by repeating an internal melisma. But the range of Hildegard's composition is much greater, quickly reaching the octave above the opening F, then in the Christe the G a step higher. Just afterward the melody falls all the way to a C below the opening F. This wide scope is primarily a function of the composer's fondness for vocal *roulade,* a sort of caressing of a prominent pitch by ornamenting it and then falling away. One of these is the central melodic figure of the work, which is heard in every phrase:

00:00, etc.

Listening Chart

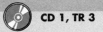 CD 1, TR 3

Hildegard of Bingen (1098–1179)
Kyrie eleison (c. 1150)

Type: Chant
Meter: Free
Key: Church mode on F
Duration: 02:08

For: unaccompanied choir, monophonic

Text: from the Latin liturgy: the first movement of the Mass Ordinary

Hildegard's Kyrie is more decorative than the Gregorian example, and the melodies sound very different owing to the particular quality of the mode on F. That, and the women's voices, give this Kyrie its particular brightness.

00:00	**Kyrie**	Starts and ends on F.
00:11		The opening "e-" of *eleison* climbs to the higher F and includes the most prominent motive (see example).
00:24	**Christe**	Climbs from F immediately to the motive, then to the highest point, G.
00:38		The *eleison* falls to the lowest point, C.
00:48	**Kyrie**	Kyrie elaborated;
01:05		*eleison,* much the same as in Kyrie I.
01:23	extended	Both subphrases elaborated, ending on F.

"Music wakes us from our sluggishness," she said. And "Music makes cold hearts warm."

 PLAINCHANT HYMN: *PANGE LINGUA* (c. 1264)

In a *hymn* the music is written to set a poetic stanza of a certain shape, and all the stanzas (or strophes) of the text are sung to the same music (see Anthology, p. 372). Here there are six lines of text per stanza with three corresponding two-part phrases of music. The melody rises immediately from the initial E to the C above it; in the second half of the phrase, the C is caressed with motion to D and back, and the succeeding phrases establish an ebb and flow that falls gently to the E where the tune began (thus mode 3, Phrygian). After the last stanza, the "Amen" affirms closure, both textually and musically.

The poem is by St. Thomas Aquinas (1225–74), a preeminent Italian theologian and philosopher of Roman Catholicism (who held, among other things, that science and theology can coexist harmoniously). Written as part of an entire communion service commissioned by the pope, it celebrates the mystery of the sacred body of Christ, as represented by the unleavened bread of the Last Supper. The feast in question is called Corpus Christi, a major celebration of the Middle Ages where the clergy, government, and citizens of a city would process through the streets bearing the host: the consecrated bread.

Pange lingua also serves as the borrowed melody in a very lovely polyphonic Mass by the Renaissance master Josquin Desprez.

Listening Chart

 CD 1, TR 4

Pange lingua (c. 1264)

For: unaccompanied choir, monophonic

Text: by St. Thomas Aquinas (1225–74), a celebrated Italian theologian and philosopher

Type: Plainchant hymn, strophic
Meter: Free
Key: Church mode on E
Duration: 01:15

Over the course of three two-part phrases, the music rises from and falls back to the pitch E. The setting is prevailingly *syllabic,* as opposed to the *melismatic* Kyries. The excerpt consists of the first and last (of six) stanzas of the hymn, with concluding Amen.

00:00	**Strophe I**	Pange lingua gloriosi	Sing, my tongue, of the glorious
00:05		Corporis mysterium,	Body's mystery,
00:11		Sanguinisque pretiosi,	Of the precious blood
00:16		Quem in mundi pretium	That on earth poured forth, as our ransom
00:22		Fructus ventris generosi	The fruit of a generous womb,
00:27		Rex effudit gentium.	The King of all nations.
00:33	**Strophe II**	Genitori, Genitoque	To the Father and the Son
00:39		Laus et jubilatio,	Let there be praise and glory.
00:45		Salus, honor, virtus quoque	Might, honor, power,
00:50		Sit et benedictio:	And blessing
00:55		Procedenti ab utroque	Proceeding from both:
01:00		Compar sit laudatio.	To both give equal praise.
01:06		Amen.	Amen.

All these chants exemplify the principles of fine song, as the music coincides gracefully with the text, properly and intelligibly articulated. The melodic contours are pleasingly shaped, each rising to high point, a kind of climax, then receding to closure. Plainchant is both sternly devout and wonderfully fluid in its ardor, saying as much about the medieval spirit as the perhaps more familiar art and architecture of the age. Go ahead and memorize one or more of these chants, singing along with the professor in class, then humming them under your tree. It's a good exercise all around, training both your ear and your memory, and you yourself will in turn become an agent of their transmission forward into still another century.

Chant is not, and never was, a bookful of music by dead people, frozen in some imagined past. Its details changed in the process of transmission, as the person who wrote down a chant in one monastery might have remembered it quite differently than another scribe hundreds of leagues away or decades later. Moreover, throughout Europe, back to the oldest Roman chant, the monasteries and churches developed their own local specialties. Some of the most advanced of these were the florid repertoire of the Milan cathedral in Italy, the monastic practices at St. Gall in Switzerland and St. Martial of Limoges in France, and the progressive music of the great cathedral of St. James of Compostela in northwestern Spain, burial place of Christ's disciple.

The newer compositions tended to be more complex and longer than the old. Dozens of new works venerated the Virgin Mary, with titles like *Alma Redemptoris Mater* ("Nourishing Mother of the Redeemer") and *Ave Regina caelorum* ("Hail, Queen of Heaven"). New musico-poetic operations along the lines of the "Cunctipotens genitor" treatment greatly expanded the repertoire of syllabic chant. The late medieval sequence or prose combined a strophic poetry of vivid images with musical settings that involved complex internal repeat schemes. The best known of these is the long *Dies irae,* which became the focal point of the special Mass for the Dead, called the Requiem. Memorize

Day of Wrath, that day / Will dissolve the earth in ashes, /
As David and the Sibyl bear witness.

Sequence: *Dies irae* (first strophe)

that phrase, too, not only since you hear it all the time in movie soundtracks, but also because it will be cropping up again when we study the Romantic composer Berlioz, one of many composers drawn to this tune for its combination of pleasing shape and instant recognition value. And the full *Dies irae* text is overloaded with images that later composers can't resist: the trumpet of the Last Judgment as Purgatory is rent asunder, a great deal of fire and screaming and tears, and supplication before a king of terrifying majesty.

We know just a little about the composers of these later chants, and a colorful lot they were. Notker the Stammerer (c. 840–912), a monk of St. Gall, boasted of having invented the sequence to keep long melodies from escaping his "poor little head." Wipo of Burgundy (c. 995–1050), to whom the Easter sequence *Victimae paschali laudes* ("Praises to the Paschal victim") is attributed, was confessor to emperors before becoming a hermit to write his scholarly tracts.

Among the other Latin texts often encountered in music study is another medieval hymn, *Te Deum laudamus* ("We praise Thee, O God"), a jubilant work often sung to commemorate grand military victories or the completion of a great church, and reset by many later composers for the same kinds of occasions. *Stabat Mater dolorosa* ("Stood the grieving Mother") is a late sequence on Mary at the Cross, its poetry likewise reset in later periods. The *Magnificat* ("My soul doth magnify the Lord") comes directly from the Bible; it is Mary's response to the archangel's Annunciation, Luke 1:46–55, and central to both the Catholic and Anglican rites.

The liturgy continues to evolve. Its content today reflects a compromise between long and short, the freedom to experiment and respect for the traditional unities of purpose, the addition of things new and the preservation of its original components.

SECULAR MEDIEVAL MUSIC.   Singing and dancing, of course, happened at every level of medieval society. Even though the music that went with it was seldom written down, we are assured of its richness through copious literary citations and not a few pictures. Epic accounts of heroic deeds, called *chansons de geste,* were recited by the wandering minstrels, or *jongleurs,* who spun their thousand-line tales night after night to improvised melodies and perhaps instrumental accompaniment. They sang, for instance, of Charlemagne's heroic commander Roland, ambushed by the Basques (Saracens in the poem) in a mountain pass but manages to sound his elephant-tusk horn in time to ward off the main army. Words of *The Song of Roland* were set down on paper in the eleventh or twelfth century. Music was surely heard with the King Arthur stories of Chrétien de Troyes (*Perceval,* c. 1170) and the Anglo-Norman romance of *Tristram and Isolde.*

In southern France, in the region and language of Provence, flourished the lyric art of the *troubadours,* who left behind a rich corpus of song but only four manuscripts containing any music. They, too, were a colorful lot. Peire Vidal, from Toulouse, had his tongue cut out by an enraged husband but nevertheless went on to "take a fancy to every woman he saw." Marcabru of Gascoigne appears to have lived with a boyfriend in the profession and was put to death by women of whom he had spoken ill. The troubadours' expressions of courtly love, including bittersweet complaints about the cool

Secular medieval music: harp and lute

response of elegant ladies to their ardent but chivalrous courtiers, were adopted in successive generations by the *trouvères,* writing in the language of the north. One important point of crossover from south to north was the Poitiers court of Eleanor of Aquitaine (1122–1204), estranged wife of Henry II of England and mother of Richard the Lion-Hearted and the duplicitous King John. Her daughter Marie, at court in Champagne, was an important patroness of the trouvères; and among the several aristocratic composers of the movement was the Chastelain de Couci, one of the powerful sires of Coucy chateau. The music of the trouvère poetry, by contrast with that of the troubadours, exists in abundance and is notated with hints of the rhythms used in its performance.

A slightly later generation of manuscript sources preserves a very small body of dance music called *estampies.* These were doubtless given a lively, highly rhythmic performance, probably with improvised percussion and lots of clapping.

POLYPHONY.   People experimenting with the performance of one-line melodies almost immediately come up with multivoiced solutions that amount to primitive polyphony. One obvious possibility is the drone accompaniment, where one singer or instrumentalist holds a long note while the tune goes on above or around it. Another is a kind of parallel polyphony, where voices double the melody not at the unison or octave but at some other interval. A third possibility is the kind of *heterophony* that results when two or more voices singing the same basic melody diverge from time to time, whether by accident of memory or purposeful design. Probably you've also had the experience of improvising a descant, or "harmonizing" a part, note against note, while somebody else sings the melody. Such practices lie at the heart of the earliest notated polyphonic practices, generally called *organum.* Examples below show excerpts of organa based on the *Kyrie Cunctipotens genitor.* The first, from a twelfth-century manuscript used by French pilgrims to the shrine of St. James of Compostela in northern Spain, shows a florid, melismatic organal voice laid over the *Cunctipotens genitor* tenor, the principal voice. The second example shows note-against-note polyphony, from a treatise of about 1100 called "How to Write Organum."

Melismatic organum (mid-twelfth century, northern France)

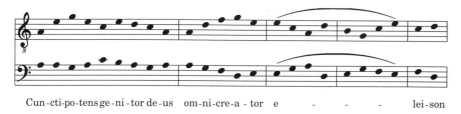

Cun-cti-po-tens ge-ni-tor de-us om-ni-cre-a-tor e - - - lei-son

Note-against-note organum (early twelfth century, northern France)

The trick, of course, was to write it down in some intelligible way. Medieval composers soon found ways of specifying rhythmic values, so that the proper relationship between the voices could be shown. First a primitive kind of score arrangement was worked out, then a method of encoding simple rhythmic patterns by note shapes. By the time its altar was consecrated in 1196, a very advanced style of notated polyphony was flourishing at the new cathedral of Notre Dame in Paris. The masters of the Notre Dame School were Leonin (in the 1150s) and his successor Perotin (turn of the century). Their two generations of Notre Dame organa, based on rhythmic embellishment of the ordinary chant melodies, were admired by theorists and copied by pilgrims to take back to their home libraries, as far away as Scotland and Italy.

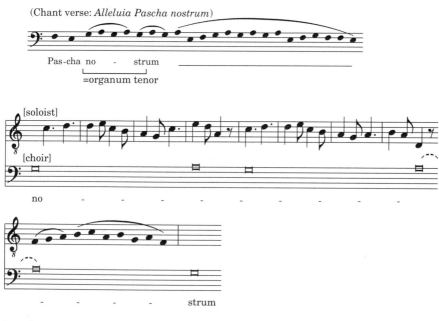

(Chant verse: *Alleluia Pascha nostrum*)

Pas-cha no - strum

=organum tenor

[soloist]

[choir]

no - - - - - - - -

- - - - strum

Leonin organum

Perotin organum

When one voice is borrowed from chant so that another can be composed above or below it, that voice is called the *tenor,* so named because it was longer, more held out (Lat. *tenere,* "to hold"), than the embellishments.

Both the music and the triumph of setting it down indicate the birth of a new musical dimension of vast significance. The thirteenth century saw the explosion of all sorts of notated polyphonic music throughout western Europe. The *motet,* with one line borrowed from chant and texted lines above it, was born of experimentation with the Notre Dame polyphonic works. Within a few decades motets were becoming increasingly secular in orientation. In the thirteenth-century motet *L'autre jour / Au temps pascour / In seculum,* for example, the tenor line, *In seculum,* comes from a Gregorian chant for Easter Sunday; the two upper lines, both in French, comment cheerily on springtime music—and lovemaking.

Tenor: *In seculum*

High voice: The other morning by a valley at daybreak, . . .
Middle voice: At Eastertide all the shepherd folk from one region
  gathered together . . .

Motet: *L'autre jour / Au tens pascour / In seculum* **(beginning)**

You can't really understand either text unless you see it, of course, and only the quick of ear would recognize the chant; this is music for the pleasure of intellectuals. Motets were easily directed to commemorative or ceremonial purpose; for instance, the murder at Canterbury cathedral of the archbishop Thomas à Becket (1170) prompted dozens of compositions over more than a century. In the motet *Thomas gemma Cantuariae/ Thomas caesus in Doveria,* about 1300, parallel poems in the two upper voices reflect simultaneously on the deaths of Becket and of Thomas de la Hale, a monk of Dover killed during a French raid in 1295.

ANONYMOUS: *SUMER IS ICUMEN IN* (c. 1240)

A merrier example of early polyphony is the famous summer canon from England, *Sumer is icumen in* (composed c. 1240 at the Reading Abbey). It's altogether secular and in a language you can grasp. Its structure is quite remarkable. The upper line is a round, with the voices entering every two bars. The lower two voices have a two-bar burden, or foot (marked *pes* in the manuscript), "Sing Cuckoo," crossing so that the second bar is a mirror image,

Manuscript source of
Sumer is icumen in

both vertically and horizontally, of the first. This results in six actual parts once everything gets going.

The Reading Rota: *Sumer is icumen in* **(beginning)**

Perhaps your class can give this simple but altogether charming work a try.

The polyphonic coming of age in the thirteenth century carried forward into the fourteenth. Although it was an era of great civil and religious unrest—the popes abandoned
Rome for the city of Avignon in southern France (1309–77), followed by the Great

Listening Chart

 CD 1, TR 5

Anonymous
Sumer is icumen in (c. 1240)
For: unaccompanied voice in six parts
Text: anonymous

Type: Double canon
Meter: triple
Key: F major-ish
Duration: 01:07

The upper line works as a round, with the voices entering every two bars. The lower line is a canonic *burden,* or refrain.

00:00	Burden	The burden, or *pes* ("foot") alone, then canonically (00:05).
00:09	**Round**	The round in four parts (00:09, :11, :13, :15); six parts in all.
00:34	again	Lead voice starts again; winds down beginning at 00:58.

Schism of rival claims to the papacy (1378–1417)—the arts saw a conspicuous refining, a softening of the Gothic severities. The century's leading composer was Guillaume de Machaut (c. 1300–77), composer to King John of Bohemia, duke of Luxembourg; later Machaut was canon of the cathedral in Rheims. (From the fourteenth century we begin to trace with relative certainty the lives and mutations of style of the notable composers.) Machaut composed a wonderful polyphonic Mass of Our Lady, sacred and secular motets, and pioneering work in the emerging *formes fixes,* or standard verse patterns, of French lyric poetry. The work of Italian composers, for instance that of the blind organist Francesco Landini (c. 1335–97), becomes increasingly prominent.

The great cathedrals began to be completed (and had long been occupied): Notre Dame of Paris, Chartres, Canterbury, Winchester, Milan, Cologne. Cities grew in size—Paris of 1350 had a population of 100,000—and artists congregated in them. An important literature in the modern languages emerged, notably with Dante's Italian masterpiece *The Divine Comedy* (c. 1310) and Chaucer's English *Canterbury Tales,* begun in 1387. The Italian painter Giotto (c. 1266–1337) helped revolutionize art with his expressive portraiture and sense of movement and natural grace; he also designed the Florence cathedral and bell tower, the architectural harbinger of the Renaissance. The manuscript books of the period are fabulous creations, lovingly hand copied on fine sheepskin parchment, the initials illuminated with fantastic miniature artworks that tell us a great deal about the times.

It was all quite pleasing to the senses, if you were lucky enough to be in the right circles and didn't mind the stink.

Pasturella pestis, "a bacterium transmitted to humans, by fleas, from infected rats," ignored distinctions of class, causing widespread sickness. The symptoms include high fever, chills, prostration, enlarged painful lymph nodes in the groin, called buboes, and hemorrhaging of black fluid. Invasion of the lungs causes a rapidly fatal pneumonia that can be transmitted by humans. In the fourteenth century they simply called it the Black Death. Between 1348 and 1350 a third of the continent's populace died of bubonic plague; some estimates suggest that over 20 years three-quarters of the population succumbed.

The plague left Italy and Sicily in 1347—but construction of the great cathedral in Siena, near Florence, was never resumed. It went on to kill everybody in the convents of Marseille and Carcassonne and ravage the clergy at Avignon; by 1348 it had reached Normandy, in northern France. The poor succumbed quickly and anonymously. Women, confined to the house, died in greater proportion than men. Queens, a king, several princes, artists, writers, sculptors, musicians, priests, and physicians all fell. The entire medical faculty of the great university at Montpellier died, as did some whole city councils; at Canterbury three archbishops in a year. When the king of France asked the faculty of the University of Paris for its report, the plague was ascribed to a conjunction of Saturn, Jupiter, and Mars in the constellation of Aquarius on 20 March 1345. "No bells tolled and nobody wept," wrote one observer, "because almost everyone expected death. People said and believed that this was the end of the world."

You can get a sense of this widespread despair from the plagues of our own time. Such horror serves as a vivid reminder that looking at a civilization through its high art tells only part of the story. One must always keep one's eyes and ears open for the whole spectrum of conditions in which a people live and work.

THE RENAISSANCE

www.prenhall.com/masterworks
timelines

The unlocking of the European imagination, the breakaway from church dogma into the golden, bustling secularity of the Renaissance, had been under way throughout the fourteenth century. In 1295, when Marco Polo returned from his sojourn at the court of the Great Khan and talked of seeing stars unknown to the savants of Europe, he alienated the church fathers (who excommunicated him) but liberated freer thinkers everywhere. In 1492, when Columbus, one of those free thinkers, happened upon other "unknown" worlds, he surprised imaginative people less than he whetted their appetites for more. Gutenberg's method of printing from movable type, perfected in the 1440s and 1450s, was put to good use in spreading the work of the philosophers, scientists, and literary giants of the secularizing movement we call Humanism. By 1543, when the Polish astronomer Copernicus demonstrated that instead of all worlds revolving around this one, our solar system was part of a universe governed by physical laws, his work could be grasped as a natural outgrowth of an era of discovery that humbled as well as thrilled the thinkers who led it. People of small minds had little choice but to watch their world be turned, in more ways than one, upside down.

The best musicians were still the product, largely, of cathedral choir schools, where they passed their long apprenticeship—from matriculating as boy soprano to their engagement elsewhere as adult professionals—mastering the liturgy and its music by singing the whole of it year after year. What we think of as Renaissance style originated midway into the fifteenth century among composers of the Low Countries and northern France. Several generations of the leading composers were trained at the cathedral of Cambrai, in northernmost France. (Medieval Flanders, the region where French and Dutch cultures intermingle, consisted of this portion of northern France and the western part of the Low Countries abutting the North Sea. Its Germanic dialect, Flemish, is still today an official language of Belgium.)

At the time, these territories belonged to the dukes of Burgundy (Philip the Good, r. 1419–67; Charles the Bold, r. 1467–77), who lavished the wealth they accrued in trade with England on the fine arts. The retinues of these and similar nobles included a private chapel consisting of singers and players under the direction of the finest chapel master they could afford. Invariably this *maître de chapelle,* or *maestro di cappella,* was a capable composer.

For instance, Guillaume Dufay (c. 1400–74), the best composer of the so-called Burgundian School, learned his trade at Cambrai, returned there between various engagements in Italy, and at length retired to Cambrai. Advancing the late medieval manner of Machaut and his followers, Dufay composed with equal success both secular song (the French chanson) and Latin sacred music. In one famous miniature illustration he is pictured with the other celebrated chanson writer of the time, Gilles Binchois (c. 1400–60), an employee of Philip the Good. The poem that goes with the picture in the manuscript suggests that both of these men knew and sometimes imitated the work of their English counterparts, especially John Dunstable (d. 1453), musician to the Duke of Bedford, near Cambridge.

Dufay and Binchois

The next generation, called the Franco-Flemish composers, begins with the work of Johannes Ockeghem (c. 1420–97), Flemish-born composer in the employ of the kings of France. Composing in the genres that had become customary—masses, motets, chansons—he asserted the principles of imitative counterpoint, text painting, and sonority that served as models for composers of the next century. Ockeghem also composed the first attributed Requiem mass. His immediate successor was Josquin Desprez (c. 1440–1521), perhaps Ockeghem's pupil and certainly his ardent admirer. Josquin's work heads a large, splendid repertoire from the decades surrounding the turn of the century.

However pious their schooling, the northerners were anything but immune to the explosion of secular power, learning, and above all wealth to be found in Italy. From the late 1400s on, the focus of the Renaissance shifts to Italy, primarily to the ducal courts of Florence, Milan, and Ferrara, and of course to the Vatican in Rome. With increasing frequency northern-trained composers made the long journey southward, serving dukes and princes and the pope, who had now returned permanently to Rome and fancied himself, not always rightly, proprietor of the best musical establishment in the world. Dufay

Ockeghem (with glasses) and his singers

held several posts in Italy; Ockeghem's contemporary Jacob Obrecht went to Ferrara; and Josquin's rival Heinrich Isaac served Lorenzo the Magnificent in Florence and after his patron's death went on to Vienna and Innsbruck. Composers in the employ of the great secular princes had little difficulty adapting their techniques on behalf of the worldly patrons of the times. Surrounded by important libraries, working alongside equally gifted poets and philosophers and architects, they were as anxious to live the modern life as anybody.

MASS, MOTET, MADRIGAL. All three major genres of the high Renaissance were for voices, unaccompanied or with the participation of a few instrumentalists. Sacred practice centered on the multimovement polyphonic mass and individual Latin motet. In secular music the early Renaissance interest in setting French love poetry led over the course of time to a genre that dominated the high Renaissance: the Italian madrigal.

Compositional technique of this period strives for the discovery of beauty through *imitative polyphony.* A *point of imitation* begins in one of the voices, is closely imitated in the shape and note values of successive entries by the other voices, and eventually reaches some form of cadence. The next point of imitation begins, usually with the next bit of text, and the movement is knitted from a succession of such phrases until all the text has been set. Throughout, the counterpoint created by the interacting voices must be circumspect; dissonant intervals, for example, must be carefully prepared and properly resolved.

Josquin: *Missa Pange lingua,* Kyrie I

Byrd: Mass in 4 Parts, Kyrie I

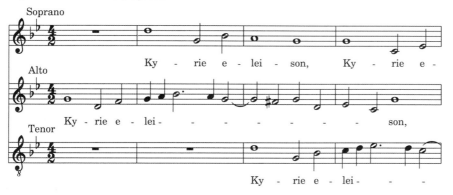

Examples of imitative polyphony

A great deal of Renaissance polyphony follows the medieval precedent of building a work around a preexisting melody in the tenor voice, often in very long notes, known as a *cantus firmus.* (The Josquin work treated next embraces one kind of cantus firmus.) In the *cantus firmus mass,* every movement makes reference to the borrowed melody and the work takes its name from that melody. Thus *Missa Ave maris stella* has the Gregorian chant "Ave maris stella" in the tenor, and *Missa L'homme armé* uses the secular song "L'homme armé" ("The Armed Man").

The word *motet* (from the French *mot,* "word") originally indicated, as we saw earlier, polyphony with texted upper voices. Motets had quickly developed into a form of high and increasingly abstract art, where a large measure of the composer's technique lay in dexterous solving of the almost mathematical problems at hand.

By the high Renaissance, the term motet was used more generally for shorter sacred pieces in Latin, mostly in four and five voices. Motets might be sung in church or for state ceremonies, or at concerts for invited guests. Many were composed for specific events like weddings or visits of state. Dufay's *Nuper rosarum flores,* for example, is for the dedication of the Florence cathedral dome, the work of the architect Brunelleschi. In an ornate manuscript given to Henry VIII by the government of Florence, the concluding motet, *Nil maius superi vident,* heaps all manner of flattery on the English king over a tenor that reads (in Latin), "Henry, by the grace of God, King of the English." The motet is probably by Philippe Verdelot (c. 1475–1552). The manuscript, now in the Newberry Library in Chicago, was probably presented to Henry in 1527–28 by a Florentine ambassador sent to London to seek money and political alliance for his new republic.

"Nymphes des bois," Josquin Desprez's chanson-motet (so called because the words are in French—thus "chanson"—while motets are usually in Latin), laments the death of his worthy predecessor, Ockeghem.

JOSQUIN DESPREZ: *DÉPLORATION SUR LA MORT DE JOHANNES OCKEGHEM* (c. 1497)

Johannes Ockeghem died in Tours in 1497 after a fine career that had begun at Antwerp Cathedral and continued in a series of excellent appointments in France. His influence was strong among the Netherlandish composers who dominated the first decades of the sixteenth century. Josquin's *Déploration,* for example, follows the precedent of Ockeghem himself, who had composed a rather similar lament on the death of Binchois.

Consider first the moving imagery in the poem by Jean Molinet. Mythological forest voices and professional singers the world over are exhorted to exchange their ordinary songs for lamentation; the late Ockeghem was a true treasure (a pun, for he was treasurer of his monastery) and master of his craft. Great is their sorrow to see him covered by earth. In the second part of the work, Ockeghem's disciples are to drape themselves in mourning garments; they include Josquin himself along with the composers Antoine Brumel, Pierre de la Rue (i.e., Pierchon, little Pierre), and Loyset Compère. Having lost their "good father," they weep bitter tears in bidding Ockeghem the farewell of the Requiem Mass itself: *Requiescat in pace, Amen* ("May he rest in peace, Amen").

The tenor voice of the *Déploration* intones the chant from the beginning of the funeral mass:

Re - qui-em ae - ter - nam do - na e - is ____

Do-mi - - - ne,

et lux ___ per-pe - tu - a lu - ce-at ____ e - - is.

Requiem aeternam dona eis Domine,	Eternal rest grant unto them, O Lord,
et lux perpetua luceat eis.	And perpetual light shine upon them.

Josquin, like Ockeghem, was a master of imitative practice. Look closely at the four lower voices in the opening measures. Not only is the tenor closely imitated by the bass three bars later, but the two voices notated here in the treble clef have the same relationship. The same note-against-note counterpoint that works for the two voices sounding in bars 1 through 3 works equally when the third and fourth voices enter. Thus the imitation is of voice pairs.

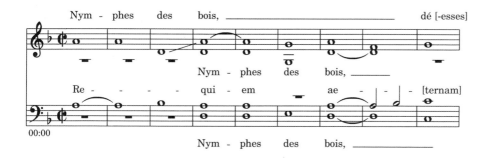

Meanwhile the *superius*—the voice on top, if you are looking at the full score—forms a tuneful melody. The phrase goes on to cadence on D, overlapping the start of the next phrase ("Chantres expers"). Here and throughout, the motet is distinguished by the graceful way the active voices move in to fill spaces left vacant when the others drop out.

Josquin's setting of the text is transparent, so that the words of the poem could be well understood. One of the humanizing features of Josquin's work is the way the expressive musical phrases mirror the meaning of the text. It is no accident that the superius rises noticeably in pitch for the words *tant clères et haultaines* ("very clear and high"), nor that the "gripping cries" that follow are so strongly set out in rhythm and reiterated pitch, decaying then into melismatic lamentation.

But the most poetic effect occurs when, at the start of the second section (or *secunda pars*), the polyphonic interaction is replaced by four-part *homophony* (the tenor having momentarily stopped), then the breathtaking falls of interlocking thirds, certain to symbolize tears.

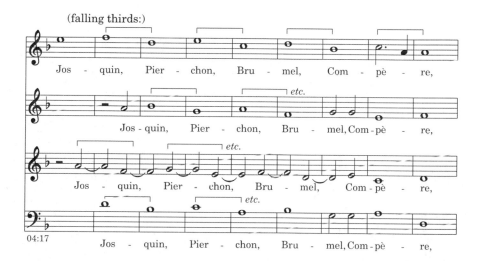

The whole passage is then repeated, followed by a homophonic statement of *Requiescat in pace* (where the tenor returns), then an "Amen" that falls dramatically by thirds again, to a hollow and quite melancholy cadence on the low A.

Even the notation is symbolic of death: Instead of the whole notes and half notes that were customary by that time, the copyist used note-values that could be written entirely in black. In Renaissance practice the music is not in score but in individual parts, and there are no bar lines. All the singers would gather around a single copy of the book—hence the large size—to read their respective parts, following (in this case) whole-note beats and subdividing them according to the meter signature, here duple. A *modern edition* puts these parts into score with familiar note shapes and, for the convenience of modern performers, adds bar lines and the necessary ties across the bar.

The performance is by the Ensemble Clément Janequin, a group founded to study and present this repertoire in what it believes to be modern approximations of original performance practice. The members are admired for their keen acuity of pitch and mastery of old pronunciations. They provide, too, the occasional sharp and flat that hones the cadence points and melodic peaks according to practices described by theorists of the time. Since these pitches didn't exist in the theoretical gamut of pitches, they are called *musica ficta*—fictive music.

Listening Chart

 CD 1, TR 6

Josquin Desprez (c. 1440–1521)
Déploration sur la mort de Johannes Ockeghem (c. 1497)

For: voices in five parts (here doubled by viols)
Text: by Jean Molinet (d. 1507), French poet and historian

Type: Chanson-motet
Meter: ¢
Key: Church mode on D
Duration: 05:54

Each new line of text begins a new point of imitation: one voice or pair of voices leading, the others imitating the leads as they spin their web. The tenor voice intones the plainchant. The uppermost voice, or *superius*, seems especially melodic.

00:00	**Part I**	Nymphes des bois, déesses des fontaines,	Melody + 2 voice pairs.
00:32		Chantres experts de toutes nations,	New point of imitation.
00:52		Changez voz voix tant clères et haultaines	Text painting: clear and high.
01:16		En cris trenchantz et lamentations,	Text painting: cries and lamentations.
01:38		Car Atropos, très terrible satrape	. . . And so on. Try now to hear the
02:05		A vostre Ockeghem attrappé en sa trappe,	cadences at the end of each line,
02:28		Vrai trésorier de musique et chef d'œuvre	as well as the bright description of
02:47		Doct, élégant de corps et non point trappé.	Ockeghem's work, then the sorrowful
03:13		Grand dommage est que la terre cœuvre.	melismas as earth covers him.
04:03	**Part II**	Accoutrez-vous d'abits de deuil:	The texture becomes homophonic.
04:17		Josquin, Pierchon, Brumel, Compère,	The falling thirds: teardrops.
04:37		Et plorez grosses larmes d'œil:	Same music as part II, li. 1
04:52		Perdu avez vostre bon père.	Same music as part II, li. 2
05:14		Requiescat in pace.	Homophonic again.
05:26		Amen.	The falling thirds descend to a low cadence.

Josquin Desprez (c. 1440–1521) is our first celebrity composer. We have a sense of the great esteem in which his works were held by the number of times they were copied in manuscript—a sure sign of musical value. The world at large was drawn to Josquin following the publication of his works, in his lifetime, by one Ottaviano Petrucci, music publisher of Venice.

www.prenhall.com/masterworks
composer profiles
Josquin Desprez

It was Petrucci's epochal invention to print music from movable type. The process took two or three passes, one to print the staves and another to print the pitches, sometimes a third for the text. Music printing has seldom looked better than it did in his very first book, a 1501 collection of about a hundred secular pieces with heavy emphasis on Josquin. (Early books of printed music, incidentally, were a luxury item, more expensive than an ordinary scribal copy. Production got cheaper, of course, as music publishing became the normal means of circulation.) Petrucci went on to publish a great deal more Josquin, notably three books of masses (1502, 1505, 1514), the first collections devoted to a single composer.

Josquin Desprez

We believe that Josquin's career took him, before he was 20, to the Milan cathedral, thence to his long service with the Sforza family there and, in the retinue of Cardinal

Opening of Josquin's *Pange lingua* Mass (see musical example on p. 84)

Ascanio Sforza, to Rome (1484); in Rome he became a member of the papal choir. He appears to have served the king of France, Louis XII, from the 1490s to past the turn of the century. In the spring of 1502 he became the highly paid *maestro di cappella* to Ercole d'Este, duke of Ferrara. Fleeing an outbreak of the plague in 1503 (he was replaced by Obrecht, who died from it in 1505), he went home to Condé-sur-l'Escaut, a few dozen kilometers from Cambrai, where he became affiliated with the local monastic order. At his death he had long been an extremely famous composer, and his posthumous reputation continued to gather. His work was admired by all the famous musicians, by the writers Castiglione and Rabelais, by Leonardo da Vinci (if Josquin is indeed the subject of Leonardo's fine *Portrait of a Musician*), and by Martin Luther, who preferred Josquin's music to any other. All told, he left 18 masses, some 100 motets, several dozen secular vocal works, and a few instrumental pieces. These works are firmly ascribed to him; a great deal more is credited him in dubious attributions.

Josquin seems to have had a healthy sense of his own worth. Searching for a *maestro di cappella* for the Ferrarese court, Ercole d'Este's agents quickly narrowed the choice to Josquin or his gifted contemporary Heinrich Isaac. One of the agents thought Isaac the better hire, finding him more prolific and of better disposition. And a good deal cheaper. "It's true that Josquin composes better," the agent wrote, "but he composes when he wants to and not when you want him to."

Sacred music after Josquin, owing largely to his example, gradually abandoned the cantus firmus tenor and mathematical device in favor of the softer edges of free imitative polyphony. Equality of the voice parts was assumed, and the preferred sonorities resulted from alternating rich, increasingly triadic, consonances with carefully handled dissonance. One revels in the sheer luxuriance of the sound and in what many consider the perfection of contrapuntal technique. The masters of this last period of Renaissance sacred music were the Roman composer Giovanni da Palestrina (1525/26–94); the Spaniard Tomás Luis de Victoria (1548–1611, trained in Rome, perhaps by Palestrina); Orlando di Lasso (1532–94), *maestro di cappella* to the dukes of Bavaria at Munich; and the English composer William Byrd.

William Byrd (1543–1623), born almost exactly a century after Josquin, watched at close range the splendid yet turbulent age of Elizabeth I. Born toward the end of Henry VIII's reign, he became an organist at Lincoln cathedral and in due time a Gentleman of the Chapel Royal, that is, the queen's musicians. In 1575 he and Thomas Tallis, the other leading English composer of the era, were granted an exclusive royal patent for the printing and sale of music and music papers, which, even though it proved unprofitable, established Byrd's centrality in English musical life. But Elizabeth I was an ardent Anglican, and Byrd an unreformed Catholic. In increasingly dangerous times he quietly maintained his religion, eventually leaving London in order to be able to worship with a small congregation in the safety of a private chapel in the countryside. Byrd contributed greatly to the keyboard repertoire and secular song, but he is at his most polished and probably his most devout in his *a cappella* (unaccompanied) sacred music for the Catholic liturgy. This includes two books of polyphonic settings of the mass propers (*Gradualia* I, 1605; II, 1607) and masses for three, four, and five voices, all written after he left London. Of the masses the first to be composed was doubtless the Mass in 4 Parts, probably in 1592–93.

www.prenhall.com/masterworks
composer profiles
Byrd

BYRD: *AGNUS DEI,* FROM MASS IN 4 PARTS (1592–93)

The last movement of Byrd's mass is one of the most exquisitely shaped movements in the Renaissance literature. Byrd is sensitive both to the gentle image of the Lamb of God and to the poignancy of the imploring "miserere" and "dona nobis pacem."

Agnus Dei, qui tollis peccata mundi, Miserere nobis.	Lamb of God who takest away the sins of the world, Have mercy on us.
Agnus Dei, qui tollis peccata mundi, Miserere nobis.	Lamb of God, who takest away the sins of the world, Have mercy on us.
Agnus Dei, qui tollis peccata mundi, Dona nobis pacem.	Lamb of God, who takest away the sins of the world, Grant us peace.

The three verses are set in a single movement, in contrast to the Franco-Flemish preference for a short movement for each. The opening point of imitation is presented, with naive innocence, by the alto and soprano, beginning with the same motive that opened the earlier Kyrie and Gloria (see the example on p. 84). Note how closely the soprano imitates the alto, breaking away only to reach the B♭ cadence.

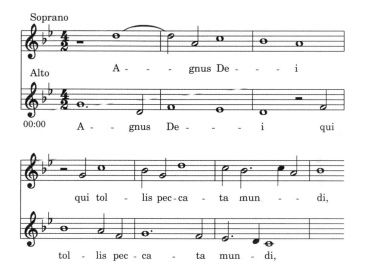

The first verse, then, is a duo, establishing a treble-dominated texture over such an extended period that the near simultaneous entries of the tenor and bass, when they finally happen, take your breath away with the resonance of the new sonority.

The second verse begins with a trio for tenor, bass, and soprano, this one drawing out the *miserere* motive by extensive repetition. As the big cadence concluding the second third approaches, the bass voice shifts forward in speed and rhythmic character, pointedly emphasizing this moment of arrival with a marvelous new pitch, A♭.

The final verse is in close four-part imitation, with a second extended point at "qui tollis peccata mundi." When the "Dona nobis pacem" is at length reached, Byrd begins to link chains of striking dissonance-consonance pairs, called *suspensions,* such that each new vocal entry draws the movement out still further. The bass voice settles again and again on the long-held D, thus acting as a strong dominant. All this seems especially powerful owing to the strong consonance of everything that has come before. And everything so far has been strongly oriented toward G minor as a tonic chord (G-B♭-D), so the closing B♮ in the soprano seems to leave the movement glowing with a golden halo. This effect of substituting a major triad in the last bar of a work in the minor key, much favored of Baroque composers, is called a *Picardy third,* or *tièrce de Picardie.*

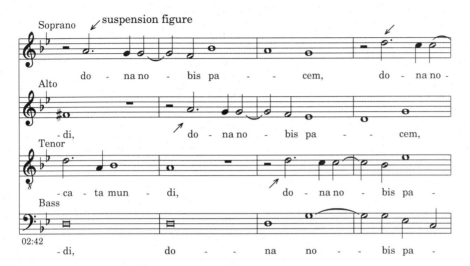

Listening Chart

 CD 1, TR 7

William Byrd (1543–1623)
Mass in 4 Parts (1592–93)
 Agnus Dei

For: unaccompanied voices in four parts (S,A,T,B)

Text: from the Latin liturgy: the last movement of the Mass Ordinary

Type: Polyphonic
 Mass movement
Meter: $\frac{4}{2}$
Key: Church mode on
 G (G minor-ish)
Duration: 04:11

Queen Elizabeth I was an ardent Anglican, and Byrd an unreformed Catholic. Accordingly this mass was composed for a small congregation's worship in the safety of a private chapel in the countryside. In the Agnus Dei, Byrd is sensitive both to the gentle image of the Lamb of God and to the poignancy of the imploring "miserere" and "dona nobis pacem."

00:00 00:25	**Agnus I**	Agnus Dei, qui tollis peccata mundi, Miserere nobis.	Duo: 2 voices (S, A).
00:47 01:17	**Agnus II**	Agnus Dei, qui tollis peccata mundi, Miserere nobis.	Trio: 2 lower voices (T, B), then S. Grows in expanse.
01:49 02:42	**Agnus III**	Agnus Dei, qui tollis peccata mundi, Dona nobis pacem.	All four voices. Chains of suspensions. Each new entry draws things out; bass keeps settling on the dominant pitch D.
03:52			Final cadence with major triad.

The overall technique of the "Dona nobis pacem" phrases is somewhat similar to the teardrop imagery at the end of Josquin's *Déploration*. Here the suggestion is of humankind revently but urgently pleading for peace.

The Byrd masses were sung in private, in hiding, and thus very possibly with one singer on a part. The performance on the CD is by a larger ensemble, the Winchester Cathedral Choir.

Much as medieval chant had spread from Italy throughout western Europe, Catholic church music came with the Spaniards to the New World. Sacred polyphony flourished in Spain in the second half of the sixteenth century, generally thought of as the "Golden Age" of Spanish cathedral music. Its composers sought a sensuous, expressive musical language that favored full consonant harmonies and the rich, blended sound of large choirs. The Golden Age coincided with the period of empire building, and as a result Iberian artistry traveled to the Spanish colonies. The works of Victoria and others were well known throughout the Spanish empire, particularly in the important musical centers of Lima, Cuzco, Montevideo, Guatemala City, and Mexico City.

The art of polyphonic composition was quickly adopted by the native population. Several gifted native composers achieved fame, including the Zapotec musician Juan Mathías (1618–67), chapelmaster at the Oaxaca cathedral, the first native American to achieve such a post.

 MARTINEZ: *AGNUS DEI*, FROM THE "ZAPOTEC" MASS (1636)

In 1636 in the southern Mexican province of Oaxaca (pronounced "Wa-*ha*-ca"), another Zapotec musician, Andréz Martinez, composed a mass that has recently come to light.

The manuscript was found in the early twentieth century by the explorer William Gates, who bequeathed it to Tulane University in New Orleans. On the front cover of the document a handwritten inscription in the Zapotec language gives the date of composition and the name of the composer. It was retrieved and studied in the 1990s by the musicologist Mark Brill (who as a graduate student helped pioneer *Masterworks* and wrote the teacher's manual for it). Here the Agnus Dei is performed by the choral ensemble InQuire, who brought the "Zapotec" Mass to life in 1999.

This simple movement shows relatively little of Byrd's high contrapuntal imitation, let alone Josquin's many levels of cross-reference. Instead its conceptual goal is to establish a tranquil, devotional atmosphere of pleasing vertical sonorities—chords, really—and elegantly contoured melody. The overall language is controlled by a system of rules, taught by the European colonizers, where every dissonance is balanced by consonance on either side and every phrase concludes in a full cadence. What results is both strongly homophonic and strongly leaning toward F major as a *key*—features of post-Renaissance musical thinking. Martinez sets only one of the three sentences in the liturgical Agnus Dei. A full

Frescoes for instructing native composers in music. Mission San Antonio di Padua, central California

rendition might have repeated the music three times, altering "miserere nobis" to "Dona nobis pacem" the third time through; or it might have used plainchant for two of the verses.

Listening Chart

 CD 1, TR 8

Andréz Martinez (fl. 1630s)
"Zapotec" Mass (1636)
  Agnus Dei

For: unaccompanied voices in four parts (S, A, T, B)

Text: from the Latin liturgy: the last movement of the Mass Ordinary

Type: Polyphonic
Mass movement
Meter: $\frac{4}{2}$
Key: Church mode on F
(F major-ish)
Duration: 01:12

Two phrases of choral polyphony, each ending in a prominent cadence. There is relatively little imitation among the voices; instead the texture is largely homophonic, and the harmonic language leans toward F major as a *key*.

00:00	Phrase 1	"Agnus Dei, qui tollis peccata mundi." The voices begin simultaneously, then diverge. Partial cadences at 00:20 and 00:29.
00:27	extension	Sopr. leads extension of the "Qui tollis" clause to full cadence.
00:42	Phrase 2	"Miserere nobis." Mostly homophonic; the cadence at 00:56 is diverted into an "Amen"-like closure.

The earliest music composed and written down in the Americas comes, then, from the first decades of the seventeenth century; this includes a handful of works in the Incan and Aztec languages composed mostly by Spaniards. Virtually all of it was descended, in approach and purpose, from the Golden-Age cathedral style.

THE MADRIGAL.   The secular repertoire for singers expanded, too, notably with the cultivation in Italy of the *madrigal*. Principles of madrigal composition were not, at first, so different from those of contemporaneous sacred polyphony, but the poetry was in modern Italian and the overall effect was lighter and faster. From the beginning, however, there was greater emphasis on homophony, and the madrigalists contributed much to the development of chord-oriented thinking. The texts, often concerned with the stings of love and sometimes its cruder manifestations, invite word painting a good deal more than the liturgical texts.

Madrigals emerged in Florence of the 1520s as lighthearted treatments along the lines of the French chanson of the same era, usually for four voices. By mid-century, Venetian madrigalists had made the genre much more serious, using intricate texts (the sonnets of Petrarch, for example) and complex declamation, counterpoint, and harmony. Five-voice madrigals became the preferred texture. In the late decades of the century, hundreds of madrigals were composed all over Italy by all the major composers. Experimentation abounded: bizarre chromaticism and dissonance in some quarters, virtuosic decoration in others, elsewhere the bright simplicity of dance music. One of the most progressive of the late madrigalists was Carlo Gesualdo (c. 1560–1613), prince of Venosa, lute virtuoso, and wife murderer. His unruly use of the chromatic pitches to illustrate texts of wrenching, fruitless love stretched everybody's notions of propriety. In short, the boldest advances in composition, many of which begin to define the new era of the Baroque, took place first of all in the madrigal.

Pastoral verse was in vogue. Many of the leading late madrigalists were acquainted with Torquato Tasso (1544–95), poet of the Este court in Ferrara (where he succeeded the great Ariosto, author of *Orlando furioso,* 1532). They drew freely on Tasso's pastoral verse and epic *Gerusalemme liberata* ("Jerusalem Delivered," 1575), about the First Crusade. And I imagine they saw life imitating art as Tasso conceived a tragic passion for his patroness, Leonora d'Este, who later became Gesualdo's second wife. Equally popular was G. B. Guarini, author of *Il Pastor fido* ("The Faithful Shepherd"), a verse play of 1590. Texts by Guarini predominate in books IV and V of the nine madrigal collections published by the last great madrigalist Claudio Monteverdi—a native Italian.

MONTEVERDI: *IO MI SON GIOVINETTA* (1603)

The five-voice madrigal "Io mi son giovinetta" ("I am a young woman") is found in Monteverdi's book IV, published in Venice in 1603. Together books IV and V (1605), set mostly to excerpts from *Il Pastor fido,* show the high point of Monteverdi's middle period. Here the text, not specifically identified, is probably also by Guarini; certainly it is a typically pastoral exchange. The shepherdess sings in pleasure at the arrival of spring; the shepherd responds by observing "the springtime of love that blossoms in your beautiful eyes." Alas, his advance is in vain: "Flee," she says, "for in these beaming eyes there will never be springtime for you."

No harm is done in this brief encounter, which lacks the bitter sighing and protestations of cruelty that darken so many of the madrigals of this period. Instead, the setting is brilliant and lively, taking its atmospheric cue from the text's focus on laughter (*rido, ridente*) and spring (*primavera*), and, of course, the girl's admonition to the shepherd: *fuggi* ("flee").

Of the five singers the top two are presumably women, the lower three, men. (Women played a much more significant role in secular music than sacred; by Monteverdi's era there were a number of very successful women virtuosi.) Accordingly, the shepherdess's initial springtime banter is given to the upper voices and the lad's response to the lower, the alto participating in both trios. The phrases tend to begin with homophonic reiterations of the G-minor triad (G-B♭-D), which we sense as a strong tonic.

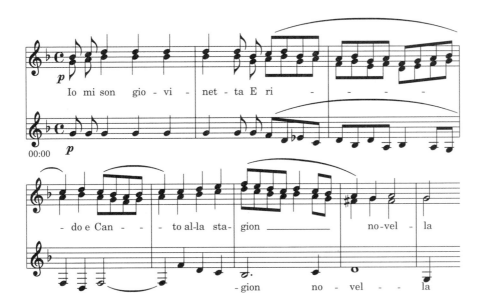

Each of these blossoms into passagework, generally descending sequential figurations related by intervals of a third (say, G–B♭ or B♭–D) and concluding with a cadence point.

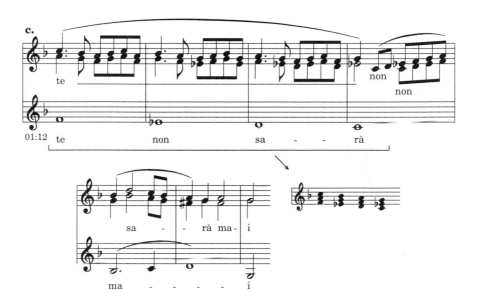

As the example shows, these treatments disguise very simple chord chains. The sequential passage, bracketed in **c.** above, represents one of the most characteristic sounds of Monteverdi at mid-career.

By the halfway point most of the material has been presented, so the second half, with its long string of *fuggis*, is occupied with the same motives in a rather more complex distribution through the five voices. In addition to the many strong cadence points on G minor, there are arrivals on B♭ and D, sonorities that function in tonal practice as the relative major and the dominant. As in the Agnus Dei from the Byrd mass, the final cadence uses a G-B♮-D triad instead of G-B♭-D, making the work conclude in the major mode. But lurking in this simple innocence is at least one pang of despair. Try to identify, just before the end, the hint of chromaticism as the middle voice descends for a moment in half steps.

Claudio Monteverdi (1567–1643), born in Cremona, was called to the Gonzaga court in Mantua, where he played in the orchestra and sang madrigals, eventually becoming *maestro di cappella.* This first period of his career is represented by the first five madrigal books; in successive stages he composed some dozen operas and superb church music. But the madrigals, and

Monteverdi

Listening Chart

 CD 1, TR 9

Claudio Monteverdi (1567–1643)
Io mi son giovinetta (1603)

For: unaccompanied voices in five parts

Text: attributed to G. B. Guarini (1538–1612)

Type: Madrigal
Meter: ¢
Key: G minor
Duration: 02:04

This five-voiced madrigal is no. 13 of Monteverdi's *Fourth Book of Madrigals,* published in 1603. The lively setting takes its atmosphere from the text's focus on laughter (*rido, ridente*) and spring (*primavera*), and the girl's admonition to her suitor: Flee! (*fuggi*).

00:00	**Part 1**	"Io mi son giovinetta E rido e canto alla stagion novella."	She: "I am young, laughing and singing in the new spring season." The three high voices.
00:08			4, then all 5 voices.
00:16		Quando subitamente . . . il cor mio.	Suddenly his heart responds to her song.
00:31		Cantò quasi augellin vago e ridente:	Transition to new section (modulation).
00:41	**Part 2**	"Son giovinetto anch'io E rido e canto alla gentil e bella Primavera d'amore	He (men's voices): "I am young, too, Laughing and singing . . . In the springtime of love . . .
00:51		Che ne' begl'occhi tuoi fiorisce."	That blossoms in your eyes."
00:58	**Part 3**	Ed ella: "Fuggi, se saggio sei,	She: "Flee, if you are wise." High voices,
01:06		Fuggi . . .	again; emphatic *fuggi* (fleeing) motives.
01:10		Primavera per te non sará mai."	"There will be no springtime for you here." Sequential cascades.
01:20	**Part 4**	"Fuggi, . . .	All five voices in an extended
01:38		Primavera per te . . ."	repeat of part 3, coda-like.

related works called *scherzi musicali,* continued long after he left Mantua. Thus, the early books seem to summarize the madrigal practice he inherited, while the later ones open up new vistas for secular singing.

Increasingly, Monteverdi flavored his madrigals with sharp dissonances to emphasize biting words in the poetry. This practice did not escape criticism from pedants wedded to rules calling for the careful treatment of preparation and resolution of dissonance that characterized the purest polyphony of the high Renaissance. In the preface to book V, Monteverdi replies to his critics by outlining what he called the "second practice," or *seconda prattica,* of harmony and then flaunts it by beginning the book with one of the offending works, previously circulated in manuscript, *Cruda amarilli* ("Cruel Amaryllis"). This work has a particularly grating dissonance just near the start at the word "Alas." Violating harmonic rules, he argues, is thoroughly appropriate when demanded by the poetic idea, in this case, cruelty. "I do not do things by chance," he petulantly observes.

The last six madrigals in book V come "with continuous bass for the cembalo, chitar-rone or other similar instrument." Instrumental parts go on to become the norm, and with that the Renaissance distinctions of genre begin to fade away. The *Madrigals of War and Love* (*Madrigali guerrieri et amorosi,* 1638), composed in Venice, are no longer amusing little works to sing after dinner but an interrelated evening's worth of advanced concert music. As you must be sensing by now, the transition of style from Renaissance to Baroque was well under way, and Monteverdi was its single most influential voice.

MUSIC WITH INSTRUMENTS. Gradually during the Renaissance we begin to recognize the growing importance of another group of professional musicians: instrumental players and player/composers. Paintings and tapestries suggest that for a very long time a few instrumentalists had been added for festive performances of church music. At court they were in great demand for chanson accompaniments and dancing. Dance music was played by bands using all sorts of musical instruments, grouped in matched *consorts* of loud and soft instruments, those for outside and those for indoors. Instruments came in sets, or *chests,* of different sizes—treble, tenor, and bass—in order that the appropriate parts would be covered. Among the winds there were recorders, double-reed instruments like the shawm (a forerunner of the oboe) and crumhorn, and brass sackbuts (early trombones). Of particular importance were the *viols,* bowed instruments of five or more strings, held between the knees (thus viola *da gamba,* "of the lap"). Frets of gut were tied to the fingerboard, against which the finger stopped the strings. Enthusiasm for the viols declined in proportion to the rise of the violin family, but the cello-sized gamba retained popularity as a solo instrument well into the Baroque.

Music for dance ensembles was soon being published in a variety of formats, along with method books called *tutors* to teach amateur instrumentalists how to play. These describe the essence of instrumental technique in words and then give music in graded lessons to be mastered and usually some examples of the kinds of things virtuoso players might improvise.

Both the organ and the harpsichord, meanwhile, developed notated repertoires of their own: the organ, not surprisingly, for services in the churches where they were built. The harpsichord had been gaining a foothold throughout the Renaissance and by the Baroque was one of the major solo instruments. Among the important pioneers of early harpsichord music were Byrd and his English colleagues John Bull and Orlando Gibbons, composers of the published *Parthenia* (1613), the manuscript *Fitzwilliam Virginal Book,* and some dozen similar collections. The virginal was a one-manual harpsichord common in England and the Netherlands, presumably favored of pure young ladies.

Cultivated people learned to read musical notation, very often well enough to accompany their singing on the lute, a fretted instrument with a pear-shaped belly, balanced in the lap and plucked with the fingers. Lute music is notated in *tablature,* where the grid shows the position of the fingers on the strings rather than the pitches. Mastery of singing with the lute was promoted by Baldassare Castiglione in his widely read treatise on how gentlemen should behave, *The Book of the Courtier* (1528). Both solo lute music and the lute song mingle characteristics of instrumental dance music and the madriga-lesque styles.

ENGLAND: THE ELIZABETHAN MADRIGAL AND LUTE SONG. Italian madrigals reached England in the 1580s and became the center of attention with a published collection called *Musica transalpina: Italian Madrigals English'd* (that is, in English translation; 1588). Thomas Morley (1557–1602), seconded by Thomas Weelkes (c. 1575–1623) and John Wilbye (1574–1638), turned these models into an English national form. English madrigal texts on the whole are somewhat lighter than their Italian counterparts, often consisting of pastoral ditties about Arcadian shepherds and shepherdesses attending to each other when they should have been tending sheep: "Fair Phyliss I saw sitting all alone" and "Where the bee sucks, there suck I." The musical treatment, however, is just as expressive as the Italian variety, with careful attention to declamation, pictorial expression of the text, rhythmic and metric delight, and overall formal balance. Merry subspecies of the English madrigal embraced "fa-la" refrains and thus were popularly called *fa-las.* The pinnacle of the movement was a collection of 25 works by the leading composers called *The Triumphes of Oriana* (1601), where each madrigal ends with the salute "Long live fair Oriana," in tribute to Queen Elizabeth I.

Madrigals were sung after dinner by gentlepersons seated around a table, reading from individual partbooks or sometimes sheets printed so that each part faced a different direction, as in the illustration on p. 101. Parts might be doubled or covered altogether by a viol player or lutenist. The English madrigal is a source of great delight, full of such double meanings as bees stinging ruby lips, and in one case a treatment of Renaissance cosmography, where the lover's heart burns with the fire of volcanoes and freezes with glacial ice.

The decline of the English madrigal coincided with the rise, in the early 1600s, of the lute song. The singer would accompany himself on the lute in songs of very serious poetic intent. Lute songs are exceptionally sensuous and of great lyricism in the vocal part; the accompaniments, simple as they sound, interact contrapuntally with the voice and can interject vivid chromatic effects.

The principal lute-song composers were John Dowland (1563–1626) and Thomas Campion (1567–1620), both also distinguished lutenist-singers.

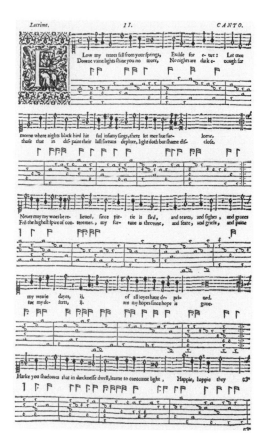

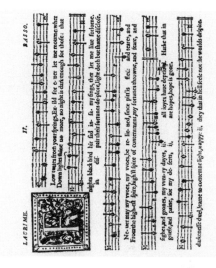

Dowland: *Flow My Tears,* with separate bass part (facing right) (note the lute tablature)

DOWLAND: *FLOW MY TEARS* (1600)

Dowland's masterpiece, still known the world over, first appeared in his *Second Booke of Ayres* (1600) and subsequently in dozens of resettings, transcriptions, and arrangements under the title *Lachrymae* (Latin for "tears"). The musical form used to deal with the five stanzas of text is particularly engaging, with one strophe repeated for the first two stanzas, a second strophe for stanzas 3 and 4, and a new strophe for the conclusion, as a kind of coda. There is a strongly sensed motion downward in nearly every sung phrase, appropriate to the lament of a man deprived of joy. This is reaffirmed by the little motive in the accompaniment that concludes each strophe:

There   let me live   for - - lorn.

Lute

00:30

The tonal shape is well defined, centering on A minor in the first strophe, with a strong move to C major at the beginning of the second and gradual return, through the use of G♯s, to the original A minor.

Listening Chart

 **CD 1, TR 10**

John Dowland (1563–1626)
Flow My Tears **(1600)**

For: tenor, lute

Text: by the composer

Type: Strophic lute song
Meter: 4/2
Key: A minor
Duration: 04:08

Dowland wrote the text and the music and would have accompanied himself as he sang, for cultivated gentlemen of the era could do such things.

00:00	**A** (St. 1)	Flow, my tears, fall from your springs! Exiled forever let me mourn; Where night's black bird her sad infamy sings, There let me live forlorn.	Three phrases of music for five stanzas of text. Note cadence figure in lute.
00:42	**A** (St. 2)	Down, vain lights, shine you no more! No nights are dark enough for those . . .	Singer ornaments new stanza.
01:24	**B** (St. 3)	Never may my woes be relieved, Since pity is fled; And tears and sighs and groans my weary days Of all joys have deprived.	Shift to major.
02:05	**B** (St. 4)	From the highest spire of contentment My fortune is thrown; . . .	
02:46	**C** (St. 5)	Hark! you shadows that in darkness dwell, Learn to condemn light. Happy, happy they that in hell Feel not the world's despite.	Return to minor.
03:28	**C** (St. 5)	Hark! you shadows . . .	Stanza 5 repeated; ornamented.

Flow My Tears, then, is for all intents and purposes in the key of A minor, with cadences that have emphatic G♯ to A motion in the soprano part. Meanwhile you should also have sensed the mutation from the hollow, open sonorities of the Josquin *Déploration* to the more familiar vertical chords you can also hear in the Byrd mass and Monteverdi madrigal. Tonality, in short, is increasingly easy to recognize; indeed, we have been using its terminology for the last dozen pages or so. Tonality is the prime indicator of the dawn of the Baroque.

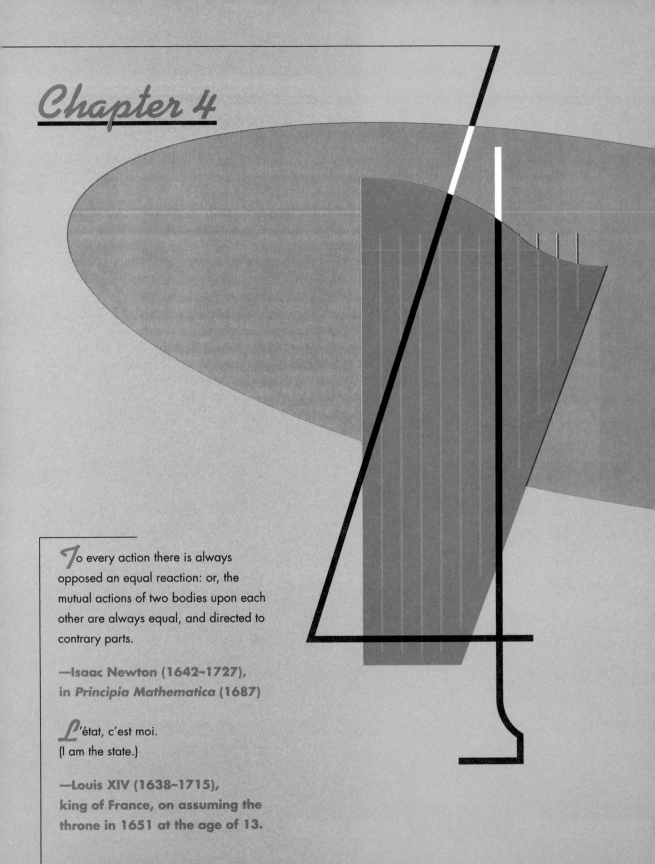

Chapter 4

To every action there is always opposed an equal reaction: or, the mutual actions of two bodies upon each other are always equal, and directed to contrary parts.

—Isaac Newton (1642–1727), in *Principia Mathematica* (1687)

L'état, c'est moi.
(I am the state.)

—Louis XIV (1638–1715), king of France, on assuming the throne in 1651 at the age of 13.

The Baroque

*T*he first of the remarks on the facing page is from a common citizen gifted with uncommon powers of observation; the second is from the most opulent of monarchs, certain that his supreme authority came directly from God. Together they say much about the climate of the 150 years that stretched from 1600 to 1750. Extending from the precipitous decline of Roman Catholicism in the late sixteenth century through the dawn of the industrial and political revolutions that concluded the eighteenth, the Baroque was a period of drastic change in the way people thought about themselves and the laws of their universe.

Saying of an epoch that it is a time of great contrasts is too commonplace, for a close look at any particular era or region will reveal all sorts of inconsistencies. But here the antitheses are particularly striking: the emergence, for example, of a powerful middle class alongside the consolidating of empires by the great feudal monarchies. Gradually the religious confrontations of the previous century were subsiding into a measure of coexistence between the largely Protestant north and Catholic south, but at the expense of endless warring over seemingly insignificant territories and successions—the Thirty Years War (1618–48), for instance. Scientists and philosophers took the opportunity to refashion their understanding of natural principles; artists responded to the modern secular climate with all manner of entertainments for a new public of ticket holders. Galileo's experiments come from the early 1600s; Molière's timeless comedies come between 1660 and his death in 1673. Yet for the most part the thinkers of the Baroque continued to be pious and God-fearing, and their religious art stands in good company with that of the Middle Ages and Renaissance.

In music the modern Italian style was exported to Germany, France, and England as talented composers who had gone to study in Italy returned home. Among these were the German master Heinrich Schütz, Handel, and later Mozart and many others. Likewise the Italian composers took to the road, Lully to France, Corelli and Vivaldi to Vienna. Just as influential were foreign publications of the Italian repertoire, as (we have seen) with *Musica transalpina* and, later, the great commercial success of the Amsterdam publications of Corelli's and Vivaldi's instrumental music. Both Germany and France developed strong national styles based on techniques that had been acquired from Italy.

The look of Europe changed greatly through the work of the Baroque architects. In 1541 Michelangelo had completed his frescoes for the pope's private place of worship, the Sistine Chapel at the Vatican, generally considered one of the triumphs of Renaissance art. He then went on to begin the rebuilding of St. Peter's, the pope's much larger public church alongside. But completing St. Peter's took more than a century, so the finished edifice has less to do with Renaissance ideals than the later passion for vista and spectacle. The dome, great piazza, and grandly curved quadruple colonnades are those of the architect Bernini, completed in the 1660s. This is a Baroque structure: ornate, gilded, spectacular, occasionally deceiving to the eye, and based on the most modern science of the time.

Not long afterward there rose from a swamp by Versailles outside Paris the grandest of all palaces, built for Louis XIV, king of France since 1661. From every vantage point it, too, was a masterpiece of perspectives—terraces giving onto formal gardens, statuary and fountains of mythical deities, reflecting ponds, and grand avenues for horseback recreation. Within there was gilding everywhere, lacquered timepieces, ornate fabrics and carpets, and for a throne room the great Hall of Mirrors. Versailles, and the extravagant life that went on there, was the epitome of all things Baroque (the word refers, it appears, to the pearly inner surface of the oyster shell). And what eyes jaundiced by the excess of its extravagance once found overdone we can now see as exceptional and even stirring.

Baroque thinking grew from the struggle between the serene purity of the sacred styles and the expressive freedoms of the secular. During the early Baroque (c. 1600–50) this dialogue was centered in northern Italy. The *mid-Baroque* (c. 1650–1700) is the period where the principles of the new music radiate outward across Europe. The *late,* or *high, Baroque* (c. 1700–50), represented notably by the music of Vivaldi, Handel, and Bach, shows a fully matured style where technical problems have been overcome and the possibilities seem limitless. The central accomplishment of the era was the perfection of major/minor tonality and a corresponding way of thinking about chords and modern harmonic progression. Contrapuntal equality of voices as an ideal gave way to a sharp focus on the outer lines: the uppermost voice (or melody) and lowermost (or bass). The Baroque era saw the crafting of an impressive body of purely instrumental music, and the birth and runaway popularity of opera.

Louis XIV,
king of France

These developments began to coalesce into a new style just about the time Claudio Monteverdi arrived to take a new job in Venice.

ENICE: MONTEVERDI AND THE OPERA

Neither opera nor the instrumental repertoire was actually born in Venice, but by the first decade of the new century no one could deny Venetian preeminence in both these pursuits. Venice, lying at the confluence of East and West, was in 1600 the pride of Italy and the lion of Europe. Great wealth had accrued in the Venetian republic, earned by a commercial and financial network that had spread by land and sea as far as the imagination dared venture: Marco Polo had begun his famous voyages from the harbor there. At the center of Venice sits the great church called St. Mark's, a bubble-domed neo-Byzantine structure that in architecture alone makes a powerful statement about the unique geographic position that had brought this city-state to power. St. Mark's served as the chapel

of the doge, the elected head of state, whose palace is adjacent. (Both are often filled with water, for Venice is sinking faster than the leaning tower of Pisa, on Italy's other coast, is leaning.) The doge, the clergy, and all their musicians and retinues would travel in barges down the Grand Canal, disembark at the vast piazza, and process into St. Mark's in some of the most spectacular parades of the era.

There flourished in Venice an advanced musical civilization as well. Music printing had been perfected in Venice a century before (see p. 88), and throughout the Baroque music students flocked to Venice to study and compose music, and the public to hear it. Composers and performers were also drawn to Venice, which hosted Handel and Domenico Scarlatti in the Baroque and in later centuries Mozart (who astounded the locals by improvising a fugue at his Venice concert), Rossini, and Verdi. Wagner died there, and Stravinsky and Diaghilev, the giants of twentieth-century ballet, are buried there. Stravinsky's opera *The Rake's Progress* was premiered in Venice, and one of his last works, a *Canticum sacrum,* was composed for St. Mark's cathedral. Several of the best living conductors studied at the Venice conservatory, and the city remains today an important locus of new music composition.

The large musical establishment at St. Mark's included a *maestro di cappella,* organists for each of the two organs, singers, and instrumentalists. Owing to the architecture and acoustic properties of the building, small groups of performers, called *cori spezzati* ("individual choirs"), were often deployed about the chancel, and the St. Mark's composers and organists thus

St. Mark's Basilica, Venice (exterior and interior)

delighted in investigating *antiphonal effects.* The St. Mark's style was fostered notably by the organist/composer Andrea Gabrieli (c. 1510–86) and his nephew Giovanni Gabrieli (c. 1555–1612). It is in Giovanni Gabrieli's singularly significant work that we first encounter scoring for specific instruments and the use of the dynamics *piano* and *forte.* The style favors homophonic sonorities over intricate counterpoint and tends thus to take its shape over a prominent bass line, a voice that now becomes first among equals. Melody and harmony veer sharply away from the Renaissance church modes toward recognizable major and minor keys. Tonality takes firm root.

Monteverdi secured his position in Venice by submitting a set of Vespers of the Blessed Virgin Mary (published 1610) in a style certain to please the authorities at St. Mark's. He thoroughly merited the appointment to this prestigious post, for he was undeniably the most gifted composer alive anywhere in Europe. It is indicative of the broad tastes of the time, however, that Monteverdi's fame thus far lay not in sacred music at all but as a forward-looking composer of madrigals like the one we considered in Chapter 3. Moreover, in Mantua, where he lived before coming to Venice, he had advanced another secular form of music entertainment, the infant genre people were calling *opera.* Monteverdi served the church with dignity, but his chief importance to Venice was that owing to his presence there it became one of the principal centers of music drama for 200 years.

Jacopo Peri
in costume

OPERA. This new medium grew out of the deliberations of a gathering of intellectuals from Florence who called themselves a *camerata* ("band of comrades"). Their stated purpose was to recover an authentic manner of performing Greek tragedy, which they took to be declaimed in speech-song formulas. The scholar in the group was Vincenzo Galilei, father of Galileo; among the others were poets, actors, and virtuoso professional singers, including the composer/performers Jacopo Peri, Giulio Caccini, and Caccini's daughter Francesca Caccini. The camerata called the Italian equivalent of their ideas about Greek declamation *recitative.* Here the dramatic text was set in speechlike rhythms, accompanied by occasional chords from an instrumental force of (perhaps) keyboard, lutes, and bass viol.

I weep not and sigh not, O my dear Euridice,
for whom I can neither sigh nor cry.

Peri: *Euridice*, an example of recitative style

Recitative was an efficient way of getting the point across, for a good deal of text could be intelligibly conveyed in a very short time. From this point on in music history, any kind of conversational delivery can be called recitative style.

The music of the first opera, Peri's *Dafne* (1598), is lost. The subject matter that lured the Florentines next was the myth of Orpheus, who used the power of harp and song to win the fair Eurydice back from the dead. From this story Peri and Caccini fashioned a new operatic entertainment to a text by their colleague Ottavio Rinuccini. *Euridice* was performed for the wedding in 1600 of Marie de' Medici of Florence to Henry IV of France. Within a year or so Peri and Caccini each published a version of the work.

You wouldn't find this music especially thrilling; its importance lies more in establishing an idea than in its aesthetic perfection. Meanwhile, Caccini developed a theory and repertoire of rather more tuneful songs along similar lines and published these *monodies* as *Le nuove musiche* ("The New Music," 1602). Monodic singing became the basis for the recitative and aria pair, the heart of Baroque opera. The declamatory *recitative* introduces the *aria* (or "air"), consisting of more formal, more rigorously composed music to full instrumental accompaniment. The strength of this pairing is that it allows the advancing of plot and context during the recitative, and in the aria the character's emotive response to the situation at hand.

Monteverdi composed his particular *Orfeo* (1607) in Mantua, to an Orpheus libretto by Alessandro Striggio. This marvelous opera begins to take wing as the wedding guests assemble in a meadow of mythical Greece. A messenger brings the news that Orpheus's bride, Eurydice, has died of a snakebite. Orpheus's anguished cry on learning the truth is a noteworthy example of the new powers of *tonal* drama, with its abrupt, wrenching move from an E-major chord to a G-minor chord.

MESSENGER: Your beautiful Eurydice . . .
ORPHEUS: Alas, what do I hear?

Orpheus descends to Hades to fetch his bride and at the River Styx lulls the boatman Charon to sleep with the beauty of his song. Here the score carries the full particulars of virtuoso work by violins, cornetti (wooden trumpet-like instruments), and the harp, as well as suggesting a reading for the very florid decoration expected of the singer.

Things turn out reasonably well. After a misadventure in which Orpheus loses Eurydice once again (during their escape from Hell, he sneaks a peek at her after being expressively forbidden to do so), the lovers are reunited in mythical Elysium with Apollo, the sun, and the stars.

Scarcely a moment of Monteverdi's *Orfeo* has anything to do with composition of the Josquin era. At every turn it seems wholly concerned with the rhythms, forms, orchestration, and vocal display of the modern era. Indeed, *Orfeo* remains firmly ensconced in the operatic repertoire.

RECOMMENDED LISTENING:

www.prenhall.com/masterworks

Monteverdi: excerpt from Orfeo *(1609)*

The early Orpheus operas had many descendants, the last and possibly best of which is *Orfeo ed Euridice* by the Classical composer Gluck (1762). Two other Monteverdi operas are preserved complete, one drawing on the Ulysses myth and the other on a story of the emperor Nero's abandonment of his wife for a mistress, Poppea. *L'Incoronazione di Poppea* ("The Coronation of Poppea," 1642) is Monteverdi's last major work.

Opera, a more promising kind of music theater than any of its many predecessors, was a hit. In 1637 the first public opera house opened in Venice, with a half dozen others springing up over the next few years. By the end of the century some 400 operas had been produced in Venice and important theaters built in the other major Italian cities. Baroque theaters were capable of spectacular scenic effect, creating nautical scenes, weather, and descents of the deities with a combination of elaborate stage machinery and optical illusion, or *trompe l'œil.* (The architects of these spectacles, incidentally, were equally at home with engines of destruction and were called upon in wartime to design and build fortifications and heavy military apparatus.) Opera in the Italian Baroque was the most lavish entertainment to be found anywhere. No wonder people came from all over Europe to see it.

Ideally, the joining of words and music on the stage makes for a more powerful experience than either alone. In practice, the history of opera is an ongoing search for the right balance. In Baroque serious opera, or *opera seria,* music rather quickly became the ruler of the words. Generations of high-priced, wildly popular professional singers developed an improvisatory performing practice ranging from gentle embellishment of individual pitches to florid ornamentation that entirely redefines the nature of the music. In the *da capo aria* (A-B, *da capo* to A), which rapidly became the norm for *opera seria,* the return of the A section was considered an opportunity for the singer to demonstrate every vocal invention he or she could muster, particularly when its prevailing sentiment (or *affect,* as the theorists called it) was sorrow or rage. Nowhere was this more extravagant than with the male *castrato* singers of the late Baroque, whose mellow high voices and strong volume earned them fortunes. They were greatly prized as lovers, too.

Instrumental players, for reasons of their own, followed suit. Theories of how to ornament were published, and a whole grammar of symbols was developed to abbreviate the most common effects. In matters of ornamentation the connection of Baroque music to Baroque art and architecture is particularly close, each having its own way of "painting the lily, gilding the gold." Do not be surprised, then, to hear in recordings of Baroque music a great deal that does not appear in the score. Notated music in the Baroque is sometimes merely the scaffold for what is actually performed, so this repertoire is more than usually recreated afresh every time it is played.

*B*ASSO CONTINUO; THE RITORNELLO PRINCIPLE

In *Orfeo* we witness the Baroque's new post-contrapuntal textures, the novel use of instrumental force, and the strong hold of tonality. Now note, as well, the organizing role of the bass part, called by the Italians the *basso continuo,* by the English the *thorough-bass.* The feature that most audibly characterizes Baroque music is this ongoing bass part: beginning at the beginning and continuing through to the end, often in more or less continuous eighth notes, driving steadily on, and serving as foundation for all that is fashioned above it.

The continuo line is played by any bass instrument present in the performing force, from a single cello or gamba to the full cello section, basses, and bassoons. Moreover there is virtually always a *keyboard* player who doubles the bass line with the left hand and with the right improvises on it, filling out the chords, ornamenting pitches, and so forth. When the composer was conducting from the keyboard, as was often the case, he improvised from the full score before him. For other performers, the continuo part would be in the form of a *figured bass,* where the numbers define the intervals above the bass note that will produce the correct chord structure at the keyboard. You saw some figured bass in the example from Peri's *Euridice* and will encounter another in the excerpt from Henry Purcell's opera *Dido and Aeneas,* considered on page 113.

Thus the *basso continuo* is usually provided by two or more players, at a minimum the keyboardist and, say, a cellist. Usually the keyboard instrument is the *harpsichord,* where quills pluck the metal strings and yield a rapidly decaying pitch of rather percussive tone quality. (Harpsichordists, too, are fond of ornamentation, for it can extend and reinforce the otherwise limited sustaining power of the instrument.) In churches the organ sometimes provided the continuo; sometimes, as in the case of the Monteverdi operas, the bass force would be joined by lutes and archlutes. *One of the surest ways to recognize Baroque music is to hear the presence of the basso continuo.*

Another way Baroque music is different from its predecessors is in its basic organizational plan. Whereas in the Renaissance much serious music had been built up in series of loosely related contrapuntal phrases (as in Josquin's *Déploration* and the Byrd *Agnus Dei*), the Baroque deals primarily with ritornello forms. The *ritornello*—"that which returns"—is a section that introduces a movement, then comes back over its course to serve as a point of structural reference. A ritornello will be stated at the outset in its entirety; it may return several times, usually abbreviated, and then will be heard again in full at the conclusion of the movement. Between these statements of the ritornello come various kinds of departures, but the ritornello inevitably returns to conclude the movement. Later we consider a concerto movement by J. S. Bach in classic ritornello form.

Florentine musicians (note the harpsichord)

Even the rigorous Baroque contrapuntal forms, fugue and the like, are specialized ritornello forms. This is the period of "concerted music," where large groups of musicians joined together in concord and harmony. The basso continuo was their linear common denominator, the ritornello their formal one.

By the mid-Baroque—the last decades of the seventeenth century—these practices had evolved into a style whose grasp extended throughout Europe. Heinrich Schütz (1585–1672), a student of Giovanni Gabrieli, had taken the Venetian notions of concerted sacred music northward to Dresden. The Vatican organist Girolamo Frescobaldi (1583–1643) had taught Johann Jakob Froberger (1616–67), pioneer of the mighty North German organ school. And the North German organists had been fed in equal measure by the thriving school of Dutch composers headed by the Amsterdam organist Jan Pieterszoon Sweelinck (1562–1621). Components of Italian opera began to shape the noble French court ballet and the equally lavish entertainment the English called the masque.

As England emerged from the religious and civil disruptions where Charles I had been beheaded and a Commonwealth briefly declared, there came to the fore the short-lived but distinguished composer **Henry Purcell (1659–95)**. Trained as a chorister of the Chapel Royal, where his father had also served, he spent his life working for the English monarchs. At the age of 20 he was named organist of Westminster Abbey, in three years' time organist of the Chapel Royal, and a year later Keeper of the King's Instruments. He composed coronation music for James II and funeral music for Queen Mary II (d. 1694), wife of William III. Purcell wrote fluidly and quite originally in all the genres, and the acuity of his ear for the rhythm of English words makes his work in that language quite memorable. Both at court and as a theater composer he paved the way for Handel's conquest of London a few decades later.

Purcell embraced Baroque rhetoric somewhat reluctantly but soon came to excel at it. The musical elements we have been considering—recitative and aria, basso continuo,

www.prenhall.com/masterworks
composer profiles
Purcell

ritornello practice, the new tonality—provide the raw materials for his wonderful opera *Dido and Aeneas.*

PURCELL: "WHEN I AM LAID IN EARTH" (DIDO'S LAMENT) FROM *DIDO AND AENEAS* (1689)

Dido and Aeneas, an hour-long theatrical composed for a girls school near London, is the first true opera in English. Everything about it is small of scale, from the number of roles to the size of the orchestra. The story, one of the finest sagas of tragic love in all literature, comes from Virgil's Latin epic *The Aeneid.* Aeneas, wandering with his band of survivors from the pillage of Troy, takes refuge in the harbor at Carthage and there falls in love with Dido, the Carthaginian queen. His destiny, however, is to establish a new civilization in Rome, and following the dictates of the gods and his conscience, he abandons her. Grief-stricken, Dido prepares her funeral pyre, then commits suicide.

The libretto was fashioned by Nahum Tate in picturesque, sometimes rather comical English. Its sequence of arias, choruses, and dance is of memorable good humor: Witches cackle and sailors dance. But the gods and goddesses achieve their fateful end, and events begin their plummet toward Dido's death scene.

The recitative preceding Dido's final aria is for obvious reasons slow and lugubrious, achieving its impact by its inexorable downward fall from the C with which it opens to the D where it ends. The sudden shift from the E♮s of "invades me" to the biting E♭s of "Death" turn a C-major triad into a minor sonority to very powerful effect.

Dido's lament is built on a recurring bass pattern, which repeats in five-bar cycles. We call this kind of bass a *basso ostinato* ("obstinate bass") or, more particularly, a *passacaglia.* Purcell invented neither the technique nor the specific pattern, but this particular passacaglia is the most famous of them all.

The bass line moves chromatically downward from the tonic G to the dominant D, then drops to cadence and repeat. Purcell's chief means of keeping this repetitive scheme taut is by leaving some musical issue unresolved at each point of repetition. The melody is open-ended and for the most part stays away from the tonic G, reaching a climactic, even terrifying, high point at the last "Remember me." In the orchestra part, a pitch often becomes dissonant when tied across the bar, another case of the suspension and resolution practice we saw in the Byrd mass.

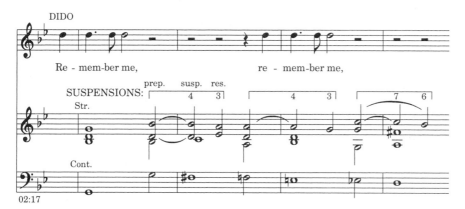

The suspensions resolving downward (as they most often do) emphasize the sorrow, and the same teardrop imagery is quite prominent in the final chorus, "With Drooping Wings."

Listening Chart

 CD 1, TR 11

Henry Purcell (1659–95)
***Dido and Aeneas* (1689)**
　From act II: "Dido's Lament"

For: Dido (soprano), strings, continuo

Text: by Nahum Tate (1652–1715)

Type: Recitative and aria
Meter: $\frac{3}{2}$
Key: G minor
Duration: 04:08

The story comes from Virgil's epic narrative *The Aeneid* (c. 30 BC), "modernized" by the librettist to suit the tastes of the time and place. Learning that Aeneas will leave her to achieve his destiny, the grief-stricken Dido prepares to kill herself. In the recitative she turns for support to her attendant Belinda; the aria, over an unvarying chromatic bass figure, is her heart-rending final lament.

00:00	**Recitative**	Thy hand, Belinda; darkness shades me:	Singer and continuo (lute, cello),
00:19		On thy bosom let me rest:	speech rhythms. Slow downward fall
00:29		More I would, but Death invades me:	reflects the dramatic situation.
00:39		Death is now a welcome guest.	Poignant minor chord for "Death."
00:54	**Aria**		The passacaglia bass alone.
01:08	phrase 1	When I am laid in earth,	She begins.
		may my wrongs create	
		No trouble in thy breast;	
01:43	phr. 1 rep.		First phrase repeated.
02:17	phrase 2	Remember me, but ah! forget my fate.	Suspensions in strings.
02:56	phr. 2 rep.		Second phrase repeated.
03:32	orch. close		Orchestral close dwells on the
			wrenching suspensions.

Composers found in basso ostinato patterns like the passacaglia an obvious technical challenge, and for some people that kind of challenge frees the imagination. A famous later example, also a lament, is the crucifixion passacaglia from Bach's B-Minor Mass. Bach also composed a huge Passacaglia and Fugue for pipe organ and, in his second partita for violin, a closely related movement type called the *chaconne*.

www.prenhall.com/masterworks
recommended listening

RECOMMENDED LISTENING:

Pachelbel: Canon in D (c. 1700)

More intricate still are the kinds of operations afoot in a work that has become a kind of theme song of the Baroque, Pachelbel's Canon for three violins and continuo. In a canon, remember, what is stated by the leading voice must be scrupulously followed by the successors. (*Rounds,* like "Three Blind Mice" and "Sumer is icumen in," are one kind of canon.) With Pachelbel you have both the canon and a kind of passacaglia bass. In this case the ostinato pattern is only two measures long.

These pitches imply a rudimentary chord progression, the simplicity of which facilitates in some measure what goes on above. The cycle repeats 28 times, over which the three violins move in strict canon, the first violin leading, the second following (exactly, all the way through) two measures later, and the third entering two measures after that.

The cleverness comes in the way Pachelbel arranges the new episodes in the first violin, so textural changes, duo combinations, and dialogue fall naturally out of the scheme. On paper this is all quite clear and quite impressive; without the score, however, you cannot necessarily sense which of the three violin parts is which, nor who's leading and who's following. The net effect is one of constant mutation within a very static framework, a simultaneous complexity and simplicity that every listener can grasp and enjoy. Other than that, I cannot say for certain how the Pachelbel Canon achieved its modern celebrity. It appears to have made the Top Ten of Baroque music beginning in 1969 and was subsequently used in a movie soundtrack and a Jell-O commercial. In the dozens of its recordings the original score is almost always rewritten, probably to compensate for a rather tame middle section.

Pachelbel, organist of Nuremberg, exerted a strong influence on the development of Johann Sebastian Bach by virtue of his geographic proximity to the Bach family and the more direct connection that he was the teacher of Johann Christoph Bach, the brother who raised young J. S. after his parents died. One of Pachelbel's sons came to the New World, working in New England and Charleston, South Carolina.

BAROQUE INSTRUMENTS. The Baroque orchestra abandoned the more primitive Renaissance instruments in favor of their technically improved successors, and a reasonably standard orchestral configuration began to be assumed. The violin family—violin, viola, cello—represented an advance over the viols in acoustic properties and refinement of construction. Where the viols had six strings and frets, the violins were unfretted with four strings, thus simplifying the mechanics of playing and in turn broadening the technical possibilities. A true Baroque violin is noticeably different from its modern counterpart, however, with shorter neck and fingerboard, a squatter bridge, and of course gut strings. (The Romantic era's interest in bigness caused virtually all existing old violins to be rebuilt with longer necks and more resonant bridges and prompted the development of a longer, more powerful bow.) The period from about 1660 to 1725 constitutes the heyday of the great violin-making families of Cremona in northern Italy: the Amati, Guarneri, and Stradivari dynasties. Theirs are the instruments for which a vast corpus of sonatas and concertos was fashioned by the late seventeenth-century violinist/composer Arcangelo Corelli (1653–1713) and his many followers.

The double-reed instruments—oboes and bassoons—began to take recognizable shape, although the complex metal key systems are an advance of the nineteenth century. Bach, in particular, writes lovely parts for other members of the oboe family: the alto *oboe d'amore* and the tenor *oboe da caccia* ("of the hunt"), an early English horn. The other prominent woodwind instruments were the flutes: the recorders and, more and more, the transverse flute made of wood. Horns and trumpets, both valveless, were

www.prenhall.com/masterworks
woodwinds
oboes and bassoons

Yuzuko Horigome playing a Stradivarius violin crafted in the Baroque period

greatly valued by composers for their ability to evoke the outdoor sentiments: sounds of the hunt, the battle, or simple jubilation. The grouping of three trumpets with timpani became a musical symbol of royalty, often heard in the big Baroque festive pieces. And professional trumpet players developed dazzling skills in the higher octaves, where scale-work is possible on natural instruments. Composers, accordingly, wrote them good material.

www.prenhall.com/masterworks
instruments
keyboards

The harpsichord was perfected in the seventeenth century with the one-manual Flemish instruments of the Ruckers family. The English and French of successive generations preferred the bolder two-manual design, which culminated in the work of the Parisian builder Pascal Taskin (1723-93). The second half of the Baroque was also the golden age of the pipe organ in the north, where Dutch builders had long plied their magnificent craft. The German builder Arp Schnitger and his sons designed the kinds of instruments Bach and his contemporaries aspired to command.

For the orchestra there developed a large repertoire of concertos and suites, and the orchestra also served as the usual accompaniment force for sacred choral works and theater music. Solo and chamber-sized compositions for the instruments were called *sonatas* (from *sonare*, "to play," as cantata is from *cantare*, "to sing"). The *trio sonata* was avidly cultivated, establishing the common Baroque texture of two high voices and a bass voice. (But note that a trio sonata typically has *four* players, the three soloists and the keyboard player.) Corelli's sonatas distinguish between the grave sonatas *da chiesa* ("of the church") and the lighter sonatas *da camera* ("of the chamber").

www.prenhall.com/masterworks
recommended listening

RECOMMENDED LISTENING:

Mouret: Rondeau from First Symphonic Suite (c. 1729)

A good example of Baroque instrumental music is the theme music for the public television series *Masterpiece Theater.* This is the Rondeau from the First Symphonic Suite of Jean-Joseph Mouret (1682–1738).

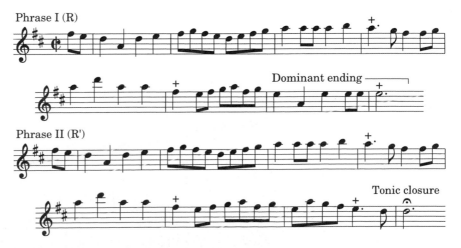

Mouret: Rondeau, the opening ritornello

The *rondeau,* or rondo, is a simple form where the ritornello appears after each departure episode: R-A-R-B-R, and so forth. The martial character of this work is achieved through the use of the trumpet and timpani in the ritornellos; in the interludes, the trumpet drops out and the focus shifts to the oboes and strings.

Mouret came to Paris in 1707, where he composed court music, conducted opera, and eventually served as director of a famous series of solemn Lenten programs called the Concert Spirituel. He is one of the several composers in music history who went mad, finishing his days in the insane asylum at Charenton.

Mouret was one of the more modest figures in the flourishing tradition of music around the royal court of France during the period of its maximum influence, the reigns of Louis XIV and XV. The preeminent French composer of that period was Jean-Baptiste Lully (1632–87), an Italian—Giovanni Battista Lulli—who had come to France in 1646 to help Mademoiselle de Montpensier with her Italian. Ma'am'selle, as everybody called her, was a cousin and bride apparent of Louis XIV. Louis himself was a splendid dancer and capable musician with a good eye for talent, so it is no surprise that Lully was soon assimilated into the royal court. His critical accomplishment was to commingle French ballet and Italian opera, first working in tandem with Molière on their famous *comédies-ballets* (e.g., *Le Bourgeois Gentilhomme,* 1670), then composing a series of operas in French which he called *tragédies-lyriques* (e.g., *Armide,* 1686). Louis required music for nearly every waking hour, including serious concert music every evening but Saturday, and saw to it that the best French musicians were in his employ: the harpsichordist François Couperin (1668–1733), lutenists, the celebrated gambist Marin Marais (1656–1728; Lully's pupil and subject of the film *Tous les matins du monde*), and the multi-talented child prodigy Elisabeth Jacquet de La Guerre (1659–1729).

VIVALDI, BACH, HANDEL

The various branches of the so-called high Baroque (c. 1700–1750), are best followed in the work of the Italian Antonio Vivaldi, the German Johann Sebastian Bach, and the adopted Englishman George Frideric Handel. The Parisian Jean-Philippe Rameau, (1683–1774), was of no less accomplishment and also the most important theorist of his day, but there are significantly fewer performances of his music in modern times.

Whether for weekly church services or courtly entertainment, a large proportion of the music of this period was composed rapidly, played a few times at most, then shelved for reuse later on or simply laid to rest. Vivaldi, Bach, and Handel all worked this way, each of them composing many thousand pages of music, willingly rewriting old material for different occasions, and not infrequently gathering some other composer's work into their own. What distinguishes them from the hundreds of lesser composers of the time is the way each perfected the styles and genres in which he worked. All three achieved fame commensurate with their abilities, and in each case that fame has been enduring.

ANTONIO VIVALDI (1678–1741). A singularly worldly priest with a striking shock of red hair, Vivaldi wrote and conducted the music for a Venetian school for foundling girls called the Pietà. Venice in the Baroque was known for its all-female orchestras, a by-product of an orphanage movement that by Vivaldi's time sheltered thousands. (The foundling hospitals took in boys as well, but most of them were trained as artisan craftsmen.) Vivaldi's Sunday concerts were popular and well attended, widely recognized as a major component in the musical life of a city still considered the musical mecca of Europe, with a musicians union that numbered 300 professional instrumentalists and singers.

Although Vivaldi wrote in all the customary genres, producing nearly 100 operas, cantatas, and sacred music (including the popular "Vivaldi Gloria"), he is remembered primarily for the orchestral music he composed for his young women. Taking as his precedent the orchestral works of Corelli, he composed a huge number of concertos for one or more soloists and string orchestra, some 500 or 600 works in all. Vivaldi is open to the criticism that his prolific output was due to routine use of the same formulas and mechanics much of the time, in effect writing the same work over and over again. But his ideas of harmonious interaction between soloists and orchestra are very attractive, and his music is nearly always vibrant, elegant, and well shaped. The descriptive concertos called *The Four Seasons,* op. 8 (1725) were the best-sellers of their era. And his better music has lasted quite well by virtue of its catchy melodies and rhythmic vitality. Everybody likes him, and Vivaldi addicts are not uncommon.

Nevertheless Vivaldi was something of a scoundrel, unpopular among his colleagues and given to fiscal irresponsibility. Although his fees were high, his expenses were enormous, and he died in poverty.

Vivaldi

JOHANN SEBASTIAN BACH (1685–1750). Bach was born into a dynasty of church musicians active in north Germany that began with his great-grandfather Hans Bach and extended to the several of Bach's sons who became distinguished composers. Following the death of his parents, he was raised and educated by his brother Johann Christoph and later became a choral scholar in Lüneburg. By the age of 18 he was earning his own living. As a journeyman organist and composer, he rose rapidly through the ranks, serving churches in Arnstadt (1703–1707), Mülhausen (1707–1708), and Weimar (1708–17), and composing for them many of the great organ solos that appear to constitute the majority of his early work. These positions he won through competitive auditions; and in contests, consultations, and recitals across Germany he became famous as one of the brilliant organists of his generation. Through his travels he became personally acquainted with the best of his contemporaries, notably Dietrich Buxtehude, the music master at Lübeck (c. 1637–1707), and Georg Philip Telemann (1681–1767).

Bach's employment records in Arnstadt record that he went to Lübeck "to learn one thing and another about his art," expecting to stay four weeks and staying four months; his obituary says that he went, "what is more, on foot." His primary reason for going away was surely to hear Buxtehude play, but Bach was possibly also interested in the matter of Buxtehude's succession. A condition of employment at Lübeck was for the incoming organist to marry his predecessor's eldest daughter. (Handel and the composer

Johann Matheson had withdrawn their candidacies on learning the rules of engagement; a suitable organist and husband was at length found in Buxtehude's own assistant.)

Telemann befriended Bach after he became Kapellmeister in Eisenach, Bach's hometown. Later Telemann was the preferred candidate for the job in Leipzig that eventually went to Bach, choosing instead a similar but better paid position in Hamburg.

Bach's appointment as conductor to the court musicians of the Prince of Cöthen (1717–23) was a major turning point. Adept at composing what was asked of him, he began to focus on instrumental music, composing there the Brandenburg Concertos, the orchestral suites, solo pieces for cello, violin, and lute, and an important body of harpsichord music.

In 1723 he moved to Leipzig to become cantor of the St. Thomas Church and music director of its boys school, a post he held the rest of his life. This, too, was a fine job, with the extra advantage of requiring from his pen mostly Protestant church music, to which he was by artistic inclination and religious belief strongly drawn. He plied his trade in the bosom of what appears to have been a loving family. Certainly it was large, with 20 children (by two successive wives), 9 of whom lived to adulthood and helped him copy the music for his mounds of cantatas for Sunday services, major works for the Christmas and Easter seasons, music for ceremonies and festivals, and pieces for the instruction of his family and pupils.

J. S. Bach

In summary, Bach was a star organist, a master composer, the most capable contrapuntist of his age, and a gifted educator. A devout Christian, he regarded his talents as gifts from God, and took care to note "Jesus, save me" at the beginning of his scores and "God be praised" at the end.

Toward the end of his life Bach became engrossed with the idea of pursuing the various genres to their outer conceptual limits. To this end, he composed *The Art of Fugue,* containing dozens of ways to treat the same very simple fugue subject (see pp. 128–29); the *Goldberg Variations,* an aria with 30 variations for two-manual harpsichord, named after his pupil Johann Goldberg (intended, one account has it, to be played for Goldberg's patron, who suffered from insomnia); the *Musical Offering,* 13 contrapuntal movements to a theme by Frederick the Great, King of Prussia; and the B-Minor Mass, a compilation and rewriting of previous sacred compositions into a complete Latin mass of formidable dimensions. The B-Minor Mass is a curious work in that Bach's intentions for it, other than as a private intellectual exercise, are unclear. We have no documentation regarding what it was to be called or by whom it was intended to be performed. Bach and his musicians were Protestants, but the full mass sets the Catholic liturgy. Ultimately such questions are of little import, since taken together these summarizing works say virtually all there is to say about high Baroque counterpoint. They crown Bach's magnificent career.

Despite a prevailingly pious disposition, Bach nevertheless had his colorful side. He was given in his youth to temper tantrums (hurling his wig, in one not particularly well-documented story, at an unsuspecting student) and yelling epithets at a "nanny-goat bassoonist" (*Zippelfaggott*) with whom he was quarreling—another reason he was anxious to leave town and get to Lübeck. His file shows reprimands for secreting girls into the choir loft and disrupting the congregational singing of chorales with long organ improvisations over the fermatas (holds) that come at the end of each line.

Having lived a full life, Bach essentially completed what he had to say as a composer. By the time of his death, younger artists were investigating radically new ways of thinking about music. And so it is that Bach stands, with scarcely a rival, at the pinnacle of the Baroque.

His works are identified by BWV number, which refers to a catalog by the scholar Wolfgang Schmieder, the *Bach-Werke-Verzeichnis.* The catalog is arranged by genre and thus does not reflect chronology; indeed, Bach chronology is a complicated business at best and has only recently begun to be fully understood.

www.prenhall.com/masterworks
composer profiles
Handel

GEORGE FRIDERIC HANDEL (1685–1759). Like Bach, Handel lived a long and prosperous life, but the country he dominated with his music was far removed from the sober world of the Lutherans. Handel, too, was born in north Germany, near Hamburg, but unlike Bach he was drawn primarily to the theater and secular forms. To pursue this interest he traveled to Italy (1706–1709) to acquire the style of opera and cantata at its source. The work of Alessandro Scarlatti (1660–1725), composer of operas, cantatas, and oratorios, greatly influenced him in his younger years; from Corelli and others he mastered the essence of the concerto style. In 1710 he became Kapellmeister to the elector of Hanover, a duchy in north-central Germany.

As a visitor to England in 1711 and again in 1712 he enjoyed artistic and social successes during a sojourn so long that it threatened his standing at home. But in 1714 his employer, George, elector of Hanover, was invited by Parliament to become George I, king of England. Handel never went back to Germany.

In England Handel composed anthems, ceremonial works, and entertainments for his employers: *Water Music* for royal barge progresses, *Music for the Royal Fireworks,* and so on. By far his most important work, however, was in the perfection of the Italian *opera seria.* For much of the century, Italian opera, centered in Venice and Naples, had been buffeted by attacks and reforms, efforts to purify what were regarded as its excesses, and most recently the assault of the comic styles called *opera buffa.* Handel, meanwhile, worked easily within its conventions of plot and form. As director and principal composer of The King's Theatre in the Haymarket, he produced 39 operas that met with considerable financial success. Among these perhaps the most often performed today is *Giulio Caesare* (1724), based on the story of Caesar and Cleopatra. Altogether Handel was a decidedly secular character, at home in cosmopolitan surroundings (speaking, it is said, five languages badly), a shrewd businessman who enjoyed his measure of luxury.

In the late 1730s Handel felt, with good reason, that the London public had begun to tire of Italian opera and thus turned to concentrate on a new genre, the English oratorio. These works for soloists, large chorus, and orchestra were welcomed by a public that extended much further than the operagoers. The 21 oratorios, among them *Israel in Egypt* (1738), *Messiah* (1741), and *Judas Macchabeus* (1746), are his last big works.

Handel died a venerated man, in some respects the darling of English society. It was Handel, more than anyone else, who internationalized the Italian style. Between them, Bach and Handel—the severe church composer and the elegant society musician—represent most of the avenues of high Baroque musicianship worth pursuing in a general studies course.

THE BAROQUE CONCERTO

The predominant orchestral genre of the period involved the amiable encounter of soloists and the full orchestra. The Baroque concerto has three movements, fast-slow-fast, the outer movements big ritornello forms and the middle one typically a freer aria form. The general theory is one of alternation between the ritornellos provided by the full orchestra, or *ripieno,* and departures by the soloists, or *concertino.* The continuo players carry all the way through underneath, but in the solo breaks the bass ripienists drop out, leaving the keyboard and the principal cellist.

Frederick the Great of Prussia, playing a flute concerto in a chamber of his palace, Sans Souci

The Baroque concerto comes in two closely related branches, solo and *grosso*. A *concerto grosso* requires more than one soloist, very often two violins (and continuo)—that is, the configuration of the trio sonata, the primary chamber style of the Baroque.

Bach's six Brandenburg Concertos, each for a different solo force, represent an advanced, highly stylized version of the concerto grosso. Their stature in the concerto grosso literature is analogous to that of *The Art of Fugue* in counterpoint. Bach's experiments with instrumental color in the Brandenburgs are very fine: in the Second an unusual solo force of flute, violin, oboe, and high trumpet; in the Fourth permutations of pairs of violins, violas, and cellos; in the Fifth a fancy solo harpsichord part (which Bach himself would have played) that quite overshadows the violin and flute solos.

The fast movements of a Baroque concerto typically begin with a full orchestral ritornello of 16 bars or so, firmly rooted in the tonic key. The solo episodes are punctuated by shorter orchestral passages based on the ritornello, leading away from the tonic key with modulatory passages that reach a subsidiary key area. At the center of the movement there is usually a full ritornello in the related key, such that the second half of the movement constitutes a return to tonic, marked by a strong harmonic arrival and a restatement of the opening ritornello. The solo passages, then, tend to be *modulatory;* the longer orchestral ritornellos recognize rooting in a central key area. Meanwhile the thematic material is quite limited. The orchestra and solo themes trade about and sometimes parry for authority but are seldom fully integrated; the opening orchestral ritornello always, so to speak, wins. But this is not considered a defeat for the soloists, who typically play along in the opening ritornello and join in the close.

 BACH: DOUBLE CONCERTO IN D MINOR, BWV 1043 (C. 1720)

I. ALLEGRO

You'll probably recognize the main theme of the opening movement of what everybody calls the "Bach Double" because every violin student trained in the Suzuki method knows it by heart.

That four-bar theme is the basic ritornello. But Bach makes of the opening orchestral tutti something much grander, principally by treating the ritornello figure as a *fugue* subject. The opening gambit in the first violins on D is answered by the same melody on A in the seconds, followed by a return of the subject on D in the bass instruments and another statement on A.

RITORNELLO:

(We consider fugual procedure more thoroughly in a few pages.) The soloists have a different main theme, which they seem to toss back and forth. Their parts are tightly interwoven, as subject and counterpoint invert and the roles of leader and follower switch. Meanwhile even the shortest orchestral interjections draw on motives from the ritornello.

Solo theme

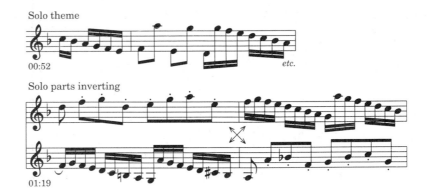

00:52   etc.

Solo parts inverting

01:19

By the middle we have progressed from D minor to A minor; the music then turns back toward the tonic key, arriving back in D minor for the last solo and closing ritornello.

During the Baroque the conventional method of getting around among the keys was by the "circle-of-fifths" pattern, where the tonic (I) of each V–I progression becomes dominant (V) of the next V–I.

Bach always manages this superbly, often having the soloists twinkle their way through a cloudy texture of pedal points and chromatic alterations. This is what occurs just after the center ritornello (02:05 ff.), for instance. Also note the prominent D-major cadence at the end, another example of the Picardy-third close we noted with the Byrd *Agnus* and the Monteverdi madrigal.

The performers on this recording of the Bach Double are Itzhak Perlman, Isaac Stern, and the New York Philharmonic conducted by Zubin Mehta. Perlman, Mehta, and Daniel Barenboim (now conductor of the Chicago Symphony) were at the time of this recording a Gang of Three *enfants terribles* of classical music, just achieving superstardom. Stern was the nation's best-known violin virtuoso. It's a pleasing group, the sort of billing that catches the eye and sells tickets (and CDs). All the performers here lean to the big philharmonic sound.

Listening Chart

 CD 1, TR 12

J. S. Bach (1685–1750)
Double Concerto in D Minor, BWV 1043 (c. 1720)
  Movement I: Vivace

For: solo violins I-II; string orchestra, continuo

Type: Baroque concerto first movement
Meter: ¢
Key: D minor
Duration: 03:52

Everybody calls this piece the "Bach Double," one of the greatly famous works in the Baroque repertoire. Composed and first performed in Cöthen, it would have been played by some 18 musicians. The first movement is an excellent example of Baroque ritornello practice.

00:00	**Opening Ritornello**	D minor. The ritornello is fugal: violins II have the theme (scalar rise, then leaps) on D; then vns. I on A (00:10), brief episode, continuo on D (00:23), vns. II on A (00:33—hard to hear), vns. I on D (00:43).
00:52	**Solo**	D minor. Violin solos I, II, firmly rooted in the tonic. Vn. I states the solo theme: scalar descent leads into very characteristic leaps; Vn. II solo does same (01:03), as Vn. I goes on in counterpoint.
01:14	+ Rit. motives	Modulatory. 2 bars of orchestra answered by 2 bars of soloists, twice. That is: fragments of the ritornello underpin the tonal migration now beginning: the tonality cycles out of D and into:
01:34	**Solo**	A minor. Otherwise the treatment of the solo work is as before.
01:56	**Center Ritornello**	A minor. A single phrase in the new key.
02:05	**Solo**	Modulatory. Circle-of-fifths motion of soloists over long notes (pedal points) in orchestra (*piano*), cycling out of A minor and into G minor.
02:19	+ Ritornello	G minor.
02:29	**Solo**	Modulatory. The process begun at 02:05 continues, cycling out of G minor toward D.
02:53	+ Rit. motives	Modulatory. The treatment is quite similar to 01:14 above.
03:14	**Solo**	D minor. Recapitulation of 00:52.
03:36	**Closing Ritornello**	D minor. A single phrase of the ritornello, now an octave higher than at the beginning.

The vast majority of Vivaldi's several hundred concertos are for violin, cello, or bassoon, with a few each for flute, piccolo, oboe, and lute or mandolin. Doubtless this reflects the artistry of the personnel at the Pietà, where he was contracted to write two concertos a month. Indeed Bach's model in concerto composition was the work of Vivaldi; he was intimately familiar with some of the Vivaldi concertos, and copied several out in longhand. One of Vivaldi's best concertos, in A minor, is at least as often performed in Bach's splendid organ transcription (BWV 593) as in its original form.

Handel, too, wrote fine solo concertos and concerti grossi. The two sets of 12 concerti grossi, ops. 6 and 12, embody a remarkable freedom of form and substance in comparison to the Vivaldi style. In many ways they are as good as the Brandenburgs.

UGUE

Another mode of composition prominent in the middle and high Baroque was the *fugue,* the most rigorous and demanding manifestation of imitative counterpoint. The principal theme of a fugue is called its *subject,* stated at the outset, usually by itself. This is followed by an *answer* of the same material a fifth (five steps) above.

Bach: Fugue in C Minor, from *The Well-Tempered Clavier,* book I

Meanwhile the first voice continues in counterpoint over or under the answer; if this material is reiterated often enough to become thematic, it is called a *countersubject.* The series of subjects and answers goes on until all the voices of the fugue have entered. This is the fugue's *statement,* or *exposition,* a counterpart of the full ritornello that opens the concerto forms.

Passages that lack the subject-answer material are called *episodes,* and the fugue is built (again, quite like a concerto first movement) of alternating statements and episodes. Each successive statement tends to explore a new key area, and the episodes serve to effect the modulations. You get strong signals as a fugue approaches its conclusion: Things happen faster and the texture grows more complex. One might, for example, hear a *stretto* toward the end, where the subjects and answers compress, not waiting for the previous voice to be done. Organist/composers developed the concept of the dominant *pedal point,* where the player plants his or her left foot on the dominant pitch and improvises over it, often with exotic chromaticisms, building strong tension before the release of the final cadence. Thus, organ or no, the arrival at a sustained dominant pitch in the bass as part of the cadential process is called a pedal point. Prolonging the final tonic pitch in the bass is, then, a *tonic pedal.*

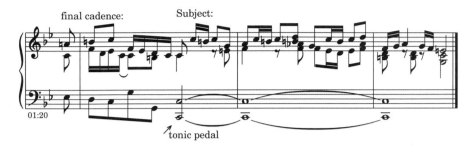

Bach: Fugue in C Minor from *WTC* I, conclusion

Fugue subjects lend themselves to all sorts of manipulations, among which the most common are their *augmentation* and *diminution* into longer or shorter note values than previously encountered (see the example from Fugue IX of Bach's *Art of Fugue*). In advanced fugal treatments the subject might be given in inversion (Fugues III, V) or even backward, in retrograde. In double fugue, two voices begin simultaneously, each as much subject as countersubject (Fugue IX). There are even *permutation fugues,* where the subject and all its countersubjects are stated simultaneously, then rotated round in all their possibilities.

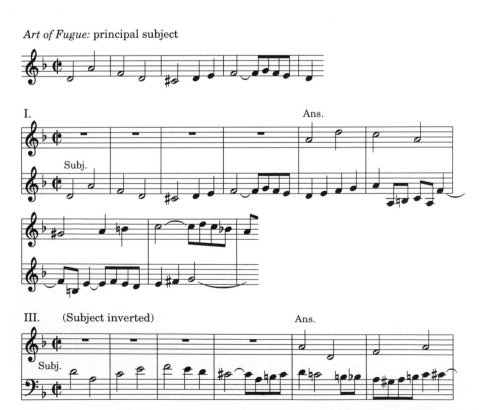

Fugues are difficult to compose because of the way every detail must be designed to fit together, and the ability to write technically correct fugal counterpoint is, still today, one benchmark of a composer's coming of age. Full-blown fugues happen less and less after the Baroque, but the subject-answer relationships of *fugal texture* have been easy to recognize in music ever since the Baroque era.

Bach's great fugues for pipe organ are preceded by loud, improvisatory introductions. The traditional opening is the *toccata,* inherited (like most everything else in the Baroque) from Italy, in which the volume is loud and the passagework fast, thereby calling attention to the presence of the organist in the organ loft. A quieter opening might be called a *prelude,* a more extended, methodical one a *fantasia.* Bach uses all these titles: Toccata and Fugue in D Minor (BWV 565), Fantasia and Fugue in G Minor (BWV 542), and the very fine Passacaglia and Fugue in C Minor (BWV 562). Most of the big organ pieces come from Bach's Weimar period or earlier.

Book I of *The Well-Tempered Clavier* comes from the outpouring of instrumental music Bach composed during his employment in Cöthen.

V.   (Subject inverted, mirrored)

IX.   (Double fugue: subject I, augmented + subject II)

**BACH: FUGUE IN C MINOR FROM *THE WELL-TEMPERED CLAVIER*
(BOOK I, 1722)**

Well-tempering was a technique for tuning keyboard instruments that approximated the theoretical ideal of *equal temperament,* where every half step is equidistant from its neighbors (see p. 22). The net result is that all 24 keys are equally well in tune and thus equally usable. Before that time, scales with more than a few sharps or flats were so out of tune as to be useless for much other than special effects. Bach's purpose in *The Well-Tempered Clavier* was to demonstrate the musical importance of this mechanical advance, to which end he composed 24 preludes and fugues, one each for every major and minor key, thus Prelude and Fugue No. 1 in C Major, No. 2 in C Minor, No. 3 in D Major, and so forth. A second book in the same format was completed about 1740.

The fugue *subject* (see p. 127; the complete work appears in the Anthology, p. 376) carries through to the downbeat of bar 3, with the *answer* beginning immediately. The interlude in bars 5 and 6, a *sequence* of three exchanges between the two voices where the *motive* comes from the subject, precedes the entry of the third voice at bar 7.

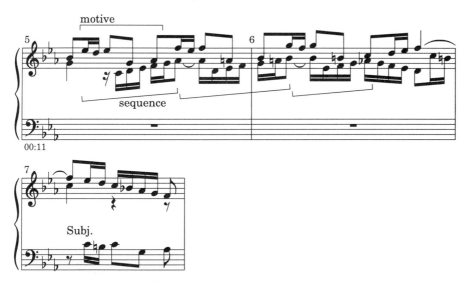

Just over the barline between mm. 6 and 7 there is a momentary foreshadowing of the third voice, a kind of *false entry* put there to delight and possibly perplex you. The full exposition, then, shows this to be a three-voice fugue.

Afterward, statements of the subject or answer occur at mm. 15 (middle voice), 20 (upper voice), 26½ (bass), and 29½ (upper voice), this last as part of the final cadence. On the whole, however, this is a rather loose fugue, more concerned with the exchange of sequential material than in alternating complete statements with extended episodes. One admires the conceptual unity and strong sense of personality established in very short order. This continues throughout the cycle, so listening to the whole book at one time is a great deal more interesting than you might think. The pieces work equally well on harpsichord or piano.

Listening Chart

CD 1, TR 13

J. S. Bach (1685–1750)
Fugue in C Minor from *The Well-Tempered Clavier*, book I (1722)
For: harpsichord or other keyboard

Type: Fugue (3 voices)
Meter: C
Key: C minor
Duration: 01:34

A three-voice fugue: top, middle, bottom.

	Exposition	The exposition presents the entries of the three voices.
00:00	Subject	Middle voice alone.
00:06	Answer	Upper voice; the middle voice continues in counterpoint.
00:11	Extension	Sequential treatment of the main motive.
00:17	Subject	Lower voice; the two upper voices continue in counterpoint.
	Continuation	The passages of sequential figuration gradually become as important as the
00:23	Episode	subject. The sequences carry the tonality from C minor toward E♭.
00:28	Subject	On E♭, top voice.
00:34	Episode	Passagework in the upper voice, parallel thirds in the bottom voices.
00:39	Subject	On G, middle voice.
00:45	Episode	More motivic sequences.
	Conclusion	
00:53	Subject	On C, upper voice.
00:59	Episode	Quite like the episode at 00:34; the movement clearly drawing to a close.
01:12	Subject	On C, lowest voice, leads to final cadence.
01:20	Cadence	The cadence ends in a low-C pedal, over which you hear the original
01:23	Subject	subject in the top voice. Note the Picardy third (C-major) cadence.

Go back, now, and listen to the opening ritornello of the Double Concerto (p. 123) until you are certain you hear the subject-answer setup.

You saw earlier the famous subject of *The Art of Fugue,* to which later composers often allude one way or another. Consider one other very short tune, the one built on the pitches B-A-C-H, for in German pitch parlance B equals B♭ and H equals B♮.

Bach: *Art of Fugue*, no. XIX (middle)

Bach himself turned the tune to good use on a couple of occasions. But I mention it here because ever since the Baroque, composers have used fugue to salute the past and demonstrate their mastery of compositional technique. When they do, they invariably think of Bach and now and then weave his musical signature into their work.

THE SUITE OF DANCES

Parallel to the history of sonata and concerto runs that of another multimovement genre, the *suite of dances.* Hundreds of suites were composed for every conceivable instrumental force, soloists (keyboard, violin, cello, lute) and chamber ensembles as well as the symphonic groupings. Bach's four orchestral suites (BWV 1066–69) are at the heart of the repertoire, as are the many and diverse suites of Handel.

In most suites a formidable overture is followed by a series of dance-based movements of varying tempo and character but always in a binary structure. The harmonic progress is to a closely related key and back.

	‖:	A	:‖:	B	:‖
Major key:	I	⟶	V	⟶	I
Minor key:	i	⟶	III	⟶	i

The movement names are those of dance steps inherited from the various national styles, each with its particular meter and prevailing rhythm. Here's a list of some of the most common:

Allemande	German	stately duple meter
Courante	French	faster duple
Sarabande	Spanish	slow $\frac{3}{4}$
Gavotte	French	fast duple with upbeats
Bourrée	French	fast duple
Minuet	French	stately triple
Gigue	English	fast, merry $\frac{3}{8}$ or $\frac{6}{8}$

To a certain extent the choice and order of the dances is traditional, based on the notion of contrast between the movements. But composers also felt free to drop in less customary movements. Bach's Badinerie is merely a "plaything" for the solo flute; in another suite he includes a polonaise, a Polish character dance. (But the titles French and English Suites applied to some of his harpsichord works are not his own and do not describe character at all. Bach also uses the title Partita for some of his suites.)

Dances might also come in pairs, as for example Gavotte I and Gavotte II. In performance each dance would be played through with its repeats, followed by a *da capo* to the first, played without repeats. The result is identical in form to the Classical minuet-and-trio.

The *overture* to a suite is usually the so-called *French overture,* where a pompous dotted-rhythm opening is followed by a faster, imitative center section and concluded with reference to the dotted-rhythm opening. This had its origin at Versailles, where the king's taking of his seat was a matter of formal protocol—the pompous beginning—as was nearly every other function of the royal day.

 BACH: "BADINERIE" FROM ORCHESTRAL SUITE NO. 2 IN B MINOR, BWV 1067 (C. 1735)

Think again about the Badinerie, which we first examined in Chapter 2 on p. 57. Now you can more comfortably file it in your mental database as a *two-part dance form from a Baroque suite of dances.*

Listening Chart

 CD 1, TR 14

J. S. Bach (1685–1750)
Orchestral Suite No. 2 in B Minor, BWV 1067 (c. 1735)
  "Badinerie"

For: flute, strings, continuo

Type: Binary dance
Meter: $\frac{2}{4}$
Key: B minor
Duration: 01:29

Bach's suites begin with a fancy overture followed by a selection of two-part dances. The Second Orchestral Suite, in eight movements, features a solo flute and concludes with this delightful Badinerie ("plaything"), a favorite of players and the public alike.

00:00	A	Solo flute states the theme in B minor, 4 bars; the response extends itself in
00:06	→ V	the move to V and is thus twice as long (8 bars), cadencing on V.
00:16	A rep.	
00:32	B	Solo flute begins in V minor (F♯ minor), with a brief *piano*.
00:45	→ I	At this little interlude, the music begins to wend back toward I, with
00:58	B rep.	brightly ornamented closing figures in the flute.

www.prenhall.com/masterworks
recommended listening

RECOMMENDED LISTENING:

Handel: Music for the Royal Fireworks *(1749)*

 HORALE, CANTATA, ORATORIO

The theologian Martin Luther (1483–1546), a professor at the University of Wittenberg in north Germany, nailed his 95 theses on the door of the Schlosskirche on 31 October 1517. (This was still in the Renaissance; Josquin died in 1521, the year Luther was excommunicated.) By the late 1600s, the Lutheran church was firmly established in north Germany and with it important new musical practices. One of the tenets of Protestantism is direct participation of the congregation in worship. Simple hymn tunes were found for devotional poems in the vernacular—German, in this case—rather than Latin, and the congregational singing of these hymns occupies a central position in the Lutheran liturgy. German composers delighted in drawing on the *Protestant chorale,* owing to the ease with which the tunes could be recognized and thus the sense of their texts implied. Organist/composers would fashion keyboard preludes around the chorales—bright and excited for the Christmas song *In dulci jublio* (the traditional "Good Christian Men Rejoice"), brooding and melancholy for the crucifixion chorale *O Haupt voll Blut und Wunden* ("O Sacred Head Now Wounded"). More extended treatments were called the chorale partita and the chorale fantasia.

A church concert, c. 1730

In the *chorale cantata,* developed by the German composers from Italian forerunners, a chorale appropriate to the liturgy would be used as the reference point for a multimovement work involving soloists, chorus, and orchestra. Often there is a big opening movement for chorus and orchestra, analogous to the overture in a suite, that embraces the first stanza of the chorale. Solo recitatives and arias separate settings of the successive chorale stanzas. The cantata usually concludes with a simple homophonic setting of the last stanza of the chorale, where the congregation might have joined in singing. Most sacred cantatas are specific to a particular Sunday in a local church's calendar, thus serving to instruct the faithful by expanding on the biblical texts of the season—just like Gregorian liturgy.

Bach's primary duty at St. Thomas's church in Leipzig was to conduct a cantata every Sunday. Many of these half-hour works he composed himself, starting on Monday, having his wife and children copy the parts for midweek rehearsals, and somehow managing to get it all rehearsed for Sunday morning performance. All told, more than three years' worth of Bach's cantatas are preserved, and there are perhaps another hundred that have not come down to us. Among the most familiar are Cantata 140: *Wachet auf, ruft uns die Stimme* ("Sleepers Wake"); the Easter Cantata 4: *Christ lag in Todesbanden* ("Christ lay in Death's dark bonds"); and Cantata 80: *Ein' feste Burg ist unser Gott,* to Luther's famous chorale "A Mighty Fortress Is Our God."

 BACH: FROM CANTATA 80: *EIN' FESTE BURG* (C. 1734)

I. CHORUS

The words and possibly the music of the venerable hymn are by Martin Luther himself.

Ein' fe - ste Burg ist un - ser Gott, ein' gu - te Wehr und Waf - fen;
er hilft uns frei aus al - ler Not, die uns jetzt hat be - trof - fen.

Der al - te bö - se Feind, mit Ernst er's jetzt meint, groß' Macht und viel' List

sein' grau - sam' Rü - stung ist, auf Erd' ist nicht sein's - glei - chen.

[traditional translation for hymn singing:]
A mighty fortress is our God,
A bulwark never failing;
Our helper He, amid the flood
Of mortal ills prevailing:

For still our ancient foe
Doth seek to work us woe;
His craft and power are great,
And, armed with cruel hate,
On earth is not his equal.

Chorale tune: *Ein' feste Burg*

Bach's cantata for Reformation Sunday consists of eight movements: chorale settings at the beginning, middle, and end (movts. 1, 5, and 8) and for the soloists two arias, a recitative, and a duet to texts of a contemporaneous librettist. All five of the solo movements, and the chorale harmonization at the end, come from an earlier work of c. 1716.

The first movement is a grand mixture of concerted practice, fugue, and the chorale genres. Each phrase of the chorale tune serves as the subject of an extended point of fugal imitation.

Tenor
Subj.
00:00 Ein' fe - - - - - ste Burg ist un - ser

Alto Ans.
Ein' fe - - - - ste Burg ist un - ser Gott,

Tenor
Gott, ein' gu - te Wehr und Waf - - - - - [fen]

Meanwhile, at the climax of each section, the chorale phrase on which the subject was based is presented as a long-note canon between the high winds and the pedal part.

00:27

Double bass, **Chorale tune**
organ pedals

Listening Chart

 CD 1, TR 15

J. S. Bach (1685–1750)
Cantata 80: *Ein' feste Burg* (c. 1734)
Movement 1: Chorus

For: chorus (S, A, T, B); 2 oboes, strings, continuo
Text: by Martin Luther (1483–1546).

Type: Oratorio excerpt: opening chorus
Meter: 𝄴
Key: D major
Duration: 04:50

Each line of the chorale tune *Ein' feste Burg* is treated fugally, culminating in a long-note canon between oboes and continuo.

00:00	Line 1	Ein' feste Burg ist unser Gott,
00:27	Canon	
00:38	Line 2	Ein' gute Wehr und Waffen;
00:59	Canon	
01:14	Line 3	Er hilft uns frei aus aller Not,
01:41	Canon	
01:53	Line 4	Die uns jetzt hat betroffen.
02:13	Canon	
02:28	Line 5	Der alte böse Feind,
02:50	Canon	
02:58	Line 6	Mit Ernst er's jetzt meint,
03:16	Canon	
03:23	Line 7	Groß' Macht und viel' List
03:38	Canon	
03:44	Line 8	Sein' grausam' Rüstung ist.
03:59	Canon	
04:08	Line 9	Auf Erd' ist nicht sein'sgleichen.
04:29	Canon	

At the beginning and for the second big section the fugue statements are quite strict. As the chorale settles into shorter phrase fragments, Bach uses a variety of other imitative relationships, but by then the polyphonic interchange is so intense you don't really notice the difference.

The cantata closes with a four-part harmonization of the Luther chorale, the instrumentalists doubling the vocal lines. This approaches the version of "A Mighty Fortress" still sung as a Protestant hymn. Never forget the centrality of the chorale cantata—dominant genre of Bach's Leipzig years—to a true picture of Bach. With the first movement of *Ein' feste Burg,* for example, we see many of the compositional priorities of the B-Minor Mass beginning to take shape.

The two preserved *passions* by Bach are extensions of the cantata idea based on the Good Friday biblical texts. An Evangelist (tenor) declaims the chosen Gospel text in recitative, with soloists taking roles of Jesus, Pontius Pilate, Peter, Judas, and the minor characters as they speak. The chorus provides the noisy interjections of the crowd and the quarrelsome Pharisees, and offers the long opening and closing choruses and the devotional chorales that conclude each section. The arias set texts supplied by librettists that reflect on the meaning of the episodes in the passion story.

Both passions come from the first years of Bach's tenure in Leipzig. The *St. Matthew Passion* is a very large setting with two choruses and orchestras and an additional boy choir in the opening movement; the *St. John Passion* is smaller and perhaps more cerebral. Both are deeply moving, so inspired in the imagery of the recitatives and layout of the arias and ensembles that one has the impression they spring from the core of Bach's faith. The orchestration in the passions is also fascinating, featuring elaborate solo work in the aria accompaniments. Among these are arias where the lute, viola d'amore, and gamba make what is essentially their last stand in the central literature.

The passion as a genre is one descendent of the Italian *oratorio,* a sacred dramatic work for soloists, chorus, and orchestra similar to Baroque opera but lacking its sets and costumes. The name comes from the monastic oratory, or prayer room, where the first oratorios were given.

Probably Handel's most provocative contribution to the history of music was Anglicizing the oratorio and refashioning it in modern terms. Why he shifted so quickly in the 1740s from opera to oratorio as his principal mode of expression is a matter of speculation; up until then he had written comparatively little sacred music. Possibly it was due to his advancing years, for it is not uncommon that secular people are drawn into the spiritual realm as they see death approaching. Certainly, as we have observed, there were market considerations at work: The potential public for an oratorio was larger than the dwindling population of London opera lovers, and the productions were cheaper. Handel was not inclined to the lesser comic opera style of Pergolesi's *La Serva padrona* (1733) or the new ballad opera (e.g., *The Beggar's Opera,* 1728), both of which he considered vulgar. Finally, there may have been an important social consideration at issue, with Handel's sympathy turning toward the emerging middle class.

Whatever the spectrum of his thoughts, he forged of them something both radically modern and financially viable. Handel captivated his audiences with almost madrigalesque text painting, as in the music for the plagues in *Israel in Egypt,* and heroic military effects; additionally, there are unmistakably proud references to the royal court and the enterprises it held dear. The static elements of serious opera are abandoned, and for the most part the focus lies squarely on the big choruses and the superb orchestral work.

Handel's best oratorio is, of course, *Messiah,* a work that for many is treasured as a central experience of the Christian belief. *Messiah* was composed in a little over three weeks in late summer 1741 for performance in Dublin the following spring.

HANDEL: EXCERPT FROM *MESSIAH,* PART I (1741)

RECITATIVE: "THERE WERE SHEPHERDS ABIDING IN THE FIELDS"
CHORUS: "GLORY TO GOD"

Messiah is less a narrative account of Christ's life than a consideration of its redemptive meaning to the faithful. You often hear excerpts of this very long work called the "Christmas portion" and the "Easter portion," but altogether there are three parts. Part I deals with the prophecy of the coming of Christ and the nativity; Part II with crucifixion and its interpretation; and Part III with salvation from sin. The text is selected from both the Old and New Testaments.

Messiah was immensely popular from its first performance and was played many times thereafter under Handel's direction. None of these versions was exactly like any of the others: Arias would be added, subtracted, and rearranged according to the particular roster of singers involved; the orchestration would be adapted. And after Handel's death *Messiah* was tinkered with, refashioned, and otherwise modernized by those who believed that doing so was for the further glory of God, queen, and country.

After a French overture with fugal Allegro, the work proceeds in sections built of recitatives and arias and culminating in choruses that summarize one way or another the section that has come before. The big polyphonic choruses thus serve the same organizational function as the chorales in the Bach passions. Handel's subtle response to the texts keeps the oratorio enthralling despite its great length and rather esoteric musical philosophy: for example, the chromatic meanderings, in "The People That Walked in Darkness" immediately followed by the bravura treatment in the aria "For He Is Like a Refiner's Fire."

After the great chorus "For Unto Us a Child Is Born" come the nativity movements based on Luke 2:8–14, first the so-called Pastoral Symphony, an atmospheric piece that suggests the rustic tranquility of the shepherds at night. From this quiet setting the boy soprano begins the narration in recitative. Excitement mounts with the appearance of the angel of the Lord, and in contrast to the simple continuo recitative just past, there is rapid arpeggiation in the upper strings. The angel delivers tidings of great joy, again to simple continuo recitative. Violin figuration for the sudden appearance of the "multitude of heav'nly host" evokes the flutter of angels' wings. The violins envelope the recitative

and merge into the short chorus "Glory to God." The unison declamation "And peace on earth" yields to an imitative treatment of "Good will toward men."

Two trumpets, marked "from afar, and rather quietly" suggest the heavenly glory of this mystic though sleepy occasion, and toward the end the music simply dissipates as the angels disperse.

The "Hallelujah" chorus comes at the end of Part II, and we stand for that movement following a custom established by the English king, who may simply have been stretching his legs.

Despite its sacred subject matter, this excerpt shows a theatrically oriented composer, ever sensitive to the musical possibilities of a good scene and responding to texts with clever if sometimes blatant text painting. Bach, oriented to the church, responded to similarly interesting scenes—Peter's denial of Christ, more subtly, but perhaps more ardently.

After *Messiah* and the other oratorios, musicians visiting England went out of their way to hear Handel. All were greatly moved by what they heard, and several—Haydn, Mendelssohn, Berlioz—went on to recreate his success in the language of their own time. Few works in the history of music have so wide a legacy as *Messiah.*

Listening Chart

 CD 1, TR 16–17

George Frideric Handel (1685–1759)
Messiah **(1741)**
From part I: Recitative ("There were shepherds abiding in the field") and Chorus ("Glory to God")

For: soloist (S), chorus (S, A, T, B); 2 trumpets, strings, continuo
Text: from the Bible (Luke 2:8–14), asssembled by Charles Jennens (1700–73)

Type: Oratorio excerpt: recitative simple and accompagnato, chorus
Meter: C (all movements)
Key: C major to D major (recitatives), D major (chorus)
Duration: 01:20, 01:42

Handel's setting of the Biblical passage describing the angel's announcement of Christ's birth to shepherds in the field follows an orchestral interlude commonly called the "Pastoral Symphony." The recitative is sung on the recording by a boy soprano.

00:00	*Recitative*	There were shepherds abiding in the field . . .	A boy soprano narrates. Simple recitative (continuo only).
00:13	*Rec. accomp.*	And lo, the angel of the Lord came upon them . . .	Excited arpeggios in violins I and II as the angel appears.
00:31	*Recitative*	And the angel said unto them . . .	The angel's announcement: simple recitative.
01:03	*Rec. accomp.*	And suddenly there was with the angel . . .	Accompanied. Violin passagework suggests the flutter of angels' wings.
	Chorus		
00:00	Phrase 1	Glory to God in the Highest	The angels' "Gloria." Note the two trumpets.
00:09	Line 2	And peace on earth	Unison voices; tranquil string response.
00:18	Phrase 2		Restatement; ends higher.
00:35	Phrase 3	Good will toward men.	Imitative entries.
00:51	Phrases 4-5		Big restatement of all, emphatic "good will."
01:26	Orch. close		Imitative figure dissipates as angels leave.

Chapter 5

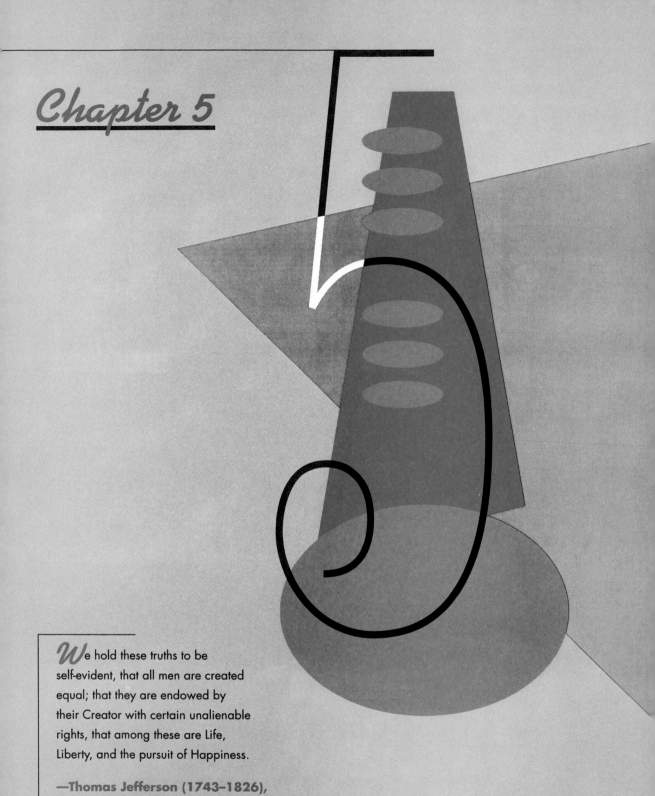

*W*e hold these truths to be
self-evident, that all men are created
equal; that they are endowed by
their Creator with certain unalienable
rights, that among these are Life,
Liberty, and the pursuit of Happiness.

—**Thomas Jefferson (1743–1826)**,
in the American ***Declaration
of Independence* (1776)**

The Classical Style

*T*o hold as self-evident truths that all men are created equal and are endowed by a benevolent creator with rights to life, liberty, and the pursuit of happiness is an Enlightenment way of thinking. Not just the philosophers and politicians thought this way: You'll enounter the same sentiments in Mozart's opera *The Marriage of Figaro* and the finale of Beethoven's Ninth Symphony. Enlightenment ideals denying the divine right of kings and promoting alternatives to feudalism steered us through our own relatively tame Revolution (1776–81) and the much bloodier and more confused French Revolution (1789–95). America, at its best a civilization of laws, rights, reason, and implicit belief in unstoppable progress, is the triumph of Enlightenment thought.

Indeed, one might well conjure up Jeffersonian images to epitomize the period: not just white wigs and fancy signatures affixed with quill pens on fine pieces of parchment but the very notion that an industrious and thinking citizen in an egalitarian society might frame great institutions, design and build noble edifices, and commit to paper hundreds of provocative observations on everything from seed germination to the immorality of slavery. Or consider Benjamin Franklin, genially and indefatigably darting from the publishing trade, experiments with optics and electricity, diplomacy, and service as postmaster of his new nation—all the while an excellent man of letters.

Following tenets espoused by the great French philosopher Voltaire, thinkers in the Age of Reason promoted learning, deductive thought, and personal industry. It was committed to social progress with the state as the agent of reform. Notions of the worth of the individual led to manifestos on the rights of man (our Bill of Rights comes from 1791, the year of Mozart's death), the vote for all men and women, and the emancipation of enslaved peoples. Thus the Enlightenment was also a code of behavior—a moral stance, a faith in the limitless potential of humankind.

Thinkers of the era formulated and then pursued the scientific method in their search for the laws and natural order of the universe, discovering oxygen (1794), a smallpox vaccine (1796), and the Voltaic cell (1800). They endeavored to perfect and codify knowledge, as in the 28-volume *Encyclopédie* (1751–72), edited by Diderot with contributions from Montesquieu, Voltaire, and Rousseau.

Many of these ideas, of course, were in direct conflict with traditional modes of European life. "To secure these rights," the Declaration of Independence stated, "governments are instituted among men, deriving their just powers from the consent of the governed." A few monarchs—the so-called enlightened despots—grasped the momentous nature of

143

all this and struggled to adapt themselves and their subjects to it: the Austrian emperor Joseph II (1765–90) and his mother Maria Theresa, Catherine the Great in Russia (1762–96), and the flute-playing Frederick the Great of Prussia (1740–86). Others, notably George III of England and Louis XVI of France (and his wife Marie Antoinette, Maria Theresa's daughter), as well as the clergy, just didn't get it.

Meanwhile the middle class—bankers, lawyers, journalists, physicians, the lesser nobility, and government bureaucrats—flourished. Industrialists harnessed scientific and technological breakthroughs like the steam engine (1769) and cotton gin (1793) with the hope of acquiring, as the shrewdest did, vast wealth. The study of economics was born and the principles of capitalism posited (Adam Smith: *The Wealth of Nations,* 1776).

In art, the Enlightenment emphasis on order and rational thought led to a simplicity and elegance of style that turns sharply away from the Baroque. Artists and architects were taken with the graceful forms of Greek and Roman antiquity, prompted in part by the excavations at Pompeii and Herculaneum. Gardens and household objects show a similar delight in symmetry and balance. Literature, having in one sense fostered this revolution to begin with, was already occupied with newer concerns. The Sturm und Drang ("storm and stress") movement in German-language prose emphasized the emotional turbulence underlying the social order, while Goethe (1749–1832) was describing the situations and feelings that would soon be at the heart of Romanticism.

Composers were sensitive to Enlightenment ideals as well. Music became less the gift of God than a luxury of the good life. We call the music of the Enlightenment *Classicism,* or *Viennese Classicism,* or (following the title of a famous book by Charles Rosen) the *Classical Style.*

Don't get tangled up with the terminology here. *Classical,* in its general sense, also means the universal concern for balance, clarity, refinement, and grace in art, which struggles for position in any age alongside the passionate (romantic) and worldly (popular), as in "classical music" versus "pop music." The designation "classic" applies to any creation that endures as a monument to its era: the Ford Mustang, for instance. With Viennese Classicism, however, we are talking of music of a particular time and place.

Vienna: Napoleon arriving at the Schönbrunn Palace

The Classical period is unlike any of the other commonly accepted style periods in that it's very short, focused on a single place (Vienna), and largely, for our purposes here, the creation of two men, Haydn and Mozart. It begins to be recognizable in the 1760s, catches fire in the 1770s, and matures in the 1780s with the joint accomplishments of the two masters. Following Mozart's death in 1791, Haydn was for more than a decade the reigning monarch of music composition. It was thought natural (and quite enlightened) that so promising a student as Beethoven should travel all the way from western Germany to Vienna for tutelage with him. Haydn, meanwhile, was not insensitive to the political and artistic changes around him—this is the period of Napoleon and Goethe—and the acute ear can tell in Haydn's late masterpieces that he was cognizant of the dawn of Romanticism. By that time Beethoven and others were boldly sweeping musical discourse into the post-Revolutionary era.

RECURSORS OF THE CLASSICAL STYLE

Where did such remarkable steps forward as the sonata form, the action opera, the piano concerto, and the orchestra-with-clarinets originate? If you know that Handel's *Messiah* dates from 1741 and Bach's B-Minor Mass from a few years later, the Haydn-and-Mozart phenomenon cannot help but seem an abrupt shift of compositional priorities. Certainly Viennese Classicism left the Baroque style suddenly and undeniably dead. But overlapping the work of the senior composers of the high Baroque, progressive younger artists—Bach's own sons not the least among them—were working in new modes of musical expression with results that were drawn directly into the Classical style. One setter of precedents, for example, came to be called the *stile galant,* an airy, elegant, and easily grasped mode of expression cultivated in France and Italy, favored by the Bach boys and received enthusiastically by Haydn and Mozart. Compared with traditional Baroque procedures, it had slower rates of chord change, less emphasis on intricate counterpoint, and little basso continuo.

We find roots of the Classical keyboard sonata in the work of Domenico Scarlatti (1685–1757), son of the Baroque opera composer Alessandro Scarlatti. Domenico Scarlatti, an Italian employee of the queen of Spain, composed more than 500 sonatas for harpsichord in which we see the tonic/dominant thematic organization and the repeat scheme common to early sonatas. The Italian composer Domenico Alberti (c. 1710–40) used a left-hand pattern of broken chords so frequently in his keyboard sonatas that it became known as the Alberti bass, a texture quite common in the piano figuration of Haydn and Mozart.

Haydn: Piano Sonata No. 59, movt. I

00:31

An Alberti bass figure

Carl Philip Emmanuel Bach (or simply C. P. E., 1714–88), the fifth child and third son of J. S. Bach, had purposely set out in his many dozens of keyboard works to free musical style from what he saw as the rigidities of the Baroque. These works are extraordinary in their sometimes wiggy freedom and spirit of experiment, wandering off into prolonged spells of distraction (*Empfindsamkeit,* "melancholy expression") and showing a palette of sonority that later composers found quite useful, especially in their more sentimental moods. C. P. E. Bach, moreover, was author of an influential volume on performance, *A Treatise on the True Art of Keyboard Playing* (2 vols., 1753, 1762). C. P. E. Bach's study was contemporaneous with other significant treatises, such as J. J. Quantz's volume on how to play the flute (1750, dedicated to Frederick the Great of Prussia) and Leopold Mozart's on violin playing (1756).

In opera, disillusionment with the strict conventions of serious opera had led to a number of reformed approaches. Pergolesi's *La Serva padrona* ("The Maid as Mistress," 1733), a short, rambunctious, and quite silly piece meant to be played in the inter-missions of more substantial fare, enjoyed unprecedented popularity and fostered all sorts of jocular imitations. In Paris it also prompted a war of pamphlets, the *querelle des buffons* of 1752–54, between supporters of Pergolesi and those of the more formal French school. Comedy and adventure onstage, notably the rescue of wrongly imprisoned heroes, came to be preferred to dramas about the old nobility. Also, the spoken text that had always been a part of lesser music theatricals now was to be heard on the opera stage. There was conscious reform, too, in the serious lyric tragedy of Christoph Willibald von Gluck (1714–87), a Viennese composer who enjoyed equal success in Paris. Every musical gesture, Gluck felt, should be motivated by the libretto. Opera allowed no room for gratuitous display—no overly embellished *da capo* arias, for instance. His *Orfeo ed Euridice* (1762) effectively dealt the final blow to *opera seria.*

In the tiny principality of Mannheim there thrived a court orchestra composed of the usual strings and pairs of wind instruments, including the clarinet. The Mannheim orchestra, numbering in its ranks several fine composers, cultivated such novel devices as the crescendo and staccato, and their technical capability was described with astonish-ment by travelers who came to hear them. Among these was the young Mozart, who clearly regarded the Mannheimers as a model to emulate.

Houdon:
Bust of Gluck

By 1750 the Viennese composers were more occupied with these kinds of modern-isms than with the music of Bach and Handel, which they knew minimally or not at all.

IENNA

But why Vienna? Partly it was the simple juncture of lifestyle and money. Vienna was the capital of what had become the most cosmopolitan empire of Europe, its influence extending eastward through Hungary, Bohemia, and Poland to Turkey and Asia, north-ward well into Russia, west to the Prussian border, and south to Venice and Milan. The

Hapsburg dynasty controlled an empire of dozens of languages where German served as the common tongue. Lesser nobility—princes, counts, margraves—flocked to townhouses and apartments in Vienna from late autumn through Lent, there to enjoy not just political solidarity and shared warmth but an uninterrupted cultural calendar as well. With the spring, they would return to their country estates to oversee planting and the subsequent harvest.

Those inclined to the pursuit of music vied to outdo each other in their patronage, engaging the better composers to produce groups of sonatas or quartets and then seeing to their first performance. In return, the works would be dedicated to them—hence Haydn's King of Prussia Quartets and Beethoven's Razumovsky Quartets and Waldstein Sonata. Those with real wealth and abiding musical passion might engage a full musical establishment with resident music master, instrumentalists, and singers. Chamber music flourished in homes and palaces, where it was played after meals with the dinner guests sometimes joining professional artists familiar to the household.

The Landstrasse, Vienna

The Hapsburgs themselves were distinguished patrons of the arts. The palace supported theater companies, concerts, a fine museum, and one of the great libraries of Europe. The empress Maria Theresa was connected by birth and marriage with much of the aristocracy of Europe and Russia; she helped to make Vienna a center of political exchange and, as a result, a crossroads of the arts.

Aristocratic patronage was critical to the emergence of the Viennese style. No less significant was the new do-it-yourself public concert called the Academy, where composers offered their work not for purses of gold coins but for ticket income. Concert music came to be as important as music for the theater and the church.

This was part and parcel of the new bourgeois way of doing things, and the middle-class subscribers to public concert series went on to become the nucleus of the philharmonic societies of the nineteenth century. They purchased pianos and other musical instruments and then bought music lessons for themselves and their families—for not a few composers, an important new income source. And they bought printed music, now published in increasingly abundant supply. In short, the public was never far from a musician's concerns, and it was by no means beneath the dignity of a composer to write for amateurs or to incorporate features into the music that the public might be counted on to like. One might even compose dance music for the pleasure garden. There lies one important explanation of the simple, direct, and altogether absorbing new style.

THE NEW STYLE. While it naturally drew on the best of past practice, Classicism represented a fundamental shift in the way composers thought about many of the parameters of music: texture, melody, rhythm, harmony, form, even the performers themselves. Classical music is a music of studied logic, in keeping with Enlightenment ideals:

Yet it is one of contrasts, too, apt to brood and ruminate. Let us examine these parameters point by point.

TEXTURE. Classical composers preferred to write in prevailingly homophonic textures, where the orderly progress of vertical sonorities (chords) is as carefully articulated as the horizontal motion. Put simply, composers of homophony write a melodic phrase, add a bass line to it, then fill in the appropriate inner part or parts: There is always a functional top, bottom, and middle. Classical texture is decidedly less busy than in, say, a chorus from Handel's *Messiah:* There is much less contrapuntal exchange and little prolonged imitation. There tends to be a uniformity of rhythmic motion among the voices, particularly those accompanying the melody; and while it still provides the structural underpinning, the bass voice is more closely integrated with the others. Think of the opening eight bars of *Eine kleine Nachtmusik* (or if you don't think you know them yet, refer back to the sample score on p. 21): four bars of unison fanfare, then the theme in the first violins with all the other voices articulating the chord progression in repeated eighth notes. Four-part quartet writing quietly supplants the Baroque trios of two upper voices and basso continuo. The string quartet (two violins, viola, and cello) becomes the ideal ensemble for chamber music.

Counterpoint continued to exist, of course, for a composer must always be sensitive to how the voices interact as they move forward. Excelling at one's counterpoint lessons remained a necessity. But more and more, complex imitative counterpoint became something one reserved to show off one's technical expertise or to evoke the language of the past.

The uniformity of Classical texture is offset by great sensitivity to tone color. Melodic solo work is distributed imaginatively among the participants, and variety in deployment among the orchestral sections (woodwinds, brasses, strings) is cultivated: Note the beautiful woodwind solos in Mozart's symphonies and concertos. Other textural effects include a wide range of dynamics: *crescendo* and *diminuendo,* and new emphasis on articulation (*staccato* and other forms of accent such as *legato* and *pizzicato*).

MELODY. Nowhere, perhaps, is the difference between the Baroque and Classical styles clearer than in the shape and content of their melodies. The most characteristic Baroque melodies are memorable in the way they telescope outward from measure to measure, in the technique called *Fortspinnung* ("spinning out"). Remember, for example, in the Bach "Badinerie" how the initial, square four-bar idea is met with wide-eyed continuance: What's interesting is how the response to the gambit *doesn't* balance it, but keeps rolling on. Classical melodies, in contrast, tend to yearn for balance and symmetry—like everything else in the style. And the tunes are shorter, more compact, reaching cadence more frequently—in a word, more popular.

The melody on page 149 is called a *period* because it describes a complete musical event and ends with a strong cadence; it consists of an *antecedent* portion of four bars and its *consequent.* The subphrases, in turn, are made up of two-bar units, each component serving to achieve balance in terms of all the other components. Such antecedent-consequent melodic relationships, and their organization into four-, eight-, and sixteen-bar segments, constitute the foundation of Classical phrase structure. That said, remember that periodicity is mainly a kind of concept or model, seldom so strict in real life as the theorists define it and almost never rigid over the long haul.

Mozart: *Eine kleine Nachtmusik,* movt. II

A Classical melody

Be on the lookout, too, in Classical melody, for subunits that lend themselves to achieving structural prominence as *motives.* These have the ability to *motivate* musical structure in parts of the form where true theme is not so significant: the bridges and transitions, for example, and of course the development. In Beethoven's Fifth, the opening gambit becomes motivic right away.

HARMONY. The Classical decades saw popular new chord treatments emerge, notably color chords embellished with extra sharps and flats, as well as provocatively new key areas in the development. Mechanical improvements in instrument making—and *The Well-Tempered Clavier*—encouraged composers to experiment with the use of key for atmosphere. You now begin to hear such keys as F♯ minor and E♭ major routinely, where the Baroque composers usually kept to keys of one or two sharps or flats, major and minor; and the way the various keys sound on the piano or in the orchestra gives them their own particular colors and symbolic associations. Regularity in the rate of chord change—called *harmonic rhythm*—is a great deal more important than in the Baroque, again in keeping with internal notions of symmetry.

But what you will note most distinctly is the inevitable departure from the tonic to a secondary key area (in major, to the dominant: C to G major, for instance; in minor, to the relative major, C minor to E♭ major) and the equally inevitable return to tonic in a balancing position about two-thirds of the way through a movement. Departure-and-return is an all-pervasive rule of Classical harmony, to which you should attune your ear as rapidly as possible. Modulation becomes an artful enterprise; development and resolution a required tactic.

RHYTHM. Rhythmic character, too, is much altered in Classical music. It isn't, of course, that there are any more note values, but rather that the Baroque composers tend to use rhythms uniformly throughout a movement, and the rhythmic character established at the outset tends to prevail (think, again, of the Bach Badinerie). This was due in large measure to the strong influence of the continuo part, which is usually quite regular in rhythmic values; the terracing of voices in the highly contrapuntal idioms has the same effect. The result is a certain mechanical quality to Baroque rhythmic patterns, which partisans hear as the musical equivalent of fine German watchworks and detractors as sewing-machine rhythm.

In Classical music, by contrast, rhythm figures prominently in the way composers establish contrast and variety. The inevitable arrival in a secondary key area tends to be articulated by a shift of rhythmic gears.

Beethoven: Symphony No. 5 in C Minor, movt. I

You will hear structurally significant pauses, rests, empty bars, and fermatas. Metric irregularity, syncopation, and hesitation all find good use. And as composers search for new rhythmic relationships, they are also willing to try new tempos, both faster than you've heard before and slower.

Many of these rhythmic features may seem quite ordinary to you, for they figure in most of the music you already know. Compared to what came before, however, they represent a substantial stylistic mutation.

NEW SOUNDS.   All of the above certainly constitutes a new world of sound. Then there are the equally intriguing new sonorities of the musical instruments themselves. Chief among these, of course, is the piano, which had emerged about 1710 in Italy and by Mozart's time was being manufactured all over Europe. Its attraction was not only that it could play both loud and soft, but that it had a stronger presence overall; and the piano's technical superiority represented the progress of the age. The Viennese fortepiano played by Haydn and Mozart and, in his early years, Beethoven, was not yet the monster contraption we know today. The structure of its frame did not yet permit the high-tension stringing that came later, and the hammer mechanism was still rudimentary. Yet the early pianos were a quantum leap forward and became the vehicle for many of the era's most representative developments.

The newest sound to be heard in the orchestra is that of the clarinet. Mozart, who belonged to a Masonic lodge with some famous clarinet players, assured it a permanent place both in the orchestra and as a solo instrument by writing conspicuously beautiful clarinet lines. Also favored by the Viennese composers was the horn, for which there were also virtuoso players around. Although the horn, lacking any valves, was still quite primitive, it was dexterous in octaves where the trumpet was not, and thus significant parts for pairs of horns, and sometimes quartets, began to be featured in ensemble music. The mechanical systems of the other woodwinds were also undergoing refinement as levers and keys were added and more efficient key layouts designed. Trombones eventually joined the orchestra. Gradually the symphony orchestra began to take shape, growing from the two dozen or so instrumentalists for whom Haydn typically wrote to the 50-member orchestra of Beethoven and then to the 100-piece ensemble of the late Romantics. Orchestration begins to be regarded as high art.

Meanwhile, the great instruments of the Renaissance and Baroque—the lute, viols, harpsichord, even the pipe organ—fell more or less abruptly into disuse. So did, with a few exceptions, the professional chapel choir, which was replaced by the chorus of amateurs. Professional singers sought careers in the theater, and it was these artists that composers engaged as soloists in their masses and other sacred music.

FORM. What characterizes the Viennese style more than anything else is the pre-eminence of *sonata form.* In fact, sonata practice was not merely a form but an all-embracing way of compositional life. Its hierarchies of logic were the stuff of the age; its concern for proportion, balance, and symmetry born from contrast are the very essence of the style. Writing a sonata entailed rigorous planning and a compositional strategy as demanding as the fugue, but along wholly different lines. Three- and four-movement compositions remained the norm, with Classical ideals determining their character and behavior. One way or another, sonata practice affected all the movements of the various genres that flowered in Vienna: the piano sonata, string quartet, solo concerto, and symphony.

HE VIENNESE SONATA

You learned the rudiments of sonata form in Chapter 2. If you don't remember its elements, consult the computer tutorial or go back and review pp. 55–57. Listen, now, to a central example of the Classical sonata, one you should have heard before: the first movement of Mozart's *Eine kleine Nachtmusik.* Consult the musical score (Anthology, pp. 378–82) as we dissect its vital parts. Remember to hum the musical examples to yourself, not skip over them. Take some time to do this right; it will make a big difference in the way you hear music in the very near future.

MOZART: *EINE KLEINE NACHTMUSIK*, K. 525 (1787), MOVTS. I, III

An excellent example of basic sonata form at work is Mozart's string serenade *Eine kleine Nachtmusik,* K. 525, finished in Vienna in 1787. The title, "A Little Night Music," identifies it as a smallish, pleasant work and a nocturne (or *notturno,* for evening performance) from the *serenade* family. Serenades, although by no means trivial, were a rather less elevated genre than the more rigorous and demanding symphony and concerto. They were for what might be considered easy listening rather than intense scrutiny. One would have heard them played from musicians' lofts at social gatherings or out of doors in a garden. Mozart wrote dozens, for all sorts of performing forces. There is much gorgeous Mozart to be found in the serenades and related genres (*divertimento, cassation*), notably in the long works for wind ensemble.

Eine kleine Nachtmusik is scored for strings alone, in four parts: violins I and II, violas, and cellos, doubled—as happens with most Classical bass lines—by contrabass viols (double basses). The clarity of the scoring contributes markedly to the character of the work. At the same time, the all-string orchestra has a very homogenous tone quality, such that the composer must seek the contrast in other parameters than the orchestration.

I. ALLEGRO

The first "theme" consists of three more or less independent elements: an opening gesture that sounds very like a fanfare, a rather more theme-like continuation, and a winsome closing gesture—a cadential figure.

The *sf* bursts (*subito forte,* "suddenly loud") and soft responses indicate the dawn of something new (00:30). During the crescendo (the first notated crescendo you have encountered in our chronological treatment) C♯s begin to be introduced (00:37). By now you should be able to sense the tonal shift happening: The C♯s are what bring the tonality out of G major (the tonic) and toward D major (the dominant). This, then, is the *tran-*

sition, or *bridge,* during which the process of modulation takes place. The rest at the end (00:46) represents a collective taking of breath before the second theme.

The second theme is gracious and courtly, contrasting pointedly with the swashbuckling assurance of the first. Thus it stands in relief or opposition to what has come before, reflecting a central feature of the sonata style. The restatement of this idea is in violins II, with a new figure in the firsts, the repeated high As.

Like the group in tonic, this second group in dominant has three elements: the main idea, its extension, and a cadential figure. The cadential figure is repeated, rearticulating and confirming what it has had to say.

Now the exposition builds in range and volume to a climax, followed by a quiet, elegant fade. Mozart's closing material is always delightful.

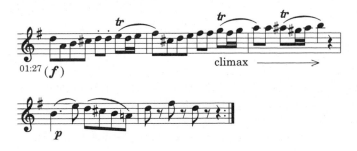

The exposition repeats, doubling your opportunity to register these things.

The sonata is, in the Classical period at least, a two-section movement. In the second section the music will be developed and recapitulated, and here (as with many works of the period) the composer calls for a repeat of the whole second half. The development begins with the fanfares again (although on D instead of G), and for a moment you may be uncertain about the direction things are taking. You prick your ears and listen attentively, convinced fairly quickly that you're in the development because of the way the bridge theme begins to be shifted around among the voices. Mozart then treats material from phrase 2 of the second theme. With the powerful E♭ in the bass (03:35) comes a signal that maximum tension has been reached, emphasized by the strong play of motives and fragments; the unison string chromaticisms lead to the dominant D in the first violins and in the basses. You just can't miss that the recapitulation is at hand.

Indeed, if you're listening intently, the inevitability of all this should be apparent to you. The instability of the development gives way to the solidarity of the recapitulation. You the listener respond with a sense of satisfaction that this most significant element of the sonata construction has been achieved.

Remember that in recapitulation, for the second group to stay in the tonic key, there have to be alterations to the bridge. Its original purpose was to go somewhere; this time it must *not* go anywhere. Mozart marks time for a moment with a clever sleight of hand, then presents the second theme beginning on D, so it comes out in G, the proper tonic.

Here, a special moment: The little concluding sigh (05:20) is stretched almost romantically with chromatics down and scales up, then there's a bold confirming tutti—a coda—of six bars, reminding you a little of the opening fanfares.

Now go back and listen to this work again with the chart in front of you, cuing up passages as you like. You should be able to hum most of this movement through from memory. Go back and read the commentary and try to hum the musical examples, nodding to yourself as you understand what's happening.

The strength of the sonata is the freedom with which its elements can be manipulated. The sonata is viable and durable because of its very simplicity; there is a universality in its process of statement—tension—resolution. As the decades go by, it will prove how malleable it can be in the number of its themes, its length, character, and dramatic purpose.

Listening Chart

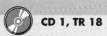 **CD 1, TR 18**

W. A. Mozart (1756–91)
***Eine kleine Nachtmusik*, K. 525 (1787)**
   Movement I: Allegro

For: strings

Type: Sonata first movement
Meter: C
Key: G major
Duration: 05:43

Mozart and his contemporaries often wrote serenades for gatherings in a noble person's salon or gardens, lighter fare than the formal concert repertoire. We know little about the composition of *Eine kleine Nachtmusik*, except that there was once another minuet attached and that the concluding rondo is based on a Viennese song Mozart used again in the opera *The Magic Flute*. The first movement is a gallant, compact sonata form.

	Exposition	
00:00	Th. I.1	G major. The first theme has three elements: this little fanfare,
00:07	Th. I.2	a surging, merry main theme, and
00:17	Th. I.3	a cadential figure. Violins I dominate the melodic work.
00:30	Bridge	The *sf* bursts and C♯s indicate something new: transition to
00:47	Th. II	D major; gracious and courtly, contrasting pointedly with what has come before. Restatement (00:54) in vns. II, with new figure above in vns. I.
01:00	Cl. th.	Two 4-bar subphrases, one lyrical and soft, the other bold; repeated (01:14).
01:33	cad. fig.	A confirming cadential figure.
01:36	Exp. rep.	The exposition repeated.
03:13	**Development**	The short development starts with the fanfares (on D, not G, momentarily disorienting), then treats the first half of the closing theme. The bass E♭ (03:35) and unison string chromatics suggest motion toward:
	Recapitulation	
03:49	Th. I.1	G major. As before.
03:56	Th. I.2–3	As before.
04:20	Bridge	Modified in its last bars to stay in G major (the tonic key, or I).
04:34	Th. II	G major. Otherwise as before.
04:47	Cl. th.	As before, except:
05:20	sigh	The concluding sigh is stretched with chromatics down and scales up.
05:30	**Coda**	Six-bar tutti.

III. MENUETTO: ALLEGRETTO

You can see how strongly sonata as a principle affects Classical composers in the way they treat the minuet-and-trio. By the late eighteenth century the minuet, inherited from the Baroque, was an old-fashioned, almost stock sort of movement. Putting a minuet between the slow movement and the finale satisfied the perceived need to have something relatively straightforward and stately before the rigors of symphonic conclusion. Sonata practice is suggested by having the first phrase or elements of it incorporated at the end of the second, in what we have called *rounded binary* procedure:

‖: A :‖: B a :‖

The beginning of the second strain, moreover, often has a feeling of harmonic unrest equivalent to a mini-development. The first strain, in this case, has a white-wigged, pompous feel to it; the second strain is a little smoother and more relaxed.

Trios are nearly always more pacified and restrained than minuets, often through the use of rustic effects (bagpipe-like drones, perhaps, and a tune in a solo voice) or music-box treatments. The latter is the case here, with a single-voice tune in the violin (*sotto voce* means "undervoiced," or whispered) and a rather routine accompaniment. As in the

Listening Chart

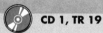 **CD 1, TR 19**

W. A. Mozart (1756–91)
Eine kleine Nachtmusik, K. 525 (1787)
   Movement III: Menuetto: Allegro

  For: strings

Form: Minuet-
  and-trio
Meter: ¾
Key: G major
Duration: 02:03

Make certain you have grasped the organization of the Classical minuet-and-trio: ¾ meter, the repeat scheme with *da capo* as outlined below, and often a return in the second phrase of material from the first (B = **ba**, for example) thus *rounding* the binary form.

	Minuet	
00:00	A	G major. A stately 8-bar phrase.
00:10	A rep.	
00:21	B	The departure, in legato 8ths, touches on related keys, then embraces
00:26	a	a rounding of the binary form with recapitulation of the A.
00:32	B rep.	
	Trio	Somewhat more restrained; like a music-box tune with simple accomp.
00:42	C	D major (V).
00:54	C rep.	
01:05	D	Touches on A major (V of V), then embraces
01:10	c	a rounding of the binary form with recapitulation of the C.
01:22	D rep.	
	Minuet da capo	No repeats in minuet *da capos*.
01:39	A	
01:50	B	

minuet proper, the first theme returns, very slightly disguised by the addition of the A♯ in m. 29—a bit of seasoning one might well savor.

This kind of minuet treatment happens hundreds of times over in the Viennese period, and even in Haydn and Mozart, third movements begin to grow rather routine. Not surprisingly, the minuet-and-trio was the first of the Viennese movement types to lose its appeal. Beethoven was soon suggesting interesting alternatives.

*M*OZART AND HAYDN

The lives of Mozart and Haydn epitomize, each in its own particular way, the societal currents of their time. Haydn lived obediently in the system but rose above it. The volatile Mozart quit it and tried to go freelance, not very successfully. (Beethoven, who wasn't very good at *ancien régime* behavior, succeeded admirably in the era's looser climate of equality and the open market.) Haydn was nearly 25 years older than Mozart and thus had been at his trade for some years before the young prodigy first came on the scene. For Mozart, Haydn was, at the start, just one of many models whose accomplishments he emulated and absorbed. In the 1770s the two developed a friendship that broadened into artistic brotherhood; by the 1780s, when both were flourishing in Vienna, they studied and compared each other's music—sometimes dedicating similar works to each other. One senses little rivalry between these two masters, the one comfortable in his maturity and position, the other in the certainty of his powers. Neither seems ever to have been short of imagination or at a loss for things to do.

www.prenhall.com/masterworks
composer profiles
Haydn

FRANZ JOSEPH HAYDN (1732–1809). The genial Haydn, known to his disciples as "Papa," spent the bulk of his career in domestic service. Most of his life he worked for the princes Esterhazy, wealthy landowners in Vienna and Hungary, before whom he and his musicians were cautioned to appear in their powdered wigs and fresh hosiery. Outliving Mozart by nearly two decades, Haydn became the most celebrated composer of his time, sojourning twice in England in the high style the British accorded persons of great attainment, and given an honorary degree from Oxford University. So far as we know, fame had little effect on his basic humility, and he retained his allegiance to the Esterhazy family until the end. He characterized himself as a simple God-fearing craftsman, and on the whole his attitude toward his art and the world around him was not so different from Bach's.

Haydn was born in modest circumstances and raised in a small village, surrounded by peasants for whom he conceived a lifelong affection. His musical talents took him to Vienna, where he trained as a choirboy at St. Stephen's Cathedral (as did his brother Michael, also a fine composer). In 1761 he was first employed by Prince Paul Anton Esterhazy, scion of a noble family glittering with wealth. Esterhazy and all his entourage wintered in the family townhouse in Vienna, then in good weather wandered from one to another of their castles. Their dream estate was Eszterháza in western Hungary, constructed during Haydn's tenure with the family.

Under the prince's successor Prince Nikolaus, the property came to have its pleasure garden, theater and concert hall, and a dormitory for the orchestral musicians engaged and sustained by the household. Haydn would rehearse the orchestra, repair and tune its instruments, attend to its music library, compose for it, and at night lead it (from the keyboard, or playing the violin) in concerts and operas. (We know, too, of occasions where he played in a string quartet with Mozart and two other noted Viennese composers, Vanhal and Dittersdorf. He also enjoyed playing the timpani, for which he wrote some fine licks.) On Sundays there would be Mass with music. At midday during the week he might be summoned to play duets and trios with his patron, an amateur of the *baryton,* an unusual instrument descended from the viol da gamba family. For the prince's pleasure Haydn composed five books of trios for violin, baryton, and cello. For the theater he composed some operas and music for marionette shows—slight and inconsequential works in comparison with Mozart's theater pieces, but appropriate to the nature of his service. The total schedule, with its daily routines, the concerts and theater and masses, and the necessary composing, seems by modern standards crushing.

Haydn

Yet these were the expected duties of an eighteenth-century *Kapellmeister*—master of a large corps of musicians, ready and capable of performing almost anything, as was Haydn to compose it. One has the impression of a jovial individual with good business acumen and a healthy attitude. Keeping musicians well trained and in a positive frame of mind is not always easy, and he knew how to make a point in their behalf. For instance in 1772, when Prince Esterhazy dawdled too long at his country estate while the musicians were anxious to get back to their wives and children in Eisenstadt, Haydn composed and conducted a symphony at the end of which the musicians, one by one, snuffed out their candles and left the room. The prince took the point and had the carriages readied for departure the next day. The Symphony No. 45 in F♯ Minor has ever since been called the "Farewell."

Haydn literally forged the sonata style, breathing into it a vitality that took it well beyond its relatively tame predecessors. His solutions integrated form, force, and substance to produce instrumental music of unparalleled internal coherence. His sense of motive is quite powerful, and he had a good feel for rhythm and drive. You are reminded forcefully of his own modest roots and his ear for the primitive formulas he heard about him: Hints of village song and gypsy music pervade his work. You can't miss his good humor—one of the things that makes it possible to distinguish between Haydn and Mozart. Most of all you are taken by his remarkable melodic fertility and orchestrational skill, even with the limited orchestra he had at hand.

Viennese Classicism reached its maturity in the late 1770s and the 1780s, mostly owing to the work of Haydn and Mozart. After 1790 things changed: Haydn went to London (1791–92, 1794–95), Mozart died, Beethoven moved to Vienna (1792). Across

Europe the Napoleonic conquests began and in a few years reached Vienna's gates. Haydn, meanwhile, thrived.

www.prenhall.com/masterworks
composer profiles
Mozart

WOLFGANG AMADEUS MOZART (1756–91). You may know by now the essence of Mozart's story: His gifts were admired throughout Europe even during his early childhood, he died young, the music he composed during his short life is, almost without exception, inestimably sublime. There's a degree of perfection in his work that has little parallel in music history.

It all goes to prove something about the advantages of good heredity and careful upbringing. His father, Leopold Mozart, of Salzburg, was a master teacher of the violin and author of a treatise on how to play it. Mozart's sister was also a child prodigy. In 1762, when Mozart was 6 (and Haydn just beginning to work for the Esterhazy family), Leopold led the children on the first of the concert tours that eventually presented Wolfgang in virtually every important city of Europe. Among the monarchs who heard him play were Maria Theresa of Austria, Louis XV, and George III. Not to mention Haydn, who later remarked to Leopold Mozart, "Before God and as an honest man I tell you that your son is the greatest composer known to me either in person or by name. He has taste and, what is more, the greatest knowledge of composition."

There was good entertainment to be found in Mozart's ability to improvise fugues on difficult subjects given to him by the local *maestro di cappella* and his ability to jot down from memory music he had heard only once. But the important thing was that he

The Mozarts: Nannerl, Wolfgang, and Leopold, with a portrait of their late mother

absorbed at their sources all the elements that went to make up art music of the time, from Italian opera to clarinets. In a generation or two after Mozart, the world having begun to grow smaller, many composers traveled through Europe as a matter of course, particularly Mendelssohn, Berlioz, and Liszt. But none of these quite matched Mozart in his ability to synthesize the international vocabulary.

Mozart's relationship with his employer in Salzburg, the sinister Archbishop Colloredo, was stormy, in part because his innate republicanism made him an unlikely candidate for the kind of servitude implied by his job. Quitting the archbishop's court in 1781, Mozart went to Vienna to seek his fortune, hoping to secure a post at the imperial court. A court appointment never materialized, but within a few months Mozart had found a wife, Constanze, who was a soprano. All three of her sisters—Josepha, Aloysia, and Sophie—were capable sopranos as well, and Mozart went on to compose the coloratura part of the Queen of the Night, in *The Magic Flute,* for Josepha.

One could not call Mozart's life in Vienna a failure. He was a major figure in the local concert life, and his appearances at the keyboard in his own piano concertos were greatly popular. The subscription concert series in which he presented much of his best orchestral work succeeded well, for the most part, at the box office. The majority of his work was bought by the publishers. In Prague he was more popular still: In 1786 there was an important performance of his opera *The Marriage of Figaro,* followed by commissions for *Don Giovanni* and the symphony now known as the "Prague," No. 38 in D Major, K. 504.

The young Mozart

By virtue of his ability to keep the whole of a movement in mind while he wrote down its constituent parts on paper, Mozart brought to sonata practice a great sophistication of internal design. The potential of themes and motives is progressively at issue, the development becoming a place for working out the implications of the stated material. All the genres he touched profited from his work; in two of them, the piano concerto and the opera, he is unrivaled even by Haydn. All told he composed over 600 works, including sonatas, quartets, symphonies, sacred music, and operas. These are identified nowadays with K. numbers, after the catalog of his works by Ludwig von Köchel. The K. numbers are chronological through the Requiem, K. 626, such that K. 191 (a bassoon concerto) is a relatively early work; anything in the K. 600s (*The Magic Flute,* the Clarinet Concerto, *Ave verum corpus*) is among his last.

Haydn and Mozart, incidentally, were both Freemasons, as eventually was Mozart's father Leopold. Although a secret fraternity, the Masons were devoted to good things: moral behavior, loyalty to the church and the state, charitable causes, and each other's welfare. Mozart's opera *The Magic Flute* is from one perspective an allegory of Masonic symbols and ideals, and from time to time he wrote for specific Masonic occasions.

Exhausted by the rigors of his 1790 visit to Prague, and suffering from what appears to have been rheumatic fever, Mozart died before turning 36, having had virtually no life other than as a fast-lane prodigy. Constanze's widowhood was no bed of roses: She sold the remaining rights to her husband's music and most of his estate, then was forced to beg others to organize concerts to benefit the Widow Mozart and his son. Constanze remarried in 1809, and the son died in 1844, putting an end to the short-lived family dynasty.

 ## *C*LASSICAL GENRES

THE STRING QUARTET. The idea of a string quartet arises naturally out of part writing for four string voices, as in *Eine kleine Nachtmusik*. In the best quartet writing the homogeneous tone quality of the four instruments is not so much a limitation as an opportunity. Textural interest is achieved through the contrast of homophonic passages with highly contrapuntal ones, solo work, registral change, and the occasional use of mutes and pizzicato. At the beginning, Haydn's quartets gave strong prominence to the first violin; when he started to favor a philosophical equality of the participants, the mature string quartet began to emerge.

The typical four movements of a string quartet are similar to those of a symphony: a big sonata at the beginning, a slow movement, a minuet-and-trio, and a finale, often highly imitative. Quartets tend to come in groups of six, for dedication to a particular patron. (Baroque concertos and sonatas had come in dozens.) Haydn began to write quartets in the summer of 1757 for the simple reason that he had the four necessary players in residence. In his op. 33 quartets of 1781, he developed the third-movement *scherzo,* a kind of jocular minuet, and experimented with fugal finales. By the mid-1780s, Haydn's quartets and Mozart's were cross-pollinating each other, thus establishing a mature genre.

Altogether there are some 64 Haydn string quartets, ranging from the early ops. 9, 17, and 20 to ops. 76 (six quartets from 1797, dedicated to the Hungarian count Joseph Erdödy) and 77 (two last quartets, from 1799, of a planned set for Prince Lobkowitz). Mozart wrote 26 quartets, including a group dedicated to Haydn in 1785. Among the other pioneers of the string quartet were the Czech-Viennese composer J. B. Vanhal (1739–1813) and the Italian Luigi Boccherini (1743–1805), both of whom composed more than 100 string quartets.

 ### HAYDN: FROM STRING QUARTET IN C MAJOR, OP. 76, NO. 3 ("EMPEROR" 1797)

II. POCO ADAGIO, CANTABILE

The third of the op. 76 quartets is a sprawling, eclectic work, by turns folklike and noble. After four decades of quartet composition, the 65-year-old master still seems to be brimming over with imaginative things to say. Haydn's music of the period is strongly patriotic. Napoleon had reached Austro-Hungary in 1796, and Haydn knew that his Hungarian patrons, both Esterhazy and Erdödy, had committed monetary support to the Austrian cause. His imperial hymn of 1796, *Gott erhalte Franz den Kaiser* ("God preserve the Emperor Francis"), was by the spring of 1797 being sung in the streets of Vienna, and it seems likely that the first theme of the quartet makes reference to the title in an anagram: G-E-F-D-C.

Movement II is a theme with variations based on Haydn's imperial hymn, which later became the Austrian national anthem. (For a brief time, with brasses, drums, and cymbals, it became the Nazi war cry "Deutschland über alles"; it also serves for the hymn "Wondrous Things of Thee Are Spoken / Zion City of Our God"). The theme is stated homophonically, marked *dolce* ("sweet") and *cantabile* ("singingly"). A 16-bar period A-A-B-C, suitable for a four-line poetic stanza, is extended to 20 bars by repeating the last unit: A-A-B-C-C. Haydn's curious barring, implying upbeats at the beginning that don't really exist, allow the half-note cadences to fall on beat 1.

Classical practice tends to vary themes by progressively complex ornamentation. Toward the end there is nearly always a shift to the minor mode, a signal the end is at hand. Here Variation I is a duo for the violins, with the theme in the second violin and a sixteenth-note figuration in the first. Variation II, with the theme in the cello, investigates syncopated counterpoint. Variation III, theme in the viola, turns darkly chromatic. The last variation incorporates elements of each of the preceding units: the prevailing homophony of the theme, bits of the chromaticism and syncopation and sixteenth-note motion. Moreover, it begins in the minor mode. The closure is quite remarkable, with the meandering chromatic accompaniment of the last subphrase calmed by the first violin's long downward fall and placid cadence. Note particularly the crescendo-decrescendo effect in the last two bars.

Composers of the Viennese school were as adroit at variation practice as Bach had been. One way Mozart earned his reputation as a musical genius was his talent for spur-of-the-moment theme variations suggested to him by a member of the audience.

Listening Chart

 CD 1, TR 20

Franz Joseph Haydn (1732–1809)
String Quartet in C Major, op. 76, no. 3 ("Emperor;" 1797)
Movement II: Poco adagio; cantabile

For: string quartet (2 violins, viola, cello)

Type: Theme and variations
Meter: ¢
Key: G major
Duration: 07:06

The theme is stated homophonically, then recast in four variations that feature each member of the quartet. In the last variation note the remarkable synthesis of the elements: chromaticism, syncopation, mix of the minor and major modes, and a delicious meandering closure, with crescendo-decrescendo in the last two bars.

	Theme	
	Theme	The theme is Haydn's imperial hymn, *Gott erhalte Franz den Kaiser*
00:00	**A**	("God preserve the Emperor Francis"). Homophonic, *dolce, cantabile*.
00:15	**A**	
00:29	**B**	
00:49	**C**	
01:05	**C**	The repeat of C extends the 16-bar period to 20 bars.
01:24	**Variation I**	Duo for violins; theme in vn. II, figuration in vn. I.
02:31	**Variation II**	Theme in cello; syncopated counterpoint.
03:50	**Variation III**	Theme in viola; richly chromatic accompaniment.
05:12	**Variation IV**	Comingling of the elements: homophony, chromaticism, syncopation, figuration. Starts in minor. Note the remarkable close.

His typical style can be heard in his variations K. 265/300e on the tune you know as "Twinkle, Twinkle, Little Star," and Europeans know by the French title "Ah vous dirai-je maman." A few years later the Viennese publisher Anton Diabelli conceived the notion of publishing a volume to which all the local composers would contribute a variation on a waltz tune of his own composition. Beethoven responded not with one but with the 33 Diabelli Variations, op. 120. One of these cleverly reshapes the Diabelli tune so that it also varies the melody of a famous aria from Mozart's opera *Don Giovanni.* Here you get a taste of what's to come in variation practice, where the musical organism itself undergoes radical transformation.

Remember that the string quartet is but one of the many chamber aggregations for which the Classical composers wrote. There are trios with and without piano, piano quartets and quintets (that is, three or four string players with piano), and, notably, Mozart's quintets: two for two violins, two violas, and cello (K. 515 in C major and 516 in G minor, 1786–87) and the Clarinet Quintet in A minor (K. 581, 1789; for clarinet and string quartet). Beethoven's "Archduke" Trio, op. 97 (1811), named after its dedicatee Archduke Rudolph of Austria, is for violin, cello, and piano.

The string quartet was one of Beethoven's strongest genres, progressing from the Haydn-and-Mozart idiom of the six quartets op. 18 (1798–1800) through the mature quartets written for Count Razumovsky, op. 59 (1805–1806) to the formidably abstract series he composed at the end of his life, ops. 128 and following. After Beethoven, the popularity of the quartet declined somewhat, although most of the Romantics tried to keep their hand in. In the late nineteenth and early twentieth centuries, the genre flourished anew with contributions by Brahms, the French (Fauré, Debussy, Ravel), and, most especially, the six fine quartets of Béla Bartók.

THE PIANO SONATA.　　The piano was developed in the first decade of the eighteenth century by the harpsichord maker Bartolomeo Cristofori of Florence, who called his instruments *gravicembali col piano e forte* ("keyboards with soft and loud"). His hammer mechanism involved an imaginative action called escapement, where a springs-and-levers arrangement causes the hammer to strike the string and immediately fall away; when the finger is lifted from the key, a damper falls onto the string and stops the sound. Additionally, various kinds of pedals or knee-activated levers allowed the entire damper apparatus to be kept disengaged, thus prolonging the sound; and for shifting the hammers sideways so that only one (or two) of the three strings for each pitch were struck, thus muting the overall volume. The result was an instrument with substantially increased possibilities of volume, touch, and expressive color. Bach was the Leipzig representative of an early German piano maker; his son J. C. Bach favored the piano in his public concerts. By 1775 or so the victory of the piano was complete, not only in Vienna but in Berlin, Paris, and London as well. Important piano factories sprang up in all of those cities.

One would not call the first solo piano sonatas a gripping sort of music. That was not the point. Symphonic music and opera dealt in the grander issues, while piano music was for the pleasure of those who played it. Haydn reveled in composing piano sonatas, where we often find him at his most witty and playful.

HAYDN: FROM PIANO SONATA NO. 59 IN E♭ MAJOR (1790)

I. ALLEGRO

Haydn's works have been numbered in different ways. One edition calls this sonata no. 59, while Haydn's cataloguer Hoboken lists it in position 49, and *The New Grove Dictionary of Music and Musicians* considers it no. 44 of 47 authentic sonatas. For our purposes it's enough to know that this is a late sonata, the next to last of the ones in E♭. It was composed for the wife of Prince Esterhazy's physician, a gifted singer and pianist.

Listening Chart

 CD 1, TR 21

Franz Joseph Haydn (1732–1809)
Piano Sonata No. 59 in E♭ Major (1790)
   Movement I: Allegro

For: piano

Type: Sonata
Meter: ¢ 3
Key: E♭ major
Duration: 04:28

This work, which comes relatively late in Haydn's output of some four dozen piano sonatas, was apparently composed for Maria Anna von Genzinger, wife of Prince Esterhazy's physician and a gifted singer and pianist. The recording, from the late 1950s, is by the weird but wonderful Glenn Gould, a pioneer in modern techniques of studio recording.

	Exposition	Gracious and lively, a many-themed Allegro: sonata form can be playful.
00:00	Th. I	E♭ major. Bursts of 16ths in the r.h., sharp responses in the l.h., a gallant 12-bar phrase.
00:14	Bridge	The new rhythm is striking, thematic in quality, but transitional to:
00:28	Th. II	B♭ major. Begins as Th. I (see ex.), but in dominant (V); the new
00:31		melody comes next, with prominent Alberti bass figuration.
00:48	Cl. th. pt. 1	Closing material consists of cadential figures and the emphatic
00:56	Cl. th. pt. 2	short-short-short-long motive, much favored of Beethoven.
	Development	
01:14	part 1	Based on bridge: modulatory, unstable.
01:32	part 2	A hint of Th. I (in minor), then the Alberti bass figure (from Th. II).
02:03	part 3	The short-short-short-long motive treated; hints of Th. I (02:26).
02:32	cadenza	An improvistory cadenza to end the development.
	Recapitulation	
02:39	Th. I	E♭ major. As before.
02:53	Bridge	As before, until altered at 03:00 (to stay in tonic).
03:10	Th. II	Skips theme, goes right to Alberti bass.
03:26	Cl. themes	
03:47	extended	
03:55	**Coda**	Based on bridge, with brusque cadential rip at the end.

Haydn's ebullience is much in evidence here, beginning with the perky opening gesture. It's necessary to remember, in sonatas like these, the difference between *theme* and *theme group:* The movement has many thematic ideas, but the second group (Th. II, as we call it in the charts) actually begins with the motto from Theme I. The important thing is the arrival of the new key, B♭, signaled by the bridge motive's ending on a fermata.

The B♭ section is quite extended, first with passagework over an Alberti bass (see p. 145), then with the short-short-short-long rhythmic figure much favored by Beethoven, here serving as part of the closing material. The development amalgamates the motto opening, Alberti-bass passages, and the short-short-short-long motive, concluding in a flowery cadenza point. When the recapitulation is done, a substantial coda turns back to investigate the bridge passage once more, as though cognizant that it was left out of the development. The movement uses the new piano well, with idiomatic figuration (note the very last right-hand rip, for instance) and modern dynamics and articulations.

Haydn wrote about four dozen piano sonatas, Mozart some 21, along with sonatas for violin and piano. The 32 Beethoven sonatas remain at dead center of the piano repertoire. Additionally, Beethoven composed 10 sonatas for violin and piano and five for cello and piano. Of these the favorites are the "Kreutzer" Sonata for violin and piano, op. 47, dedicated to the French violin virtuoso Rodolphe Kreutzer, and the op. 69 cello sonata.

THE SOLO CONCERTO.   Having soloists play with backup orchestras is of course an old idea; remember the hundreds of concertos from the Baroque, both solo and grosso. What happened in Vienna was the merger of the concerto as a genre with the all-pervasive sonata practice. An intimacy of relationship between soloist and orchestra is in keeping with the basic equilibrium of the Viennese style, and while the soloists (including Mozart and Beethoven themselves) were famous performers, the cultivation of flamboyant virtuosity is a product of the next century. The three-movement norm, fast-slow-fast, is retained from the Baroque, although the length is greater. A Mozart concerto lasts about a half hour.

Concerto first movements have a particularly appealing structure where the sonata is adapted on behalf of the soloist. Recall that in a symphonic first movement the sonata exposition invariably repeats. In the concerto the mechanical repeat is abandoned in favor of a scheme whereby the orchestra presents most of the main thematic material in its own complete *tutti* or *orchestral ritornello* before the soloist first enters.

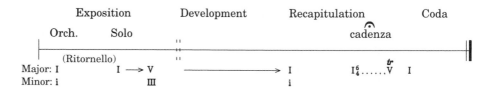

You usually hear the traditional first and second subjects and closing material, but in the orchestral ritornello *everything stays firmly rooted in the tonic key.* After the big orchestral cadence the soloist enters with a version of the main theme; *the long-delayed motion to the dominant, required of the sonata, is left to the soloist*—or at least to the solo portion. This gives the soloist's half of the overall exposition a particular formal role to play.

The development and recapitulation proceed as in any sonata but with the added possibility of solo-tutti dialogue. There will be a summary orchestral tutti to conclude the recapitulation. But its forceful, seemingly final cadence is magically interrupted, and the soloist alights on a further improvisation, the *cadenza,* not written out in Mozart's time, but rather indicated with a fermata in the score and parts. The soloist is to discover in his or her improvisations what possibilities still lurk in the given material and seek to display the registral and technical capabilities of the instrument as well as whatever measure of virtuosity the performer deems appropriate to the work. At length the pianist settles on a trilled supertonic pitch in the right hand and the dominant-seventh chord in the left, and the orchestra uses the trill as a cue to enter and finish up with a quick, usually peremptory coda. The cadenza point looks like this:

Mozart: Piano Concerto No. 25 in C Major, movt. I

But in fact a good five minutes or more of improvisation by the soloist can take place during that single bar marked "Cadenza." Cadenzas are among the great pleasures of concertgoing, with all sorts of opportunities for adventure and artful digression. What seems to be the cadenza trill, for example, can prove to be a false lead as the soloist darts merrily away into something new, and the closing orchestral tutti sometimes turns into a coda altogether different from what has come before.

Quite soon, you'll find the soloist entering in the first bars—the "orchestra's" ritornello—as though anxious to break in. This happens both in Beethoven's Fourth Piano Concerto and in his Fifth, the "Emperor"; thereafter it's common, as in both the Schumann Piano Concerto and the Mendelssohn Violin Concerto. The potential of the performing force, with its soloist and orchestral winds, is much greater than in the Baroque concerto, offering possibilities for conversation, rivalry, and even outright disagreement between the participants.

Concerto slow movements are often binary or abbreviated sonata forms with the soloist given aria-like material, somewhat along the lines of the Baroque slow movements.The third movement is often some sort of rondo form, where the composer works with alternations of both theme group and solo/tutti episodes. The *sonata-rondo* is common, with progress from tonic to dominant in the expository material, development, and recapitulation that stays in tonic. If there's a third-movement cadenza, it is usually quite brief, perhaps a run-and-trill. Spur-of-the-moment improvisations elsewhere are perfectly acceptable. For one thing, Mozart, having been the soloist, sometimes leaves only sketchy indications of the piano part in his manuscript, so filling in empty spots is essential. In any event you sense Mozart's personal presence at every turn, feeling somehow closer to the essence of his artistry in the concertos than anywhere else.

The Mozartian concerto went on to have many imitators and descendants. A few composers—Schubert, Berlioz, Verdi, Wagner, Mahler—showed little interest in the piano concerto. Otherwise nearly everybody afterward went out of their way to write them: Beethoven, Schumann, Mendelssohn, Chopin, Liszt, Brahms, Tchaikovsky, Bartók, Stravinsky, and Prokofiev. Modern orchestra concerts rely heavily on the concerto repertoire, which brings the stars to town and the public to the hall.

For Mozart the initial choice of key goes a long way toward defining the character of the music. C major is the royal key, one of grandeur and victory. It lends itself to trumpet work, thus fanfares, thus open triadic structures and bold proportions; it can also be put well to naive effects. All this is to be found in the atmosphere of the C-Major Concerto K. 503, the last of Mozart's 12 great piano concertos (K. 449 to K. 503) of the mid-1780s.

 MOZART: PIANO CONCERTO NO. 25 IN C MAJOR, K. 503 (1786)

I. ALLEGRO MAESTOSO

Now take in the concerto first-movement organization and try to conceptualize how it differs from an ordinary sonata allegro. Keep in mind that this particular example is a very big movement with many thematic elements and motives. The orchestral ritornello has a two-part *first theme:* the fanfares and the connecting oboe-and-bassoon turns; the *bridge* involves two important motives, a short-short-short-long figure and upward rocketing scales; the *second subject,* a little march in C minor (incorporating the short-short-short-long rhythm), gives way to an important *closing figure.* This makes for a total of six important motivic elements in the ritornello alone. *But the ritornello stays very closely centered on C, the tonic key.*

The solo role seems quite tentative at the pianist's first wispish entries but rapidly assumes critical importance in the eliding passagework and then with new themes. The first of these, curiously, is an episode in the middle of the bridge and in the unexpected key of E♭. Finally the soloist reaches the true second group, *in the key of G major.*

Br. (E♭) episode

04:33

05:13 *legato*

The exposition concludes with the long trill in the piano and a closing section drawn from the orchestral tutti (Bridge 1 and 2, above) with big G-major cadences.

What has been conspicuously omitted from the soloist's portion of the exposition is the minor-mode march, Theme II (orch.) above, and the development turns immediately to treat this passage, to the near exclusion of everything else. At length the horns settle on a dominant pedal point, and you know the recapitulation must be next. The piano participates all the way through the recapitulation, and the many themes all appear, including both the E♭ episode and the march, now transformed into the major mode.

Pay particular attention to where the cadenza falls: right at the end, when virtually everything is over. Murray Perahia's cadenza on the CD starts with a vigorous fantasia on the various short motives, then turns to investigate the solo second theme and the ritornello's march theme, finding and musing over the now familiar short-short-short-long rhythm. Cadenzas often veer sharply in thematic content and harmony from one issue to the next as the soloist digresses from one subject to the next; the keyboard texture is thicker, too, since there is no orchestra to fill in.

Pause to admire the many new sounds you hear in this movement: the martial qualities of the brass and drums, the feathery piano work, and above all Mozart's creative use of the harmonic palette to splash all sorts of punctuating color about.

Listening Chart

 CD 2, TR 1

W. A. Mozart (1756–91)
Piano Concerto in C Major, K. 503 (1786)
   Movement I: Allegro maestoso

For: piano solo; flute, 2 oboes, 2 bassoons; 2 horns, 2 timpani; strings

Type: Concerto first
  movement
Meter: C
Key: C major
Duration: 15:17

A Classical concerto is easily distinguished from a symphony of the same period, owing not just to the soloist but also to the absence of a minuet, the lighter finale (often a sonata-rondo), and the *concerto first movement,* where instead of a repeated exposition, the orchestra presents the main thematic material in its own complete orchestral ritornello before the soloist first enters.

	Orchestral Ritornello	
00:00	Th. I	Bold C-major arpeggiations with woodwind rebounds. A hint of minor, then:
00:33	Br. 1	A new figure, staccato upbeats. Short-short-short-long motto.
00:47	Br. 2	Section closure: fast scales over motto; long extension, then big cadences with cascading strings. Motto.
01:32	Th. II orch.	Minor-mode march (C minor), then major mode. A very important theme.
02:01	Cl. th.	Brass fanfares, then legato figures and elegant brass response. Extended (02:31) with busy reiteration of motto.
02:47	**Solo Exposition**	The final cadences of the ritornello prolonged by the initial piano entries.
03:26	Th. I	C major. Begins as before; piano joins in second phrase, then takes over.
03:59	Br.	As before; this time a new transition yields an:
04:33	Br. episode	E♭-major episode. Sounds like a Th. II, but isn't—wrong key.
05:13	Th. II solo	G major (V). The true new theme, gracious, gentle, contrasting— tinged with minor at the end; big extension (05:44); trilled cadence.
06:33	Close	The same as the section closure figure at 00:47.
07:05	**Development**	The entire development is concerned with the minor-mode march theme. Relationships much the same as in orchestral ritornello (01:32). Ww. episode (07:23) joined by soloist (07:46). Dominant pedals (08:40).
	Recapitulation	
08:54	Th. I	C major (I). As in the solo exposition (03:26).
10:02	Br. episode	As before, in E♭ major; takes a questioning new direction at the end.
10:39	Th. II solo	C major. The minor-mode march now major (11:15); gathers to:
12:38	**Cadenza**	Three sections reviewing motives, Th. II solo, and Th. II orch.
14:34	**Coda**	Largely the same as 02:01.

RECOMMENDED LISTENING:

Mozart: Piano Concerto No. 25 in C Major, K. 503, movts. II–III

THE SYMPHONY.   The term *sinfonia* originated in Italy, as did some of the prevailing ideas about the overall purpose and character of multimovement instrumental works. With Haydn and Mozart, the symphony reaches its ordinary configuration of four movements, usually an ambitious sonata first movement, a slow movement, minuet-and-trio, and sonata finale. As we noted earlier, the Classical orchestra numbered about two dozen, with pairs of winds, timpani, and perhaps four to six string players per part. Orchestral concerts of the period now regularly featured overtures, concertos, and symphonies, perhaps a pair of each, and often arias for guest singers or virtuoso variations for a featured instrumentalist.

In due time the words "symphony" and "symphonic" come to describe large-ensemble work: symphony orchestra, symphony hall, symphonic music in general.

Together Haydn and Mozart composed some 150 symphonies, and there are hundreds more from the many other composers of Austro-Hungary. The first 80 or so of Haydn's 104 symphonies were for the Esterhazy musicians, a smallish band; with Haydn's ascendancy to international fame the symphonies become bigger and greatly more important. Symphonies 88 through 92 were commissioned by others for performance in Paris and elsewhere; the last dozen, 93 through 104, were for his triumphant London seasons and have been known ever since as the "London" symphonies. Of Mozart's 41 symphonies, the early ones seem to take second place aesthetically to the piano concertos. This relationship was reversed with the "Haffner" Symphony, No. 35; possibly Mozart had simply run out of steam where it came to piano concertos, or the public had begun to tire of them. A half dozen more dazzling symphonies were forthcoming before his death.

MOZART: SYMPHONY NO. 40 IN G MINOR, K. 550 (1788)

I. ALLEGRO NON TROPPO

The G-Minor, No. 40, is the middle (with nos. 39 and 41, the "Jupiter") of the three symphonies Mozart composed in the summer of 1788; these were the first he had written for the Vienna public since moving there in 1781. We don't know the particular reasons behind this astonishing product of six week's work, but with composers such summer activity generally means they are thinking about the forthcoming concert season. The clarinet parts were added later, perhaps in 1791, and the flute and oboe parts redistributed accordingly. Like the others, the G-Minor is a complex work of memorable themes and strongly felt formal design. The first movement has an agitated, troubled quality about it, allayed only slightly by the delicate second theme. The opening theme is an excellent example of Viennese Classical symmetry, and the very first gesture (bracketed in the example) quickly becomes the overarching point of reference—a strategy much like that in Beethoven's Fifth.

Tension and unrest can be sensed in the other movements as well: in the poignant dissonances of the Andante, the syncopations and stern key of the minuet, the rocketing subject of the last movement, and its intense contrapuntal treatment. These are all hints of the overt Romanticism that would preoccupy the generations after Mozart.

Listening Chart

 CD 2, TR 2

W. A. Mozart (1756–91)
Symphony No. 40 in G Minor, K. 550 (1788)
Allegro non troppo

For: flute, 2 oboes, 2 clarinets, 2 bassoons; 2 horns; strings.

Type: sonata
Meter: ¢
Key: G minor
Duration: 08:12

The taut structure and strong reliance on the opening motive and its fragmentation make this, the most famous Mozart first movement, the obvious precursor of Beethoven's Fifth.

00:00	**Exposition**	G minor. Two bars in the middle strings, fretful and agitated.
00:01	Th. I	A deftly shaped though melancholy theme. Shortly after the restatement (00:24), the theme veers into:
00:33	Br.	The bold orchestral *tutti* effects the modulation, concluding with an empty bar (where Szell wheezes) just before Th. II.
00:52	Th. II	B♭ major (relative major of G minor); longer note values, more chromatic. The restatement (01:01), reverses roles of winds and strings.
01:21	Cl. th.	A conventional cl. th. with scalar descent to the new tonic, extended by treatment of the opening motto.
02:02	Exp. rep.	The exposition repeated.
	Development	Concerned almost entirely with Th. I and the motto.
04:07	pt. 1	Harmonically unstable, investigating other key areas.
04:21	pt. 2	Low strings, answered by violins; strong counterpoint.
04:49	pt. 3	Th. I systematically fragmented, anticipating recapitulation.
05:06	transition	Urgent, troubled outbursts of the motive, receding into:
	Recapitulation	
05:21	Th. I	G minor. Much as before, with new bassoon countermelody.
05:55	Br.	Starts exactly as before, then greatly extended.
06:37	Th. II	G minor. Th. II in the minor mode.
07:12	Cl. th.	Much as before, though in G minor.
07:44	transition	Emphasizing the turbulent elements again.
07:50	**Coda**	Tender, almost Romantic closing gestures.
08:00	cad. fig.	Closes, however, with bold, emphatic strokes.

www.prenhall.com/masterworks
recommended listening

RECOMMENDED LISTENING:

Mozart: Symphony No. 40 in G Minor, K. 550 (1788), movts. II–IV
Mozart: Symphony No. 41 in C Major, K. 551 ("Jupiter," 1788)

MOZART OPERAS

From early childhood Mozart had been surrounded by opera. The bulk of it was in Italian, with *opera seria* still the reigning genre. Its music consisted of recitatives and arias for each of the important singers, with now and then a duo or brief chorus; the last finale might find the chorus offering the moral of the story in a little quatrain. The overture was, likely as not, in the French fashion, and the piece appended at the front of one opera might just as well serve for any other. By Haydn and Mozart's day, comic opera, or *opera buffa,* had become a popular rage as well. Extensions of the lighter fare included theater works constructed of street songs (*ballad opera*) and fast-paced works in the vernacular German with spoken texts in lieu of recitatives (*Singspiel*). Here low comedy was the order of the day: bumbling noblemen, wronged noblewomen, cocky servant girls, the arrival of a notary or military officer who either sorts things out just in the nick of time or else puts yet another fly into the ointment.

It was Mozart's particular genius to be able to gather these disparate elements into a vital new rhetoric where the serious and the funny coexisted, the net result much truer to life. Once he was done, the old distinctions of genre had little validity left: Mozart, venerating the past scarcely at all, saw nothing to keep him from mixing, matching, and mingling elements as he went. And while he wrote ably for Italian libretti, his two German-language operas *Die Entführung aus dem Serail* ("The Abduction from the Harem") and *Die Zauberflöte* ("The Magic Flute")—helped break the hegemony of the Italian lyric stage.

He also had a great gift for settling on subject matter of real significance and was lucky in his choice of collaborating librettists. The most capable of his Italian librettists was Lorenzo da Ponte. The librettist of *The Magic Flute,* Emanuel Schikaneder, was the proprietor of the theater company that produced the opera, and he himself sang the role of Papageno.

In both *Le Nozze di Figaro* ("The Marriage of Figaro") and *Don Giovanni,* Mozart deals with the most pressing social issue of his day, the matter of class distinction. The aristocrats habitually take advantage of the working classes, and the peasants invariably outfox them. Yet there's high comedy and slapstick in both operas, with repeated episodes of mistaken identity, a great deal of hiding behind things, broken pottery, and a pistol or two. *The Magic Flute* opens as a comedy, with storybook characters and enchanted toy instruments, but soon turns into a serious treatment of the tenor's journey toward spiritual purification.

What makes these operas special is their vigorous forward motion; characters evolve and plots advance *during* the music. The ensembles and act finales become scenes of rank confusion, as the characters group and regroup in every permutation, the dramatic situation changing every few dozen bars. Different texts are sometimes sung simultaneously; you can't always make out the words, but you get the point. There's a passage in *Don Giovanni,* for example, where a minuet, contradanse, and allemande go on simultaneously: three little orchestras, three pairs of characters, three parts of the palace. And it all fits together.

Each of the operas has a short but important overture at the beginning. Although these are not medleys of the tunes to follow, as you'd hear in the potpourri overture to a Broadway play, each makes direct allusion to what follows.

www.prenhall.com/masterworks
recommended listening

Recommended Listening:

Mozart: Overtures to **The Marriage of Figaro,** *K. 492 (1786) and* **The Magic Flute,** *K. 620 (1791); arias from* **The Marriage of Figaro,** *and* **Don Giovanni,** *K. 527 (1787)*

Mozart's operas go on a very long time—about four hours with intermissions—and you have to come to grips with their leisurely pace, relic of an era when time passed more slowly than it does now. But they are absolutely central to the history of theater, holding their own alongside the work of Sophocles, Shakespeare, and Molière.

HAYDN AFTER MOZART. In September 1791 Mozart was in Prague, where he heard a performance of *Don Giovanni* and completed a last *opera seria, La Clemenza di Tito,* which he conducted on opening night. He was back in Vienna for the first performance of *The Magic Flute* on 30 September. Meanwhile, he had been visited by a mysterious stranger bearing a commission for a Requiem Mass. Before the Requiem was done, he succumbed to overwork and bacterial infection (not poisoning by his rival

Salieri, as a popular movie would have it). He was left in an open collective grave outside Vienna to await the spring thaw.

(I hope you will take an early opportunity to see, or see again, the movie *Amadeus,* available at your local video shop. Remember that the facts, plot, and characterizations are the playwright's. In truth, Salieri was a distinguished and highly qualified musician who left a great deal of good in his wake. But many of the images in the film are first-rate: the outdoor concerts with Mozart conducting from the keyboard, the look of a theater of the era, the way the emperor is always surrounded by his sycophants. And several of the lines given to Mozart—"I beg Your Majesty's pardon: There are precisely as many notes as needed."—are firmly ensconced in the Mozart lore.)

Haydn's employer Prince Nikolaus Esterhazy had died in 1790, and the chapel was allowed to decline. Thus freed of his most pressing obligations, Haydn accepted the invitation of the impresario Salomon to visit England and present his works to the English public. For his London sojourns of 1791–92 and 1794–95, Haydn composed his celebrated "London," or "Salomon" Symphonies, the 12 that conclude his work in the genre. The nicknames added to these—"Surprise" (no. 94), "Clock" (no. 101), "Drum Roll" (no. 103)—not only helped the public distinguish them but indicate the great affection in which these works were held.

But even after the triumphs of London, Haydn was far from done. In England he had heard Handel's *Israel in Egypt,* and he returned home with a libretto for an oratorio of his own. A new Prince Esterhazy, moreover, now wanted annual masses for chorus and orchestra. Accordingly, Haydn composed six magnificent masses in the late 1790s and, in 1798, his stunning oratorio *The Creation.* It lovingly adopts the general design and the text painting of the Handelian model, but at the same time hints at the new century's radical ideas about harmonic and orchestral vista. *The Creation* was recognized from the

Esterháza: exterior

beginning as the masterpiece of a beloved composer who by that time had no equal in the world of music. Haydn's last public appearance was for a performance of *The Creation* on his 76th birthday. Salieri conducted; and among the princes and poets who stood at the door to greet him was his formerly petulant charge, Beethoven. Then he was seated in an armchair and borne into the hall to fanfares of trumpets and drums and joyous shouts of "Long live Haydn!"

He lasted a little over a year longer, passing away peacefully in May 1809 at the age of 77. Napoleon's forces had just occupied Vienna.

Chapter 6

*I*m wunderschönen Monat Mai,   In the lovely month of May,
Als alle Knospen sprangen,   when all the buds were bursting,
Da ist in meinem Herzen   then with my heart
Die Liebe aufgegangen.   love broke forth.

—Heinrich Heine (1797–1856), in *Buch der Lieder* (1827)

Romanticism

*W*hen, exactly, Romanticism starts—the kind of Romanticism you hear and feel in the lines from Heine's poem—is anybody's guess. Whether Beethoven and Schubert are best categorized as late Classical or early Romantic composers is for you to work out in your own mind; certainly they both represent turning points in the history of musical style. Both lived and worked in the aftermath of a genuine turning point in political history, the French Revolution of 1789.

*T*HE FRENCH REVOLUTION; NAPOLEON

The Oath of the Tennis Court, pictured on page 180, had nothing whatever to do with sport. On 20 June 1789 the deputies of the Third Estate (or lower house), denied their right to meet in the king's assembly hall, gathered in the adjacent stadium and vowed not to leave Versailles until Louis XVI granted the nation a constitution guaranteeing a representative government.

There was no music at Versailles that day. But the Oath of the Tennis Court, and the tumult that followed, affected artists everywhere ever after. It showed that working people had begun to put into practice what the Enlightenment philosophers theorized and the writers and poets celebrated. The delegates went on to make declarations of civil rights and universal suffrage and sought freedom for enslaved peoples. Even Haydn sensed a proud republicanism rising within him, and Beethoven was positively inundated in the currents that came to be called Romanticism.

The rise of Napoleon in the wake of the long, drawn-out Revolution greatly complicated the international scene. Visions of Charlemagne danced in his head as, acre by acre, he moved across Europe toward England and Russia, overrunning the German principalities and the venerable Austro-Hungarian empire. By 1810 he controlled the whole continent, as symbolized by his marriage to Marie-Louise, daughter of the Austrian emperor Francis I, and the birth of an heir in March 1811. Napoleon's undoing began in the summer of 1812, as he led his Grande Armée of 450,000 north from Poland toward Moscow. The Russians retreated before him, scorching the earth as they went. After the savage battle of Borodino that September, the citizens of Moscow abandoned and set fire to their city, thus forcing Napoleon's deadly retreat in the bitter winter cold. His army was reduced to 10,000 men.

David: The Oath of
the Tennis Court

David: Napoleon

The continent quickly turned against him, and even the French became discontent. What remained of the Grande Armée was devastated at the battle of Leipzig in October 1813; in April 1814 Napoleon finally abdicated and withdrew into exile on the Mediterranean island of Elba.

He stayed less than a year. Regathering his legions as he traveled from Cannes to Grenoble, he reached Paris in a month. Allied forces quickly massed against him. These he engaged in Belgium in June 1815, first defeating the Prussians, then meeting the Duke of Wellington's English army at Waterloo. Victory was nearly his when Prussian reinforcements arrived to turn the tide of the battle. This time the victors took no chances, banishing Napoleon to St. Helena in the distant south Atlantic, where he died in 1821.

Napoleon and the French Revolution were facts of life in Haydn's later decades and through much of Beethoven's adult life. Once Napoleon was gone, his legend captured the imagination of an era. To be sure, the Napoleonic experience exposed the frailties of Enlightenment institutions, but it also gave Romanticism its quintessential hero.

 EETHOVEN

www.prenhall.com/masterworks
composer profiles
Beethoven

The notion that the young **Ludwig van Beethoven (1770–1827)** would "receive Mozart's spirit from Haydn's hands," as it was put on the eve of his move from Bonn to Vienna, was insulting to everybody involved. By then Beethoven's genius was well established. In 1787, during a visit to Vienna, he had already met Mozart and probably had some lessons with him. He had a long list of publications and performances to his credit. The musical establishment of Bonn had been proclaiming him a second Mozart for years. But in 1792 Beethoven went to Vienna and never returned to Germany.

His time as Haydn's pupil was not a success. The master was more interested in London than in teaching; the student was arrogant and impetuous—purposefully misspelling Haydn's name, for example. They had only a few good lessons together, and Beethoven's formation was completed with other teachers. Nevertheless, his emergence as a major figure in Viennese musical life was swift. By the turn of the century he had composed more than a dozen fine piano sonatas and was completing his first symphony and the impressive set of six string quartets soon published as op. 18.

One might even say that Beethoven took Vienna by storm. Prone to boorishness and slovenly homemaking—the Franco-Italian composer Cherubini called him "an unlicked bear"—he nevertheless captivated the Viennese aristocracy. Nobles like Count Razumovsky and Count Wielhorsky helped keep him solvent with commissions and offers of lodging. Three aristo-

Beethoven

crats joined to give him a regular pension in 1809, demanding only that he remain in and around Vienna.

Despite his minimal formal education—he was mathematically illiterate—Beethoven read widely, garnering in due course a good command of the current literature. He was a shrewd, sometimes slick, businessman in his dealings with publishers and promoters. Both the success of his freelancing and the ease with which Beethoven used his musical genius to gain access to the upper classes show the striking effects of post-Enlightenment social change.

But Beethoven was also socially maladjusted. His romantic life consisted mostly of pointless desire for aristocratic ladies, and his inner circle consisted uniquely of male buddies. He appears to have had virtually no sex life (but somehow managed to contract syphilis). He was obsessed with the need to build a legend around himself, claiming that he was of noble ancestry and regularly adjusting his age downward. A typical letter from Beethoven catalogs his brilliant successes, then complains bitterly of his abject misery.

The extent of Beethoven's accomplishment, perhaps unparalleled in the history of music, tends to excuse his pathology. It was he who brought to the Viennese style the giant aspirations of the new age, infusing it with all the turmoil that lay within him. In scope and purpose his style was, from very nearly the beginning, heroic.

We see the new shape of things first of all, in the piano sonatas from the turn of the century.

RECOMMENDED LISTENING:

Beethoven: Sonata No. 8 in C Minor, op. 13 ("Pathétique," 1799)
Beethoven: Sonata No. 14 in C♯ Minor, op. 27, no. 2 ("Moonlight," 1801)

www.prenhall.com/masterworks
recommended listening

Beethoven's works of 1800 and 1801, the end of his first period, already show him effecting a profound mutation of Viennese Classicism. Even if you have no idea what comes next, you cannot fail to note the new, almost angry impetuosity, as well as the conspicuous experimenting with form. Yet nobody was prepared for what did come next, the hour-long Symphony No. 3 in E♭ Major of 1803, called the "Eroica."

THE HEROIC PERIOD (1803–14).   Around the turn of the century Beethoven had to accept the terrifying knowledge that he was going deaf—a secret that could not be kept indefinitely. This was at the center of his thoughts as he retreated to the hillside village of Heiligenstadt above Vienna to compose his third symphony. In October 1802, his despair burst forth in a letter to his brothers Karl and Johann:

> O, you men who believe or declare that I am malevolent, stubborn or misanthropic, how greatly you wrong me! You do not know the secret cause behind the appearance. . . . For six years I have been suffering an incurable affliction, aggravated by imprudent physicians. Year after year deceived by the hope of an improvement, finally forced to contemplate the prospect of a lasting illness, whose cure may take years or may even be impossible, born with a fiery, impulsive temperament, sensitive, even to the distractions of social life, I was yet compelled early in my life to isolate myself, to spend my life in solitude. Even if at times I wished to overcome all this, oh, how harshly I was driven back by the double grievous experience of my bad hearing, and yet I could not prevail upon myself to say to men: speak

louder, shout, for I am deaf. Oh, how could I possibly admit to being defective in the very sense which should have been more highly developed in me than in other men, a sense which once I possessed in its most perfect form, a form as perfect as few in my profession, surely, know or have known in the past. Oh, I cannot do it.

He considered suicide, but chose instead to live heroically for his art. Soon enough he had to give up playing the piano in public, doomed to a life of ear trumpets, botched operations, and finally the loss of the outside world.

Who can say for certain how the epochal events leading to the Heiligenstadt Testament—the new century, Napoleon, encroaching aural darkness—settled into Beethoven's already complex psyche? After Heiligenstadt we like to see in Beethoven a new determination to meet and overcome the adversities of fate, and to find in that struggle the central theme of his work. Certainly he had reached a turning point. The magnitude of the artistic issues he then goes on to confront and resolve is all but beyond measure. Everything afterward is bigger and more important.

The "Eroica" Symphony introduces the period and gives it its name. Beethoven had originally intended the work to celebrate Napoleon, but he (like everybody else) became disenchanted with the imperial aggression and so refashioned his title page—in a huff, so the legend goes. Each movement of the "Eroica" rewrites in some way the Viennese style, making it longer, noisier, and more descriptive, looser in a few ways and much tighter in all the rest. The first movement is a mega-sonata with a panoramic development and a long, developmental coda. New themes break out in unexpected places, and the recapitulation becomes an opportunity to expand on details of the exposition, not merely repeat it. The movement, played with its repeats, lasts nearly as long as a whole symphony of the 1770s; more significantly, the balance of the sonata movement is altogether different, with the structural fulcrum moved from the end of the exposition to the moment of recapitulation.

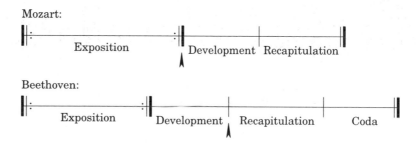

The second movement of the "Eroica" is a funeral march for a dead hero, with fanfares and suggestions of drum tattoos and at the end a dissolution as the procession passes away; later composers took this effect as an invitation to build picture music into their symphonies. The third movement is not a minuet-and-trio but its faster and cleverer descendent, the scherzo. The finale is an expansive set of variations, beginning with a one-voice harmonic outline and only gradually gathering up a proper theme.

Everywhere you look in the "Eroica" you will find radical ideas. The power of motive comes to supplant that of theme, and the *process* of working things out takes precedence over lyric refinement. It becomes nearly unthinkable to listen to one movement of a Beethoven symphony without hearing all four.

Among the central works of the heroic period are Symphonies 3 through 8, the "Waldstein" and "Appassionata" piano sonatas (ops. 53 and 57), and the string quartets op. 59, commissioned by the Russian count Andreas Razumovsky. Beethoven composed only five piano concertos, but all five are central to the repertoire, and the fourth and fifth (op. 58 in G major and op. 73 in E♭ major, called the "Emperor") are jewels of the middle period. Given the typical character of the big heroic works—vigorous, often strident, by turns urgent and anxious—the studied restraint of the Fourth Piano Concerto (and particularly its solo part) is remarkable indeed. We sense that something unusual and expansive is at work when the piano soloist opens the first movement, seeming to muse on a simple homophonic chord progression in the tonic key. The second movement has angry blasts from the strings, soothed and then thoroughly tamed by the pianist's serene responses, thus setting the stage for an airy concluding rondo.

Toward the end of the period comes Beethoven's only opera, *Fidelio,* a German-language work of long genesis and multiple versions that ended up with four overtures: the one it retains today and the Leonore Overtures Nos. 1 through 3, so called because the opera was originally titled *Leonore.* (The title character Leonore, a soprano, dresses as the boy Fidelio to rescue her husband from jail.)

RECOMMENDED LISTENING:

Beethoven: Sonata No. 23 in F Minor, op. 57 ("Appassionata," 1804–1805)
Beethoven: Piano Concerto No. 4 in G Major, op. 58 (1806)

The Fourth Piano Concerto was first heard by the public at Beethoven's concert of 22 December 1808, where the entry of the piano in the first bar must have prompted a collective gasp. There were doubtless other gasps that day, for on the same program were the first performances of both the Fifth and Sixth Symphonies and the Choral Fantasia, op. 80. One wonders how even the Viennese could have begun to comprehend the magnitude of what they were hearing.

BEETHOVEN: SYMPHONY NO. 5 IN C MINOR, OP. 67 (1808)

In Chapter 2 you took note of the form and breakneck speed of the first movement and of how the famous motto opening dominates the proceedings. In the Fifth Symphony the concept of *cyclicism,* where the movements are unified by thematic recurrence, makes a memorable debut (see Listening Charts, pp. 188–91). For it is the motto opening—Fate, said Beethoven, knocking at the door—that keeps insinuating itself, and which the symphony seems to want to overcome. This notion of symphonic genres posing and resolving artistic issues over the course of all the constituent movements is one of Beethoven's signal contributions. In the first movement "Fate" pervades all the themes.

You can't miss the signs of Beethoven's intent to establish a motto here: the loud volume, the unison scoring, the fermatas, and above all the placement at the very opening of the work. Not until the music takes wing after the second fermata do we really sense a first theme. The motto has already achieved a kind of overriding force. It goes on to shape the bridge and then to figure as a response from cellos and double basses to the second theme, as though refusing to become lost in what had traditionally been material of studied contrast to what had come before.

Note particularly in the first movement the driving development section, where the bridge passage gets reduced to its middle two notes in the process called *fragmentation*. The palpitating remains of the bridge stretch the tension level to the breaking point: The Fate motive intrudes and the recapitulation explodes. When he is done recapitulating, Beethoven is not content with a tidy closing up of the movement. Instead the motto continues to pound away and sweeps into a long and forceful revisiting of the bridge material that gives the coda what amounts to an all-new weight and meaning.

The Andante is a set of variations in A♭ major. (Beethoven's choice here of a major key to the flat side of C minor—four flats instead of three—is also Romantic, and it lends a decided gentleness, perhaps reassurance, to the stormy proceedings.) The thematic material is quite long by virtue of the modulatory bridge passage and arrival in C major for heroic fanfares with brass.

At first the variations seem merely to ornament the theme, but by the end a more organic transformation—a dissolution, in fact—is taking place. Note the very prominent allusion to the Fate motive just before the final cadence.

The third movement lies midway between a minuet and a scherzo, its initial theme virtually identical to the one at the start of Mozart's G-Minor Symphony, movement IV. Immediately, however, the Fate motive breaks in, this time quite intrusively. The scurrying fugal trio, unlike any trio heard before, then draws our undivided attention, at least in part owing to the comedy of the scrambling double basses.

At this point Beethoven's Fifth undertakes a series of dazzling ploys. The expected *da capo* occurs, but pizzicato, *pianissimo,* abbreviated and tamed; the Fate motive heard so forcefully in the horns before is now a mere peep in the oboe. The *da capo* shrinks into a mysterious pedal point with timpani. And from this blossoms, without pause, the finale. Everything about the fourth movement bespeaks victory over Fate: the C-major key (so the symphony has lifted from C minor at the beginning to C major at the end), the military tune, and the quite thrilling entry of trombones, piccolo, and contrabassoon—all making their debut in the symphony orchestra, by way of the opera-pit orchestra and military band.

The scale, too, is broad and unhurried, in stark contrast to the first movement; each theme unfolds at its leisure. And between the development and the recapitulation, we are reminded of how the Fate theme was overcome in the scherzo by a distant reminiscence in $\frac{3}{4}$. At the end the closing theme doubles in speed, a sensationalizing opera-house effect known as a *stretto close.*

Twice already in his symphonies, in the "Eroica" and the Fifth, Beethoven has stretched the very concept of the symphony. In the contemporaneous Sixth Symphony ("Pastoral"), he does it again, with pictorial movements evoking scenes of peasant life, complete with descriptive movement titles, birdcalls, and a storm—this last an extra movement before the finale, bringing the total to five. Together the Third, Fifth, and Sixth Symphonies have established the concept of narrative in symphonic music.

But composition did not come easily to Beethoven. During long walks in the countryside, he would conjure up new themes and motives and jot them down on staff paper that he carried in his pocket. Then he would return to a cluttered desk, sit down, and rework every idea from its core, trying out dozens of alternatives, selecting some and discarding others. Only gradually would he arrive at a reading that might lead to a workable draft. What Mozart discovered in a trice Beethoven took a year to perfect. Meanwhile, Beethoven's secretary, a slippery fellow named Schindler, quietly bundled up

Listening Chart

 CD 2, TR 3

Ludwig van Beethoven (1770–1827)
Symphony No. 5 in C Minor, op. 67 (1808)
  Movement I: Allegro con brio

Type: Sonata
Meter: ²⁄₄
Key: C minor
Duration: 07:37

For: 2 flutes, 2 oboes, 2 bassoons, 2 horns, 2 trumpets; timpani; strings. Last
  movement adds piccolo, contrabassoon, 3 trombones.

The Fifth Symphony, from Beethoven's "heroic" period, takes wing from the famous
motto you hear at the top. "Thus," said Beethoven, "Fate knocks at the door."

00:00	**Exposition**	Two statements of the "Fate" motto to open.
00:06	Th. I	Extended into a true theme. Mottos recur; theme works toward:
00:43	Br.	Horns, *forte:* the Fate motive plunges downward to modulate.
00:46	Th. II	E♭ major (rel. major of C minor). Lyric theme; motto rhythm in bass.
01:07	Cl. th.	Reconfirming major key, heroically, with the motto.
01:27	Exp. rep.	The exposition repeated.
	Development	
02:54	motto	Gruff bursts of the motto in horns, then low strings, for transition.
02:58	pt. 1	Treatment of first theme. Crescendos (03:17) to hammering tuttis.
03:30	pt. 2	Treatment of bridge. Tension begins to build with the:
03:41	pt. 3	Fragmentation of bridge. Decrescendo to urgent *pp*, interjections of motto.
04:12	transition	Dominant harmony achieved: more hammering of the motto, transition to:
04:17	**Recapitulation**	Tutti statement of the motto.
04:25	Th. I	C minor (I). New ww. counterpoint, added oboe cadenza (04:36).
05:12	Br.	As before, but in bassoon instead of blaring horns.
05:15	Th. II	C major. Much as before.
05:41	Cl. th.	As before. The issue is to get the tonality back to minor. This occurs when
	Coda	a long and forceful coda emerges
05:58	pt. 1	from the pounding: anything but routine.
06:14	pt. 2	Br. motive intensively revisited, as though in another development.
06:30	pt. 3	Extended forceful cadential material.
07:05	motto	The motto pounds away, retreats for a moment, then closes the movement.

all this material (with the thought of selling it, after the master's death, for his own
profit). Consequently, many hundreds of pages of Beethoven's sketches have been preserved, providing a foundation for the modern study of compositional process. Generally
speaking the sketchbooks show hard work, to be sure, but also an obsessive need to follow through on musical implication, to remember to say what has gone unsaid.

LATE BEETHOVEN (1817–25).   Gradually, as his deafness overtook him, Beethoven's artistic priorities changed. Having mined the symphonic genre thoroughly, he
turned to other modes of expression. With *An die ferne Geliebte* ("To the Distant Beloved," 1816) he forged the first *song cycle,* where the constituent songs are linked in
a unified musical fabric. Song cycles went on to become a favorite genre of the next
generation. Returning, after a long hiatus, to write for solo piano, he composed the three

Listening Chart

 CD 2, TR 4

Ludwig van Beethoven (1770–1827)
Symphony No. 5 in C Minor, op. 67 (1808)
  Movement II: Andante con moto

Type: Theme and variations
Meter: $\frac{3}{8}$
Key: A♭ major
Duration: 10:03

For: 2 flutes, 2 oboes, 2 bassoons, 2 horns, 2 trumpets; timpani; strings. Last movement adds piccolo, contrabassoon, 3 trombones.

What is different from the theme and variations of the Haydn quartet is the *process* through which each variation culminates in the C-major fanfare and the way the movement dissolves toward the end.

	Theme	Material to be varied includes the
00:00	Th.	main theme (cellos, violas), an open-ended lyric phrase, completed with:
00:24	Cad. fig.	a strong cadential figure. From this there emerges a
00:53	Br.	bridge from A♭ major to the heroic key of C major, and a
01:14	Fanfare	fanfare in C—Fate transformed by victory, you might say.
01:58	**Var. I: Th.**	Th. in cellos and vlas. as before, but now in 16ths. Clarinet countermelody.
02:18	Cad. fig.	Flute and ww., then strings, then in dialogue.
02:49	Br.	As before.
03:10	Fanfare	As before; a broadened, exquisite retransition (03:26).
03:51	**Var. II: Th.**	Th. still in cellos and vlas., now in 32nds; flute joins countermelody.
04:09	Th.'	A second statement, upper strings with ww. filigree.
04:27	Th.''	A third, climactic statement, th. in low strings. Rises to a grand fermata (04:47).
05:04	Br.	Ww., searchingly: quite different, and much longer. Horns lead into the:
05:50	Fanfare	Main climaxes. Retransition moves toward minor mode. Minor statement of:
06:36	**Var. III: Th.**	Th. in ww. Extended with interplay of scalar figures.
07:17	Th.	Surging, finale-like full orchestra statement in major.
07:40	Cad. fig.	Wws., quietly; the strings respond tenderly.
08:09	Coda	Bassoon solo over jaunty accompaniment (pizz. bass).
08:35	Cad. fig.	The last of these, in violins, emphasized by a lovely Romantic sigh (08:52).
09:11	Cadences	Ww.; growing in intensity, brass alluding to Fate motive at end.

last sonatas, ops. 109 through 111, and the *33 Variations on a Waltz by Anton Diabelli,* op. 120, works that show the concepts of continuous and progressive variation beginning to dominate his compositional thinking. These pieces unleashed the majestic accomplishment of Beethoven's last years: the huge *Missa solemnis* for soloists, chorus, and orchestra (op. 123, 1823), the Ninth Symphony (op. 125, 1824), and the wonderfully abstract late string quartets (ops. 127, 130–33, 135).

At first impression, the Ninth seems primarily a return to the tried-and-true heroic idiom of the Third and Fifth, as the work evolves from its mysterious trembling opening to the dancing delight of the last coda. But the massiveness of the Ninth Symphony suggests more yet, particularly in view of the big finale with soloists and chorus that lasts nearly as long as all the other movements combined. Gradually you become aware of its cosmic struggles, as D minor and B♭ major wrestle for control, and grasp the impact of

Listening Chart

 CD 2, TR 5

Ludwig van Beethoven (1770–1827)
Symphony No. 5 in C Minor, op. 67 (1808)
  Movement III: Allegro

For: 2 flutes, 2 oboes, 2 bassoons, 2 horns, 2 trumpets; timpani; strings. Last
  movement adds piccolo, contrabassoon, 3 trombones.

Type: Scherzo-and-
  trio
Meter: $\frac{3}{4}$
Key: C minor
Duration: 05:30

The atmosphere seems a far cry from that of the Haydn-and-Mozart minuet, and the
trio's fugue subject as stated by cellos and double basses is almost comic. But this is
where Fate seems definitively to be tamed, and thus the movement is a cornerstone of
the Romantic practice.

	Scherzo	
00:00	A	Th. in low strings: *pp,* mysterious, minor, halting.
00:20	B	Stern fanfares based on the Fate motto, as though it were reasserting control.
00:41	A'	The "repeat" (written out) has several new details, notably its
01:04	B'	different and more insistent treatment of the motto, now more controlling.
01:25	transition	Begins as a restatement of A, becoming a transition as the motto skips away.
01:53	motto	Fate, again, as closing material.
	Trio	C major. Fugal entries in strings.
01:59	C	Subj. in cellos and basses, answered by violas and bassoon;
02:14	C rep.	then subj. in vns. II, answer, vns. I.
02:30	D	The second strain, much longer, extends itself into merry imitative episodes.
02:58	D rep.	Written out and reorchestrated, flute solo dissolves into pizzicato transition to:
	Scherzo	C minor. For a few moments, much as before. But the pizzicato with bassoon
03:29	A	makes things sound nowhere near so sinister, and
03:51	B	the Fate motive has lost its grip; it seems tamed, deflated.
04:12	A'	Thoroughly quiet, now, and seeming to ebb away. Suddenly, dramatically:
04:47	transition	Timpani begin a "motto ostinato"; pedal points in bass; then a thrilling
05:24	cad. fig.	arrival on dominant pedal and a big crescendo into the finale, which begins without pause.

Beethoven's decision to make the hammering scherzo the second movement (and not
the third), so turmoil is still at issue before the taming begins. Then you admire how all
this sets up the utopian vision presented in the finale, which suggests a world of brotherhood and peace blessed by the gaze of a benevolent creator. This amazing movement
seems to summarize the whole of Viennese practice.

RECOMMENDED LISTENING:

Beethoven: Symphony No. 9 in D Minor, op. 125 (1824)

In 1824 Beethoven attempted to conduct the first performance of the Ninth from sight
and his mind's ear, but it was the concertmaster who actually controlled the players. At

www.prenhall.com/masterworks
recommended listening

Listening Chart

 **CD 2, TR 6**

Ludwig van Beethoven (1770–1827)
Symphony No. 5 in C Minor, op. 67 (1808)
   Movement IV: Allegro

Type: Sonata
Meter: ¢
Key: C major
Duration: 08:31

For: 2 flutes, 2 oboes, 2 bassoons, 2 horns, 2 trumpets; timpani; strings. Last
   movement adds piccolo, contrabassoon, 3 trombones.

A heroic, mighty march, very much in C major. The trombones finally enter, as do the
piccolo and (less audibly) the contrabassoon. Both the enlarged orchestral force and
the overall motion from the C minor of movement I to the victorious major mode here
resolve the symphonic struggle, a point made again with the reminiscence of a passage
from the third movement. Beethoven's Fifth proves to be coherent, unified discourse
where the four movements must be considered as a whole.

	Exposition	
00:00	Th. I	C major. Triadic, swashbuckling.
00:33	Br.	Another noble melody, begun in horns. The contintuation moves to:
00:59	Th. II	G major (V). Strings, with prominent triplets; these have potential to be fanfares.
01:25	Cl. th.	A strong mid-register theme for rich closure, but it abruptly veers off.
01:55	**Development**	Sudden turn of harmonic events indicates the start of development.
02:00	pt. 1	Treating Th. II. Wanders harmonically, and extends with ww. figuration.
02:23	pt. 2	Growing urgency and much trombone, Fate ever more prominent.
02:58	pt. 3	Dominant chord over a G pedal point. Recap. expected.
03:30	pt. 4 (recall)	Sensational delay of recap. by quotes of Fate from movt. III, subdued.
	Recapitulation	The delay makes the recapitulation seem especially grand.
04:09	Th. I	C major (I). As before.
04:42	Br.	Much as before, altered to stay in C major.
05:13	Th. II	As before, gathering energy with the string passagework.
05:39	Cl. th.	As before, but (from 06:01) much longer, with great flourishes of brass.
06:40	**Coda**	Long and involved. Bassoon, horn calls; prominent piccolo trills (07:07).
07:23	Stretto	Accelerates in a *stretto* to twice as fast.
07:32	Cl. th.	Now twice as fast as before.
07:47	Cad. figs.	Trumpet flourishes, gleeful exclamation points.

the end Beethoven had to be stopped from conducting and shown the applauding audience. His body, weakened by cranial infections, syphilis, and the everyday illnesses of
the era, gave out three years later in March 1827. (The autopsy report, dwelling on the
gush of black body fluids, is best reserved for the strong of stomach.) At his death
Beethoven had a Tenth Symphony in thc works, but it is difficult to deduce from the
scraps what he might have had in mind.

    It seemed nearly impossible for the next generation of composers to fathom what
might come next. Everywhere you look, over the next decades, there is the unmistakable stamp of Beethoven. When Mahler, at the beginning of his First Symphony, opens
with unison As, then a motive that falls from A to E, it is clearly in homage to the very

similar opening of Beethoven's Ninth. When Brahms, in his First Symphony, composes a hymn into the last movement, there are similarities with Beethoven's Ninth that, he noted, "any donkey can see." Minuets were essentially dead forever. Symphonies might now come in any number of movements, or with stories attached, or with texts and choruses. Cyclicism became a matter of course.

Also then there was the jinx of dying after nine symphonies. Schubert, Bruckner, and Mahler each followed suit.

SCHUBERT

The last of the Viennese composers born in the eighteenth century was Franz Schubert (1797–1828), the only one who was actually a native of Vienna. He was trained at the cathedral choir school, where after dinner he would join the school orchestra as a violinist, reading Mozart, Haydn, and early Beethoven. This led in turn to his membership in an orchestra of family and friends that sometimes read his own compositions. For a short time Schubert worked as a schoolteacher, following in his father's footsteps, but he soon abandoned the profession for full-time composition. His was a quiet, introverted personality, unconcerned with fame and fortune, and consequently ignored by the establishment. He met Beethoven only once or twice; his symphonies were performed in a serious public concert only toward the end of his life.

As a composer of art songs, or *Lieder,* however, Schubert's reputation extended far and wide. An invitation to an evening devoted to Schubert songs, a *Liederabend,* was greatly prized. Schubert would play the piano, and the famous baritone Johann Michael Vogl would often sing. Chamber music and solo piano works rounded out these amicable gatherings. The Schubertiad became a concert type all its own.

www.prenhall.com/masterworks
composer profiles
Schubert

A Liederabend, with Schubert (in spectacles) at the piano

All told, Schubert composed more than 600 songs, ranging from his very earliest compositions to his last. He set poetry of all sorts, from light ditties to works by Shakespeare and Johann Wolfgang von Goethe, the great poet and founder of the German brand of Romanticism. Schubert was exceptionally gifted in fashioning piano parts specific to the poetic text, integrating the accompaniment into a mélange of poetry and sung melody to great dramatic effect. Thus under-the-window serenades have guitar-like figuration in the piano, and the famous *Ave Maria* features arpeggiations in the manner of a harp. Using the piano as a source of symbols and images is a Romantic way of looking at things, and a far cry from Haydn and Mozart.

 SCHUBERT: *GRETCHEN AM SPINNRADE* (1814)

In Schubert's op. 1, composed when he was 17, we find "Gretchen at the Spinning Wheel." Gretchen is the girl in Goethe's *Faust,* and in this song she muses over her absent loved one as she spins. The right hand of the piano evokes the motion of the wheel in its rapid circular figurations, while the drone figures in the lower part, for the left hand, suggest the treadle. The refrain is simple: Her heart is heavy, her peace is gone, nevermore to return. Between refrains she begins to ponder, as one often does, the lover's physical attributes. It's no coincidence that the minor mode of the refrain now turns to major, nor that you get a hint of churchliness at "Sein hoher Gang" ("his noble form"). Her passion mounts, and with it the melodic contour; at the line "And, *ach,* his kiss!" the spinning stops. Then, in fits and starts, it resumes its melancholy way. Gretchen becomes lost in thought, and the last refrain halts in mid-verse.

A similar, rather grander accomplishment is the ballad *Erlkönig*, also to a Goethe text and also a very early work. Here a man on horseback gallops homeward through the forest with his son in his arms. A wicked apparition, the Elf-king, woos the child, who cries out in horror; the father says, as fathers do, that it's only the wind. As in *Gretchen*, the piano provides the setting, in this case the galloping of the horse. Meanwhile, each of the four characters (narrator, Elf-king, father, child) is placed in a different vocal register for the singer, and the key turns to major when the Elf-king tries to abduct the boy. When they get home, the boy is dead.

Listening Chart

 CD 2, TR 7

Franz Schubert (1797–1828)
***Gretchen am Spinnrade* ("Gretchen at the Spinning Wheel," 1814)**

For: voice and piano

Text: from *Faust* (1808), by Johann Wolfgang von Goethe (1748–1832)

Type: Strophic Lied
Meter: ⁶⁄₈
Key: D minor
Duration: 03:47

Central to the impact of the Schubert songs, or Lieder, is the way the piano part participates in the telling of the tale. Gretchen spins as she anticipates the arrival of her lover. This wonderful song, composed when Schubert was 17 (as his opus 1), is not only blissfully Romantic but frankly erotic.

00:00	**Refrain**	*D minor.* The piano represents the spinning wheel: pedal and treadle in the left hand, wheel in the right.
00:21	**Departure 1**	*Modulatory.* Reflecting on her lover's absence; rises in pitch as Gretchen's agony mounts; stays mostly in minor-mode key areas.
00:53	**Refrain**	*D minor.* As before.
01:12	**Departure 2**	*Modulatory.* "Waiting by the window."
01:28		When her thoughts turn to his arrival, and to his body, the key reaches a nearly religious F major.
01:53	climax	"Ach, sein Kuss!" ("ah, his kiss"): in her ecstasy, she stops spinning.
02:05		She resumes spinning
02:13	**Refrain**	*D minor.* As before.
02:33	**Departure 3**	*Modulatory.* "My breast yearns for him."
02:45		Pedal points (leading back toward D minor). "To kiss him as much as I want; to die beneath his lips."
03:12		The vocal line climaxes again on a high A.
03:25	**Refrain** (fragment)	*D minor.* The refrain fades away, as though Gretchen is lost in her reverie.

Schubert contributed substantially, too, to the maturation of the song cycle. The wonderful *Winterreise* ("A Winter's Journey," 1827) is a series of 24 songs treating the cold, cold pilgrimage of a man who has lost his lover: Everything he sees reminds him of her. The cycle *Die schöne Müllerin* ("The Beautiful Miller's Girl") consists of 20 songs to texts of Goethe.

After writing six little symphonies in the Haydn-and-Mozart style on which he was raised, Schubert could no longer avoid the need to come to grips with Beethovenian precedents and thus set about composing what he called "a big symphony." Given the severity of the task he had set for himself, and that he composed in fits and starts anyway, it's not surprising that he should have given up on some of his attempts. The "Unfinished" is the fourth of his five efforts to write his big symphony. It was not interrupted by his death; he simply abandoned it.

Schubert seems to have abandoned the B-Minor Symphony out of fear that he was not up to its technical demands, for he subsequently began counterpoint lessons. Nobody quite knows why the men to whom he left the manuscript retained it for so long in silence, for the two complete movements of the "Unfinished" symphony testify to a splendid composition in the making. You can hear a four-movement completion, for enough of the scherzo is left that it can be filled in, and a movement from Schubert's *Rosamunde* music fits nicely for a finale. But nowadays we generally content ourselves with the two finished portions.

www.prenhall.com/masterworks
recommended listening

RECOMMENDED LISTENING:

Schubert: Symphony No. 8 in B Minor ("Unfinished," 1822)

Schubert did finally finish a big symphony, the Ninth, often called the "Great C-Major." Like Beethoven's Ninth it is a monster work of metric vigor and formal imagination. Mendelssohn learned of its existence shortly after Schubert's death (at age 31 of typhoid complicated by syphilis) and conducted the first performance in Leipzig in 1839.

Schubert's symphonies made the rounds too late to have served as models for the first generation of the Romantics. The generation that formed around Liszt during his middle age, however, knew enough of Schubert's orchestral music to count it the equal of his chamber music and songs.

In virtually all of Schubert we can see, in retrospect, Romanticism taking hold. With the near simultaneous deaths of Beethoven and Schubert, Viennese Classicism came to an abrupt end. Yet the style of the early Romantics dominated musical thought for more than a hundred years, well into the twentieth century. Sonata form and the symphony orchestra and Mozart opera were the seeds from which germinated, then grew like Jack's beanstalk, the industrial-strength styles of next generations.

OMANTICISM

Spring. Sometime in February you begin to anticipate release from the dreariness of winter, for little is so certain as that Nature every year will be born anew. Spring's burst of wondrous beauty is one of life's central pleasures. Easter and other rites of fertility and rebirth coincide by design with the season of flowers. And along with the fruit trees there inevitably blossoms romance.

Like others of his generation, Robert Schumann (1810–56) celebrated springtime and the other marvels of Nature in his composition. You sense his pleasure from the beginning of the great song cycle *Dichterliebe,* the text of which comes from Heine, cited at the beginning of this chapter, yet even in the first bar you also feel twinges of melancholy and perhaps a suggestion of despair. Romantic music is like that: plumbing the emotional heights and depths, seeing a crimson sunset as both thrilling and tragic—as willing, in fact, to deal in witchcraft as with the varied ecstasies of a springtime love affair.

Mardi Gras, the Tuesday before Ash Wednesday, is typically chilly, with spring and all its promises still far away. Lent begins the next day; among its other deprivations in those days was the annual closure of theaters and concert halls in the European capitals. The high season of indoor society peaks in the Carnival week leading up to Mardi Gras. In Vienna they call this time of year Fasching, the period for fancy-dress balls and, perhaps, an invitation to waltz at the Imperial Palace. In *Carnaval,* for solo piano, Schumann invites us to one such festivity.

 SCHUMANN: FROM *CARNAVAL* (1835)

ARLEQUIN—VALSE NOBLE; CHIARINA—CHOPIN.

In a series of descriptive miniature vignettes—*scènes mignonnes,* as he calls them—Schumann portrays the guests at his imaginary ball and now and then suggests their flirtations. Some of the guests are costumed as characters of the Commedia dell'Arte, the old Italian street theater. There is Harlequin the clown, costumed in a fabric of multicolored diamond patterns; Pantaloon, in his stirrup trousers; Pierrot, in a floppy tunic of moon-white silk and big black buttons; the beautiful Columbine, and so forth. In addition, there are Schumann's friends Chopin and Paganini as well as Clara (called Chiarina) and another girlfriend Ernestine (called Estrella), to whom Schumann was briefly engaged. All are members of Schumann's imaginary Band of David, or *Davidsbund,* who take a stand against the Philistines of Music. Both Schumann alter egos are present: the pensive Eusebius and the flighty, eccentric Florestan. These are the names Schumann signed to his music criticism, depending on whether its content was prevailingly analytical or, instead, emotive in response. Modern psychoanalytical criticism enjoys connecting these alter egos with Schumann's complex and eventually suicidal psychology.

Equally vital to the nature of the composition is Schumann's choice of four pitches to serve as an organizing motive for the work: A-E♭-C-B♮. The full subtitle of *Carnaval* is *scènes mignonnes sur quatre notes* ("little scenes on four pitches"). (We call these kinds of movements descriptive miniatures, and often talk of the Romantic character piece. Romanticism is as much about fleeting moments and nostalgic reminiscence—often on the part of solitary artists, presumably at their desks, keyboards, . . . or spinning wheels—as it is about heroic, gigantic, overarching world-views.) You will remember from the end of Chapter 4 that in German music notation the pitch B♮ is called H. E♭ is called Es. Thus S-C-H represents the beginning of Schumann's name, and A-S-C-H alludes to Ernestine's hometown, Asch. From this second motive, with its easily recognized intervals, Schumann fashions the melodies of many of the 19 vignettes:

Schumann lets the movement titles shape the character of each piece. "Eusebius," where seven eighth notes are fitted into a bar of $\frac{2}{4}$, then five sixteenths to a quarter-note beat, is quietly thoughtful. "Florestan" charges about the disparate registers of the piano and darts suddenly into a motive from an earlier series of piano miniatures, *Papillons* ("Butterflies," op. 2).

Near the center of the work come two of the finest portraits, the passionate waltz suggesting Clara and the nocturne-like movement for Chopin, both of them pianist/composers. The various movements are in two parts, typically rounded: A ‖ B A, often with repeats or a *da capo.* At the beginning of *Carnaval* is a big prelude; to conclude, a "March of the Davidsbund Against the Philistines," with a silly tune in the left hand, a fossil from the seventeenth century for the Philistines. The march winds up with a flood of reminiscences of the earlier movements.

The music of the 1830s and 1840s bursts with so many advanced ideas—music as high literature, as autobiography, as chronicle of our most personal spiritual journeys, full of poetic longing and memory of lost moments of bliss—that another significant mutation of style has to be acknowledged. The Classical virtues were neither forgotten nor abandoned, but Beethoven, wellspring of it all, had shown the way to new avenues of composition, avenues so seductive that no forward-looking artist could pass them by. Romanticism in music then, is also a period of coming to grips with Beethoven.

Listening Chart

 CD 2, TR 8–11

Robert Schumann (1810–56)
Carnaval (1835)
   Arlequin—Valse noble; Chiarina—Chopin

For: piano

Type: Two-part rounded binary form
Meter: $\frac{3}{4}$, $\frac{3}{4}$, $\frac{3}{4}$, $\frac{6}{4}$
Key: B♭ major, B♭ major, C minor, A♭ major
Duration: 01:02, 02:05, 01:26, 01:06

Carnival season, the time of merrymaking that culminates in Mardi Gras. The 21 miniatures describe the guests at a masked ball. The "dancing letters" A-S-C-H are those of Schumann's name and Asch, hometown of an enamorata. As the pitches A, E♭, C, B♮, they constitute the organizing motto of these "little scenes on four notes."

00:00	**A**	*Arlequin.* Harlequin is a comic clown figure. The primary motive embraces the motto: A-S-C-H. Bumptious, with bursts of *ff*.
00:12	**B**	Focuses on the outbursts (4 bars × 2), then a lyric interlude (4 bars).
00:25	**A'**	Just as before.
00:37	**BA'** rep.	The entire section repeated.

00:00	**A**	*Valse noble.* A lyric, passionate waltz, with octaves in the r. h., standard waltz accompaniment in the l. h. Opens with the motto. 4 bars × 2.
00:12	**A** rep.	Ms. Licad repeats the first strain, not so marked in the score.
00:24	**B**	Interlude: 4 bars × 4
00:48	**A'**	Return is *p* for 8 bars, *ff* in octaves for the last 8 bars.
01:14	**BA'** rep.	The entire section repeated.

00:00	**A**	*Chiarina.* Portrait of Clara, or, better, Robert's longing for her. Melancholy waltz in minor: 8 bars × 2, *p*, then *ff*.
00:22	**B**	Interlude: 8 bars
00:32	**A'**	Return: 8 bars × 2, *p*, then *ff*.
00:52	**BA'** rep.	The entire section is repeated.

| 00:00 | **A** | *Chopin.* Portrait of a celebrated Davidsbünder. Compound triple meter, arpeggiated left hand. Note the particularly characteristic Chopin arabesques. |
| 00:30 | **A** rep. | |

Clara and Robert Schumann

UROPE AFTER NAPOLEON

The Romantics in France described themselves as frail children born of loins exhausted by the French Revolution; in Germany, they were stepchildren of Goethe, whose Faust sold his soul to the devil, Mephistopheles, for a transitory return of his youth. When they were not consorting with witches and devils, or experimenting with chemical substance, or longing on some volcano for a lost loved one, the Romantics were being heroic. Everybody wanted to be the Napoleon of his or her particular walk of life. The virtuoso performers were particularly capable practitioners of Romantic heroism. The violinist Paganini, the pianist Liszt, and a host of operatic sopranos and tenors conquered the world, finding in their art the means to live better and more lavishly than even ministers and bankers. Paganini, of gaunt, bent frame and jet black hair, cultivated his diabolic image and jealously guarded the technical secrets of what was widely regarded as violinistic magic. A degree of charlatanism cannot be denied here, but then, as now, the dividing line between art and entertainment, or between selling music and selling snake oil, was very faint.

They got around, using all the modern conveniences of travel: to Russia and Turkey, to distant parts of the United States and South America, and now and then to the South Seas. Nor did they hide from the public's adulation and scrutiny; while not quite flaunting their sex lives, they were certainly unashamed of their unusual relationships. Berlioz's mistress traveled with him as Madame Berlioz years before his first wife died. Liszt and a married countess bore illegitimate, highly publicized children, of whom the youngest, Cosima, went on to leave her husband, the great pianist-conductor Hans von Bülow, to become Wagner's mistress. (To be fair, she eventually became the very doting Frau Wagner.) It's not that these things hadn't happened before, of course, but that it was all reported in the papers.

They were highly educated, often at the university, and less beholden than their predecessors to employment in the chapels of kings and princes. They made their living by hard work in more or less open markets. And while a few of them went mad and/or tried to do themselves in, the fact is that most of the great Romantic composers died quietly of old age in their own beds, or else died too young of diseases (like syphilis, which deafens you before it kills you) that we can now cure with a round of antibiotics.

Their models were Beethoven, each other, and the work of their counterparts in the sister arts. Increasingly they regarded the German composer Carl Maria von Weber (1786–1826) as a spiritual godfather. The multitalented Weber—composer, pianist, critic, and conductor—got around as well, and had been able to oversee good productions of his operas in the European capitals before his untimely death. By mid-century his work had grown as popular in many quarters as Beethoven's. Weber's masterpiece *Der Freischütz* ("The Free Shot") is the cornerstone of Romantic subject matter and compositional practice.

Der Freischütz is the story of a handsome lad but rather poor marksman who strikes a Faustian bargain with the Black Huntsman: Six bullets will go where he wants them to, allowing him to win the shooting contest and thus his bride, but the seventh will go where the Black Huntsman directs—the new bride, of course. The setting is a forest in the depths of which lies the Wolf's Glen. There transpires the great scene of the bullet casting, with spirits that say "Uhui," the charge of a wild boar, passage of a fiery stagecoach, and last of all the appearance of the Black Huntsman, Samiel, in a frenzied, driving storm. This scene seized the imagination of the Romantics, who were forever trying to recreate its heart-stopping effects.

One musical detail of this work, in particular, was widely imitated. Samiel's presence is suggested by a mysterious plunking of timpani and double basses and a menacing chord:

So used, this chord of the *diminished seventh* (F♯-A-C-E♭) is both perplexing and spooky. Both its harmonic implication and its association with a particular character represent a point of departure for the magical, ghostly aspect of Romanticism.

The general story of Europe in the nineteenth century is one of coping with the leftovers of the Napoleonic conquests. On the one hand, citizens asserted their right to civil liberties and freedoms with growing stridency; on the other, the political need for military security, especially in the weaker principalities and kingdoms Napoleon had already once overrun, led to well-intentioned alliances that ended up provoking a new round of aggressive imperialism. As the century progressed, the great European empires—British, French, Austrian, and Russian—managed between them to lay claim to virtually all of Europe as well as a good part of Asia and Africa, including the fallen empire of the Ottoman Turks. In both Germany and Italy, meanwhile, the concept of forming a true nation based on a common language was gaining momentum. Both had been loose conglomerations of city-states and feudal holdings, functioning for the most part without the advantages of federation. In Germany the general tendency was for the little governments to give way to the hegemony of Prussia, the nation around Berlin controlled by the Hohenzollern family. As Prussian power grew, the dialectic was increasingly a power struggle between Berlin (Germany) and the old Hapsburg empire in Vienna (Austro-Hungary).

In Italy, movement toward national unification was complicated by Rome's being the seat of the Catholic church and one of Europe's great private landowners; north Italy belonged at the time to Austria, as part of the post-Waterloo settlement. Meanwhile, in the subjugated cultures like Bohemia, Poland, and Hungary, there was emerging fierce nationalistic pride and the beginnings of various independence movements, again based on a common language. A tiny populace like the Finns, for example, bounced back and forth, from the French to the Danes to the Swedes to the Russians. It was these last who came to regard Sibelius's tone poem *Finlandia* as seditious.

There was little stability in the nineteenth century, and what there was, within the established empires, however enlightened, could not last. Already in 1830 there were new anti-royal stirrings, when a brief but significant revolution removed the restored Bourbon monarchy in France and replaced it with a slightly more republican form of government under Louis-Philippe (a cousin of the Bourbons, from the Orléans line). Further revolutions swept the continent in 1848, without clear result. The pushing and shoving went on and on, but the political earthquake did not come until the second decade of the twentieth century, when World War I and the Russian Revolution caused all the boundaries of Europe to be redrawn and most of the titles lost.

These currents of nationalism affected music as well; art and politics mingled as never before. Verdi, Smetana, and Sibelius all became national symbols, and in some quarters their music was branded as insurrectionist. Russian intellectuals by mid-century saw more clearly than most the political value of a well-organized national musical establishment (see Chapter 7). Musicians adapted to the changing surroundings however they could, and the more progressive ones took advantage of modern transportation, industry, and communication to take the world under their wing. One would not, as Bach had done, sit out the better part of one's life composing music to the glory of God and for the local boys' school, satisfied at one's lot.

The first generation of Romantic masters—Schumann, Mendelssohn, Liszt, Berlioz, and Chopin—knew and for the most part liked each other. Their paths crossed often, in Paris and London, in Berlin, Leipzig, and Weimar. Later, their successors gathered at Wagner's majestic opera house in Bayreuth. It was in Paris in the late 1820s and early 1830s, however, that they began to identify each other as kindred souls. In February 1826, Berlioz spent the better part of two days pursuing Carl Maria von Weber around Paris, where the master was stranded while a blacksmith repaired his carriage wheel. The chase was in vain, but the incident shows just how seriously the young Berlioz already took Weber's work.

PARIS: BERLIOZ, LISZT, CHOPIN

Hector Berlioz (1803–69), the son of a provincial physician, had come to Paris in 1821 to study medicine. Discovering at the city morgue that he lacked the necessary stomach for the profession, he gradually turned to composition. His scientific study, however, left him with a lifelong interest in mechanics and physics that stimulated the writings that made him the Romantic era's leading expert on the modern symphony orchestra.

Although Berlioz had the good fortune to attract the attention of a gifted teacher at the Paris Conservatoire, the repertoire that surrounded him was scarcely rich with promise. He learned little Haydn and Mozart, neither Bach nor Handel. Instead he pieced together his notions of musical beauty from the operas of Christoph Willibald von Gluck and the progressive Gaspare Spontini and from a Frenchified and bastardized version of *Der Freischütz.* These he heard at the opera house and retained in his mind's ear; at the Conservatoire library he pored over Beethoven scores, trying to imagine how they must sound.

What Paris lacked in knowledge of the Viennese School—during its flourishment the French had, after all, been caught up in political and social revolutions of their own—it made up for in other kinds of intellectual ferment. This was the Paris of the writers Hugo and Balzac and Stendhal, of the painters Delacroix and Géricault, a city enraptured by the arrival at the Louvre of the treasures of antiquity and by the translation (by the 34-year-old Champollion, 1824) of the Rosetta Stone. Berlioz was a young man of insatiable curiosity and prodigious memory, quick to absorb the latest literary rages, such as Goethe's *Faust* in its new French translation. He was also prone to excessive petulance, nosebleeds, temper tantrums, uncontrollable stammering, and the occasional fainting spell.

By 1827, when an English theater troupe arrived to perform Shakespeare in Paris, Berlioz's emotional and intellectual life had reached fever pitch and maximum impressionability. He was already memorizing his Shakespeare line by line; when a lovely young Irish actress named Harriet Smithson appeared as Ophelia in *Hamlet,* then Juliet,

Hector and Harriet

then Desdemona in *Othello,* he succumbed to her spell altogether. The next Paris season saw the beginnings of the Société des Concerts du Conservatoire, the Paris Conservatory Orchestra, and its systematic study of the Beethoven symphonies. Berlioz was there for every concert, as he had been for every play. Shakespeare and Beethoven—and Paris— were his finishing school.

Berlioz's courtship of Harriet began poorly ("Beware," she said, "the man whose eyes bode no good.") So it was in an agonized and agonizing frame of mind, barraged by *Faust* and Beethoven's "Eroica," that he embarked at the age of 26 on his first symphony. Here he would paint what he called his "infernal passion." He called this symphony of desire and hallucination an "Episode in an Artist's Life" and subtitled it "Fantastic Symphony in 5 Parts." This is the celebrated *Symphonie fantastique,* without a doubt the most provocative first symphony ever composed.

 BERLIOZ: FROM *SYMPHONIE FANTASTIQUE* (1830)

V. DREAM OF A WITCHES' SABBATH. All kinds of novelties made this work the rallying point for the new Romantic movement. For one thing it is *programmatic;* that is, it evokes a narrative story printed in the program distributed to the public at concert time. In movement I, the artist is overcome by reveries and passions induced by his unrequited love. In movement II, a waltz, he sees his beloved at a ball; in movement III, she comes to mind during a scene in the country. Movement IV turns abruptly to the grotesque, as he dreams in an opium hallucination of being guillotined for murdering the object of his passion. This leads directly into the bizarre finale, where he finds himself at a witches' Sabbath. The music theme identified with the Beloved is trivialized into a common dance. A roar of approval greets her arrival, and she joins in the devilish orgy.

In his Pastoral Symphony (No. 6) Beethoven had already given titles to movements and countrified the symphonic ideal; in the Fifth Symphony, he had unified his work musically with multiple references to the Fate motive. Berlioz's tactic was to present an entire narrative in his symphony and to unify his story with a recurring musical motive drawn from the main theme of the first movement. This *idée fixe,* as he calls it, is the musical symbol of the Beloved, which haunts the music as thoughts of Harriet haunted its composer.

Allegro agitato e appassionato assai ($\downarrow$=132)

This *idée fixe* is an unusual melody, typical of Berlioz's freewheeling notions of form and shape. Like the artist's love life it delays resolution as long as possible, bubbling over and back, and extending ever outward from its center until coming reluctantly back to rest. Some reference to it appears in each movement: mingled with the waltz music in movement II, as an interlude in movement III, a last thought in movement IV just before the fatal chop of the guillotine, then tarted up and made ridiculous in movement V.

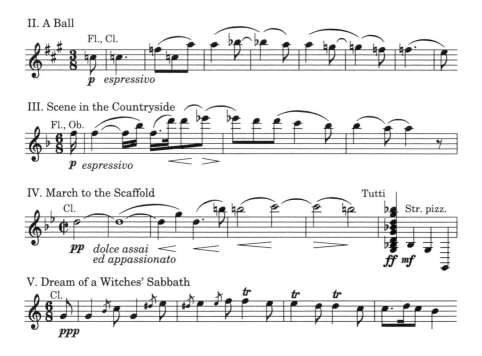

In planning the movement structures, Berlioz is similarly free from Classical constraints. In the first movement, for example, we see the rudiments of a kind of sonata form, and the point of recapitulation is clear. But the sections are carved out more to emphasize the atmospheric and psychological content than to achieve an overt elegance of structure. At the end of the March to the Scaffold there is overt pictorialism: a last view of the Beloved, the guillotine's drop, and the hurrahs of the crowd over the drum roll. And the three delightful pizzicato notes just after the guillotine clearly represent the head falling into a basket. (Old-fashioned writers complain terribly about how you're not supposed to need the program to enjoy the music, but if you don't know the story you miss this superb detail, clearly written into the music precisely for your enjoyment.)

Already in his first major work, Berlioz shows the inventiveness in orchestration that brought him his first fame. In the *Fantastique* he uses a number of instruments not heard in orchestral music before: a pair of harps in the waltz scene, English horn in the scene in the country, church bells and the piccolo (tiny) clarinet, nowadays usually called the E♭ clarinet, in the finale. Just as significantly, Berlioz is quick to use the traditional orchestral force in novel ways. The ecstatic last statement of the *idée fixe* at the end of the first movement has the strings divided into nine parts (two divisions of each section but the double basses), where usually they are divided into four. The rattling, purposefully skeletal sound you hear for a moment in the finale is produced by an effect called *col legno* ("with the wood"), where the strings players bounce the wood of their bows against the strings. In both the third and fourth movements there is progressive use of multiple timpanists playing chords: thunder in the scene in the country, drum tattoos in the march to the scaffold. The lowest brass part in the *Fantastique,* incidentally, is for a now obsolete instrument called the ophicléide (pronounced "*oph*-ih-clyde"). Typically this part is played today on a tuba, but you might occasionally see this weird and not especially satisfactory stepchild of the Baroque serpent in a historic reconstruction of the symphony.

Ophicléide

The *Fantastique* reaches its maximum power in the finale, the dramatic and structural high point of the work. (Symphonic music has, since Beethoven, been shifting its weight toward the finale.) As in the first movement, there is a very long, scene-setting introduction, here built like the Samiel motive in *Der Freischütz* around the four-note sonorities called diminished seventh chords. This particular sonority doesn't point in a single direction so much as in multiple directions; the effect is one of mysterious twinkling over the rumbles in the bass. To this atmosphere are added distant spookish calls of grotesque masculine laughter and shrill feminine giggles (upper woodwinds, with breathy glissando at the end) and their echoes. The change of meter and bouncing timpani introduce the *idée fixe,* transformed in the E♭ clarinet to a mocking dance: "It is *she* who has come." You can't miss the roar of approval, and then the "mockery of the Beloved" is repeated at full force.

Now the diabolic revelry gets underway in earnest. The sonata allegro proper begins with church bells on C and G, set irregularly into the phrase structure so they seem like they have somehow gone amok. The theme is the *Dies irae,* the Catholic chant for the dead, presented in whole notes and answered in two different diminutions, the last of which has the rhythms of the "mockery" section.

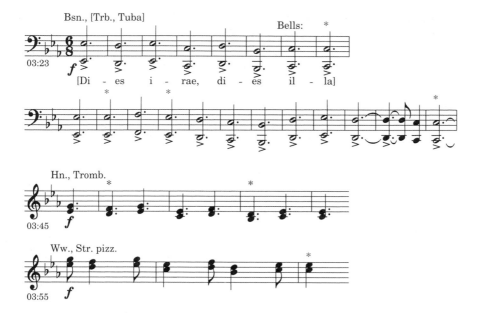

The Witches' Round Dance gains momentum and becomes the second theme. This is presented as a fugue, with proper subjects and answers, each cut off and dismissed by eruptions in the brass.

Berlioz was a master at writing fugues, having perfected his technique at the Paris Conservatoire with a noted contrapuntist, the Czech composer Anton Reicha. But where stuffier composers used fugue to demonstrate their mastery of inherited tradition and to suggest its superiority, Berlioz uses fugue to mimic churchliness and scholasticism. Here it conveys the revelry of the witches, while in *The Damnation of Faust* a chorus of drunken men sing a merry "Amen" fugue in a wine cellar.

The round dance collapses, spent, at the midpoint of the development. Then, regaining its momentum, it crescendos to the point of recapitulation. In a brilliant stroke Berlioz recapitulates the two themes, *Dies irae* and Witches' Round Dance, not consecutively, but simultaneously in what he calls a *grande réunion des thèmes:*

From there the orgy is just barely controlled. We hear the bone-rattling *col legno* passage, big explosions in the brass and nose-thumbing responses from the woodwinds, and a rollicking charge to the end, with darting piccolos and winds triumphant in the closing bar. You cannot help but heave a sigh of relief when it finally comes to an end.

RECOMMENDED LISTENING:

Berlioz: Symphonie fantastique, *movts. I–IV (1830)*

Harriet recognized her portrait and at length she and Berlioz were married, but their happiness was short-lived. Berlioz went on to a career in which he supported his composition primarily by writing music criticism for several fine papers. Parts of his life were topsy-turvy, especially monetarily, though on the whole it was probably no more tumultuous than that of Schumann (who went mad), Chopin (who declined precipitously from tuberculosis), or Liszt (who had woman problems and resolved them, once his libido had settled down, by becoming a priest). Distrustful that other conductors could ever understand his work, Berlioz drove himself to become one of the great conductors of his time, traveling all over Europe to present his own music and what he deemed the best of the rest of the repertoire, including Beethoven's Ninth. This allowed him to visit Mendelssohn, Schumann, Brahms, the great opera composer Meyerbeer, Wagner (who was conducting a rival orchestra in London), and countless other influential artists. Of his very close friendship with Liszt and his mistress you will read later. In one of his last journeys, to Russia in 1867, he had a marked effect on the emerging school of Russian nationalists, greatly influencing Rimsky-Korsakov. And if his music was admired more abroad than at home, this was a transitory phenomenon, as it has been for many other composers.

Listening Chart

 **CD 2, TR 12**

Hector Berlioz (1803–69)
Symphonie fantastique (1830)
   Movement V: Dream of a Witches' Sabbath

Type: Sonata
Meter: C; ⁶⁄₈
Key: C major
Duration: 09:47

For: piccolo, 2 flutes, 2 oboes, English horn, E♭ clarinet, 2 clarinets, 4 bassoons; 4 horns, 2 trumpets, 2 piston cornets, 3 trombones, 2 ophicléides; 4 timpani, snare drum, bass drum, cymbals, bells; 2 harps; strings

Narrative program by the composer

The composer writes: "He sees himself at the witches' sabbath, in the midst of a ghastly crowd of spirits, sorceresses, and monsters of every kind, assembled for his funeral. Strange noises, groans, bursts of laughter, far-off shouts to which other shouts seem to reply. The beloved tune appears once more, but it has lost its character of refinement and diffidence; it has become nothing but a common dance tune, trivial and grotesque; it is *she* who has come to the sabbath . . . A roar of joy greets her arrival . . . She mingles with the devilish orgy . . . Funeral knell, ludicrous parody of the *Dies irae,* sabbath dance. The sabbath dance and the *Dies irae* in combination."

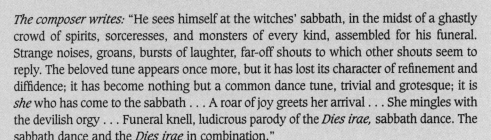

00:00	**Introduction**	Surreal rises in low strings; twinkles in high.
00:23	giggles	Fanfare effects: grotesque masculine laughter; shrill feminine giggles; echoes in horn.
00:46	repeated	Introduction repeated at higher pitch level.
01:21	mockery	Mockery of the beloved: the *idée fixe* in ⁶⁄₈ (clarinet) with grace notes and trills.
01:28	roar	A roar greets her appearance.
01:39	*idée fixe*	Full statement of the "mockery" *idée fixe,* now in E♭ (high) clarinet; bassoons gurgle pleasantly.
02:28	transition	Foreshadowings of the witches' round dance that will follow.
02:56	**Exposition**	Church bells (on C and G) introduce:
03:23	Th. I	3 phrases of the *Dies irae* (plainchant for the dead), each stated 3 times in shorter note values, the last in rhythms of the "Mockery"; bells continue.
04:59	Br.	Foreshadowing of the witches' round dance, with trumpet flourishes.
05:16	Th. II	The witches' round dance, treated as a 4-voice fugue with brass interjections, syncopated. Veers into an episode (05:44), then stretto restatements (06:04).
	Development	
06:19	pt. 1	Brass calls; woodwind cascades.
06:44	pt. 2	Fragments of the round dance in the bass; French horn squawks from afar.
07:00	pt. 3	Fragments of the *Dies irae* in the bass.
07:15	pt. 4	The drive to recapitulation is now clear; note the percussion roll.
07:44	climax	A harsh climax, bold in both metric and harmonic tension.
07:54	**Recapitulation**	The tonic (C major) returns, the round dance resumes.
08:01	*réunion*	The *Dies irae* over the round dance, a *grande réunion des thèmes.*
08:29	*col legno*	The bone-rattling effect: "with the wood" of the bow.
09:06	Coda	Flamboyant close with bass drum rolls and shrill piccolo.

In a series of giant pieces, Berlioz continued to work at the outer edge of musical thought for most of his career. In his viola concerto for Paganini, titled *Harold in Italy,* he calls for the soloist to stand apart from the orchestra, witnessing the scenes with Romantic aloofness. His Requiem Mass for a state military funeral requires a chorus of hundreds and, among the orchestral players, four brass choirs placed about the perimeter of the performing force and a battery of 16 timpani and (twice) a crash of 10 pairs of cymbals. His symphonies are capped by *Roméo et Juliette* (1839), which climaxes, in the style of Beethoven's Ninth, with a big choral finale, sung by not one chorus but three: Montagues, Capulets, and narrators, along with a bass soloist in the role of Friar Lawrence. The triumph of Berlioz's middle period was his setting of Goethe's *Faust,* which he called *La Damnation de Faust.* This work was also composed for an enormous performing force and with a very free view of genre that mingles both operatic and symphonic elements. In the masterpiece of his last years, the five-act opera *Les Troyens,* Berlioz set his favorite parts of Virgil's *Aeneid,* a Latin epic on the fall of Troy and its aftermath, complete with the Dido and Aeneas story. The libretto was his own work.

Satirical view of Berlioz conducting: "Concert of gunfire"

FRANZ LISZT (1811–86). Just after the first performance of the *Symphonie fantastique,* in December 1830, a striking young man with shoulder-length hair sailed backstage and dragged Berlioz away to make friends. This was the 19-year-old Hungarian pianist Franz Liszt, already well along the trajectory that would make him, in a few short years, the most dazzling of all the heroic virtuosos. (His closest rival was the Mephistophelian violinist Niccolò Paganini. But Paganini soon fell ill with throat cancer and disappeared, while Liszt lasted most of the rest of the century.) The direct result of this meeting was that Liszt arranged and published the *Fantastique* for piano solo, and Schumann's newspaper review of the Liszt arrangement first brought Berlioz to international attention. The friendship between Liszt and Berlioz lasted right through to Berlioz's death, although toward the end it was somewhat compromised by Liszt's enthusiasm and Berlioz's ambivalence toward Wagner.

Liszt was the arch-virtuoso. He had fabulous digital dexterity and good compositional sense, but at the same time he was a great showman whose majestic carriage and undeniable sexuality captivated the imagination of the era. He had come from Austro-Hungary to Paris hoping to establish his career. Peppering the classical repertoire with his own fantasias on popular opera tunes of the time proved to be an important box-office draw, and not just the wizardry of his technique, but the passion he unleashed gave his solo piano recitals a major place in nineteenth-century concert life. As piano

Paganini

The young Liszt

The abbé Liszt, with his
pupil Alexander Siloti

techniques were refined and the grand piano became ever more powerful, Liszt became
a kind of vagabond minstrel king of the Romantic movement, wandering the world to
play for ever wider audiences.

Of Liszt's countless amorous dalliances, the most lasting at the beginning was with
Marie, the Countess d'Agoult, who bore Liszt their three children. Their departure from
Paris to Switzerland so Marie could give birth outside the glare of publicity began his
years of vagabondage—or, as he put it, pilgrimage. During one of his tours, in Kiev in
1847, he met the woman with whom he would spend the next important chapters of his
life: Carolyne, the Princess Sayn-Wittgenstein. They arranged to relocate to Weimar, the
capital of Saxon Germany, he to serve as Kapellmeister at the grand ducal court, she to
join distant relatives.

The young Liszt had proclaimed "I am a Hungarian" to the audience at his very first
public concert. For Liszt, as for many very famous people, the growth of international
celebrity was accompanied by a growingly acute sense of his own ethnic roots. He frequently called on Hungarian idioms in his compositions, and in the later chapters of his
long life he was pleased to return humbly to Budapest for extended periods of residence.
In some respects he was the first of the nationalists, whose work dominates the pages of
our next chapter, even though Hungarians closer to home would soon complain that the
world knew its Hungarian music only from the work of the expatriate Liszt and the Hungarian Dances of Brahms, a foreigner.

In his 19 Hungarian Rhapsodies for solo piano, Liszt drew on a vast store of gypsy
and Magyar folk tunes and dances that either lingered in his memory or lay at hand.

These he would knit freely together in a manner not so different from the opera fantasies but always emphasizing folk-like improvisational practices and the strongly felt rhythmic pulses inherent in folk dance. Liszt's dazzling technical prowess, not to mention his ear for a good tune, is apparent at every turn in these pieces. He seems to have all 88 keys of the piano under his fingers at once as he pounds out chords of six and eight pitches for pages at a time, moves through the passagework with thrilling speed, and returns again and again to his particular specialties, the multi-octave rocket and repeated-note ricochet:

Liszt: Hungarian Rhapsody No. 2

He cultivated, too, cadential arabesques meant to sparkle like water dancing in a fountain.

You can imagine that audiences first hearing this sort of thing, and not seeing the music, might well have imagined themselves in the presence of some devilish force. (Paganini never showed anybody the solo part of his showpieces and wouldn't even distribute the orchestra parts until the dress rehearsal.) That these effects could be accomplished at all, let alone written down, opened up tremendous possibilities to progressive composers and set the technical standard to which all later pianists had to aspire. That is why everybody thinks of Liszt as the father of modern piano technique.

RECOMMENDED LISTENING:

Liszt: Hungarian Rhapsody No. 2 in C♯ Minor (1847)

However difficult they were, however enlightened, Liszt's pre-Weimar piano fire-works might as well be seen as so much pop music. (Hungarian Rhapsody No. 2 was composed just after Liszt's arrival in Weimar, but it was not published until 1851.) Liszt himself came to see his early works in precisely this light. In Weimar, anxious to establish for the world a venue for what he called the "artwork of the future," he settled consciously and quite conscientiously into becoming a composer of more serious music. His models were the Schubert piano works, Schumann, the Berlioz orchestral repertoire, and early Wagner. Thus emerged his great Piano Sonata in B Minor (1853), which collapses its multiple movements into one big, cyclic affair. The notions of thematic transformation and metamorphosis he developed in Weimar represented one of the major steps forward in compositional thinking of the time. Taking Berlioz as his precedent, he wrote big symphonic poems and multimovement symphonies to programmatic end, notably the one-movement *Les Préludes* (1848) and the *Faust Symphony* of 1857, with movements titled Faust, Gretchen, and Mephistopheles.

Thematic transformation is at issue, too, in Liszt's Piano Concerto in E♭ (1849), the first performance of which was conducted by Berlioz during one of his frequent visits to Weimar. (Berlioz's Weimar sojourns came at a critical time in his artistic development, and his great opera *Les Troyens* was born in part from the repeated proddings of Liszt and the princess.) From Weimar Liszt reigned over a movement called Futurism. Around him gathered disciples committed to composing progressive music. They produced significant and often controversial new works (Wagner's *Lohengrin,* Berlioz's *Benvenuto Cellini,* Peter Cornelius's *Barber of Baghdad*), and proselytized through mounds of written journalism. Wagner, rightly, came to dominate their attention.

Liszt's romance with Carolyne Sayn-Wittgenstein ended on a note of great excitement. Her husband, from whom she had never been able to secure a legitimate divorce, finally died, and in 1861 she and Liszt met in Rome to be married by the pope. At the eleventh hour, the long-awaited marriage ceremony was canceled, apparently owing to the intervention of her jealous relatives at the Vatican. Thereafter the princess lived in virtual seclusion in Rome, where she wrote vitriolic tracts about the weaknesses of Catholicism. Liszt, for his part, took minor orders in the clergy and went on to lead what he called his "tripartite life," commuting between Rome, Weimar, and Budapest, where the new Conservatory had apartments for him in the building.

It was during the post-Weimar period that Liszt accomplished his most progressive musical thinking. In late piano works like *Nuages gris* ("Gray Clouds," 1881) and *La lugubre gondola* ("The Lugubrious Gondola," 1882) he seems to plumb the outer limits of tonality, and the ramifications of this work were noted particularly by Debussy at the end of the century. Naturally there were Catholic works, too, including oratorios and a mass. Meanwhile Liszt retained his hegemony as emperor of Romanticism (Clara Schumann, probably, was its empress). The antithesis of the self-aggrandizing Wagner, he welcomed by word and deed all who came his way. He was consulted by everybody and exerted strong influence on such diverse members of the younger generations as the

French composer Camille Saint-Saëns, the Norwegian Edvard Grieg, and an American or two. Uneasy at first about having become Wagner's father-in-law, he eventually developed a certain rapport with the establishment at Bayreuth. It was there, visiting Cosima, that he died, three years after Wagner. He is buried in a Bayreuth cemetery.

www.prenhall.com/masterworks
composer profiles
Chopin

FRYDERYK CHOPIN (1810–49). Another Paris expatriate was the Polish pianist Fryderyk (or Frédéric) Chopin. He had risen to prominence at the Warsaw Conservatory and subsequently enjoyed a brilliant debut, and his first publications, in Vienna. Like Berlioz, his experience of the Viennese School was minimal. Unlike the others, however, he was uncomfortable as a lion of the concert hall. His was a more intimate Romanticism, expressing the delicate side of the Romantic equation. Virtually all of Chopin's work is for piano alone.

Chopin (an early daguerreotype)

Alone in his studio Chopin discovered a new rhetoric for the piano, where the pianist was not so much its master as its poet. His music breathes with new freedoms in its improvisatory arabesques, use of tonality that features passive harmonic relationships over urgent ones, and fresh piano sonorities. His very free attitude toward the passage of time in music—rhythm and meter—led to the notion of *tempo rubato* ("robbed time"), where length can be borrowed from one beat and given to another and where events in the right hand need not overlap precisely those in the left. You sense this primarily as a stretching of dominant harmony that prolongs the unrest. In one sense, rubato merely recognizes a performer's tendency to emphasize delicious moments by dwelling on them, especially in Romantic music. This sort of rubato is common in nearly all orchestral and operatic performance.

Chopin was a pioneer in the composition of smallish works, often dance-based forms. Many last less than five minutes, few more than ten. These include waltzes, Polish dances called the *polonaise* and *mazurka, impromptus* ("improvisations"), and the slightly longer and richer nocturnes and ballades. Additionally, there is a set of Preludes in every key, although whereas Bach's preludes and fugues in the *Well-Tempered Clavier* proceed by chromatic scale (C major and minor, C♯, D, and so on), Chopin's are ordered by major and their relative minor keys in a circle of fifths (C major, A minor, G major, E minor, D major, and so on).

CHOPIN: MAZURKA IN A MINOR, OP. 17, NO. 4 (1834)

The mazurka, perhaps Chopin's favorite genre and certainly his most personal, is a Polish dance in triple meter, usually featuring a dotted eighth and sixteenth on the downbeat (as in this selection). Otherwise the definition of a Chopin mazurka is very vague. Some are stately in tempo, others very fast; some quite complex, others naively simple. He thought of the mazurka style as beginning with Polish rhythms and motives, and then allowed his fancy to carry him wherever it would. Altogether Chopin composed some 56 mazurkas, usually in groups of three or four to be dedicated to a particular patron or admirer.

The form in this case is a simple A-B-A, the key progress A minor–A major–A minor.

A (Dance; A minor)

00:07

B (Trio; A major)

01:50

This apparent simplicity of form allows other elements of the structure their full measure of play. For one thing, the sonorities themselves are quite imaginative. The A-minor tonality, for example, seems unusually questioning by virtue of its consistent avoidance of the true tonic triad, A-C-E, in favor of a substitute, A-C-F (the triad of F major, F-A-C, respelled in its first inversion so the F is on top). This is perhaps most obvious in the first four bars, repeated as the last four. One is left, quite romantically, with issues unresolved.

03:50   *sotto voce*

In the A part the right hand has a single line, the melody, but this is rich with invention as the tune plays out in all manner of willowy ornamentation, accentuated by rubato performance. The B part, as in the trio of a dance form, has a quite different character owing to its shift to major mode and thicker chords; additionally, the prevailing direction reverses as the theme falls and rises instead of rises and falls. There are two different sorts of ostinatos here: the quarter-note drones in the bass (a fifth, A–E) and the eight-bar phrase itself, cycling through four times with varied closes at the end of each repetition.

Listening Chart

 **CD 3, TR 1**

Fryderyk Chopin (1810–49)
Mazurka in A Minor, op. 17, no. 4 (1834)

For: piano

Type: Dance-and-trio
Meter: $\frac{3}{4}$
Key: A minor
Duration: 04:08

The mazurka, Chopin's most personal genre, is a Polish dance in triple meter. For Chopin the mazurka takes wing from Polish rhythms and motives, then is carried by the composer's fancy in whatever direction seems fitting. The form here is a simple A-B-A, the key progress A minor–A major–A minor.

00:00	**Intr.**	A 4-bar introduction, mysterious in that it focuses on the pitch F, not a member of the tonic triad.
	Dance	
00:07	a	A single-line melody in the r. h. over 3-note chords in the left: two 8-bar phrases.
00:37	a'	Reornamented; the ornamental arabesques (00:51*ff.*) seem like lacework.
01:07	b	An 8-bar interlude, focusing on V.
01:21	a''	Reornamented, more or less as before.
	Trio	A major (the parallel, not the relative, major of A minor), a kind of trio.
01:50	c	Drone fifths (A–E) in the left hand, falling melody in the right; both these contrast with
02:03	c'	the atmosphere of the A part. The first 4 bars of the 8-bar phrase are identical on all
02:15	c	four passes; the second 4 bars vary in c' and c'' for harmonic reasons.
02:27	c''	Crescendo to climax.
	Dance	A minor. Back to the quiet, dreamy reverie of the first part. The ornamentation
02:41	a'''	continues to change.
03:12	**Coda**	Two 8-bar phrases over a tonic pedal in the l. h.; reminiscences of a, dying away.
03:50	close	The introductory motive—and all its mysteries.

Quiet, dreamy revery is just as representative of Romantic thinking as an orgy of witches. Romanticism is a time when the miniature and colossal cohabit.

Chopin was a darling of the upper class, members of which paid him lavishly for giving them lessons. They would court him assiduously to appear at their teatimes and *soirées musicales*. The famous novelist who called herself George Sand took him as a lover—she smoked the cigars; he played the piano. This arrangement lasted well enough, but in the end, after a tempestuous vacation in Majorca, she tired of and dismissed him. There followed Chopin's precipitous decline, during which his tuberculosis worsened and he was forced to flee to England to escape the 1848 revolution in France. Overtaxed by the demands of life there, he returned to Paris a dying man, and lived only a few weeks longer.

"Hats off, gentlemen," said Schumann of Chopin: "A genius!"

EIPZIG: SCHUMANN AND MENDELSSOHN

Another boundary that separates Classicism from Romanticism in the German-speaking countries is geographical. After Beethoven and Schubert the focus shifts from Vienna to a belt of important cities in north-central Germany: Leipzig, Dresden, and Weimar. (Leipzig and Dresden were the first German cities to be connected by a railroad, of which the musicians made good use.) By the 1840s this area had eclipsed Paris and London too as the epicenter of progressive art. It was in Leipzig that Schumann and Mendelssohn cultivated the Romantic repertoire, Dresden where the Wagner operas began in earnest, and Weimar where Liszt courted the Futurists.

Until its devastation in the Allied bombings of World War II and subsequent neglect during the East German period, Leipzig was one of the major intellectual corners of Europe. Bach spent much of his career here, and Leipzig had enjoyed a fine university and associated musical life since the Middle Ages. Leipzig was also a center of book publishing and its offshoot, music publishing. The firm of Breitkopf und Härtel came to prominence in the nineteenth century as publisher of the most beautiful editions of the Viennese and German composers, having perfected a process of copperplate engraving using elegant music fonts and a style of page layout that remains unparalleled today. In 1850 Breitkopf und Härtel began to publish the complete edition of J. S. Bach, followed by similar *Gesamtausgaben* (as complete editions are called in German) of Mozart, Schumann, Brahms, and others.

Since 1743, moreover, there had been an important series of concerts in the guild hall, or Gewandhaus, of the Leipzig cloth merchants. The Gewandhaus concerts continued in a succession of halls; from these was born the Gewandhaus Orchestra, among the most celebrated of the many fine orchestras of the century. Mendelssohn became its conductor in 1835, and Schumann's First Symphony and many other significant works were first performed there. Shortly after his arrival in Leipzig, finally, Mendelssohn and his associates planned and oversaw the establishment of the Leipzig Conservatory. This confluence of major orchestra, music publishing house, and conservatory is throughout the nineteenth century an indication of a city's artistic coming of age, occasioning much the same civic pride as professional sports do in America today.

ROBERT SCHUMANN (1810–56). Schumann's parents owned a bookshop and lending library where he doubtless acquired a certain portion of his bookish inclinations. His tenure as a law student at the University of Leipzig was not a success, and a year at the University of Heidelberg confirmed his intention to become a musician. It was for this reason that he returned to Leipzig and undertook serious piano study with the noted piano teacher Friedrich Wieck. Schumann was by this time already troubled with the symptoms of the psychological distress that ran in the family, and his tempestuous emotional life was greatly complicated when he began to fall in love with Wieck's teenage daughter, Clara. Simultaneously he developed a curious, doubtless psycho-

somatic, paralysis of the right hand that made him abandon his aspiration to a career as a piano virtuoso.

Meanwhile, his compositions began to attract attention, as did his literary gifts. In his mid-20s he founded an influential music newspaper, the *Neue Leipziger Zeitschrift für Musik* ("New Leipzig Newspaper for Music"), to which he contributed insightful, imaginative criticism of music. Writing under the pen names Florestan, Eusebius, and Master Raro (his effusive, pensive, and academic characters, respectively), he canonized, one by one, the avatars of new music, notably Berlioz, Chopin, and Brahms. Schumann's marriage to Clara in 1840, after a long courtship and many legal entanglements, unleashed the decade of his great masterpieces: songs and piano works, chamber music, and wonderful orchestral music in which he wrestled, like other composers of the era, with the implications of Beethoven. In 1844 the Schumanns moved a few dozen kilometers to Dresden, where they lived for six years.

By the time the couple moved across Germany to Düsseldorf, on the Rhine, Schumann's final mental collapse was well under way. He was irritated by street noises and ringing in the ears and suffered episodes of irrational behavior, so his success with the orchestra he had been engaged to conduct was minimal. One ray of light during this troubled period was the young Johannes Brahms, who had come to study piano in the Schumann household and whom the master confidently proclaimed to be Beethoven's successor. But Schumann's decline could not be halted: After an unsuccessful attempt at suicide (by throwing himself into the Rhine), he was confined to the local insane asylum. For most of the two years he was there, Clara was prevented from visiting him lest he become overexcited; in his final days they met one last time.

Brahms had meanwhile quietly become the man of the house, and he and Clara developed a profound, lifelong attachment to each other. In the decades after they separated, each enjoying the triumphs of their profession, they were content to exchange a radiant correspondence.

Schumann's wonderful Piano Concerto in A Minor, which Clara popularized in solo appearances throughout Europe, achieves a depth of passion and a warmth—a satisfaction level, you might say—for which there is little precedent in the concerto literature, and which surely has much to say about both Robert and Clara. But in granting the solo part such clear preeminence the composer makes some trade-offs: For all the lovely solo work, the orchestral material here is for the most part not especially interesting. The same slackness in the orchestral part, never found in Mozart, troubles the Chopin concertos as well. It's a problem composers like Brahms went far out of their way to avoid.

Still, Schumann's overall way of thinking about a concerto, with the soloist as hero, reflects the Romantic attitude toward life itself. The point here is not what fetching collaboration can be achieved but instead how to elevate a single player above the crowd. Try to listen to the Schumann Piano Concerto and the Mendelssohn Violin Concerto in one sitting. Then reflect on the several ways that nineteenth-century ideals have affected composers' ideas about what a concerto is supposed to be.

RECOMMENDED LISTENING:

Schumann: Piano Concerto in A Minor, op. 54 (1845)
Mendelssohn: Violin Concerto in E Minor, op. 64 (1844)

www.prenhall.com/masterworks
recommended listening

FELIX MENDELSSOHN (1809–47). Despite his close association with the Gewandhaus Orchestra, Mendelssohn, too, was a vagabond. It was a habit that began before his 21st birthday, as his parents bankrolled his grand tour of Europe, the capstone of a marvelous education in languages, arts, and letters. (Mendelssohn's father was a successful Berlin banker; his grandfather, the philosopher Moses Mendelssohn.) In Italy he met (and detested) the young Berlioz, although they shared an aversion to Rome; in France he appeared with the Société des Concerts. But it was for England and Scotland that he developed his strongest affection, over the course of ten different visits during his career. His 1829 visit to Scotland resulted in the lovely programmatic overture *Fingal's Cave* (1832) and his "Scottish Symphony," No. 3, finished in 1842. Later he tutored Queen Victoria and became a favorite at her court. And in Birmingham in 1846, shortly before his death, he presented one of his last masterpieces, the noble oratorio *Elijah.*

In Germany, too, Mendelssohn wandered, commuting often between Berlin and Leipzig. For Berlin, in his 20th year, he conducted the remarkable performance of Bach's *St. Matthew Passion* that spurred the revival of interest in Bach that has lasted ever since. The King of Prussia's interest in his career led to Mendelssohn's incidental music for Shakespeare's *A Midsummer Night's Dream,* first performed at the palace in Potsdam in 1843. (The *incidental music* for a play consists of an overture, a brief *entr'acte* to precede each of the remaining acts, and music for any songs and processions that take place on stage: hence, in this case, the famous Wedding March.) Mendelssohn had composed the overture to *A Midsummer Night's Dream* long before, when he was 17, flush with excitement over his discovery of Shakespeare. This work, too, is a benchmark of Romanticism, opening with twinkling "once-upon-a-time" chords, then building a bustling sonata from evocative themes, including a donkey's whinny (representing Bottom the Tailor, who turns into an ass).

Mendelssohn's orchestral music—five major symphonies, programmatic overtures, and concertos—and his volumes of *Songs Without Words* for piano solo achieved a popularity in the nineteenth century that was unrivaled by any other composer. Those who were still looking for a successor to Mozart found one in Mendelssohn. He was susceptible to the Romantic notions of free form and vivid imagery but unprepared to let them overcome his equally strong sense of fastidiousness. His music almost never oversteps its bounds or becomes outrageous; it seldom puzzles and never frightens you. But taken on its own terms, without comparing it to Berlioz or Liszt, Mendelssohn's work stands proud. There are few musical moments in the century purer than the opening of the *Midsummer Night's Dream* Overture, few works lovelier than the middle movement of Mendelssohn's Violin Concerto, few chamber pieces finer than his great Octet of 1825.

*R*OMANTICISM, AGAIN

Romanticism in music is, then, first of all a matter of subjective emphasis on the feelings and passions of a life, typically the artist's own life. In nineteenth-century music, you are never far from autobiography. A composer's struggles with adversity, his love life, and increasingly his death and transfiguration to a better beyond come to dominate his artistic purpose. The spiritual journey takes precedence over the purely cerebral. Frequently there is a concern with nature (water music, thunder) and its supernatural extensions (ghosts and goblins, heaven and hell). Whatever the setting, if we look hard enough, we will find a Romantic hero, probably longing for something he has lost.

As the arts cross-fertilize, music becomes richer than ever with images and more dependent than ever on texts. The intellectual issues associated with music that endeavors to express nonmusical subject matter are many and formidable. But typical and expected tactics include the "once-upon-a-time" unveiling and the reminiscence of pleasures past. Romantic music, as you now know, loves to tell a story. Hence the tone poems, programmatic overtures, and movement titles with which the era abounds.

Romanticism speaks to us directly and deeply; nearly everybody likes Romantic music, at least until its tendency to excess begins to wear. Music was greatly popular with the new middle class of the nineteenth century. Concert tickets sold briskly, as did sheet music of excerpts and arrangements from the latest operas. Bourgeois families took their children to music lessons, and many people, including unmarried (and unchaperoned) women, joined local choral societies. Manufacturers dreamed of supplying a piano to every parlor in the land, a goal they came very close to achieving until the record player came along in the twentieth century. Throughout Europe, town councils oversaw the building of new lyric theaters and concert halls.

People tended to think big. To be the Napoleon of one's profession was a common desire. Bigness was also a response to social changes. Industry was booming, its noises louder than ever before. Projects were grandiose: the big cities were redesigned and railroads and canals built. Lighting was brighter. And there were many, many more people. Aspirations for the public health, education, and social welfare were high, too. All this made for a music of increasing size, affecting everything from the volume of the instruments and singers to the size of the halls and theaters.

Expansiveness changes form, for as movements get longer they risk getting lazier. You may be sensing, too, formidable changes in harmonic practice, as composers become more fluent in reaching distant key areas, and more daring in the use of complex, sometimes ambiguous chord forms. The chromaticism is intense, the chords multidirectional, the palette of sounds much broader. Not just the bigness of the Romantic orchestra but its mechanical improvements greatly changed its sound, with new, louder violins, fully chromatic woodwinds and brass, the pedal harp, and a growing percussion battery. While sonata-like forms, and above all the need to recapitulate for closure, retain their strong grip, exceptions to the rule are quite common. The urgency of form, as it was practiced by the Viennese Classicists, dissipates noticeably in the early Romantic period. The new freedoms were so universally investigated that only a few decades later tonality itself was threatening to become unglued.

ROMANTIC OPERA

By the 1830s every European metropolis had one or more opera companies, their repertoire fed by a seemingly inexhaustible supply of lyric delights from Italy. In dozens of houses from Naples to Venice to the celebrated La Scala of Milan, the opera business was thriving. Fabulous tenors and sopranos surfaced afresh with each new season. Composers were prolific and well paid. Tickets were cheap. The publishing house of Giovanni Ricordi (1785–1853) produced scores and parts for rental by the world at large. Exported Italian opera—the works, the singers, and even the composers—rivaled olive oil and Parmesan cheese as necessities of civilized life.

Italian opera in the Romantic period had much the same allure as the movies do today. And as in the film industry, high art took a back seat to hundreds of more formulaic and more popular works, and the public was often more interested in the stars than the particulars of their material. Yet for all the composing that simply put a new spin on last season's smash hit, the Italians managed to keep their lyric theater thriving and to dominate the world's stages with it. They had, after all, invented opera. The *bel canto* composers Rossini, Donizetti, and Bellini, all of whom became international superstars, constitute the first wave of the Italian school. Giuseppe Verdi dominated the second half of the century, and Giacomo Puccini took the style into the twentieth.

Bel canto means "beautiful singing." The ideal is the long vocal line, exquisitely controlled in its unfolding, and reaching a climax in the singer's most thrilling register. Vocal display is encouraged as the singer is given cadenza points and florid finale work, and the virtuosi felt free to add a great deal more ornamentation as they went. Often the *prima donna* (the lead soprano) and *primo uomo* (the tenor) are given an entire *scena,* like a soliloquy in Shakespeare. Left alone at center stage during a long orchestral introduction, they engage in a leisurely aria and often wind up with vocal fireworks in the section called the *cabaletta.* The effect is purposefully show-stopping. For example, the Mad Scene from Donizetti's *Lucia de Lammermoor*—in which Lucy, having stabbed her new husband on their wedding night, appears, quite loony, before the wedding guests in her blood-stained nightgown—lasts a good fifteen minutes and is inevitably followed by five minutes of thunderous applause. (The singer, having collapsed, waits through it in a heap on the floor.)

Bel canto operas are constructed as a series of movements, or numbers; hence the term *number opera.* The general deployment of numbers is predictable: a big aria in each act for the leads, arias for the male and female companions, the love duet, the men's chorus and women's chorus, and the crowd scenes. The delight comes in how composers inject novelty into the conventional schemes. Lucy going mad is a fine idea, as is that of

Figaro, Rossini's cocky barber of Seville, bragging of how his chic clientele calls at him from every corner of the neighborhood. The situations get ever more exotic as the century progresses, with the whiff of camels in Verdi's *Aida* and of girls smoking cigarettes in Bizet's French opera *Carmen*.

It was the Italian composer Gioachino Rossini (1792–1868) who formulated the *bel canto* style. Jovial in both his private and professional life, he excelled in comic opera laden with ridiculous situations. Rossini is a master of soprano coloratura, the comic bass, and the ensemble finale—and, in general, moving at lightning speed. He composed with Mozartian facility, preferring, as we noted earlier, to rewrite a page that had fallen onto the floor rather than go to the trouble of getting out of bed to pick it up. His operas are preceded by brilliant overtures, a half dozen of which make the Rossini overture one of the staples of the light classical repertoire.

Rossini accrued great wealth and prestige from his output of 1810–1823, allowing him to travel the world and develop a taste for its luxuries. Finding in Paris a genial welcome and excellent financial incentives, he composed his masterpiece, *Guillaume Tell* ("William Tell"), to a French libretto after Schiller's play concerning the legendary hero of Swiss independence. (The famous overture to *William Tell*, by the way, is *not* in the traditional format of the comic opera, but rather a potpourri of scenic evocations that concludes with the celebrated Allegro that you probably associate with the American Wild West.) On the profits of *Tell*, Rossini retired in his 50s to enjoy Parisian society. From time to time he would compose a little to entertain his many admirers, but he never again came close to regaining the rhythm of his work from the 1810s.

www.prenhall.com/masterworks
composer profiles
Bellini

Rossini's successors Vincenzo Bellini and Gaetano Donizetti imitated his example both artistically and fiscally, each becoming in due course a celebrity. The short-lived **Vincenzo Bellini (1801–35)**, a Sicilian, favored dramatic tragedy, the outgrowth of the old *opera seria*. The gravity of these sad tales, where both the soprano and the tenor usually expire before your eyes, is a far cry from Rossini's effervescence. The dramatic subject matter encouraged Bellini's keen sense of atmosphere and pacing, of purity in the declamation of text, and most especially of how to build a ravishing melody from the customary four-bar units of Italian song. His use of key is quite dramatic; for example, keys with many flats are chosen for the passages of greatest lyric intensity. It was Bellini who brought to *bel canto* a seriousness of purpose.

 BELLINI: "CASTA DIVA," FROM *NORMA* (1831)

In this aria the high priestess Norma cuts the sacred mistletoe and implores the "chaste goddess" of the moon to bring peace to her people. Taken separately the elements that make up the aria seem so conventional as to be almost trivial. Nothing could be more ordinary than the $\frac{12}{8}$ underpinning that carries through from beginning to end, the same kind of figuration a Sicilian mandolinist would automatically feel beneath the fingers:

The basic tune is simple, too, cobbled together of four-bar units. But Norma's gentle orna-mentations of the melody begin to hypnotize us early on. As the second big phrase begins, we sense the start of an exquisitely paced rise to climax: The chromaticism inten-sifies, the range edges upward. Norma's high B♭ is reached through a dramatic run and ravishing syncopations (an effect considerably augmented by the soprano, whose vibrato widens to include a G♯). And the cadence itself is drawn out not just by the huge ritard singers always take, but also by the fall of an octave and a half from the high B♭ to the tonic F. Both Verdi and Wagner were smitten with these few measures, finding in them a control of musical materials unmatched anywhere else in the *bel canto* repertoire.

The chorus, like so many gondoliers, provides a codetta-like closure, undulating from tonic to dominant and back. Over this Norma settles, birdlike, warbling the little roulades of coloratura singing at its most attractive. The second strophe proceeds quite similarly;

this time after the high B♭ there is a brief cadenza and final cadence. (Actually, this is not all: The scena continues as Norma declares the ritual done and then unleashes a flamboyant *cabaletta* reminding her listeners of her power to levy war.)

Norma is a Druid high priestess in ancient Gaul, c. 50 B.C. While the Gallic forces are at war with Rome, Norma has borne the Roman proconsul Pollione two children. Pollione, meanwhile, has sought the attentions of Norma's apprentice, Adalgisa. The reconciled Norma and Pollione eventually go to their deaths by burning on a funeral pyre, there to discover a more perfect love.

Bellini knew and wrote for the dazzling prima donnas with which his era was richly endowed. *Norma* was for the great soprano Giuditta Pasta (called simply "Pasta"); his Romeo and Juliet opera, called *I Capuleti e i Montecchi,* was for the sisters Giulia and

Listening Chart

 CD 3, TR 2

Vincenzo Bellini (1801–35)
***Norma* (1831)**
   "Casta diva"

Type: Opera aria, strophic
Meter: $\frac{12}{8}$
Key: F major
Duration: 05:26

For: Norma (sopr.), chorus (S, S, T, T, B); 2 flutes, 2 oboes, 2 clarinets, 2 bassoons; 4 horns; strings

Text: by Felice Romani (1788–1865), after a play by Alexandre Soumet

Ancient Gaul, ca. 50 B.C. The Gallic warriors are at war with Rome. Their high priestess, Norma, cuts the sacred mistletoe and asks the goddess of the moon for peace. "Casta diva" is a superb example of Bellini's melodic style, carefully building long lines from short units, with the beauty of the vocal ornamentation always paramount.

00:00	**Strophe I**		Arpeggiated mandolin-like accomp.
00:06	phrase 1	Chaste goddess who bathes in silver	2 half phrases, rising in ambitus.
00:30		These ancient, hallowed trees,	
00:52	phrase 2	Turn thy fair face upon us,	The rise continues, extravagantly
01:06	build	. . .	extended (with syncopated A♮s to the
01:22	climax	Unveiled and unclouded.	high high B♭—the moment so admired
			by Wagner, and others)
01:45	**Interlude**	. . . *etc.*	Chorus vamps: I-V-I-V
01:56	coloratura		with gentle soprano ornamentation.
02:33	cadence		
02:44	**Strophe II**		Str. II begins identically to str. I.
02:49	phrase 1	Temper thou the burning hearts,	
03:14		The excessive zeal of thy people.	
03:36	phrase 2	Enfold the Earth in that sweet peace	Richer scoring than strophe I: adds
03:50	build	. . .	flute, chorus.
04:05	climax	Which, through thee, reigns in heaven.	
04:30	cadence . . .		
04:43	**Cadenza**		
05:00	. . . cadence		

Giuditta Grisi. The *bel canto* operas, associated as they were with the idols of the lyric stage, became in due course vehicles for successive generations of virtuosi, including the French mezzo Pauline Viardot and her sister Maria Malibran, and their successors Jenny Lind (the "Swedish nightingale," presented to American audiences by P. T. Barnum of circus fame) and Adelina Patti. Any opera lover will delight in tracing these nearly royal successions for you. In the twentieth century the *bel canto* operas served Maria Callas, who galvanized the world with her combination of acting and singing, the Australian diva Joan Sutherland, and the American Beverly Sills, called "Bubbles" (because she sang in a famous television commercial for the detergent Rinso Blue), now a director of Lincoln Center in New York. Here the singer is Renata Scotto, a native Italian known particularly for her interpretations of the great tragic roles of Verdi and Puccini.

The beauty of the singing is everything in this sort of opera. The orchestra and conductor must follow the rubatos and ornamentation, *colla parte* ("with the singers"). The composers themselves bowed to the stars. "Casta diva" was rewritten for Pasta, the original key of G having been too high for her, and subsequently seven more times to suit the various singers cast in the part.

The other artist central to the success or failure of an opera is its librettist. Fashioning an effective libretto is a deceptively complex task, requiring a knack for reducing the source story to a few hundred lines, the ability to make the necessary arias and duets seem appropriate and natural, and not least of all a willingness to retreat to second place once the composer begins work. Composers then adjust the libretto, sometimes adding lines of their own. But good librettists could make serious money and secure a certain amount of fame as well. In this period the big name was Felice Romani, librettist of both Bellini's *Norma* and of Donizetti's *L'Elisir d'amore* ("The Elixir of Love") and several of the Verdi operas. (*L'Elisir d'amore* was fashioned, in turn, after the work of the most celebrated of the French librettists, Eugène Scribe.) The librettist, paid up front, often made more money from an opera than its composer did.

Both composer and librettist were sensitive to the need for memorable stage pictures. Audiences held these in their minds and, perhaps more importantly, so did the journalists. A gravure in one of the new illustrated newspapers of a thrilling final tableau might guarantee an opera's financial success. The sets and costumes, called the *décor,* were typically designed and built by the theater's resident artisans; the stage director, too, usually came with the house.

Lots of other people had a hand in the character of an opera, not only demanding changes but ultimately legislating its success or failure: the stars, the government's censors (who would forbid anything they thought might embarrass the royalty or clergy), and of course the audience. The audience ranged from the claque—rowdies paid to applaud their employer—to the aristocrats, who preferred that the memorable material in an opera come in Act II or later, so they could enjoy their dinner and not miss anything important by arriving late. After the performance all manner of assignations took place between gentlemen of the audience and their mistresses in the cast, chorus, or *corps de ballet.* None of this had much to do with art, but it was part and parcel of the social fabric of the time.

Nor was Italian opera Romanticism's only form of lyric theater. At the Paris Opéra, where everything had to be in French, a genre of lyric tragedy developed that came to be called *grand opera*. This was dominated by the Judeo-Franco-Germanic composer Giacomo (i.e., Jakob) Meyerbeer and the librettist Eugène Scribe (*Le Prophète, Les Huguenots, L'Africaine*). Grand operas were very long, very serious, and very theatrical. Gas lighting made it possible to lower the auditorium lights and provide such novel effects as scenes in the moonlight and fiery explosions. One Meyerbeer opera has a famous ice-skating scene; another has a theater-sized ship that crashes on the rocks. Alas, few people today remember much of the music. But all the greats—Rossini, Bellini, Donizetti, and later both Verdi and Wagner—aspired to compose for Paris, where the production practices had set the stage, so to speak, for the fabulous theatrical breakthroughs just around the corner.

Chapter 7

The men and women perceive with awe the light in the sky, in which now appears the Hall of Valhalla, where the gods and heroes are seen sitting together. Bright flames seize on the abode of the gods.

—stage direction for the final tableau of Wagner's *Götterdämmerung*

Through whirling clouds can be glimpsed now and again waltzing couples: . . . a fantastic and fatal Dervish's dance.

—from Ravel's notes for *La Valse*, a "choreographic poem" originally called *Wien* (Vienna)

Götterdämmerung

*L*ate Romanticism was precisely that: fantastic and fatal. Ravel's *La Valse,* composed just after World War I, looks backward at the sparkling *fin de siècle* and *belle époque* as though it were a dead civilization. Wagner, whose conceptions uncannily transcend his time and place, seems to predict the fall of Europe: art music's Valhalla, the abode of its gods. After 1914 nothing would ever be the same.

On the one hand, the revolutions of 1848 in France, Austria, Germany, and elsewhere, were mostly skirmishes lacking clear-cut outcomes. Only a few governments changed substantially. On the other, the uprisings signaled sweeping mutations in political ideology. They also reflected the basic change in social fabric that had been underway since the Industrial Revolution. The second half of the nineteenth century is a time when the great powers—the British, French, Russians, Germans, and Austrians—consolidated their empires, while minority populations increasingly greeted them as outsiders and looked to their own nationalistic roots.

The late nineteenth century is one of the richest periods in music history. Opera houses continued to thrive, and the lyric theater was perhaps the primary venue for the entertainment of the privileged classes. The orchestras of the great philharmonic societies came into their own, regularly selling out their subscriptions and at length constructing the near perfect concert halls of the era. (The Concertgebouw in Amsterdam dates from 1888, Symphony Hall in Boston from 1900.) The conservatories had by late century turned out several generations of virtuoso players. In Germany and the Austro-Hungarian empire in particular, few cities were without an opera company and symphony orchestra, and young composer/conductors like Mahler and Richard Strauss followed a reasonably predictable career ladder from small towns like Kassel to Budapest and Munich, then Vienna or Berlin. Seldom were economic conditions so favorable to art music.

Composers, meanwhile, had learned to manipulate both tonality and the vast forces at their disposal to powerful ends. Still captivated by the narrative possibilities of music, they developed concepts of motivic allusion and transformation to tell their tales, using ever more complex harmonic structures. Meanwhile, the nationalist composers increasingly sought ways that music could be used to achieve political ends. Composers of implicitly philosophical bent were especially conscious of their role in forging the future of art. They believed in progress toward a utopia where music reigned supreme.

Which, in a way, they had already found. As the world flung itself closer and closer to global conflict, the more advanced composers began to feel that the customary genres and forms had been essentially mined out, and that indeed the possibilities of tonality itself were beginning to be exhausted. Even before the first shot of World War I had been fired, listeners in Paris were rioting in the streets over barbarisms in a ballet! This was Stravinsky's *Rite of Spring,* where, for many, modernism begins.

ERDI AND WAGNER

At mid-century, however, these weighty issues were only just beginning to come into focus. At the opera house, progress was still the order of the day. Not only the production techniques but the dramatic structure of opera were substantially refined. During the 1850s two major new composers emerged as leaders of the modern lyric theater: Giuseppe Verdi, an Italian whose work began from *bel canto* thinking, and Richard Wagner, who looked to Weber as his model. Their prevailing attitudes toward music and theater could not have been more different, yet each contributed majestically to the art. So much more advanced was their work over the competition that they have virtually no rivals from the 1850s until the end of the century. If Wagner represents the more significant step forward in technique, it is Verdi whose works took Europe by storm. There were a good hundred performances of Verdi for each production of a Wagner opera.

GIUSEPPE VERDI (1813–1901). The remarkable thing about Verdi is how this very simple man managed to transform a convention-laden style into a style that even today seems quite progressive. In an Italian opera, as we have seen, one expected a sequence of relatively specific features—an overture, recitatives and arias for the principals, love duets, and ensemble finales. The magic lay in the Italian predilection for melody, always tuneful and hummable, and generally bright, and in its presentation by the star performers. Italian opera, as Verdi inherited it, is great fun. You know the story is only a story, and that it's not over until either the soprano or the tenor, often both, expire before your eyes.

www.prenhall.com/masterworks
composer profiles
Verdi

Verdi

Verdi absorbed these conventions fully, not worrying half so much as Wagner did about a composer's need to be radical. But he had a very astute inner sense of dramatic force; he knew how to use musical materials to delineate character and the high points in his sometimes improbable plots. He collaborated unusually closely with his librettists. The result represents a clear advance for opera as drama. Verdi's characters seem more real, the situations they face truer to our own experience.

Verdi was born into the rusticity that characterized much of provincial northern Italy in the early 1800s, and he achieved his place in the world of music largely by dint of very hard labor. He called the period where he rose to the top his "galley years," composing a major opera every nine months or so. By the early 1840s he had conquered the great opera house of La Scala in Milan, and his work was beginning to be performed all over the world. The trio of operas produced in the period 1851–53—*Rigoletto, Il Trovatore,* and *La Traviata*—is as enviable a two years' accomplishment as you will find in the annals of music.

Take time to discover Verdi's wonderful *La Traviata,* about the love affair between Alfredo, scion of an aristocratic family, and the Paris courtesan Violetta. The story is that of Alexandre Dumas (the younger), *La Dame aux camélias* ("The Lady of the Camellias"), after the flower Violetta removes from her bodice and gives to Alfredo. You know when Violetta coughs into her hankie early on that all is not well, and the plummet from their rapture at the close of Act I to her death from consumption in Act IV is precipitous and tragically thrilling. Here Verdi follows his typical first-act scheme of a magnificent ensemble opening, soprano and tenor aria, and love duet. The setting is a soirée at Violetta's mansion, with dancing and cards and assignations; among its wonders are the great drinking song ("Libiamo, libiamo") and Violetta's *scena* "Ah, fors'è lui."

After a tragic first marriage in which his wife and both his children died of infectious disease, Verdi found domestic happiness with the soprano Giuseppina Strepponi, who became his second wife. He also grew wealthy, investing his earnings in a farm outside Milan where he found a level of tranquility enjoyed by too few other composers. But in the 1850s and 1860s Verdi's career was one of nonstop deadlines, with the inevitable assaults on his equilibrium caused by the rigors of preparing the first performances of each new work. While the money was good and his fame grew—he received commissions from the czar of Russia (*La Forza del destino,* 1862) and the viceroy of Egypt (*Aida,* 1871, for the opening of the Suez Canal)—the fatigue was substantial, too. After *Aida* he retired, reemerging only when it was absolutely necessary. One such occasion was the death of the Italian nationalist poet Alessandro Manzoni, following which Verdi composed his epic Requiem Mass of 1874. It took the collusion of Verdi's wife, Giuseppina, his publisher, and the composer/librettist Arrigo Boito to convince him to compose another opera. Quietly but insistently they brought the old man around to the notion of an opera on Shakespeare's great tragedy *Othello.* The work quite revivified his genius, and *Otello* (it lacks the *h* in Italian) is on everybody's list of the top ten greatest operas of all time.

 VERDI: FROM *OTELLO* (1887)

LOVE DUET (OTELLO, DESDEMONA, ACT I): "QUANDO NARRAVI"

The military hero Otello, a Moor (or black man), has been awarded the governorship of Cyprus by the Republic of Venice. His beautiful Venetian wife, Desdemona, is the passion of his life. But the villainous Iago, an embodiment of evil, sows the seeds of disaster by suggesting a romance between Desdemona and Otello's trusted lieutenant, Cassio. Otello's jealousy consumes him: He smothers Desdemona, then, comprehending Iago's ugly plot, stabs himself. In his dying moments, as the curtain falls, he kisses the lifeless Desdemona one last time.

You have to get used to dead bodies in the opera house. Final curtains usually fall on a tragic tableau with the orchestra throbbing away on a huge minor-key final cadence. *Don Giovanni* is swallowed live into a fiery hell for his misdeeds; Mimi in Puccini's *La Bohème* peters out from consumption, as does Violetta in *La Traviata;* Carmen is stabbed to death by the jealous Don Jose just outside the bullring; and Madama Butterfly commits hara-kiri before our eyes. At the end of Wagner's *Ring of the Nibelung,* as we will soon discover, pretty much everybody is gone but the common people and the Daughters of the Rhine. (If you're sensitive to this sort of thing, you leave the theater in a daze, even after standing and cheering as the fully restored singers take their curtain calls, and wake up the next morning still trying to sort out your feelings.) Toward the end of *Otello,* Verdi makes the story exquisitely pitiful by composing the great scene where, in a dark premonition, Desdemona sings the "Willow Song" of a woman abandoned by her lover, says her prayers in a simple but haunting *Ave Maria,* and then falls into a fitful sleep dressed, no less, in her wedding nightgown.

The love duet that concludes Act I shows how scrupulously the librettist and composer treated the hallowed Shakespeare text, even though making a duet from what was originally a monologue. (Both texts are given in conjunction with the chart on the CD-ROM/Website.) As a child Desdemona had listened with wide-eyed delight as Otello recounted his adventures to her father: of deserts, cannibals, and the clash of arms. She wept at his defeats. "She loved me for the dangers I had passed," says Otello, "and I loved her that she did pity them." Verdi and Boito make of this sublime text the lovers' central exchange:

OTELLO: E tu m'amavi per le mie sventure
          ed io t'amavo per la tua pietà.
DESDEMONA: Ed io t'amavo per le tue sventure
          e tu m'amavi per la mia pietà.

Verdi reaches this moment expertly indeed. A cello quartet sets the tender scene, and we sense the ensuing conversation less as preliminary recitative than as the undeniable stirring of passion, especially when both singers are given breathtaking lifts into their high registers. In "Quando narravi," the F-major duo on Otello's adventures, the orchestral fabric reflects the changing character of every line of text, from the clash of arms to the shimmering sands of Otello's African homeland. As the climactic couplet is reached, the lovers' vocal lines at last entwine, and they arrive at the cadence point in close harmony.

Now all the elements of the scene coalesce to heighten the rapture of their kiss. Onstage the clouds disperse into starry night, and Verdi so arranges the tonality that each new key area seems to float over the previous one: C major for their prayer, a moment of breathless panting, and then a thrilling lift into E major. As Otello asks for a kiss, *un bacio,* the orchestra throbs the kiss music.

And as the lovers retreat to their chamber, the music floats to a high D♭ cadence, with reminiscence in the cello section of the duet's first bars.

Act IV opens forbodingly in the orchestra as the maid Emilia helps Desdemona prepare for bed. Troubled with premonitions, Desdemona asks Emilia to lay out the nightgown from her wedding night, then sings a song from her youth of a woman crying by the weeping willow tree ("The Willow Song"). This is once interrupted by a thump in the night—Otello, in fact, coming to murder her: but Emilia dismisses the noise as that of the wind. Left alone, Desdemona kneels at her *prie-dieu* to say her prayers; an *Ave Maria* of shattering serenity. But a moment later Otello creeps in, and the climax and dénouement take their ghastly course. Shakespeare's last couplet for Otello ends with the final kiss:

> I kiss'd thee ere I kill'd thee.
> No way but this,
> Killing myself, to die upon a kiss.

So does Verdi's music. Having drawn a dagger and stabbed himself, Otello takes a last kiss from the lifeless corpse and himself falls dead, as the orchestra recalls the *bacio* theme from the love duet. The curtain falls. If you needed proof that music is capable of enriching even one of the best stage plays, here it is.

At the age of 79, Verdi wrote one last opera, the comic masterpiece *Falstaff* (1893), based on Shakespeare's *Merry Wives of Windsor*. (Both of Verdi's late Shakespeare operas thus were completed after Wagner's death in 1883.) This brought to 28 the num-

Listening Chart

 CD 3, TR 3

Giuseppe Verdi (1813–1901)
Otello (1887)
From Act I: Love Duet ("Quando narravi")

For: Otello (ten.), Desdemona (sopr.); piccolo, 2 flutes, 2 oboes, English horn, 2 clarinets, bass clarinet, 4 bassoons; 4 horns, 2 piston cornets, 2 trumpets, timpani, harp; strings

Text: by Arrigo Boito (1842–1918), after Shakespeare's *Othello*

Type: operatic scene
Meter: C
Key: (G♭ maj.,) F major, (then C, E, D♭ major)
Duration: 10:26

Cyprus at the end of the fifteenth century. Otello, a Moor, has been victorious in battle and proclaimed governor-general. The love duet that concludes Act I shows how scrupulously the librettist and composer treat the hallowed Shakepeare text, while making a duet from what was originally a monologue. "She loved me for the dangers I had passed," says Otello, "and I loved her that she did pity them."

00:00	**Introduction & Recitatives**	Cello quartet, setting the tender scene. Note, throughout, the text painting and stunning use of vocal color and range.
00:39	Otello	G♭ maj. The calm of night; after the battle (01:15), infinite love.
01:42	Desdemona	"My superb warrior." She reminds him of how he used to
02:15	transition	tell his story while she listened. "Do you remember? . . . "
02:36	**Otello's Tales**	"Quando narravi," F maj. The duo on Otello's deeds is fashioned from Shakespeare's monologue (see text) by alternating lines of text.
	Desdemona	When he narrated his tales, she listened, rapt and ecstatic.
03:17	Otello	Tales of battle, of assaulting bastions as arrows whizzed past.
03:39	Desdemona	His (African) homeland; being sold into slavery.
04:16	Otello	Her tears and sighs at his story brought him Paradise.
04:51	Desdemona	From his dark temples radiated bright nobility.
05:00	Both	She loved him for the dangers he had passed, And he loved her that she did pity him. (Big F-maj. cadence.)
05:57	**Their Prayer**	(Note the dramatic shifts of tonality, rising toward closure.)
	Otello	"Let Death take me in the ecstasy of this supreme moment."
06:56	Desdemona	C maj. (As the moon rises): "May our love survive forever."
07:17	Amen (both)	"May Heaven answer this prayer."
07:46	ecstasy	Breathless joy: orchestral panting.
08:10	kisses	E maj. The *bacio* theme: "a kiss, another kiss."
08:50	starlight	D: "It's late." O: "Come. Venus is shining." D: "Otello!"
09:51	Coda	D♭ maj. The cello figure from the opening.

ber of his major works for the stage. In its own way the Verdi repertoire seemed to later composers as invincible as the Beethoven symphonies had been. Verdi's clearest successor is Giacomo Puccini, composer of *La Bohème* and *Madama Butterfly*. If Puccini lacked Verdi's gift for profundity, he was equally successful with sentiment; for example, there are any number of parallels between the love scene of *Otello* and that of *Madama Butterfly*.

RICHARD WAGNER (1813–83). Among the several revolutions of 1848–49 was an uprising in Dresden against the Saxon king. There at the barricades—in a signal tower actually—was the young court composer and conductor Richard Wagner, whose future had until that week seemed assured by virtue of the progressive operas he had created in Saxony. These were *Rienzi* (1842), *Der fliegende Holländer* ("The Flying Dutchman,"1843), and *Tannhäuser* (1845). He had just finished *Lohengrin* and had started to plan a work on the death of the Norse hero Siegfried as well. Now there was a Wanted poster with his picture on it, and he was forced to flee the city.

This unusual turn of events left Wagner without formal employment. As a self-motivated intellectual, he was content to make this hiatus in his career a time for inner reflection on the philosophy of theater—and content to freeload off his friends to make ends meet. Already in his works to 1848 you can grasp the essence of the Wagnerian style: his reliance on ancient legends for subject matter, on the composer himself as librettist, on harmonic daring, and his frequent use of recurring motives to emphasize the underlying themes of the story. He wrote a spate of books and essays summarizing his thoughts, then seven operatic masterpieces that shook musical thinking at its foundation.

Wagner called his theoretical formulation *Gesamtkunstwerk,* or "total art work," by which he meant that opera—or what he preferred to call music drama—was a forum where the perfect mingling of music, acting and dance, poetry and prose, plastic art, and architecture could be achieved. Going to the opera was for Wagner tantamount to a religious experience,

Wagner

and it was no accident that he chose as his subject matter old European and Norse legends. His libretti developed a style of short, very rhythmic lines, strong on alliteration (which he found quite musical) and short on end-rhyme (which he did not). The texts tend to be highly symbolic, with strong emphasis on, say, light-and-dark / day-and-night. Over the long haul—and Wagner operas are *very* long—there is enough repetition and retelling of stories that you can't miss the point. The logical extension of all this is the notion that Wagnerian opera needs celebrating in a temple devoted solely to its own apotheosis; thus Wagner eventually had his Festspielhaus (Festival Performance Hall), too.

This is undeniably heavy stuff. Wagner was strong-willed at the least, more often leaning toward megalomania. Wagner's was a personality of many contradictions: He was brilliant, greatly disciplined in work habits, self-indulgent, thoroughly unpleasant, and at times vicious. He thought the world owed him wealth and fame for his genius. But it's his very self-centeredness that makes Wagner work so well, for the result is opera of exceptional musical and dramatic coherence. If you are of a mind to be moved by this sort of thing, the essential truths of Wagnerian opera—in *The Ring of the Nibelung* a monarch who can no longer control his empire; in *Tristan und Isolde* a carnality that can only be fulfilled in death—stay with you a long, long time.

Wagner was a successful composer with a decent track record by the time he fled Dresden in 1849. But it was the work he conceived and composed in exile—the four operas in the cycle he called *The Ring of the Nibelung* (1851–76) and the great Romantic tragedy *Tristan und Isolde* (1859)—that brought him into the front rank of the European musical establishment.

THE RING OF THE NIBELUNG.   Of all the colossal works of the nineteenth century—Berlioz's Requiem, the grandest of the grand operas, Mahler's "Symphony of a Thousand"—none surpasses in nobility of concept Wagner's great *Ring of the Nibelung,* a cycle of four operas involving hundreds of musicians (and dozens of stagehands) and lasting the better part of a week. Attending a complete *Ring* someday is an experience you must set your sights on, for there's nothing quite like the thrill of seeing it through, discovering as you go just how important you, the audience member, are to its overall effect. In the meantime, bear with me while I recount the high spots of its very complicated but very fine plot.

The Nibelung in question is an ugly dwarf named Alberich, who in the opening moments of the first opera, *Das Rheingold* ("The Rhinegold"), steals the gold at the bottom of the river Rhine, symbol of the perfection of Nature. The gold is watched over by three rather naive Rhinemaidens. As the curtain comes up we find them swimming around the gold, the first of many sensational stage effects with which the *Ring* is richly endowed. To steal the gold, Alberich forswears love, a curse that passes to all who come to hold it.

The scene shifts to Valhalla, a mountaintop castle just finished for the gods by the giants Fafner and Fasolt. When a dispute over payment erupts after the necessary gold runs short, the giants abduct Freia, whose golden apples give the gods their perpetual youth. The threat of old age and death prompts Wotan, king of the gods, and his side-kick Loge, the messenger of fire, to descend to subterranean Nibelheim. There they trick Alberich and steal the ring he has forged from the gold. Fafner kills Fasolt and spirits the gold away to a cave, where he protects it in the form of a giant dragon. The gods cross a rainbow bridge to occupy their new castle.

Die Walküre ("The Valkyrie"), the second opera, opens during a driving rainstorm. A beautiful young man with golden hair is being hunted down by the dogman Hunding and his hounds. He takes refuge in a treehouse, where an equally beautiful young woman, Sieglinde, bids him welcome. Intrigued by this representative of so obviously a heroic tribe, she drugs her husband—none other than Hunding—and dallies with the visitor in the front room. The rain ceases and spring blows in. The gorgeous couple fall madly in love, and at length the young man pulls a magic sword from the trunk of the tree. In so doing he recognizes his kinship with Sieglinde: They are brother and sister of the great tribe of Wälsungs. He takes the name Siegmund.

Fricka, Wotan's wife, learns of this affair and forbids the seven Valkyries, who are protectresses of great warriors and—to Fricka's irritation—Wotan's daughters by another liaison, from protecting Siegmund. Wotan reluctantly carries this message to the eldest Valkyrie, his favorite daughter, Brunnhilde. But seeing Siegmund and the now pregnant Sieglinde losing ground to Hunding, she holds her protective shield over Siegmund. The angry Wotan, charging in on his steed, chases Brunnhilde away and shatters the magic sword with his spear, fashioned from the World Ash Tree. Hunding gives Siegmund a fatal blow, and in the next instant Wotan himself strikes Hunding dead. Sieglinde flees into the woods, there to give birth to her child.

The famous "Ride of the Valkyries" is that of the frightened girls fleeing their angry father. Wotan finds Brunnhilde on a mountaintop and in the stirring finale punishes her by taking her godliness away. When she wakes from her magic sleep, she will be a mortal. He summons Loge to surround the sleeping Brunnhilde with magic fire, turns his back on the scene, and trudges sadly away. Only a hero can penetrate the fire and take Brunnhilde for his wife.

In *Siegfried,* the child of Siegmund and Sieglinde has grown to young manhood and is now a glorious adolescent clothed in an animal hide. Sieglinde has died in childbirth, and Siegfried has been raised by Mime, a Nibelung. Mime (pronounced "*Mee*-muh") has tried unsuccessfully to recast the shards of the magic sword; now Siegfried does it effortlessly, even lustily. They set off to the dragon's lair to regain the gold. In slaying the dragon Fafner, Siegfried tastes its magic blood, enabling him to hear the words of a songbird. The bird urges him to go to Brunnhilde's mountaintop. There he discovers womankind and takes Brunnhilde as his bride, sealing their marriage with the cursed Ring of the Nibelung.

Brunnhilde

In *Götterdämmerung* ("Twilight of the Gods") Siegfried descends to the Hall of the Gibichungs, a Rhineland tribe, and quickly falls prey to their treachery. Using his magic helmet to disguise himself as the Gibichung prince, he abducts Brunnhilde from her rock. Brunnhilde, however, turns violently on Siegfried for taking part in the Gibichungs' trickery and colludes in their plot to kill him. On a hunting trip along the Rhine, the Gibichungs murder Siegfried, and his body is borne back to the hall to a dark orchestral dirge. Brunnhilde, having surmised the awful truth, orders Siegfried's body to be placed on a huge funeral pyre. Mounting her trusty horse, she charges into the fire. The gold ring returns to the grateful Rhinemaidens as the Rhine overflows its banks and the hall of the Gibichungs collapses into it. Simultaneously, we see Valhalla afire in the heavens, with the gods seated at a table awaiting the end of the world.

There are as many levels of meaning in this awesome myth as in James Joyce's *Ulysses,* and it's just as complicated. The tale centers on Wotan, a leader who, once having embarked on deceit, is powerless to control the developments he has unleashed. One can't miss the stern warnings about the cost of interfering with Nature. There is a strong emphasis on the idea of a master race, which you are likely to find appalling, especially if you know how the Nazis went on to exploit it. But this was part and parcel of the superman philosophy of Friedrich Nietzsche, who strongly influenced Wagner at the time *The Ring* was being composed.

Wagner conceived all this himself, taking the story from several different sources of Norse mythology. The operas consist of self-contained acts where the music runs continuously from prelude to curtain fall, and even the internal scene changes are covered with orchestral music. The individual scenes embrace the usual arias and duets and big visual pieces, but the seams between them are smoothed over, as is the difference between recitative and aria, by Wagner's routine avoidance of anything that feels like a strong cadence point. His main tool for managing this is a kind of chromatic harmony where a simple sliding chromatic motion and the use of ambiguous sharps and flats allow him to float over the certainties of old-fashioned fifth-related key areas.

Consider, for example, Wagner's strong reliance on the so-called diminished seventh chord (that of Samiel in *Der Freischütz,* p. 200). This is a four-note chord built of minor thirds, for example C-E♭-G♭-B♭♭. Only three of these chords exist, for after you build them on C, C♯, and D, they begin to repeat themselves.

=E♭-G♭-B♭♭-C
=C-E♭-G♭-B♭♭

Moreover, since the intervals in the chord are equidistant, any one of its members can be thought of as its bottom note, or root. Thus a single chord points in four simultaneous directions and by simple chromatic oozing to one of the other two possibilities can be made to point to any one of the 12 keys in a few seconds' time. If you find a keyboard and experiment with these chords, you'll be making Wagnerian sounds quickly.

Additionally in Wagner a fabulously intricate web of counterpoint makes all sorts of subsidiary dramatic allusions. Wagner's operas are not about venerating the singer but venerating the artwork; you are less drawn to the component parts than to the power of the composite. But if any element stands out above the others, it is the orchestral fabric, for the orchestra is the agent for conveying Wagner's rich theory of the Leitmotiv.

THE LEITMOTIV.   Wagner relies on a repertoire of short musical motives associated with specific characters, ideas, and actions in the story. These are called *Leitmotivs.* (*Leit* in this case means "leading" or "principal"; hence Leitmotivs are "principal motives.") You probably already know the Valkyries' tune and the motive drawn from it.

Lebhaft

Brass

Valkyries' motive:

Typically you first discern a motive when it is associated with a powerful visual or plot element, such as the Rhine, the gold, Valhalla, or the sword in the tree. The presentation is usually so forthright as to be blatant and is repeated several times so you get the idea. Thereafter the motive can be used in the orchestral texture to provide a level of commentary that goes beyond what you're seeing onstage. If a motive is already strongly associated in the listener's mind with, say, an oath taken, it becomes sensational if heard when that oath is broken. When Wagner draws the Leitmotivs into a counterpoint of musical allusions, the dramatic power can be overwhelming. This is precisely what happens in the last scene of *Ring,* where a half dozen major issues need settling in the ten minutes before the final curtain.

WAGNER: BRUNNHILDE'S IMMOLATION (FINAL SCENE), FROM *GÖTTERDÄMMERUNG* (1876)

By the last scene of *Götterdämmerung,* every spectator has understood that the ring is cursed and that only by returning the gold to the Rhine can Nature's equilibrium be restored. It falls to Brunnhilde, who has emerged as the heroine of the cycle, to do the honors. This she accomplishes by self-immolation on Siegfried's funeral pyre. (The scummy villain Hagen actually has the last line, a forlorn "Give back the ring!" but this is scarcely heard over the din and is omitted from the recording.)

The excerpt begins as Brunnhilde signals some men to bear Siegfried's body to the funeral pyre and simultaneously removes the ring from his finger. Contemplating it, she resolves to cast the ring back to the "wise sisters of the water's deep, the swimming daughters of the Rhine," from which the gold was robbed. Suddenly the watery accompaniment is interrupted by the big brass figure associated with Wotan's deceitful treachery, a sort of orchestral "I told you so," as Brunnhilde seizes a torch and hurls it into the pyre. She sends the ravens of death to convey the news to Valhalla, then summons her steed Grane and rides to her death:

Heiajoho! Grane!	Heiajoho! Grane!
Grüß deinen Herren!	Greet your master!
Siegfried! Siegfried! Sieh!	Siegfried! Siegfried! See!
Selig grüßt dich dein Weib!	Your wife joyfully greets you!

But it is the orchestra that says most of what needs saying. Among the motives in play are the following, given in the order they come once Brunnhilde seizes the firebrand:

(Remember that you can cue these motives up from the CD-ROM/Website.) Note in particular that the tumbling-down motive of the gods' twilight is a kind of inversion of the Rhine music; thus, Valhalla, built on deceit, collapses into Nature. Note, too, that the "main" theme, that of Brunnhilde's dying love for Siegfried, has for all intents and

Listening Chart

 **CD 3, TR 4**

Richard Wagner (1813–83)
Götterdämmerung (1876)
Act III, concluding portion of final scene: Brunnhilde's Immolation

Type: operatic finale
Meter: mostly $\frac{4}{4}$
Key: D♭ major
Duration: 10:40

For: Brunnhilde (sopr.); piccolo, 3 flutes, 3 oboes, English horn, 3 clarinets, bass clarinet, 3 bassoons; 4 horns, 3 trumpets, bass trumpet, 4 trombones, 4 tubas, contrabass tuba; 2 pairs timpani, triangle, cymbals, 6 harps; strings

Text: by the composer

The excerpt consists of the last 11 minutes of Wagner's four-opera cycle *The Ring of the Nibelung,* first presented in August 1876 at the brand new Festspielhaus in Bayreuth.

00:00	**Part 1**	Brass fanfares as Siegfried's body is set on the pyre;
00:18	G/R	Twilight of the Gods motive down, answered by Rhine motive up.
00:29		Brunnhilde contemplates the "terrible ring," resolving to return
00:51	RM	it to the "wise sisters" (watery motives); her fiery death will
02:20	G/R	cleanse the curse, the robbed gold washed back into the Rhine.
	Part 2	
02:43	T	Orch. introduction recalls the treachery. She seizes a torch.
02:55	MF	"Fly home, ye ravens; tell the gods what you have learned."
03:10	"	"Fly first to Brunnhilde's rock to fetch Loge and his fire."
03:34	G/R	"The end of the gods draws nigh."
04:01	**Part 3**	She hurls the torch into the pyre, which takes flame.
04:20	W	She greets her Valkyrie's steed, Grane, which she will ride into the
04:50	L, S,	fire, there to find redemption in love for Siegfried, the fallen hero.
	W, MF	The counterpoint of motives thickens notably.
05:26	L	"Feel how my bosom burns. Flames carry me to his embrace."
05:58	S, L	"Ho-yo-to-ho!" (the Valkyrie's call). "Grane, greet thy master."
		"Siegfried! Siegfried! See! . . . Thy wife joins thee!" The massive cadence is disrupted when . . .
06:17	W	She charges into the fire. (End of Brunnhilde.)
	Part 4	Orchestral finale.
06:25	MF	The fire consumes her, filling the stage and terrorizing the crowd.
06:51	G	The fire is extinguished in a cloud of smoke as the Rhine overflows.
07:06		The Rhinemaidens appear riding the waves near the pyre.
07:27		Hagen plunges in after the ring; they drag him under.
07:45	RM	Swimming happily, they hold up the ring: Nature restored.
07:54	V	In the red glow we see the gods seated at table in Valhalla.
08:04	R, L	The motives intertwined: gods, Rhinemaidens, mortal lovers.
08:44	V	Bright flames seize on the abode of the gods.
09:33	S, G	Last climactic statement of Siegfried's motive, another cadence, ebbing into
09:46	L	reminiscence of the love music, decrescendo leading to
10:04		final cadence, as curtain descends to a last crescendo.

Key to Leitmotivs: G = twilight of gods; L = redemptive love (of Brunnhilde and Siegfried); MF = magic fire; R = Rhine; RM = Rhinemaidens; S = Siegfried; T = treachery (Wotan's theft of the gold); V = Valhalla; W = the Valkyries (Walküre), Brunnhilde as Valkyrie.

purposes been reserved for this point the end of the opera. Once Brunnhilde has finished, the music comes to its thrilling climax in a complex web of associations, outdoing even a Berliozian *réunion des thèmes* as the music seems to gather up the gods, Rhine-maidens, and mortal lovers in a sea of orchestral sound. Wagner is a master of the growling brass French horn and trombone/tuba register, here resonating in heroic volume. Meanwhile, we ordinary people, along with the Gibichungs, watch and listen with awe as the bright flames seize on the abode of the gods. Allow the music to wash over and through you, and let your imagination provide the rest. However inventive the stagecraft with which all this is accomplished in the theater, the most rewarding production is in your own mind's eye and ear.

So radical were the implications of Wagner's thoughts, and so complex, that during the course of composing *The Ring of the Nibelung* Wagner had to pause and reconsider where he was going. His private life had taken a new direction, too, when he left his first wife Minna and took up with Mathilde Wesendonk, wife of one of his wealthy patrons.

Thus it happened that between *Die Walküre* and *Siegfried* Wagner interrupted work on *The Ring* to compose what is doubtless his finest single accomplishment, *Tristan und Isolde*. In this saga drawn from medieval French legend, the vassal Tristan is bringing Isolde from France to England to be the bride of King Mark. Owing to Isolde's magic potion, however, she and Tristan fall in love on the boat. In Act II, after Isolde has married, the lovers tryst through the night, ignoring the repeated warnings of Isolde's maid, and are interrupted by the wronged husband and his men at dawn. Tristan is gravely wounded. In Act III, having fled to France, Tristan languishes near death, although certain in the knowledge that Isolde will eventually come to his side. She arrives just at the moment of his death. In the famous *Liebestod* ("Love-Death") with which the opera concludes, Isolde, cradling Tristan's head in her arms, rejoices that in death the lovers will discover a bliss that was denied to them in life. She then swoons, lifeless, over his body.

The frank sexuality of *Tristan und Isolde* was daring indeed. A measure of the story was autobiographical; Wagner seems to be "composing away" his naughty affair with Mathilde Wesendonk. But *Tristan* is equally daring in structure. There are only the two title roles and a few supporting characters, and virtually no stage action at all. The opera is an intense psychological drama along what we can now recognize as very modern lines.

Tonally the opera is one of the significant works of the century, particularly in the famous "Tristan" chord heard in the opening bars of the prelude:

MIDI 7.01

It's a sonority so complex in implication and so frequently diverted that it becomes the very essence of dangerous, unfulfilled sexual longing. And when at length the chord does resolve in the final tableau, it passes *through* the A minor it implies to rise chromatically into B major—and symbolically to the higher plane of the lovers united in death.

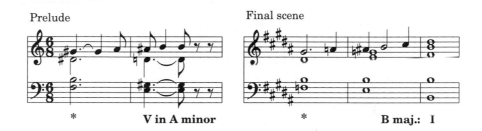

After *Tristan* and *The Ring,* Wagner composed two last operas, *Die Meistersinger von Nürnberg* (1868) and *Parsifal* (1882). The latter, completed a few months before he died, is his treatment of the legend of Percival, legendary knight in search of the Holy Grail, the chalice from which Christ offered the wine at the Last Supper.

Die Meistersinger, with its famous C-major prelude, is Wagner's only comic opera. Again the subject matter is medieval, in this case a reasonably factual look at a guild of artisans devoted to the highest craft of singing. The moral of the story is that beauty makes its own rules. The apprentice singer Walther, by following his instincts instead of the old-school practices, composes the best song and thus wins the prize: the hand of the beautiful Eva.

At length Wagner was allowed to return to Germany, and in Munich he attracted the patronage of the king of Bavaria, Ludwig II. His romance with Cosima Liszt von Bülow led to her divorce and a second marriage for them both. From 1866 they lived in a villa called Tribschen on the banks of Lake Lucerne in Switzerland. Their son Siegfried was born in 1869, and a year later they were married. It was for the most part a blissful, rather saccharine arrangement. For Cosima's birthday (Christmas Day) in 1870, for example, he secreted a chamber orchestra into the house to wake her with his *Siegfried-Idyl,* in honor of their love child. For his birthdays, she, in turn, would dress the children up as characters from his operas.

Meanwhile, leaders in the Bavarian village of Bayreuth, where the king had one of his many palaces, invited Wagner to locate the opera house of his dreams there. On a hill above the town he oversaw the building of his virtually perfect music theater, the Festspielhaus. Furnished entirely in wood, with a huge orchestra pit and the latest in stage machinery, it became the center of Wagner's world, offering the first complete *Ring* in 1876. No other composer's work has ever been heard at the Festspielhaus, and the operation is still controlled by the Wagner family.

Bayreuth has always regarded the Wagner repertoire as work in progress, and although the productions have often been controversial, they have never grown stale. In 1976, for example, the centennial production of *The Ring* was given to the French director Patrice Chéreau and conductor Pierre Boulez, who stretched the work into a Marxist manifesto, featuring a dam on the Rhine, steel ovens, and Wotan as a robber-baron capitalist in white tie and tails. Although the production was hissed from beginning to end

Bayreuth

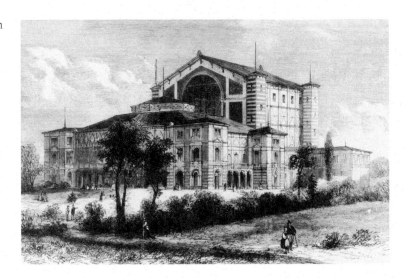

in a tumultuous opening week (and Wieland Wagner, Wagner's grandson, was roundly booed at a board meeting of the Friends of Bayreuth), the crazy approach succeeded admirably, as the video recording proves. The closing tableau of *Götterdämmerung,* with the hungry, desensitized proletariat staring blankly out into the house, is unforgettable.

Wagner's lovely, understated villa Wahnfried ("House of Joy") lies behind the royal palace in Bayreuth along the gardens. He and Cosima rest in an idyllic peace there in a garden gravesite. Liszt, who died in Bayreuth three years after Wagner, while visiting Cosima, is buried in the town cemetery a few blocks away.

The musical world toward the end of the nineteenth century revolved around Wagnerism. Everybody who was anybody went to Bayreuth and came back changed: Tchaikovsky and Grieg, for example. Composers' careers were established by being able to sight-read his difficult scores at the piano. In Paris, where Wagner had always been miserable, a *Revue wagnerienne* figured prominently in the intellectual life of poets and artists alike.

Yet while Wagner's own music is convincing almost anywhere you open a page, imitation Wagner is for the most part dreadful. It was not especially difficult to imitate Wagnerian volume or length or chord structure, and certainly not the motivic references, which had been around a long time. But Wagner's perfection of pacing and overall finesse eluded all but a few. Much work from the generation in his direct shadow is prolix and too loud. The symphonies of Anton Bruckner (1824–96), who idolized Wagner, are often that way, and Wagnerism stymied a whole generation of French composers, including at times even the best of them, César Franck and Camille Saint-Saëns.

By contrast, Georges Bizet, in his wonderful opera *Carmen* (1875), composed and produced before the late Wagner repertoire was commonplace, assimilated some of the most promising practices of both Wagner and Verdi as he knew them. *Carmen* is an opera of decided realism and progressive tendency. Several different levels of licentiousness (from the sexual adventure of the story to onstage smoking) come into play in *Car-*

men, and at the end she lies murdered on stage at the hands of her jealous lover, Don Jose. Parisian audiences found these assaults on their gentility rather too much, so at first *Carmen* was a colossal failure. Within a decade, however, *Carmen* shared the spotlight with late Verdi and late Wagner as guideposts to the future.

By and large, Wagnerian opera as a genre had a single successor, the theater work of Richard Strauss, treated below. The matter of coping with the broad range of musical issues engaged by Wagner, meanwhile, advanced first in Vienna, then in Paris once more.

*B*RAHMS, MAHLER, AND STRAUSS

As the century progressed, Vienna continued to savor the great composers and institutions of her distinguished past. The philharmonic societies grew strong and the state opera house was unsurpassed. In the press there was lively criticism of the locals and the many visiting foreigners, along with enthusiastic publicity when musical detective work uncovered additions to the repertoire, notably Schubert's lost works. Vienna tends to be conservative, preferring veneration of its accumulated artistic wealth to provocative or dangerous modes of expression. That is why Brahms, who at least on the face of it seemed to epitomize the time-honored principles of the past, found a good home there. It helps to explain the phenomenal success of the barons of the waltz business, the Strauss family, of whom Johann Strauss II became the uncontested "Waltz King" the world over. It explains, too, some of the turbulence surrounding the Vienna tenure of Brahms's most obvious successor, the composer/conductor Gustav Mahler. And it makes the confluence in the next generation of the pioneers of atonality all the more noteworthy.

JOHANNES BRAHMS (1833-97). I doubt if in the long run Beethoven, being Beethoven, gave much thought to his obligations as heir to Mozart and Haydn. Having been anointed Beethoven's successor weighed heavily on Brahms, however, and slowed the development of his self-assurance. But the result was worth the neurosis, for the four Brahms symphonies lie at the very heart of late nineteenth-century orchestral music.

www.prenhall.com/masterworks
composer profiles
Brahms

The lineage from Schumann to Brahms is as direct as if they were close kin. Brahms had been born into a not especially successful family of Hamburg musicians and spent his formative years doing piano hack work in Hamburg saloons. Then he came under the influence of the violin virtuoso Joseph Joachim and during their recital tours met the reigning musical aristocracy. With Liszt, unaccountably, the relationship fizzled. With the Schumanns it caught fire and burned brightly for the remainder of Robert's days. Brahms became a student of Robert and was treated nearly as a family member in the Schumann household. He helped Clara hold the family together during Schumann's decline and became in every respect his protégé and artistic heir.

After Schumann's death, Clara enjoyed a majestic widowhood, and she had a hand in encouraging a number of masterpieces by the composers who revered her. Brahms, for his part, became a confirmed and rather eccentric Viennese bachelor as his good looks declined into the unkempt chubbiness of his later years. In Vienna he conducted choruses, played the piano and contributed handsomely to its repertoire,

Brahms

composed in a broad spectrum of forms and genres, and participated in all sorts of good works. He became the central orchestral composer of his age.

The orchestra for which Brahms wrote was by late-century standards small, consisting of the usual strings with pairs of winds sometimes extended with contrabassoon, four horns, three trumpets, three trombones (nobody writes more dramatically for three trombones than Brahms), and very modest percussion. From this essentially conservative ensemble he coaxed a rich, idiomatic sonority, recognizable for the warmth of its string writing, especially in cellos and violas, and the gracious use of the woodwind choir. There is a dignity and sweep to Brahms and a wonderful freedom of register, where melodies move *through* the orchestra instead of being confined to the range of a single instrument.

Brahms was passionately curious about the musical past. He conducted choral works of the Renaissance and Baroque, collected composers' autographs, and supported the new profession of Musikwissenschaft—musicology. His interest in older music drew him to the passacaglia, which he uses and sonatafies in the finale of the Fourth Symphony, rooted in a bass he had found in Bach. It led him to write a German Requiem to texts from the Lutheran Bible (not the Latin rite), following a precedent set by the German Baroque composer Heinrich Schütz. And when he was perfecting his orchestral style, it gave him the idea for one of his major works of the period, the Variations on a Theme of Haydn, op. 56A. (Op. 56B is the same work for two pianos.)

BRAHMS: FROM VARIATIONS ON A THEME BY HAYDN, OP. 56A (1873)

THEME—VARIATIONS I–III—FINALE

In one of those historical twists that make Musikwissenschaft so interesting, the theme Brahms used is not by Haydn after all. What intrigued him about this St. Anthony Chorale was its unusual five-bar phrase structure.

The extended closing figure, with its repeated bell tones, was his own addition.

The St. Anthony Chorale, having come from a divertimento for winds, is stated simply by the woodwind choir. In the eight variations that follow, you very quickly become aware of Brahms's broad definition of variation practice, for by the halfway point it becomes difficult to track the original melody or to grasp with precision the relationship of what you are hearing to the original theme. In other words, Brahmsian variation is a highly developmental process expressed in the growth and mutation of all the building blocks of the work.

In Variation I, for instance, you can successfully hum the original melody back to yourself while the music plays. Brahms, meanwhile, focuses on other matters, such as the insistent five-stroke bell figure and the rhythmic tension between triplets in one group of strings and duplets in the other. The minor-mode Variation II focuses on the rhythmic cell of the theme's first three notes; then Variation III, in gentle legato textures, begins to brood and probe the sentimental features that will be developed from the seemingly square source. Starting at this point, the exact repeats are often abandoned in favor of written-out material, and the variations become full-scale submovements with radical changes of character. The ear is taken more by the differences than by the similarities.

For the finale, Brahms extracts from the bass line of the chorale a passacaglia bass, likewise in five-bar cycles:

The passacaglia sounds 16 times before being swept into a majestic recapitulation of the St. Anthony Chorale. During the first several cycles, Brahms adds layer upon layer of orchestral force, in fine imitative counterpoint, until all the instruments have entered. Here, at cycle 7 (00:59), there emerges over the passacaglia bass its own diminution, a figure that will, after the contrastive center section (01:19), effect the retransition to the chorale tune.

The grand, flowery conclusion is decorated with lacy trails of scalar sixteenths. This is characteristic of Brahms's rapturous closes (a spirit to which Mahler will later aspire); compare the effect with the cascades at the end of his famous *Academic Festival* overture.

Listening Chart

 CD 3, TR 5-9

Johannes Brahms (1833–97)
Variations on a Theme by Haydn, op. 56a (1873)
  Theme: Chorale St. Antoni (Andante)—I. Poco più animato—
  II. Più vivace—III. Con moto—Finale: Andante

For: piccolo, 2 flutes, 2 oboes, 2 clarinets, 2 bassoons, contrabassoon; 4 horns, 2 trumpets; timpani, triangle; strings

Type: Theme and Variations
Meter: ²⁄₄ (Th., Var. I-III), ¢ (Finale)
Key: B♭ major; Var. II in minor mode
Duration: 02:00, 01:16, 00:56, 01:54, 03:44

The St. Anthony Chorale, though probably not by Haydn, offers particular interest for variation in its five-measure phrase lengths and repeated notes (like tolling bells) at the end. After the theme come eight variations and a big contrapuntal finale on a passacaglia bass. The excerpt includes the theme, variations I–III, and finale.

00:00	**Theme**	Andante. 10-bar theme A (5 + 5), departure and return (B = b + a' + cl. fig.).
	A	Homophonic woodwinds and horns with pizz. cello and bass; good
00:20	A rep.	example of antecedent (*p*) and consequent (*f*).
00:40	B	Oboes lead the departure, *p*, answered *pp*;
00:57	a	rounded by full ww. and brass, then a
01:05	cl. fig.	grand extension of 4 bars, as though a peal of bells, and a diminuendo
01:19	B rep.	of five strokes, reflecting the 5-bar phrases of the theme.
	Var. I	
00:00	A	Poco più animato. The 5-stroke bell figure introduces the variation and
00:13	A rep.	becomes its main motive. Strings, legato, rising and falling.
00:25	B	Bold strokes of brass, then a long fading descrescendo. In the strings,
00:50	B rep.	tension between 4 eighth notes (vns.) and 6 sixteenths (vla., cello).
	Var. II	
00:00	A	Più vivace. Minor mode. Features the theme's dotted-8th-and-16th
00:09	A'	rhythm. Clarinets and bassoons gallop with the figure; pizzicato in bass.
00:18	B	Legato responses to the *forte* outbursts of the main motive. Again, a
00:36	B rep.	diminuendo, folding-up close.
	Var. III	
00:00	A	Con moto. Returns to major mode; theme in expansive legato phrases.
00:18	A rep.	The repeat written out, with flutes and bassoons in decorative dialogue.
00:36	B	Romantic, chromatically inflected treatment of the head motive.
01:13	B'	As before, decorative dialogues for the repeat: low strings, then ww.
	Finale	Andante. Governed by a five-bar passacaglia, based on chorale theme.
00:00	part 1	8 cycles of the passacaglia: a big orchestral crescendo, smooth and gorgeous,
00:39		then tutti, with timpani; dotted figure becomes imitative in upper instruments.
01:19	part 2	Contrastive center section: decrescendo; triplet-dominated dialogue.
02:08		Minor mode: in variation practice, nearly always suggesting end at hand.
02:35	part 3	From the gruff tutti, the woodwinds emerge with the major-mode head motive.
02:48		Full-blown recapitulation, with cascading winds.
03:05		The original closing figure, with upward rockets in strings.
03:13		Bell tones ebb away; last rocket (03:29) to big tutti close.

Organic variation and transformation of given material, as Brahms practiced it, became a cornerstone of Viennese compositional practice in the new century.

The First and Second Symphonies (in C minor, op. 68, 1876; and D major, op. 73, 1877) followed in due course. Brahms had prepared diligently for his debut as symphonist, thinking his way carefully through the issues of musical vocabulary as they had mutated since Beethoven and Schumann. There are many parallels between Brahms and Beethoven, but the principal structural debt is probably to Schumann. The famous "Brahms sound" is uniquely his own, a function not merely of the way he regards the orchestra but also of an expansive view of form that brings his symphonies to 45 or 50 minutes in length. Many themes find their way into Brahms's orchestral movements, making them sound unhurried, rhapsodic, free of some of the urgency of Viennese sonata practice. At the same time, the multimovement works have a clear overall coherence, a sense of interconnection from beginning to end. Brahms's view of thematic recall is much less sweeping than Wagner's Leitmotivs and Berlioz's *idée fixe,* but in all the Brahms symphonies the intermovement relationships are so strongly established that the four movements can belong only to each other.

www.prenhall.com/masterworks
recommended listening

RECOMMENDED LISTENING:

Brahms: Symphony No. 3 in F Major, op. 90 (1883)

The Third and Fourth Symphonies come from the first half of the 1880s. Even though Brahms then ceased to compose symphonies, he nevertheless continued to write symphonically—that is, to compose orchestral works of grand scale and gesture. This is the case with both the Second Piano Concerto—a formidable work in four movements that seems to keep trying to become a symphony with piano—and the unusual Double Concerto for violin, cello, and orchestra, his last orchestral work. Additionally there is a large Brahms repertoire of piano solos, chamber music, and Lieder, and the important German Requiem (1868), a mid-career work for chorus, soloists, and orchestra that, like the Haydn Variations, shows great genius just reaching its full potential.

People liked to think of Wagner and Brahms as rival commanders on some imagined field of musical battle, or as spokespersons, respectively, for the musical left and right. That characterization is useful only in that it emphasizes the great difference of musical purpose that separated their intellectual worlds. Both scoffed at the notion that they were, in any real fashion, rivals. Moreover, the kinds of paths to the future that Brahms showed in his orchestral writing were in their own way just as important as Wagner's. And it was certainly more practical to belong to the Brahms camp. Many, many more composers—among them Dvořák, Tchaikovsky, and Elgar—aspired to emulate Brahms's example than Wagner's.

GUSTAV MAHLER (1860–1911). A generation younger than Brahms, Mahler was the next major symphonist in the Viennese tradition. Seething with inner turmoil— over life and death, his own Jewishness, fears of sexual inadequacy, and so on—Mahler was the titan of Austro-Hungarian music at the junction of the centuries. Schoenberg said, rightly, that if Mahler had lived a little longer it would be thought that he, and not

Schoenberg, had discovered the voice of the twentieth century. As one of the two or three most important conductors of his age, Mahler was a direct participant in the intellectual ferment that closed Romanticism, and his immense musical canvases reflect the sometimes terrifying conundrums of that brilliant but violent time.

He rose quickly through the ranks of orchestras and opera houses (Kassel, Prague, Leipzig, Budapest, Hamburg) to the Vienna Opera. There he revivified the house, especially in the period of his collaborations (1903–1907) with the designer Alfred Roller, with whom he produced vital new readings of Mozart, Beethoven, and Wagner. But Mahler's tastes were expensive and his ethnic origins a liability in that growingly anti-Semitic epoch. He was unpopular with the Vienna Philharmonic. To escape this deteriorating environment, he accepted engagements in New York to conduct the Metropolitan Opera and the Philharmonic. His experience there was unhappy on several counts, but mostly because his health was rapidly declining. In late February 1911 he gave up New York to return to Vienna, but died just after reaching home.

Mahler was one of the dwindling band of composer/conductors who could manage the demands of both careers. From 1901 he returned every summer to his villa in the Austrian Alps, working in his "composing hut." During the concert season he would correct and polish his drafts. Only a compulsive personality would have kept at such a schedule so diligently.

In 1902 Mahler married Alma Schindler, a woman of similar artistic temperament who helped sustain his creativity. The marriage was tempestuous, however, and troubled him enough to prompt him to spend an afternoon in consultation with Freud, in 1910. The death of his elder daughter in 1907 coincided with the onset of the heart condition that hastened his end.

Virtually all Mahler's composition investigates the relationship of song and symphony. Of opera he had doubtlessly had enough by conducting other people's work; he had even less to do with chamber music than Wagner. The symphonies take their course as chapters in Mahler's epic internal struggles: the First and Second Symphonies a long study of life, death, and the promise of resurrection, the Fifth through Seventh a kind of trilogy concerning darkness turned to light. Some of this Mahler sets forth in program-like explanatory notes and movement titles, supplied after the fact to lead concert audiences through his daunting designs. The rest becomes clear from his correspondence and the memories of later associates. While Mahler's symphonies are not storytelling works in the sense of the *Fantastique,* they are deep psychological studies that return to the origin of Romantic thought: the heroic struggle.

Recommended Listening:

Mahler: Symphony No. 1 in D Major (1888)

www.prenhall.com/masterworks
recommended listening

In the period after the First and Second Symphonies, Mahler's intellectual world was dominated by a collection of poems from German folklore called *Des Knaben Wunderhorn* ("The Youth's Magic Horn"). Fashioning music for the poems seemed irresistible, and during the "Wunderhorn years" these songs of trumpet-playing corporals and childlike views of heaven and hell found orchestral settings and worked their way into his symphonies. Mahler's Fourth, for example, concludes with a quiet movement for soprano and orchestra, a song of wide-eyed delight at the joys of heaven. His later *Kindertotenlieder* ("Songs on the Death of Children") and other songs to texts of Friedrich Rückert are increasingly sinister, and the symphonies from the Fifth through the Ninth grow progressively cerebral and abstract. Mahler's next-to-last finished work, part song cycle, part symphony, is *Das Lied von der Erde* ("The Song of the Earth"), settings of ancient Chinese poetry in German translation for tenor, contralto, and orchestra. He left the beginnings of a tenth symphony, which has been fleshed out by disciples and is occasionally heard in the concert hall.

Mahler

So personal and so difficult is Mahler's later work that his untimely death threatened its oblivion. The Mahler symphonies were kept alive by Willem Mengelberg of the Concertgebouw Orchestra in Amsterdam, who offered the first Mahler cycle in 1920. In the 1960s Leonard Bernstein became a sort of high prophet of Mahler in the United States and left an influential recording of all the symphonies. Another ardent champion was Bruno Walter (1876–1962), Mahler's assistant conductor in Hamburg, who also produced an impressive discography.

Besides Mahler the other great post-Wagnerian was **Richard Strauss (1864–1949)**, who, by contrast, lived to popularize his own works—well past the end of World War II. In his first period Strauss was equally post-Lisztian, achieving his celebrity through a series of single-movement symphonic poems: *Don Juan, Death and Transfiguration, Till Eulenspiegel's Merry Pranks,* and *Also sprach Zarathustra.* Here the sequence of recognizably symphonic submovements (allegro, slow movement, scherzo, finale) is more or less retained, but they are folded into an overarching programmatic design.

Also sprach Zarathustra ("Thus Spake Zarathustra"), for example, finds its point of origin in Nietzsche's book of the same title. The curtain-raising beginning, which you know as the loud music from the film *2001: A Space Odyssey,* is that of the prophet Zoroaster rising up to descend to earth. *Till Eulenspiegel's Merry Pranks,* once you have learned what they are, can easily be heard, right down to his last distant giggle on the hangman's gallows.

The downside of the Strauss symphonic poems is that they are all variants of the rapidly waning birth-to-death idiom: youthful exuberance, the discovery of love, battles with adversaries, the finding of wisdom, the pain of death mingled with the promise of a transfigured existence. Considered singly, the Strauss tone poems work extremely well. In their totality, the idea gets old soon enough, and Tchaikovsky and lots of others in the period were doing the same kind of thing at the same time.

It got old for Strauss, too, and at mid-career he abandoned the symphonic poem and became primarily a composer of operas. His intense, fabulously adorned music was altogether suited to the theater, and there he was able to develop as personal and idiomatic a style as Mozart, Verdi, and Wagner had found. In *Der Rosenkavalier* ("The Knight of the Rose") the music glistens with the brilliance of the silver rose presented, in Act II, to the young Sophie as a token of her engagement. This is as much a matter of musical color as of key and melody; all three leading characters—the Feldmarschallin (a field marshal's widow), Sophie, and the teenage rose-bearing knight, Octavian—are soprano parts.

Strauss and his wife Pauline, who in her time had been a fine singer, lived to enjoy their grandeur. It's part of his legend that at the very end of his life Strauss composed four wonderful orchestral songs, ostensibly on Nature and the passing of the seasons, but in fact a glamorous *adieu* to life and to the Romantic century, where he walks hand in hand with his loved one toward the rosy morning of afterlife. These *Four Last Songs* were first performed posthumously, by the soprano Kirsten Flagstad with Wilhelm Furtwängler conducting (London, 1950).

Richard Strauss, incidentally, was not related to the waltz-composing Strausses of Vienna.

HE NATIONALISTS

Nationalism was first and most urgently expressed in central Europe, playground of the world powers. You saw its beginnings in the music of Chopin, a Pole, and Liszt, a Hungarian. But it was the Czechs who forged the earliest viable school of nationalist music, and for overtly political purpose. Czech music is that of the people of Bohemia and Moravia. (In the colonizing days of the United States, Moravian missionaries came to Georgia, Pennsylvania, and North Carolina, bringing with them a handsome musical establishment, which still thrives.) Bohemia is a land of some interesting mythology, but more significantly the scene of the heroic revolution of the Christian Hussites, who sought religious liberty for Bohemia after their leader, the reformer Jan Hus (1369–1415), was burned alive. Its great river, the Moldau (or Vltava), is dear to the imagination of the Czechs and putative home of sprites and nymphs.

Terezie Rückaufová as Mařenka in *The Bartered Bride*

BEDŘICH SMETANA (1824–84). The Bohemian composer Smetana devoted his life to promoting and building a National Theater in Prague, then to writing operas that might be performed in it. The original structure burned down a couple of years after it opened, as theaters of that period were prone to do; the replacement still stands, proudly, as one of Prague's many monuments to musical civilization. But in 1866, when Smetana introduced his masterpiece, *The Bartered Bride,* the company was still called the Provisional Theater.

 SMETANA: "FURIANT," FROM *THE BARTERED BRIDE* (1866)

What was politically significant about *The Bartered Bride* was its local color: peasant subject matter, Czech language, and superb dance music. In the Furiant, for example, the focus is on treating triple meter in both its half-note and quarter-note multiples, setting up strong *hemiola* relationships. The dance takes place in the local tavern.

The Bartered Bride concerns the young lovers Jeník and Mařenka, whose promise of happiness seems compromised when the village marriage broker arranges a match between Mařenka and the wealthy landowner's son. Jeník barters away his bride for 700 florins on the condition that the groom be the landowner's son. Then he takes both the bride and the money, for it turns out that he is himself the long-lost elder son.

The form is the traditional dance-and-trio, with some novel twists. The waltz-like trio, for instance, is built over a four-bar repeating figure in the cellos that sounds at first like a theme and then, once the woodwinds begin to urge themselves into some romantically distant tonal regions, like an ostinato working hard to stay in touch with the proceedings. Smetana proceeds to investigate all the possible harmonic interpretations of the little motive.

And once the main dance theme has returned and the dance-trio-dance form is thus assured, the motive blares forth again from the brass, in a bold *réunion des thèmes.*

The music that established Smetana's international presence, however, was his series of six symphonic poems on Bohemian subject matter, *My Fatherland.* Of these the second, *The Moldau,* retains exceptional popularity. It describes the course of the Bohemian river from its origin in two springs on through its majestic arrival in Prague, where it flows past the mighty citadel of the Bohemian kings. One of the main reasons *The Moldau* is so popular is that it's simple and direct—innocent, you might say. You're welcome to follow the changing riverscape in your mind's eye, and the lovely main theme—that of the river itself—lends itself to big crescendos and sits well over running-water figuration. This theme serves to anchor the symphonic poem by returning between the other rhapsodic episodes: a passing hunt, the polka of a peasant wedding, nymphs bathing in the moonlight, the rapids. At the end, *The Moldau* reaches its greatest breadth and passes the Vyšehrad castle. The river flows gently away.

Listening Chart

 CD 3, TR 10

Bedřich Smetana (1824–84)
The Bartered Bride **(1866)**
    Ballet from act II: Furiant

Type: Dance-and-trio
Meter: $\frac{3}{4}$
Key: F major
Duration: 02:09

The dance takes place in a tavern, the music focusing on hemiola effects and an unusual trio ostinato.

00:00	**Introduction**	Sets forth the metric hemiola, and jolted by the empty bars.
	Dance	A highly stylized descendant of the 3rd-movement dance type.
00:05	A	An 8-bar phrase (4 + 4), stating the main theme.
00:11	B	Departure (B) and return (a): thus the rounded binary typical
00:14	a	of two-part dance forms.
00:20	B rep.	
00:29	transition	Two bars of rebound.
	Trio	D♭ major. Gentler and waltz-like, abandoning the bumptious hemiolas.
00:31	C	The 4-bar ostinato in cellos and bassoons continues through C and D.
00:45	D	Again, departure and rounding return (00:57), thick with harmonic wandering.
01:00	D rep.	
01:15	transition	Long crescendo with triangle as the main theme regains its grip.
	Dance d. c.	
01:29	ABa	Much the same as before.
01:42	A + trio	The trio's ostinato returns in a kind of *réunion des thèmes*.
01:53	**Coda**	Big tutti: Note the fine percussion: timpani, triangle, cymbals, bass drum.

RECOMMENDED LISTENING:

Smetana: **The Moldau** *(1874)*

www.prenhall.com/masterworks
recommended listening

Smetana would have been of more use to the nationalist movement had he not gone crazy, the indirect result of syphilis and the direct result of a high whining in his ears. By the premiere of his opera *Libuše* in 1881 he had become something of a street person, and was not offered a ticket to his own show.

But by that time the principles of Bohemian nationalism had been well understood, and other composers had begun to take up the cause. Chief among these was **Antonín Dvořák (1841–1904)**. His popularity during his own lifetime can be compared with that of Weber and Mendelssohn, and today many people are likely to name Dvořák with Brahms and Tchaikovsky as the triumvirate of great late-century symphonists, forgetting, I am sorry to say, Mahler.

Dvořák, like Verdi, was a simple man. His musical proclivities were the same as Smetana's, and his technique was more polished. His rise to success in Prague was thus meteoric. Brahms learned of his work and the two became friends, giving Dvořák a useful connection in the world that opened outward from Vienna.

The Slavonic Dances op. 46 (1878; a second set is op. 72, 1887) earned Dvořák his international following and a certain measure of wealth. They were modeled after Brahms's Hungarian Dances and, like them, circulated widely in publication as piano duets; they remain today near the top of the list of best-selling classical recordings. Dvořák's prolific period from 1883 to 1895 yielded the mature symphonies (nos. 7–9), three concert overtures, and a cello concerto. During this time he made three major visits to England, was appointed professor of composition at the Prague Conservatory, and was awarded two honorary doctor's degrees (at Cambridge, and Prague, both in 1891). In 1892 he accepted an invitation to come to New York as director of an institution called the National Conservatory of Music. Between their time in the metropolis and summer holidays in the Czech community of Spillville, Iowa, the Dvořáks learned at least the high spots of American folklore: the pioneer spirit, Longfellow's poem *Hiawatha,* and what was then being termed the Negro spiritual.

Dvořák called the symphony he composed here "From the New World." Additionally the wonderful Cello Concerto was written in the United States, as was a string quartet, now called the "American." The interesting thing about all these works is that the folk-like elements are as Bohemian as they are American. You may think you hear strains of "Swing Low, Sweet Chariot" in one of the themes of the "New World" Symphony, and it's true that the main subject of its second movement became the pseudo-spiritual "Goin' Home." But that's as far as it goes: The "New World" is not so much a catalog of Americanisms as a big cyclic work with recurring motives, Berlioz- and Liszt-fashion, and what is American about the music is a strongly sensed but rather vaguely defined outdoor character.

All of which proves a simple truth about nationalistic styles. Whatever culture they say they represent, they tend to boil down to the same characteristics: strongly felt dance patterns, village band effects, and melodies based on exotic pitch collections. Where language or subject matter is involved, the nationality is clear. But if you stop to think about it, a polonaise, a mazurka, a Hungarian rhapsody, and a Slavonic dance have much in common.

Dvořák went back to Prague to serve as director of the Conservatory and to finish his days in the peasant simplicity he had come to love. Of his several successors the most interesting was Leos Janáček (1854–1928), another self-effacing composer who burst into the world's consciousness with the Prague performance of his opera *Jenůfa* in 1916. Its success, coupled with a platonic love affair that began when he was in his 60s, led to an artistic rebirth with the curious effect that virtually all of his lasting works postdate his 65th birthday.

In developments elsewhere, Italian nationalism played itself out, not surprisingly, on the opera stage. In Norway the career of Edvard Grieg (1843–1907) roughly paralleled that of Dvořák. Grieg's most famous work is his Piano Concerto, modeled on Liszt and Schumann; his best music is probably to be found in his piano miniatures, notably the Norwegian dances. The *Peer Gynt* suites come from his incidental music for the play by the great Norwegian writer Henrik Ibsen (1828–1906). You will read a little later of the next generation of nationalists: the Hungarians Zoltán Kodály (1882–1967) and Béla Bartók (1881–1945) and the Finn Jan, or Jean, Sibelius (1865–1957). Roughly contemporaneous too were the Iberians: Albéniz, Falla, Rodrigo, Turina.

While we are thinking along these lines, ponder for a moment the British imperial style, as represented Sir Edward Elgar (1857–1934). The *Pomp and Circumstance* marches and *Imperial March* are the musical artifacts of Queen Victoria in all her glory, of the British experience in India and elsewhere throughout the world. The *Enigma Variations* (1899), meanwhile, have an important place in post-Brahmsian variation practice. Elgar's followers were Ralph Vaughan Williams, Gustav Holst, and eventually Benjamin Britten.

It may surprise you not to see an American nationalist school taking shape in the very period when the United States emerged from its cocoon and started to become a world power (taking the Philippines, Cuba, Puerto Rico, and Guam away from Spain in 1898, for example). But American composers of classical music continued to look to Europe for models, and true Americana was born in grittier venues than opera houses and concert halls.

USSIAN NATIONALISM: THE MIGHTY HANDFUL

Russia had emerged in the eighteenth century into the community of civilized European nations—though still curiously prone to government by assassination—and by the end of the nineteenth century was a powerhouse of new music. Moscow, St. Petersburg, and Riga (in Latvia) were regular stops for western European artists on tour. Liszt came to Russia, for example, and so did Wagner and Berlioz and the Schumanns. There were important opera houses employing foreign artists in all three cities.

The Russians learned a great deal from this influx of foreigners, but the invention of a national school was their own work, carefully planned, much discussed among friends and in the press, and carried out with military precision. Administrative expertise was brought to the movement by the pianist/composer Nicolai Rubinstein, and the polemics supplied by the journalist Vladimir Stasov, while various noblemen paid the bills. Step by step the Russians established national conservatories, philharmonic societies, and music journals in the two capital cities, and they encouraged music publishers to take native composers under their wing. (This is much the same strategy that Mendelssohn and his associates had advanced in the 1830s and 1840s to make Leipzig the center of the musical universe.) They also deliberated the principles of a national music, looking especially to develop opera on local subject matter. There is no dearth of local color in the case of Russia, which sits at the confluence of Asia and Europe. An inbred sense of panorama and wilderness is a part of every Russian.

For a spiritual godfather, Russian composers looked to Mikhail Glinka, composer of the Russian-language operas *Ruslan and Ludmila* and *A Life for the Tsar.* (The overture to *Ruslan and Ludmila,* a popular curtain-raiser at orchestra concerts, bespeaks the verve and tunefulness of the incipient style, and has a strong family resemblance to similar works by the Czechs.) The central composers in the school were dubbed by Stasov the "Mighty Handful" (*moguchaya kuchka*), or "The Five": Alexander Borodin, Modest Mussorgsky, Nicolai Rimsky-Korsakov, and the lesser known César Cui and Mili Balakirev. Borodin (1833–87), a brilliant scientist by profession, worked much of his adult life on *Prince Igor,* a local-color opera on the warring of rival tribes in central Asia. The great tableau from Act II is a suite of Polovtsian Dances, which first alerted the Parisians to the magnitude of musical developments to the north. (You will recognize tunes like "Stranger in Paradise" in the Polovtsian Dances, for Borodin's music was the starting point for the entirely unrelated Broadway musical *Kismet.*)

Mussorgsky

One of the noblest voices of Russian nationalism was that of Modest Mussorgsky (1839–81). Self-taught, thoroughly primitive, he was at the end ravaged and maddened by alcoholism, as his portrait suggests. His subject matter is thoroughly and provocatively Russian, and his melodic idiom and harmonic daring has come to characterize much of what we mean by Russian nationalism. Mussorgsky's opera *Boris Godunov,* about the medieval czar driven mad by guilt over having murdered the rightful heir, is in some respects the movement's most characteristic work: primitive in sonority, driven by patterns of Russian speech, and hypnotic in dramatic intent.

But of the Mighty Handful the first among the equals was Nicolai Rimsky-Korsakov (1844–1908), the longest running, most prolific, and most broadly exposed composer of the group. Both Mussorgsky and Borodin died with their work in disarray, and it was Rimsky-Korsakov who had *Prince Igor, Boris Godunov,* and Mussorgsky's *Night on Bald Mountain* finished and saw to their production and publication. This self-effacing work alone has earned Rimsky-Korsakov an enduring place in the story of Russian music—even if his adjustments tend to blur Mussorgsky's stern, often dissonant voice, and today we tend to prefer our Mussorgsky, when we can get it, pure.

Rimsky-Korsakov was a fine composer as well. While his operas have not survived into the modern Western repertoire, the orchestral showpieces are frequently heard. In *Scheherazade* you hear the brilliant side of the Russian style, here evoking the *Arabian Nights.* The poetic device is to have the voice of *Scheherazade* portrayed by the violin; the lithe, sinewy phrase becomes her tale-telling motive that returns again and again as the four orchestral movements wend their course. The excellence of Rimsky-Korsakov's orchestration was much admired, for he was diligently attuned to what the gifted instrumentalists around him were able to do. He particularly enjoyed peppering his works with virtuoso cadenzas for the principal players.

Rimsky-Korsakov, finally, was the best composition teacher of his time and place. Among his students was the twentieth-century master Igor Stravinsky.

CHAIKOVSKY, PUCCINI

What of the most important Russian of them all, Piotr Tchaikovsky (1840–93)? Simply put, his goals and priorities were broader than those of the Mighty Handful, and he was not especially welcome in their circle. Tchaikovsky's inner sympathies lay more with the great European symphonists—he favored bold, discursive sonata forms prone to dart down unexpected paths—than with the more direct and certainly more ornamental inclinations of his countrymen. Like Mahler, Tchaikovsky had a generally tragic attitude. He had a right to his despair. His personal life story included an apparently unresolved homosexuality, a poorly conceived attempt at marriage, a bittersweet romance by correspondence with an aristocratic patroness (Nadezhda von Meck, who later would employ Debussy as piano teacher for her children), and a couple of suicide attempts. We cannot avoid finding psychological turmoil at the root of the last three of Tchaikovsky's six symphonies (especially the last, called *Pathétique*), and perhaps in the famous Piano Concerto as well. Yet Tchaikovsky also wrote waltzes, marches, serenades, and the beloved Christmas ballet *The Nutcracker*—music of innocence and even glee.

Tchaikovsky

 ### TCHAIKOVSKY: *ROMEO AND JULIET* OVERTURE-FANTASY (1869)

Tchaikovsky's orchestral works follow ordinary sonata design with groups of themes that develop and recapitulate in more or less the usual manner. But with Tchaikovsky the themes always take precedence. Form and harmonic organization are harnessed to promote the narrative impact of the melodies. The love music in *Romeo and Juliet,* its second theme, ends up swamping the strife of the first theme, in keeping with the moral of the story; likewise, in keeping with the old love-in-death apotheosis at the end, it is transformed at the end into a celestial setting, complete with harp. In a way this is Tchaikovsky's weakness, for one is seldom captivated by the formal adventure of his one-movement works. Yet he has a knowing way of stringing tunes together and is an expert at blockbusting sound effects, as in the famous cannon fire and cathedral bells at the end of the *1812 Overture*.

RECOMMENDED LISTENING:

Tchaikovsky: Violin Concerto in D Major, op. 35 (1878)

Tchaikovsky was a prolific composer whose work also includes substantial contribution to the opera repertoire (*Eugene Onegin*, 1879; *Queen of Spades*, 1890) and of course the ballet (*Swan Lake*, 1877; *Sleeping Beauty*, 1890; and *The Nutcracker*, 1892). With these he dominated the czar's opera house and the famous Bolshoi and Mariinsky companies.

Listening Chart

 **CD 3, TR 11**

Piotr Tchaikovsky (1840–93)
Romeo and Juliet Overture-Fantasy (1869)

For: piccolo, 2 flutes, 2 clarinets, English horn, 2 bassoons; 4 horns, 2 trumpets, 3 trombones, tuba; timpani, percussion; harp; strings.

Type: sonata
Meter: $\frac{4}{4}$
Key: C major
Duration: 19:19

Tchaikovsky's overture-fantasy on the great tragedy of Shakespeare is characterized particularly by its majestic love theme—the second theme of the sonata form. The introduction, suggestive of plainchant, evokes Friar Lawrence in his cell; the sonata form begins with the sword-fight music.

Slow **Introduction**		
00:00	pt. 1	Low ww. suggest a chant phrase; continuation in strings.
01:10	pt. 2	Second phrase, high ww., cello ctrpt.; harp cadences.
02:03	pt. 3	Violins pizz.; the chant in high ww. Same continuation as before.
03:05	pt. 4	Similar to pt. 2, in high strings. Timpani introduces transition.
03:56	transition	Material gathers in intensity and speed; timp. roll; regathers.
Exposition		
05:15	**Th. I** a	The furious swordplay of Capulets and Montagues.
05:38	b	Fugal treatment of the theme. Cymbals = clash of swords.
06:16	a	Theme restated as climax, with cymbals.
06:37	transition	Fragments away, the strife settling, into:
07:26	**Th. II** c	Love music of Romeo and Juliet: English horn and violas suggest Romeo's register.
07:48	d	The delicate violin palpitations suggest Juliet's uncertainty, which blossoms into:
08:31	c	Her statement of the love theme, high winds. Horn throbs. — Interstatement. — Restatement.
09:32	**Cl. th.**	A tranquil closure, with lovely bassoon and English horn work.
Development		
10:35	part 1	Th. I (vns.) and introductory chorale (horn) commingled.
11:48	part 2	Th. I elements exchanged; frenzied string scales.
12:02	part 3	Brass eruptions, swords clashing again. Furious charge into:
Recapitulation		
12:35	**Th. I**	As before. But the interlude is Juliet's (see d, above).
13:33	**Th. II**	The love theme, seemingly at full volume and passion . . .
14:13	climax	Another, even more climactic, statement of the love theme.
14:56	review	The third statement of the love theme yields to a review of the other elements in the sonata and collapse to timp. roll.
16:23	**Coda**	The death sequence. Rattle of death in the timpani ostinato.
17:17	cont'd.	Woodwind chorale, as though suggesting funeral music.
18:10	apotheosis	The star-crossed lovers united in paradise.

Scholars are still speculating on and researching the cause of Tchaikovsky's death, generally attributed to cholera contracted from tainted water. One theory holds that Tchaikovsky was ordered to commit suicide, following a homosexual liaison, by a tribunal of classmates from the School of Jurisprudence he had attended. Whatever the case, he died a little over a week after the first performance of his *Pathétique,* a symphony with a program he preferred to leave enigmatic. That performance was a failure, but a few days after his death it was triumphantly received.

Nowadays we tend to be more comfortable with a factual acknowledgment of artists' sexual inclinations and expect that that information might lead us to some deeper understanding of their art. We are not shocked to discover that our favorite artists have sex lives, and we take it as probable fact that homosexuality is common among artists. But until the second half of this century the homosexual had little choice but to live in secrecy and terror. In England, for example, the sodomy laws that brought Oscar Wilde to public spectacle and subsequent ruin a few years after Tchaikovsky were still in force when the English composer Benjamin Britten and the tenor Peter Pears began to live together in the 1940s. Equally celebrated musicians of their generation were thoroughly closeted.

Verdi's successor, **Giacomo Puccini (1858–1924)**, was a box-office magnet. Critics, uncomfortable with his vast commercial success, have noted the dramatic limitations of Puccini's operas, as though he had found in the *bel canto* tradition a series of buttons he could push to good effect at the cash register. The Berkeley musicologist-critic Joseph Kerman became famous (in part) for calling Puccini's *Tosca* a "shabby little shocker." It's true that Puccini is long on panting love duets and death scenes where the heroine props herself up in bed to sing one last time. Pavarotti's career is built on a half-dozen Puccini showstoppers. But most stage music, Broadway shows included, depends on such features and has for centuries; one might as well complain that Richard Strauss operas over-sentimentalize the noble Wagner truths. And the stories of Puccini's two best operas—in *La Bohème,* romance and death among struggling artists in nineteenth-century Paris; in *Madama Butterfly,* after a play by the American writer David Belasco, the tragic affair between a U.S. Navy lieutenant and a Japanese geisha—are, all told, great fun, even though both heroines expire by the final curtain.

www.prenhall.com/masterworks
recommended listening

RECOMMENDED LISTENING:

Puccini: Excerpts from Madama Butterfly *(1904)*

Based on the success of *Madama Butterfly* in New York, the Metropolitan Opera invited Puccini to compose a work especially for the house. He chose another play by Belasco, *The Girl of the Golden West,* set in a California mining community. (Among the characters in this unlikely story for Italian post-Romanticism are Minnie and Nick, owner and bartender, respectively, of the Polka Saloon.)

The Italians called their operas that dealt with the harsh realities of life *verismo.* Puccini touched on verismo in *La Bohème* and the others, but the better summary of his overall style is that it represents the last breath of true Romanticism.

PARIS, AGAIN: DEBUSSY, RAVEL, THE BALLETS RUSSES, STRAVINSKY

When we think in linear, chronological order about music after Beethoven, we tend to see dynastic arrangements like those of Schumann-Brahms-Mahler or Weber-Wagner-Strauss. This tends to make the dawn of so fascinating a composer as Claude Debussy seems a good deal more disruptive than it actually was. In France, since the heady decade of the *Fantastique* and Chopin, and Liszt all mingling together, music had gone confidently ahead. The French never doubted the primacy of their operatic stage, and one has the feeling that bringing Verdi and Wagner to Paris was deemed as much a favor to foreigners as an opportunity for the locals. French composers were just as motivated by the dream of a billing at the Opéra as Brahms was by the necessity to write, as it were, Beethoven's Tenth. Berlioz's lyric tragedy *Les Troyens* ("The Trojans") was followed by the best of all the *opéras comiques,* Bizet's *Carmen* (*L'Arlésienne,* "The Maid of Arles"—was merely a play with incidental music by Bizet); Charles Gounod's *Faust*—French opera's all-time greatest hit—and *Roméo et Juliette;* and Saint-Saëns' *Samson et Dalila.* All of these managed to answer the French demand for spectacle and ballet with music that held its own in the increasingly competitive world market.

But the better French composers were thoughtfully considering other areas of the repertoire as well. César Franck (1822–90) was an important composer for pipe organ, an instrument undergoing its own sort of Renaissance at the time, largely through the work of the organ builder Aristide Cavaillé-Coll. A whole movement called the French Organ School emerged in the form of works for these fabulous monster instruments of the mid- and late-century. Charles-Marie Widor's "Toccata," from his Fifth Organ Symphony, is an admired example of the style. The French also continued to investigate the programmatic symphony (Vincent D'Indy: *Symphony on a French Mountain Air,* 1886) and tone poem (Paul Dukas: *The Sorcerer's Apprentice,* 1897). Franck, toward the end of his career, composed the fine Symphony in D Minor and the Symphonic Variations for Piano and Orchestra.

Camille Saint-Saëns (1835–1921), a child prodigy with gifts the equal of Mozart's, had a career spanning over 70 years, which included writing an early film score. He was a major literary figure and a sought-after piano soloist for much of his long life, the Leonard Bernstein, you might say, of his several generations. In his serious symphonies and concertos, Saint-Saëns assimilated both the great French orchestral tradition he had inherited from Berlioz and the Germanic style in a kind of Wagnerism filtered through Liszt, his close personal friend.

His *Danse macabre,* a one-movement tone poem for violin and orchestra, remains popular and is, like Mussorgsky's *Night on Bald Mountain,* prone to be heard at Halloween. *Danse macabre* marks the debut of the xylophone in the symphony orchestra, used in this case for its ability to evoke the rattling of bones; in the original score Saint-Saëns leaves a charming note describing exactly what a xylophone is.

Saint-Saëns forbade the publication of his "zoologic fantasy," *Le Carnaval des animaux,* fearing—correctly, as it turns out—that it would be preferred to his more serious work, and it did not appear in print until 1922.

Confronting Wagner, as Saint-Saëns and Franck and their circle did, was a necessary step of the era, even for the French. But the truth is that Wagnerism is basically un-French. Some of the more enterprising Parisians were working equally hard to broaden the traditional menu of opera and orchestral concerts into a thriving life of chamber music and song. Gabriel Fauré (1845–1924) was an early visionary of the modern French school, particularly in his songs and song cycles. His subtle but influential futurisms centered on pastel splashes of modality and dissonance and the idiomatic use of the French language itself. He was also politically active on behalf of French music, as director of the Paris Conservatoire and one of the founders of the Société Nationale de Musique (1871), devoted to sponsoring first performances.

CLAUDE DEBUSSY (1862–1918). It was at the junction of the nineteenth and twentieth centuries that, born and raised in Wagner's shadow, Debussy suddenly turned anti-Wagnerian. His position was based not so much on racial origin or advanced theory as the simple fact that he found the bellowing and the animal skins distasteful. His mind was more attuned to other artistic currents around him, and he was quick to sweep a wide spectrum of modernisms into his working vocabulary. At the Paris Centennial

www.prenhall.com/masterworks
composer profiles
Debussy

Exposition of 1889, for example, he studied the underlying musical processes of the Javanese gamelan, a kind of gong-and-percussion orchestra. He knew the wonderfully modern poetry of the Symbolists: Baudelaire, Mallarmé, Rimbaud. And he seems to have had an implicit grasp of Impressionism—the style of the painters Degas, Monet, Seurat.

Debussy had a conventional music education in Paris and won the Conservatoire's coveted Prix de Rome for composition in 1884. He was engaged by Madame von Meck as a piano teacher and traveled widely with her household; he then became attached to Madame Vasnier, a Parisian architect's wife for whom he provided songs and, it appears, other favors. He scandalized his friends by dropping the first Madame Debussy for another married woman, Emma Bardac. They were married in 1908, three years after the necessary divorces and the birth of their beloved daughter, Chou-Chou.

His early works were mostly piano solos and songs to texts by the symbolist poets. In 1892 he began to compose the symphonic poem that would be seen as his first masterpiece, the *Prélude à L'Après-midi d'un faune* ("Prelude to 'The Afternoon of a Faun'"). It is a kind of reflection in musical terms on a relatively abstract poem by Stéphane Mallarmé, "L'Après-midi d'un faune."

Debussy and Stravinsky

Debussy's sound world in the *Faun* is quite different from that of the other post-Romantics we have been considering. Theme as a structural concept has an inconsequential role, and is replaced by the interaction of motive and cell; harmony is engaged less to push and pull about the tonic than to effect a much subtler floating motion. There is an incomparable play of musical light and shadow in Debussy, where willowy figures interact, gather into great wellings-up of sound, only to separate out again and die away. The brushwork is very deft and highly detailed: gesture and nuance draw our attention, not the expectation of development and recall. If you stop to ponder how Impressionist painting works, or look into the kind of literary imagery at issue in Mallarmé's poem, then you'll see how it might dawn on somebody to call music such as this Impressionistic.

The *Faun* was for its time and place radical indeed. Without a doubt it gave musical focus to the new current of artistic ideas that can be seen everywhere in the French arts at the turn of the century. Other composers followed suit, and Debussy himself pursued the rhetoric of the *Faun* aggressively as he composed his operatic masterpiece *Pelléas et Mélisande* (1902), to an important symbolist play by the Belgian author Maurice Maeterlinck.

Debussy went on to deal increasingly in music prompted by visual and scenic imagery, developing a fondness in his piano and orchestral music for the simple title *Images.* Similarly, his 1903 book of piano pieces is called *Estampes* ("Prints"), consisting of the three evocative movements "Pagodes," "La Soirée dans Grenade," and "Jardins sous la pluie" ("Pagodas," "Evening in Grenada," "Gardens in the Rain")—conversations between the piano and oneself.

DEBUSSY: *LA SOIRÉE DANS GRENADE* (1903)

Of the many exoticisms that struck the fancy of the times, one of the most pervasive was a delight in things Spanish. Spanish fever had started with visits of Spanish dance troupes to Paris in the 1870s and been fed by *Carmen;* in Russia Glinka's musical souvenirs of his visit to Spain had led to Rimsky-Korsakov's *Capriccio espagnol* and its descendants. By Debussy's time the Spanish composer Isaac Albéniz and the pianist Ricardo Viñes had settled in Paris, and in 1907 Manuel de Falla would sojourn there. What was thought of as "Spanish" music was more particularly that of Andalusia, the area in southern Spain where Granada, Seville, and Cádiz are found. This is the center of flamenco dance and gypsy song.

The dance pattern of *La Soirée dans Grenade* is a simple habanera rhythm, much like the one underpinning Carmen's famous aria and not so different from the tango rhythm we encounter a few pages hence in the *St. Louis Blues.*

That rhythm attached to repeating C♯s becomes an ostinato motive that colors nearly every measure. Debussy borrowed the idea from a rather similar habanera for two pianos by Ravel (1897).

He instructs the pianist to "begin slowly, in a nonchalantly gracious rhythm." In the first section, cells of diverse character gather in number from an initial improvisatory melody (a1) to the outbreak of what amounts to a pointedly contrastive second theme in the relative major key (b), descending in right-hand octaves from a melodic highpoint and the only *fortissimo* of the piece. But this retreats quickly into the dreamy opening melodies and key.

Toward the center comes a well-defined, convivial trio, marked "with more abandon," though nevertheless beginning *pianissimo.*

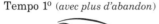

There is brief but unmistakable reference to the American idioms of tango and cakewalk, also reminiscence of a cell from the first section (a3). With the return of the opening materials and C♯ tonality the principal motives seem wispier still, and their recall is interrupted twice by a new guitar figure—as though a fleeting image has begun to disappear. What is most important about this work is the way it announces Debussy's new interest in the foundations of piano sonority. The way the hands work to create voices and evocative textures, sometimes requiring three lines of score, is quite progressive.

Debussy went on to compose two books of piano *Images* (1905, 1907), two books of programmatic *Préludes* (1910, 1913), and a very influential set of *Études* (1916: "Five Fingers," "Thirds," "Octaves," etc.).

The big orchestral works after the *Faun* are also scenic: three *Nocturnes* (1900: "Clouds," "Fêtes," "Sirenes," that is, singing enchantresses), *La Mer,* and the orchestral *Images* (1912: "Gigues," "Iberia," "Spring Rounds"). It is instructive that Debussy did not complete anything one might call a symphony: that kind of rhetoric, he clearly believed, belonged to the past.

Debussy died just as World War I was nearing its end and thus before the modernism he had done so much to foster could be defined with any real perspective. His countryman Maurice Ravel (1875–1937), younger by almost a generation, knew success in 1899, was famous by 1912, and was still a major figure in music composition in the 1930s. Moreover, it appears that many of Ravel's basic ideas about music were formed

Listening Chart

 **CD 3, TR 12**

Claude Debussy (1862–1918)
La Soirée dans Grenade (1903)

For: piano

Type: Dance-and-trio
Meter: $\frac{2}{4}$
Key: C♯ minor
Duration: 05:12

00:00	**Intr.**	The habanera rhythm becomes an ostinato on C♯.
	Dance	
00:13	a1	Improvisatory figure introduced in treble, ostinato above.
00:39	a2	Energetic strumming; ostinato.
00:50	a3	Thick chords, triplet rhythm, as though musing.
01:06	a2	The strumming figure introduces a gradual crescendo and key change to . . .
01:21	b	A major. Bigger theme, descending in octaves from the only *ff*, dissolves to . . .
02:00	a3	Ostinato again, return of the musing triplets.
	Trio	F♯ major. The change of key and atmosphere are those associated
02:21	c	with a trio. Strong suggestions of American cakewalk idiom.
02:42	a3	Cell a3 now frames the trio and brings the ostinato back for transition.
03:12	**Dance**	Returns and reminiscences.
03:16	a2	As before.
03:26	b	As before, except much softer.
03:51	g	Hints of virtuoso guitar passagework.
03:58	c, g	As before, though interrupted by more passagework.
04:19	a1	Harplike arpeggio, then fading reminiscence of the opening improvisation.
04:44	a2	Wisp of a reminiscence and cadence.

before he knew a great deal of Debussy's work. So while it's true that Debussy and Ravel had much in common where it came to the modern French style, Ravel was definitely his own man. The style of Debussy and Ravel was not erased in one fell swoop in 1913, simply pushed into second place.

SERGEI DIAGHILEV AND THE BALLETS RUSSES. The enthusiasm for Russian spectacle Parisians had shown for a couple of decades gradually turned to mania after 1909, when the St. Petersburg impresario Sergei Diaghilev first presented his Ballets Russes to the French public. Already he had brought Rimsky-Korsakov to Paris to conduct and the legendary Russian bass Fyodor Chaliapin to sing excerpts from *Boris Godunov,* accompanied by Rachmaninov. The Polovtsian Dances from Borodin's *Prince Igor* had generated the most enthusiasm, however. Taking that cue, Diaghilev formed a company of the best Russian dancers, choreographers, and designers he could assemble to take to Paris. And he had a considerable gift for assembling them.

Diaghilev's star was Vaslav Nijinsky (1888–1950), whose magical leaps and aeronautical gymnastics made him the Paganini of dance. But for his thick, muscular legs he was small and squat; onstage he seemed thoroughly androgynous, resplendent in

Nijinsky as the
Golden Slave
in *Scheherazade*

. . . as the faun in
*Afternoon of a
Faun*

flowing silks and jeweled headdresses, and decidedly feminine of gesture. Some of the modernisms he later cultivated appear to have been in imitation of a brother who had had cerebral palsy. (Nijinsky's younger sister Bronislava was also a famous ballerina.)

Nijinsky was by no means the only genius to be affiliated with the Ballets Russes. Early on Diaghilev had invited Rimsky-Korsakov's star pupil Igor Stravinsky to work for him, first to orchestrate some Chopin piano pieces for the black-and-white ballet *Les Sylphides,* then to compose his own ballet scores: *The Firebird* (1910), *Petrushka* (1911), and *The Rite of Spring* (1913). This launched one of the most brilliant compositional careers of the twentieth century. The list of Diaghilev's collaborators goes on and on. In one of his most inspired collaborations, he commissioned Picasso, the choreographer Léonide Massine, and Manuel de Falla to do a Spanish ballet that became *The Three-Cornered Hat.* Picasso painted a wonderful front drop of a bull ring and spectators, and Falla wrote additional music so the audience would have time to admire it. Picasso's canvas now hangs in the Seagram's Building in New York outside the Four Seasons Restaurant.

Shrewdly, Diaghilev also involved the best French composers in his enterprise, producing a ballet on *Afternoon of a Faun* in 1912 and commissioning the young Ravel to compose *Daphnis and Chloe.* But public interest in *Afternoon of a Faun* overshadowed *Daphnis and Chloe* in 1912 because the music was already known and loved and because word quickly spread about town that Nijinsky as the faun had made masturbatory gestures onstage. *Daphnis and Chloe* is, moreover, a relatively impractical ballet, in several respects more about symphonic composition than dance. It's a ballet that lives more persuasively in the mind's eye.

RECOMMENDED LISTENING:

Ravel: **Daphnis and Chloe,** *Suite No. 2 (1912)*

Debussy's Diaghilev ballet, *Jeux* ("Games," in this case a tennis match), was simply washed away, two weeks after its first performance, by the premiere of the work that many thinking people have regarded, ever since, as the turning point of modern ballet: Stravinsky's *Le Sacre du printemps* ("The Rite of Spring").

IGOR STRAVINSKY (1882–1971). Stravinsky attracted the attention of Diaghilev with the music he had composed for the wedding of Rimsky-Korsakov's daughter in 1908. Within a few months he had become Diaghilev's principal musical adviser, and the orchestrational drudge work for the first season led to a full ballet for 1910: *The Firebird,* drawn from a Russian legend about a prince and 13 enchanted princesses and a fantastic red bird with magic plumage. For the 1911 season there was *Petrushka,* in which puppets at a Mardi Gras fair come to life. Both showed Stravinsky's talents well: his understanding of theatrics, a technical command of writing for orchestra that puts him in the direct lineage of Rimsky-Korsakov, and an aggressively novel language of rhythm and tonality. As Petrushka is unceremoniously dumped into his room by the puppeteer, for example, we hear a forlorn motive of *bitonal* construction, the top voice outlining a C-major triad, the other an F♯-major chord.

"Petrushka" chord

In the big opening tableau at the Shrovetide Fair, the rhythmic irregularities emphasize the chaos of the scene, notably in the measures where some of the orchestra plays in $\frac{7}{8}$ while others are in $\frac{3}{4}$, then $\frac{5}{8}$ against $\frac{2}{4}$ and finally $\frac{6}{8}$ against $\frac{3}{4}$. These kinds of innovations prepared the way for *The Rite of Spring.* Stravinsky had conceived the notion of a ballet on the emergence of spring in central Asia just after *The Firebird,* but the compositional implications were so formidable that he delayed work on it until he had finished the rather more conservative *Petrushka.* After *The Rite of Spring* there could be no turning back.

TRAVINSKY: *LE SACRE DU PRINTEMPS* ("THE RITE OF SPRING," 1913)

Pagan Russia in primitive times. What Stravinsky calls "the violent Russian spring" begins to percolate, then the whole earth to crackle. Human forms emerge from wherever they have passed the winter, until the cast of young people has assembled to begin their spring games. The elders arrive, and the oldest and wisest one kisses the earth. In the second half the young girls form mystic circles in preparation for choosing one of them for the spring sacrifice. The Chosen One is anointed, then dances herself to death.

From the opening turn, a bassoon solo at the uppermost limits of the instrument's range, it is clear that something radically new is afoot. The mélange of mini-fanfares that follows in the woodwinds is typical of the score's thick and sometimes disarming textures. Take them apart, and you usually discover simple tonal cells not so different from the building blocks of Debussy's *La Soirée dans Grenade*.

Spring's awakening swells to a climax, rounded off by a return of the high bassoon. Notice how carefully the transition to the next dance is crafted. Violin *pizzicati* foreshadow the new number (and prompt the dancers waiting offstage that their time has come); a last gurgle of clarinets tumbles into an obviously cadential chord for high cellos; now the violin *pizzicati* turn suddenly and rather brutally into something altogether different.

After so abstract an introduction, the violent start of this dance of adolescent girls, and its irregularly placed accents, seemed to early listeners especially "barbaric," an adjective that has stuck with the passage ever since.

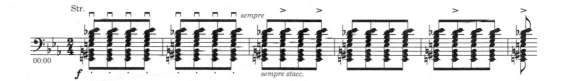

Yet here, as in the introduction, the motivic cells are actually quite naive of design, some of them based on authentic Russian melodies. (More often than not the introduction of a new cell is reflected onstage by the entry of new characters or choreographic elements.) The number takes shape as a big crescendo of these elements, with the last page occupying 30 staves of score.

For all the new and unusual sounds, *The Rite of Spring* is a clearly delineated, easily followed work. The tunes in *The Rite of Spring* are eminently hummable. It's just that the amount of space they take up, and the amount of space between them, keeps changing. You can't pat your foot in any regular fashion, but the rhythm isn't so much barbaric as what Gershwin might have called "fascinatin'."

And the overall sound is positively thrilling. The early Stravinsky ensembles, along with those of Mahler and Ravel, mark the maximum advance of orchestral expansion. It takes a good 5 percussionists, 18 brass players, and 20 woodwind players to do the *Rite* right. Even a fully stocked symphony orchestra needs about a dozen "ringers" to manage it.

You may have gleaned elsewhere that the first performance of *The Rite of Spring* caused a riot, where scandalized members of the audience spilled into the streets outside the Théâtre des Champs-Elysées in their excitement. Parisians love a scandal. Remember that it was in Paris that the *salon des refusés,* which exhibited paintings rejected for official showing, thrived, and where tongues wag every day over scandalous goings-on at the Opéra and, now, the National Library. This attitude has kept art alive in Paris for a long, long time, and it has made modern Paris a monument to itself.

Diaghilev's company held together until his death, finding welcome in Monte Carlo, Spain, and England. Nijinsky and Anna Pavlova had long since defected. Three of the female dancers went to England, where they established the classical practices of the Royal Ballet. Diaghilev's third major choreographer, after Fokine and Massine, was George Balanchine, who came to New York in 1933, revolutionizing American dance. The New York City Ballet was largely his creation, and the good health of our modern dance his—and, by extension, Diaghilev's—greatest legacy.

Listening Chart

 CD 3, TR 13-14

Igor Stravinsky (1882–1971)
Le Sacre du printemps **("The Rite of Spring," 1913)**
Introduction—Les Augures printinières: Danses des
Adolescentes ("Augurs of Spring: Dances of the Young Girls")

For: 2 piccolos, 3 flutes, alto flute, 4 oboes, English horn, E♭ clarinet, 3 clarinets, 2 bass clarinets, 4 bassoons, 2 contrabassoons; 8 horns; piccolo trumpet, 4 trumpets, bass trumpet, 3 trombones; 2 tubas; timpani; percussion; strings

Type: Ballet scenes
Meter: $\frac{3}{4}$ and $\frac{2}{4}$; $\frac{2}{4}$
Key: NA, free polytonality
Duration: 03:35, 03:21

00:00	**Part 1**	*Introduction.* High bassoon solo with chromatic ooze (clarinets). English horn cell.
00:59	**Part 2**	Eng. horn cell and the chromatic ooze. New oboe, bass clar. cells. Cadential vn. trill.
01:56		A second statement, as the cells continue to mingle: gurgling, crackling, fluttering.
02:25	**Part 3**	Waking of spring continues. Ww. and brass fanfares. Swell to climax.
03:03	**Part 4**	The bassoon figure returns. Foreshadowing (03:14), cadence (03:26) and transition to:
00:00	**Part 1**	*Augurs of Spring: Dances of the Young Girls.* Violent irregular accents, wolfing brass. Triplet trumpet call (00:19).
00:48	**Part 2**	Sassy bassoon tune, joined by trombone, oboes. Explosion and tumble.
01:24	**Part 3**	New figuration including *col legno* (01:36) leads to horn motive (01:43), taken up by the others and offset by the triplet call (01:55). Swells into:
02:19	**Part 4**	Trumpet quartet, *cantabile.* Note the tuned antique cymbals.
02:36	**Part 5**	Retreats to start big, thumping crescendo for climax.

Stravinsky progressed well beyond Russian-subject ballet to develop an encyclopedic range of interests and accomplishments. The constraints of the war years led him to develop the smaller, more conservative style that became known as neo-Classicism; later he relished his fast-lane life of big commissions and big performances. Although most of his work is prevailingly tonal, he turned with great success to serial practices at a very late stage in his career. In short, he graced very nearly everything he tried. We return briefly to Stravinsky in our last chapter. Ponder, for now, the proposition that he was the Monteverdi of his era, and that the Stravinsky ballets have a historic position analogous to the Monteverdi madrigals.

Serious young composers clamored to study and understand the wonders of Stravinsky even as their own modernist styles were emerging. Consider, for instance, the work

Stravinsky: pencil sketch by Picasso (left); Picasso and Stravinsky in a sketch by Jean Cocteau (right).

www.prenhall.com/masterworks
composer profiles
Boulanger

of the sisters **Nadia Boulanger (1887–1979)** and **Lili Boulanger (1893–1918)** of Paris. They were born into a distinguished family. Their father Ernest was a violin professor at the Paris Conservatoire, and his parents and grandparents had likewise been important musicians; their mother was a Russian princess of formidable education who married her singing teacher. Both sisters attended the Conservatoire and eventually sought, in part because their father had won it long before, the prestigious Prix de Rome in composition. Nadia entered the competition four times but never got beyond the second prize, possibly owing to gender bias among the senior composers. Lili, whose early works had already attracted critical attention, took the 1913 prize with her cantata *Faust*

Lili Boulanger

Nadia Boulanger in her prime

et Hélène—a composition "beyond compare," said the jury, which still stands out as one of the best cantatas in the history of the Rome prize. News of this signal victory by a young woman composer spread quickly though Europe and across the Atlantic, and was greeted with particular satisfaction by early feminists in the United States.

Lili Boulanger was thus for all intents and purposes a famous woman by the time she arrived in Rome, along with her mother, for her prize sojourn. The decidedly mixed welcome given the mother-daughter pair and the outbreak of war back home, complicated by Lili's periods of grave illness, made her experience abroad less than the nourishing retreat it was meant to be. But she was able to do at least some composing, and among the works she finished there was a setting of Psalm 24—"The earth is the Lord's and the fulness thereof"—for chorus, organ, and brass orchestra.

BOULANGER: PSALM 24 (1916)

Psalm 24 incorporates a text familiar from Handel's *Messiah:* "Lift up your heads, o ye gates . . . and the King of Glory shall come in." Flourishes from the brass choir, organ, and timpani frame a verse-by-verse, mostly syllabic setting of the Biblical poem; women's voices do not enter until the mid-point, as if to articulate the raising of the gates. The prevailing sonority is that of chords formed by linking pairs of perfect fifths.

When inverted, the pitches of a perfect fifth (A–E, for instance) become a perfect fourth (E–A), one of the building blocks of the ostinato underpinning the tenor solo.

Boulanger is clearly alluding to much older church styles: the phrase shapes and syllabic declamation of plainchant, the parallel fifths and fourths of the earliest polyphony, the acoustic properties of straight trumpets and pipe organ. In overall result the short piece becomes a jubilant, somewhat antique fanfare, altogether appropriate to the ceremony of approaching the great gates of a holy city.

Listening Chart

CD 4, TR 1

Lili Boulanger (1893–1918)
Psalm 24 (1916)

For: chorus, organ, orchestra (trumpets, horns, trombones; timpani; harp).
Text: from the Bible

Type: sectional anthem
Meter: $\frac{3}{4}$ mostly
Key: E minor
Duration: 03:51

A jubilant fanfare alluding to old church styles, with a prominent emphasis on chords formed of linked fifths and fourths. The brass flourishes frame a syllabic setting of the Biblical poetry.

	Part 1	
00:00	Fanfare	Jubilant brass and organ; chords of linked fifths and fourths.
00:06	Verses 1–2	"The Earth is the Lord's." Men's voices, fanfare interjections.
00:31	Verse 3	"Who shall ascend?" The bass ostinato suggests pealing bells.
	Part 2	A contrasting center section, much quieter.
00:49	Verse 4	"He that hath clean hands." Simple, solemn declamation over gentle organ support.
01:21	Verse 5	"A blessing from the Lord." Horns introduce a neighbor-note ostinato, with organ pedal-point. Tenor solo. Crescendo into:
01:47	Verse 6	"The generation of them that seek after him." Declamatory chanting rhythms; cadence in a subsidiary key area.
	Part 3	Recapitulatory.
02:20	Verse 7	"Lift up your heads." Entry of women's voices, rising melodic line, return of both the original tempo and the fanfares (02:34).
02:39	Verse 8	"Who is this King of Glory?" The melody refers to verse 3.
02:53	Verses 9–10	The repeated question-and-answer of verses 7–8 grows louder and more animated with strong emphasis on the bell-peal ostinatos. The concluding "Ah" (03:46) is a Boulanger hallmark.

Lili was in fragile health all her life. She suffered from a variety of conditions we now identify as the hereditary Crohn's disease, complicated at the end by tuberculosis. In early 1918 it became necessary to move her from Paris to escape the German bombardments, so friends and family lovingly ferried medical supplies—including ice, a precious commodity in wartime, to reduce her fever—out from town; she died in March. Among the two dozen or so works she left to posterity are songs and lyric scenes, a pair of lovely pieces for solo piano, three psalm settings including the masterpiece *Du fond de l'abîme* (Psalm 130: "Out of the depths I cry to thee"), and a "Pie Jesu" she dictated to her sister in her last weeks, probably intended for a full Requiem mass.

Nadia Boulanger, who had established herself as an influential teacher of analysis and composition, went on to become perhaps the outstanding music educator of a generation who flocked to Paris from the 1920s to the 1970s—she died at 92—to study with her, consult her, or merely to shake her hand. She was the first woman to conduct major orchestras in Paris and London and New York, promoter of interesting repertoire extending from the Monteverdi madrigals to Stravinsky's *Dumbarton Oaks* Concerto, and frequent conductor of her sister's music—including the 1968 performance on your CD. She never quite resolved the trauma of what she saw as Lili's genius interrupted by untimely death: "I live for the memory of my dear little sister," she wrote plaintively in the 1940s; in her old age she was prone to dwell too long on the subject. The personal control she exerted over Lili Boulanger's artistic estate may in fact have slowed the international reception of Lili's work, but by the early 1970s the feminist movement had found it. Lili and her music became the subject of scholarly research; her works were included on the famous record *Woman's Work* (1975); and she received coverage in such populist forums as *Ms.* magazine. Today we have both the facts and the historical distance to view Lili Boulanger as one of the dozens of composers of the 1910s (and not the only woman, either) capably engaging the sea-change of art and culture in those years: advancing in her songs intelligent musical responses to the rich poetry of her generation, and finding in her art a degree of release from a level of suffering that no one so young should have to bear.

Much like Boulanger, Maurice Ravel was content to use the more or less traditional materials of French modernism to accomplish his purposes. He was not an especially prolific composer. After World War I his works came even more slowly than before, but he went out with a bang: *Boléro* (1928), two superb piano concertos (1930, 1931), and the songs of *Don Quixote to Dulcinea* (1933).

RECOMMENDED LISTENING:

Ravel: **La Valse** *(1920)*
Ravel: **Boléro** *(1928)*

www.prenhall.com/masterworks
recommended listening

In the famous *Boléro* Ravel's idea was to fashion one long crescendo out of an "insistent melody." (Actually there are two related melodic ideas, presented over a not especially authentic bolero rhythm.) Call *Boléro* what you may—vulgar, stirring, orgiastic, nerve-wracking—the piece is serious fun. Not only has it never lost its appeal, but it markedly foreshadows modern minimalist practices in both popular and art music. It's just not the sort of piece you want to use as background music—for any activity.

"Alas," said Ravel, "it contains no music."

Part 3

Music Here and Now

Chapter 8

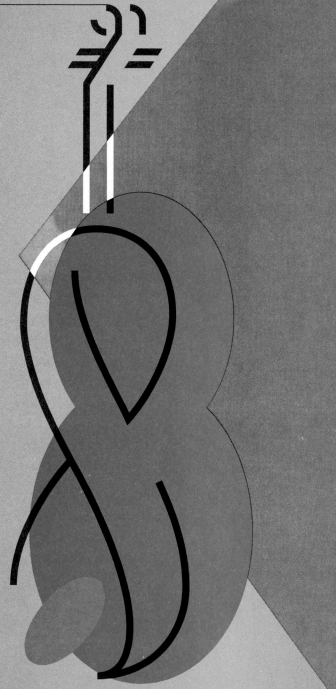

'Tis the gift to be simple, 'tis the gift to be free,
'Tis the gift to come down where we ought to be,
And when we find ourselves in the place just right,
'Twill be in the valley of love and delight.

—from "Simple Gifts," a song of the American Shakers

Music in the Land of Plenty

*I*n crossing the Atlantic Ocean to examine the music of American society, we also take a leap backward in chronology to the beginnings of the nation forged with so much optimism and courage along the North American east coast. From afar the New World was as much imagined as real, and those who came to take refuge here naturally discovered its hardships as well as its promises. Naturally, too, they arrived with song in their hearts, adapting the music of their many cultures—the Dutch and Puritan reformers, the Moravians of central Europe, the English Methodists, and increasingly the enslaved Africans—to sing of both the joys and tribulations of their lives here.

With song, as with every other pursuit of its populace, America was a melting pot. Congregational singing had by the time of the Revolutionary War produced the beginnings of a fine repertoire of choral music. The 1800s saw the growth of an important market for secular song: Civil War favorites, Appalachian tunes, cowboy ballads, parlor songs. From the rich musical practice of African Americans came spirituals and gospel and their secular equivalents, leading to the blues and jazz. Classically trained European musicians brought their virtuosity and habitual concert life, establishing enclaves of high art in the metropolitan areas. An American instrumental idiom begins to emerge in the mid-nineteenth century.

But one would not characterize American music as long on the orchestra-based genres that have dominated our last hundred pages. The nation's most indigenous music was the world of song it carried in their memory to worship, work, and play. When American art-music composers stopped needing to look to Europe for inspiration, they turned to this unique heritage of song, and it is this focus which gives the music of the twentieth-century masters Gershwin, Ives, and Copland its inimitable character. Both of America's great contributions to lighter fare—jazz and musical theater—are rooted in song. Song is America's most distinctive musical attribute.

 ONGREGATIONAL SINGING

For those who came and stayed of their own accord, America's lure had less to do with the promise of riches than the freedom to worship as they pleased. Permanent settlements took hold first in Virginia and Massachusetts, where the institutions and intelligence that defined the American way of life began to take shape. The sober New England lifestyle yielded strong church-oriented thinking. Its monuments are the sermons of Cotton Mather, Harvard College (founded 1636), the clear-headed republicanism of the eighteenth century, and the great literary movement centered around the authors of Concord, Massachusetts (Emerson, Thoreau, the Alcotts) in the nineteenth.

The Pilgrims had brought with them the psalters of English practice, where the psalms in metered English were sung to commonly known tunes printed occasionally in four parts, more often in one line, and sometimes with no music at all. In 1640 the Puritans published their new rhymed translations of the psalms, called The Bay Psalm Book (*The Whole Booke of Psalmes Faithfully Translated into English Metre*), which was in use in New England for more than a century. The new metered version of the 23rd Psalm, for example, begins like this:

> The Lord to mee a shepheard is,
> Want therefore shall not I.
> Hee in the folds of tender-grasse
> Doth cause mee downe to lie.

There is no music in The Bay Psalm Book, only references to several dozen tunes that would serve for the various meters.

By the 1720s the practice of hymn singing had declined radically into the use of a dozen or fewer hymn tunes delivered in a "Usual Way" of rote singing: ponderously slow, one-line only, with embellishments at the pleasure of the singers. To answer this deplorable state of affairs the Boston church leaders framed a singing-school movement, where "Regular Singing" from notated tune books would be taught. Instruction was given in how to read pitches and rhythms and, occasionally, how to sing in parts. The singing schools were organized by congregations much like a Bible-study course works

The New-England Psalm-Singer (1770), frontispiece: a canon by William Billings, engraved by Paul Revere

today; after a few months of instruction the students would join the church choir and go on to help train others in musical literacy.

www.prenhall.com/masterworks
composer profiles
Billings

WILLIAM BILLINGS (1746–1800). The first major composer in American history was, in true Yankee tradition, a jack-of-all-trades. By profession a tanner and later a dabbler in civil service appointments, William Billings was self-taught in composition. He had mastered the rudiments and repertoire of music in the New England singing schools and in due course became one of the wandering choirmasters of the singing-school movement, working in churches in and around Boston. In that capacity he published in 1770 *The New-England Psalm-Singer,* a collection of short church pieces introduced by tutelage in music notation couched in his unmistakably wry, rambling style. *The New-England Psalm-Singer* is epoch-making in that all the music (more than 100 psalms and hymns, 4 canons, 5 longer anthems) is multivoiced, and all of it is by Billings himself. Among its treasures is *Chester,* the tune and inflammatory text of which served as a kind of battle hymn of the American Revolution.

Let ty-rants shake their i - ron rod, And slav-'ry clank ⌐ her gall - ing chains.

We fear them not, ⌐ we trust ⌐ in God; New Eng-land's God ⌐ for-ev - er reigns.

Billings's next publication, *The Singing Master's Assistant* (1778), was a best-seller, exhausting four editions in a decade. Like its predecessor, it opened with instructions, essays, and a glossary; among the rules for regulating a singing school was "No unnecessary conversation, whispering, or laughing, to be practised; for it is not only indecent, but very impolitic." The music is on the whole bigger and better than in the first collection, centering perhaps on the captivating anthem *Lamentation over Boston,* the text paraphrased from Psalm 137 and Jeremiah:

> By the Rivers of Watertown we sat down and wept when we remember'd thee, O Boston. As for our Friends, Lord God of Heaven, preserve them, defend them, deliver and restore them to us again. For they that held them in Bondage requir'd of them to take up Arms against their Brethren. Forbid it, Lord God, that those who have sucked Bostonian Breasts should thirst for American Blood.

Billings's musical style is very stark, owing in large measure to his sparing use of chromaticism and affinity for cadence patterns that end not in triads but in open fifths. Such primitivism would not have passed muster in post-Baroque Europe (Bach's chorales of a generation earlier are a world more advanced), but it seems thoroughly in keeping with the stern New England culture.

BILLINGS: *DAVID'S LAMENTATION* (1778)

According to the Bible story, King David's rebellious third son, Absalom, was killed in battle as he hung by his long hair, tangled in a tree. David's lament, "O Absalom, my son, my son: would to God I had died for thee" (2 Samuel 18:33), exemplifies the power of language to be found everywhere in the King James translation of the Bible, especially in the Old Testament. In this case, a father's sorrow over his fallen son goes well beyond the specifics of the incident—or the moral of the story.

Billings sets the brief text in two sections. At the start of the second phrase ("And as he wept"), the music hints for a moment at a subject for imitation. Instead, the anguished homophonic cry, "Oh, my son," erupts, followed by imitative entries of "Would to God I had died," and a cadence on the open fifth A-E. The design could scarcely be simpler, yet its dramatic force is very great; it's the sort of music that rings in your mind long after the ear has registered it.

The entire second section is repeated, as is the custom with these settings. The performance here is *a cappella,* although in and around Boston the church organist might have played along.

Listening Chart

 CD 4, TR 2

William Billings (1746–1800)
David's Lamentation (1778)

For: unaccompanied four-part chorus (S, A, T, B)

Text: from the Bible (2 Samuel 18:33)

Type: Anthem
Meter: $\frac{2}{4}$
Key: A minor
Duration: 01:46

Cast in stern minor mode, David's lamentation on the death of his son Absalom is a fine example of Billings's primitive Americanism. This is the sort of music that was heard in Massachusetts during colonial times: the Old North Church, for example, where Billings served.

00:00	**Phrase 1**	The story begins in 4-part homophony.
00:17	**Phrase 2**	Basses suggest a subject for imitation, but instead:
00:25	cry	David's cry: homophonic, stark, long note values.
00:35	**Phrase 3**	Imitative entries and cadence on open fifth, A–E.
00:59	**Phr. 2–3 rep.**	The second section repeated.

Whatever money *The Singing Master's Assistant* made Billings was soon lost, and he was pursued for bankruptcy. His last work, *The Continental Harmony* (1794), was published by a sympathetic firm to help rescue Billings from poverty, and there were charity concerts for the same purpose. His fame, however, was enduring; people dubbed him, wrongly, "the rival of Handel," and, rightly, "the father of our new England music."

Billings's ideas, and his best music, were quickly absorbed into the music-literacy efforts of the 1800s. Books called *The Easy Instructor* (Philadelphia, 1801), *The Kentucky Harmony* (Harrisonburg, Virginia, 1816), *The Missouri Harmony* (St. Louis, 1820), and the like, spread the singing-school movement down the Appalachian mountains and thence into the much less literate South.

The nineteenth-century collections used a system of *shape-note notation, or fasola* notation, where the shapes of the notes suggest patterns of half steps and whole steps, the triangular *fa* serving as the tonic and scale degree 4, the round *sol* for a step above those (scale degrees 2 and 5), and the square *la* for a step above those (scale degrees 3 and 6). The diamond *mi* was reserved for scale degree 7, so *la–fa* and *mi–fa* were rises of a half step:

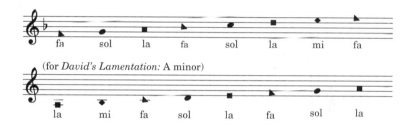

This method proved relatively accessible for sight singing and was adopted in schools and churches throughout the South and into the Midwest.

The most influential of the shape-note hymn books was Benjamin Franklin White's *The Sacred Harp* (Philadelphia, 1844), which contains, in addition to such familiar American hymns as "Amazing Grace," several of Billings's works. You see the shape-note version of *David's Lamentation* in the Anthology, p. 388. Several versions of *The Sacred Harp* remain in print and in use throughout the South.

BILLINGS: *DAVID'S LAMENTATION,* ALABAMA SACRED HARP RENDITION (RECORDED 1959)

People still go out of their way to gather and sing this venerable music from its shape-note editions. This rendition by a community sing in Fyffe, Alabama, was taped in 1959. The written text is virtually identical to that of the colonial edition, but the musical result is altogether different: They sing *David's Lamentation* faster and with no regard whatever for well-schooled vocal production. The singers tune up to the *sol* and *fa* at first; then you hear feet pounding on the floor and perhaps a rafter or two beginning to lift. "I think this is mighty fine singin'," says one old codger after another song from this same taping: "I moved 'bout 70 miles to get down here to this thing and I really think it paid off."

Alan Lomax, the distinguished American ethnologist who made the tape, was greatly moved by the meeting at Fyffe:

The voices of speakers trembled with feeling. One old gentleman told me, as he slapped his big country palm down on his songbook, "I believe that every living word in that there book is as true as gospel." The convention ended with a memorial service for members who had passed away since the last meeting, and in the closing moments tears coursed down sunburned cheeks. The Sacred Harp folk feel they belong to a big family that will someday be singing its harmony with the angels.

The repertoire of American hymns expanded throughout the nineteenth century, at preach-and-pray camp meetings and revivals, for the Sunday-school movement and the urban evangelists. By the 1870s collections of *gospel songs,* combining the attributes of conventional sacred music and popular song, were selling well. These rollicking, often sentimental hymns—from "Shall We Gather at the River" (1864) to "Blessed Assurance, Jesus Is Mine" (1873) to "The Old Rugged Cross" (1913) and beyond—are as American as, well, apple pie.

I myself grew up in this general tradition, and as a university student led a Baptist church choir in rural North Carolina every Sunday. My favorite choristers were my alto, Lottie May Lester, and her husband Melvin, a bass. They made no secret of their dislike for my frequent programming of Bach chorales and the stirring (and quite Methodist) hymns of Charles Wesley. "High Church," Melvin would grumble, and Lottie Mae would add, "Goin' down the Road to Rome." But when we settled into music of the revival tra-

Listening Chart

 CD 4, TR 3

William Billings (1746–1800)
David's Lamentation **(Alabama Sacred Harp rendition, recorded 1959)**

For: unaccompanied four-part chorus (S, A, T, B)

Text: from the Bible (2 Samuel 18:33)

Type: Anthem
Meter: $\frac{2}{4}$
Key: A minor
Duration: 01:10

As taped by the ethnomusicologist Alan Lomax at a community hymn sing in Fyffe, Alabama, *David's Lamentation* seems almost a different work—but as rapturous, in its own way, as any performance we encounter. Music belongs to everybody.

00:00	Tune-up	They find the pitch.
00:04	**Phrase 1**	4-part homophony. Enjoy the pure Alabama accents.
00:14	**Phrase 2**	Basses suggest a subject for imitation, but instead:
00:19	cry	David's cry: homophonic, stark, long note values.
00:26	**Phrase 3**	Imitative entries and cadence on open fifth, A–E.
00:40	**Phr. 2-3 rep.**	The second section repeated.

dition, and they were allowed full run of their vocal capabilities, a rapture came over the proceedings that proved to me once and for all that music belongs to everybody.

USIC OF THE SLAVES

American slaves, meanwhile, were purposefully kept illiterate, and whipped if reading materials—usually Bibles—were found in their possession. Written documentation of black Americans before the 1860s consists of bills of sale and inventories of property; there remains little by way of correspondence, memoirs, and literature, and no written music at all.

The slave trade developed its momentum in the Golden Triangle, where slaves were brought to the West Indies to grow sugarcane; the sugarcane was sold to Yankee distillers to make rum; the rum was traded in Africa for more slaves. The first slaves were introduced to growers in the American South in 1619, and the plantations rapidly became dependent on them. The American census of 1790 counted 600,000 slaves; in 1860 the official figure was 4.5 million, although the true number of slaves at the Emancipation was probably around 15 million.

Not only the languages but also the musical practice of the Africans varied from tribe to tribe. Common to African music, however, is virtuosity in drumming and percussive cycles and its strong tendency to use call and response, or leader-follower arrangements. Ethnomusicologists have demonstrated, for example, very close relationships between the calls of field hands in Senegal and the singing of illiterate chain gangs at a Louisiana prison. Musically the practice is for all intents and purposes identical. Both are versions of the *field holler,* which appears to be the common starting point for the African American musical idioms.

African and African American music are communal efforts, improvised by groups. Musical complexity results from the stacking together of rhythmic patterns—clapping,

Gospel singing in Virginia, c. 1880

foot stomping—moving in cycles, and from repetitive melodic schemes simultaneously embellished in different ways by different singers, a kind of *heterophony.* The melodies are often pentatonic (patterns of five pitches), without leading tones and thus without strong cadences. Always there is dancing. It's hard to imagine black music without body movement: Think of the hymn singing you have witnessed or participated in. Think of the Supremes.

Gradually, of course, American blacks refashioned white hymn singing to their own purposes. (One point of crossover was the pre–Civil War tent meetings, where slaves were allowed to congregate outside the tent. They would learn the hymns instantly, singing outside while the preaching went on within.) They absorbed the tonality and cadential endings of the hymns as well, strongly westernizing the prevailing modality of the African-based music they already knew. Thus the so-called Negro spiritual developed in the black churches of the deep South in part from traditional songs passed down through the generations, in part from compositional activity that assimilated the southern hymn styles. What spirituals have in common is the Christianity the American slaves had adapted to their particular situation: a view of a captured people, safe in the knowledge of finding a home with God in the promised land. This sad but powerful message is found in all the famous spirituals: "Swing Low, Sweet Chariot," "Deep River," "Jacob's Ladder."

After the Emancipation, the spiritual was quickly adapted for the public concert hall. The Fisk Jubilee Singers, organized in 1871 to raise money for Fisk University in Nashville, Tennessee, popularized spirituals in four-part arrangements during concert tours in the North and to Europe, performing for the Boston World Peace Jubilee in 1872 and before Queen Victoria. The group consisted of nine student singers and a pianist, most of them former slaves, under the direction of George L. White (1838–95). Solo recitals by black artists would always include spirituals—Dvořák heard them in New York recitals—and African American singers have traditionally included spirituals in their

The Fisk Jubilee Singers, 1871

concerts ever since. Among the most memorable of these virtuosi have been Paul Robeson (1898–1976), an actor and bass who first sang "Ol' Man River," and the soprano Leontyne Price (b. 1927), one of the great Verdi and Puccini heroines of all time and the darling of the Metropolitan Opera in the 1960s. But she and the dozens of black singers flourishing today (among them Jessye Norman, Shirley Verrett, Kathleen Battle) will tell you that greatest of them all was the contralto Marian Anderson (1899–1993). Anderson was already a star when she was forbidden by the Daughters of the American Revolution to sing at Constitution Hall in Washington, D.C., owing to their policy of racial separation. In response, the Roosevelt administration organized Anderson's famous nationwide concert broadcast from the steps of the Lincoln Memorial on Easter Sunday 1939, news footage of which you may have seen. Those images linger as much in our national memory as the very similar pictures of Martin Luther King's "I Have a Dream" speech on the same spot.

Black musicians, too, adopted gospel singing, contemporary with ragtime and the beginning of jazz. This is the raise-the-roof, holy roller style of the Pentacostal sects and the cults, with ring dancing, tambourines, swooning, and over the din the barking of the preacher. The better sopranos warble away in ecstasy while the choral accompaniment provides the rhythmic underpinning and the refrains. Black gospel is the euphoric song of good news, of praise delivered, as the Bible instructs, with timbrel and with dance, and with loud clashing cymbals.

ARLOR SONGS AND QUICKSTEPS

What passed as music of the slaves became popular among white people in the minstrel shows of the 1840s and later, unattractive affairs where white men in blackface mimicked the speech and movement of mid-century slaves with banjo songs and ballads ("There's no more work for poor old Ned / He's gone where the good darkies go") and dances like the cakewalk, meant to imitate the strutting of elegantly dressed black couples competing in a dance contest for a prize cake. "Dixie" (1859) was composed for the Bryant Minstrels, active during the Civil War. There's no denying the repulsive elements in all this, but there are hints of subtle admiration, too, especially for the good cheer and colorful dialect of the Negro. Financially, American minstrelsy was a great success. America was, after all, passing through its single greatest crisis of conscience, and the moral forces were contradictory at best.

The Pittsburgh composer Stephen Foster (1826–64), writing for a potential public of emigrant industrial workers, advanced past the "coon songs" of the generation just preceding to write in a more sympathetic, sentimental manner called "Ethiopian" songs. These include "Old Folks at Home" (i.e., "Swanee River," 1851), "My Old Kentucky Home" (1853), and his great masterpiece "Jeanie with the Light Brown Hair" (1854), yearning for the wife who left him in despair over his alcoholism. And the complete texts of these songs need substantial editing today even to approach correctitude.

But Foster was able to discover in a simplicity of means (limited range, limited pitch content, rudimentary accompaniment) a music of lasting beauty.

And many imitations. The parlor song of the 1880s and 1890s, sold as 50¢ sheet music, was a runaway rage. Nearly all are sentimental, some a little silly: The music lies in capturing the poetic idea with pleasing but elementary chords, rhythms, and tunes. With inviting titles like "Grandfather's Clock" (1876), "After the Ball" (1892), "Will You Love Me in December as You Do in May?" (1905), and charming title-page illustrations to go with them, parlor songs sold well and were popular for generations.

An indigenous instrumental idiom emerged in the music of the American military bands, given its push by the Civil War. Every regimental band had its own quickstep march, of which dozens are preserved. But these were rendered obsolete, in a trice, by the work of John Philip Sousa.

Sousa

JOHN PHILIP SOUSA (1854–1932). Sousa was born of immigrant parents, an Austrian mother and a Portuguese-Spanish father who became a brass player in the United States Marine Band in Washington, D.C., during the Civil War. The young Sousa was discovered to have perfect pitch and promising agility on the violin. After serving as an apprentice in the Marine Band during his teens, he worked for a time as an arranger and theater musician in Philadelphia; the American centennial in 1876, when he was 22, underscored his patriotic leanings.

In 1880 Sousa was appointed director of the Marine Band, its first native-born American leader. He went on to transform it in every particular, from modernizing the instrumentation to overseeing a marked improvement in musicianship. And he composed dozens of marches for the band, the first portion of the 130 or so marches he would write during his career. A good half dozen of these rank with the most famous and frequently played works ever composed by an American.

www.prenhall.com/masterworks
composer profiles
Sousa

SOUSA: *SEMPER FIDELIS* (1888)

"Semper fidelis"—ever faithful—is the motto of the U.S. Marines, and the *Semper fidelis* march has become (with *Stars and Stripes Forever* and one or two non-Sousa works) an instantly recognized trademark of the American military band.

The Sousa march is simple of design: an introduction, two 16-bar strains each repeated, then a modulation *down* a fifth to the key of the subdominant (IV) for the trio, often the most melodious and memorable segment of the march. The trio usually has two strains, sometimes separated by a vigorous interlude everybody calls "the dogfight." (And the extra chord at the end of many marches is always called "the stinger.") The first strain typically modulates to the dominant, minuet fashion; the second usually stays in the tonic.

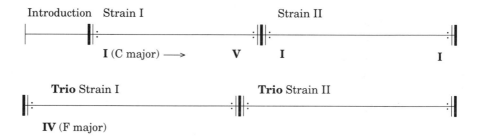

Semper fidelis is distinguished by its proud $\frac{6}{8}$ meter and resulting sense of swagger and by its unusually fine melodies. The drum tattoo between the march proper and the trio is unusual; this sets up the military tune of the trio, which is based on a bugle call:

(You'll recall that valveless brass instruments, of which the bugle is one, focus on the intervals just suggested.) This merits three, not two, passes—C, C', C"—where the plain bugle call with tuba obbligato is joined first by a filigree countermelody in the high wood-wind and then by another countermelody, this one in heroic trombones.

Note, too, the many elegant details in this performance. In the condensed published score the dynamics are only vaguely suggested, and many of the specifics of the registration—who's playing what, when—are worked out by the conductor and the players. Sousa was dead serious about making the march a work of delicacy and finesse, and good performances of a Sousa march take into account his own suave style, which can be reconstructed in part from his recordings and in large measure from the recollections of his musicians.

Listening Chart

 CD 4, TR 4

John Philip Sousa (1854–1932)
Semper fidelis (1888)

For: military band: piccolos, flutes, clarinets, trumpets and cornets, horns, trombones, tubas, percussion

Type: Sousa march
Meter: ⁶⁄₈
Key: C major
Duration: 02:45

The Sousa march consists of an introduction, two 16-bar strains each repeated, then *down* a fifth to the key of IV for the trio, often the most memorable segment. *Semper fidelis* is distinguished by its proud ⁶⁄₈ swagger, fine melodies, and drum tattoo before the bugle-call trio. Sousa thought the march a thing of delicacy and finesse, and good performances take his own suave style into account.

00:00	**Intro.**	Opening flourish and swaggering unison approach to the main theme, 8 bars. Note the particular lilt of a ⁶⁄₈ march.
	1st Strain	Two similar 8-bar phrases (a, a'), the second peaking in the high instruments
00:07	A	with answering riposte in the low.
00:23	A rep.	A second ending effects the shift to the new strain.
	2nd Strain	
00:39	B	Emphasizes dotted quarter notes. Again, two similar phrases (b, b').
00:55	B rep.	
01:12	Drum cadence	Snare drum solo separates 2nd strain and trio.
	Trio	F major, a fifth *below* C major.
01:20	C	A simple bugle call, *mf*, underpinned by a rising motive in the bass (see ex.).
01:36	C'	Countermelody ("obbligato") in the high woodwind (clar., piccolo).
01:53	C''	Countermelody 2 in tenor brass instruments.
02:09	D	Second trio strain again emphasizes dotted-quarter motion.
02:26	D rep.	Note how the bold, sharply tinted chord in the bass indicates closure.

In 1892 the elegantly monocled and mustached Sousa left the Marine Band to form Sousa's Band, a professional ensemble with whom he toured the world. Sousa's Band was as popular an attraction as Strauss or Offenbach ever were; the excitement was like that of a circus coming to town. Meanwhile Sousa fine-tuned everything about bands; for instance, the design of the sousaphone, an over-the-head tuba for marching, is his. And the important musical instrument factories that grew up in and around Elkhart, Indiana (Selmer, LeBlanc, etc.), owed their very existence to the popularity Sousa fostered for the marching band and its repertoire. Even today, when budget constraints have severely reduced public school music programs, virtually every football team in the country still has its marching band.

Sousa served in the Navy during World War I, leading massed bands in the kind of patriotic spectacles for which he had long been famous. Many senior citizens remember Sousa vividly, and not a few of his players went on to make substantial contributions to the American scene—Meridith Willson, for example, composer of *The Music Man.* But, as with every great composer, Sousa's principal legacy is the music he left behind. The well-known Sousa marches—*Liberty Bell* (of Monty Python fame), *Manhattan Beach, The Washington Post*—are of timeless delight. The comparison of Sousa, the March King, with Johann Strauss II, the Waltz King, is quite apt.

A close relative of the Sousa march is the quickstep for piano in the style called *ragtime,* one of the earliest nationwide crazes for a jazz-related idiom. Virtually identical in form to the Sousa march (and the European polka), the *rag* has a very different sound, emphasizing a high syncopation, or ragged rhythm, descended from the cakewalks of the minstrel shows.

The pioneer composer/performer of piano rags was Scott Joplin.

JOPLIN: *MAPLE LEAF RAG* (1899)

Your recording is by Joplin himself, originally made in the form of a piano roll he cut for player pianos in 1916. In this process the artist played a piano that simultaneously punched holes in a roll of paper; the master paper roll was then duplicated in quantity and sold to owners of instruments like the Pianola, popular from about 1900 through the 1920s. The idea is very old, going back to barrel organs, and the overall mechanics are a variation on the machinery that runs Swiss music boxes. (Punched paper rolls are also an ancestor of the punch-card computing machine.) More sophisticated mechanical pianos eventually permitted encoding of the soloist's touch and pedaling. These machines were used for the historic "recordings" by Mahler, Debussy, and Gershwin, among many others, and there are some equally interesting performances preserved for a reproducing pipe organ of similar design. Composers and producers also took advantage of the possibility of going back to add holes to the paper roll, creating effects impossible for a single ten-fingered player.

Joplin, like all improvisational players, adds ornaments not to be found in the published score, but by and large he is quite faithful to it. What's delightful about ragtime, and especially about the *Maple Leaf Rag,* is the happy-go-lucky sensation as the right hand goes raggedly about its business while the left hand plods away at the basic chord progression, in a kind of oom-pah bass (see Anthology, p. 389). But even in the left hand, the chord motion is not merely boom-chick, boom-chick, but rather makes syncopated ragged cycles of its own:

00:00
(and not:)

etc.

There are two strains, each repeated, and the trio in the key of the subdominant (IV). Unlike a Sousa march, however, the second strain of the trio modulates back to the original tonic key. This attitude toward the trio is much less emphatic than Sousa's, and a little disappointing; you have the sense that the second half lacks the personality of the first, and the rag doesn't really end but just stops.

"Note: Do not play this piece fast," urge Joplin's publications. "It is never right to play Ragtime fast. —*Composer.*"

SCOTT JOPLIN (1868–1917).   Joplin was born in Texarkana, where his piano lessons with a good teacher introduced him to Chopin mazurkas and Brahms waltzes. As a young man he moved upriver to Sedalia, Missouri, to study music at the George Smith College for Negroes, where he supported himself by playing his songs and marches in the local night spots (the Maple Leaf was a Sedalia dance hall). He was soon booked far and wide, and by the time of his performances at the Chicago World's Fair of 1893 he was being called the King of Ragtime.

www.prenhall.com/masterworks
composer profiles
Joplin

The *Maple Leaf Rag,* which appeared in 1899, capped his fame and made both him and his Sedalia publisher rich. On these proceeds he settled in St. Louis to become a full-time composer, turning out some 50 rags as well as songs, marches, and waltzes. In 1907 he moved to New York to establish the Scott Joplin Opera Company and produce his opera *Treemonisha* (1911), about a baby girl, Monisha, found under a tree. Its failure disgruntled him and hastened the symptoms of his syphilitic insanity; he died in a state hospital for the insane.

Modern Joplin fever began with the great popularity of a 1970 disc issued by the budget label Nonesuch Records and recorded by the musicologist Joshua Rifkin. The movie composer Marvin Hamlisch adapted one of the rags on this record, *The Entertainer,* as theme music for the popular 1974 film *The Sting.* Meanwhile a two-volume set of Joplin's works had been assembled by the New York scholar Vera Brodsky Lawrence, and *Treemonisha* was given a loving Atlanta premiere in 1972. In 1976 Joplin was awarded a posthumous Pulitzer Prize for *Treemonisha.*

Joplin

The moves of Joplin and his publisher, Sharp, from Sedalia to St. Louis and thence to New York marked a substantial climb in social and artistic prominence for them both.

Listening Chart

 **CD 4, TR 5**

Scott Joplin (1868–1917)
Maple Leaf Rag (1899)

For: piano

Type: Ragtime
Meter: $\frac{2}{4}$
Key: A♭ major
Duration: 03:13

The ragtime is a quickstep for piano closely related to the Sousa march in form, but emphasizing a kind of high syncopation descended from the cakewalks of the minstrel shows. The piano roll was made by Joplin in April 1916 and re-recorded in 1986 on a 1910 Steinway player piano.

00:00	**1st Strain**	Rag rhythms in right hand; regular eighth-note motion in left.
	A phr. 1	Like a fanfare. The hint of minor and the arpeggios lead to:
00:10	phr. 2	Repeated pounding octaves and cadence; repeated an octave below.
00:21	A rep.	
	2nd Strain	Sudden high notes and hint of chromaticism make the 2nd strain merrier.
00:43	B phr. 1	Uninterrupted, busy ragishness over 4 pairs of bars.
00:53	phr. 2	2nd phrase begins as the first; the octave eighth notes lead to the cadence.
01:04	B rep.	
01:25	**1st Strain**	Recapitulation of first strain (not repeated), in a kind of *da capo*.
	A rep.	
01:46	**Trio**	D♭ major, up a fourth (down a fifth) from A♭.
	C	Four-note chords in the right hand thicken the texture: merrier still.
02:07	C rep.	
02:28	D	Tamer. Paired 8-bar phrases, modulating back to the tonic A♭.
02:49	D rep.	

Along with it came major changes in the packaging of their sheet music. One of the early Sedalia publications shows a stereotypical "uncle" figure with woolly beard and corncob pipe, stooped over in front of a shanty with a broken door. The first edition of the *Maple Leaf Rag* shows high-stepping, high-dressed couples of African ethnicity. Later prints have a simple maple leaf, with and without a portrait of Joplin in high collar and tie. Another stage of ragtime gentrification came with Joplin's appearances at the Louisiana Purchase Exposition of 1904, the world's fair where the ice cream cone, frankfurter, and the song "Meet Me in St. Louis, Louis" made their debut. Joplin's rag for that occasion was *The Cascades,* which shows a full orchestra and upscale clientele, all white and all tuxedoed. A contemporaneous Joplin rag shows a white man on horseback, dressed in full hunt costume and with a hound at his feet.

Yet for all the gentrifying of ragtime that went on, and all the simplification of its rhythms, Europeans had difficulty making sense of the bizarre appearance of ragtime notation on the printed page. They were intrigued by it, nonetheless.

AZZ

In the world at large no musical practice so defines American identity as jazz. Few American contributions to the world's art have been so admired abroad, so envied by foreign composers (the twentieth-century masters Stravinsky and Milhaud among the first), so carefully studied, or so successful at European box offices.

But jazz is by its very nature inexact, and thus difficult to define with much precision. It is humble in its roots, yet an avenue to wealth and fame for its stars; improvised anew with each performance, but following a handful of tried-and-true formulas; done by many but mastered by an elite few; made by African Americans, but made the definition of its age by white bands—and predominantly white audiences. Jazz is primarily an instrumental idiom, but nearly all jazz is based on songs with words, and there are great jazz singers. "If you have to ask what jazz is," said Louis Armstrong, "you'll never know."

A seasoned player will tell you that jazz is a feeling, that people have it or else they don't. (And in the next breath, they'll remind you that "jazz" was originally a slang word for sex.)

Broadly speaking, jazz refers to the many varieties of music descended from New Orleans band music in the late nineteenth century. The vogue for it advanced northward along the Mississippi River, eventually reaching Chicago and radiating from there to other enclaves, notably New York's Harlem. Because jazz involves multiple instrumentalists and is seldom fully notated, it combines spontaneous improvisation with predetermined or generally understood patterning. Typically the players select a given harmonic progression in advance, often based on the harmonic scheme and phrase structure of a well-known song; this scaffold they call the chord changes. With the basic structure and perhaps the tune thus chosen, they agree on the speed and the relative roles of the players and the order they will take their solos. The rest is up to experience and the spirit of the moment, with great value attached to the discovery and innovation along the way. Not that the preplanning takes a board meeting: The leader simply murmurs an instruction: "'I Got Rhythm' in E♭, up tempo," perhaps.

For example, one might choose a song form of 32 bars, say A-A-B-A, with A called "the melody" and B being variously called the middle or the bridge. The players proceed to "count off" 32-bar choruses as they go by, according to their plan.

The standard explanation of the birth of jazz has it beginning with the mingling of ragtime and the *blues.*

THE BLUES. *Blue,* too, means lots of things. What the Germans call *Weltschmerz* (world sadness) and the French a *cafard,* ordinary Americans call feeling blue. Feeling blue can have its cosmic overtones; the resigned racial sadness implicit in the spiritual is often a good deal more explicit in the blues.

Then there are *blue notes.* While all live performance deals in manipulations of pitch, jazz goes out of its way to bend pitches out of their expected shape. This customarily involves lowering the third and seventh scale degrees by a half step into *blue notes* and inflecting any number of other pitches downward.

(The example also reminds us that the roots of jazz are strongly *pentatonic,* with much more emphasis on scale degrees 1–2–3–5–7 than on 4 and 6.) Trumpet and saxophone players cultivate very pronounced blue notes, bending them with a combination of lip, mute, and valve or key work.

A blues *text,* on the other hand, has a rigorous a-a-b scheme:

> **a** Can't go out tonight, I got those homework blues.
> **a** Can't go out tonight, I got those homework blues.
> **b** On your way, and take your dancin' shoes.

(This gem of the American repertoire was composed, I think, by my seventh grade chorus teacher, to whom I'd like to give due credit. But I can't remember her name.) It reflects in miniature a kind of structure quite common in art.

The music that goes along with a blues text is typically that of the *12-bar blues:* three 4-bar phrases in a customary chord progression.

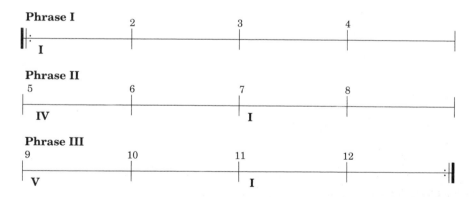

Characteristic of most blues tunes, too, is that the vocal portion fits into just over half of each four bars, typically concluding with a long tonic note. In each *break,* the instrumentalists improvise a response to the singer's proposal. Here, too, the singer might mutter an aside ("Doggone it!" or "Yes, Lord"), or someone in the backup band might compliment the soloist ("Sing it!" or "Mmmm. Sweet."). The meter is usually a lamenting $\frac{4}{4}$; as one famous player put it, "The blues is a slow story."

The grandfather of the modern blues is the famous *St. Louis Blues,* with text and music by W. C. Handy.

HANDY: *ST. LOUIS BLUES* (1914)

The lament is that of a wronged woman, whose faithless husband has left her for—indignity of indignities—a St. Louis woman: a city trollop with diamond rings and, worse, store-bought hair.

Mapped section by section, the form is not dissimilar to that of a piano rag, with two repeated strains and (acting as trio) a refrain. Both the first strain and the refrain follow the 12-bar blues scheme:

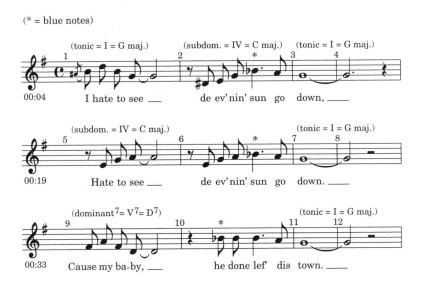

Note the spot where the prevailing strut rhythm lurches into something new, at the raggish "St. Louis Woman wid her diamon' rings." The contrastive character of this B section results in large measure from the different underlying rhythmic pattern, the tango:

From their beginning, jazz forms were subject to the strong influence of Latin—particularly Caribbean—dance steps. In New Orleans, where it all began, you are never far from Creole elements.

Here Louis Armstrong mostly fills in the spaces between the lyrics of text, as Fred Longshaw plonks out the keyboard accompaniment on a wheezy reed organ. Bessie Smith smooths out the melody, often making it into a monotone recitation, then trumpets out the start of the refrain with a fiercely guttural "I got" that can't fail to grab your attention. She's equally free with the words.

The *St. Louis Blues* represents a turn from the $\frac{2}{4}$ march to a cooler $\frac{4}{4}$ and from the untroubled merriness of ragtime to a slow ballad style where the sentiments are more deeply felt. There's a vague aftertaste of minstrelsy in ragtime, if you stop to think about it; just as tragic theater has more weight (and, ultimately, more importance) than comic, the blues seems on the whole a deeper manifestation of the African American experience.

www.prenhall.com/masterworks
composer profiles
Handy

St. Louis Blues succeeded by a brief interval Handy's *Memphis Blues* (1912), a work that had wide circulation in published form following its use as a campaign song for a mayor's election. Together the pair earned **W. C. Handy (1873–1958)** his sobriquet "Father of the Blues." Handy took pride in borrowing traditional melodies and forms, and thus one of his important contributions was the writing down of music that had long been in the air. He went on to compose dozens more popular songs in the blues style, including *Aframerican Hymn.* Additionally he was an important scholar/historian of American culture, contributing published collections (*Blues: An Anthology* and a *Book of Negro Spirituals*) and histories (*Negro Authors and Composers of the United States,* 1936; *Negro Music and Musicians,* 1944), and an autobiography, *Father of the Blues* (1941).

Louis Armstrong's Hot 5

This particular *St. Louis Blues,* as in all good jazz, owes its identity above all to the performers: Louis Armstrong (1898–1971), the cornetist, and Bessie Smith, the singer (1894–1937; she died following an automobile accident in Mississippi). Both became legends of their time. Smith was an imposing figure; her many records had phenomenal sales, and she was billed as the Empress of the Blues. Her mentor was the blues legend Ma Rainey. Alcoholism compromised her last years, but by then her 200 records and several film appearances had captured her art for all time.

Prodigious musicality took Louis Armstrong, like Smith, from the basest poverty to the pinnacle of international stardom. Armstrong played cornet in the band of his orphanage, the Colored Waifs' Home of New Orleans, to which he had been relegated for

Listening Chart

 CD 4, TR 6

W. C. Handy (1873–1958)
St. Louis Blues (1914)

For: singer and accompaniment (here cornet, reed organ)

Text: by the composer

Type: Based on 12-bar blues
Meter: C
Key: G major
Duration: 03:09

The most famous blues of them all, written by the "Father of the Blues," is here performed by two of the jazz greats, Bessie Smith and Louis Armstrong. The recording was made in 1925 in New York.

00:00	**Verse**	The verse builds an AAB block out of two 12-bar blues cycles and a 16-bar tango.
	A	The vocal portion takes about half of each 4 bars, with the trumpet licks responding.
00:04	a	Stays in I.
00:19	a	Sung bars start in IV, move to I.
00:33	b	Sung bars start in V, move to I.
	A	
00:49	a	Just as before. Louis Armstrong's responses develop in complexity.
01:04	a	
01:17	b	
	B	The tango. 16 bars: a pair of 8-bar phrases. The reed organ wheezes on.
01:32	c	
02:01	c	
	Refrain	"Got the St. Louis blues." Concluding 12-bar cycle—the most famous of them all.
02:27	d	
02:42	d'	
02:55	e	

shooting a gun during a New Year's Eve celebration. Soon he was working the honky-tonk dives of Storyville, the brothel district of New Orleans. His first recordings, which just precede this version of *St. Louis Blues,* were with King Oliver's Creole Jazz Band of Chicago (1922–23). After a stint with Fletcher Henderson's band in New York (1924) he branched out on his own with the Hot 5 and Hot 7, based again in Chicago (1925–28). By the 1930s Armstrong had become a superstar, as much for his gargle-throated singing as for his phenomenal trumpet playing. He was called Satchmo, for Satchel Mouth, and it was a term of endearment. He made his valedictory appearance in the 1969 film version of *Hello, Dolly*—since by that time Armstrong's 1964 recording of the title song had become the only one anybody cared about.

NEW ORLEANS. Questioned about where jazz began, old-timers respond to the effect that it was always there. Perhaps that poetic proposition is the real truth, but the more useful observation is that Satchmo and his generation had found it in the night spots of New Orleans. The New Orleans, or Dixieland, band consisted of a lead cornet or trumpet, trombone, clarinet, and the rhythm section: piano, guitar or banjo, bass, drums. If the band were marching, as to a graveside, the string bass part would be played on tuba and the piano dispensed with. King Oliver's Creole Jazz Band, active from 1915 in New Orleans and then (after the brothels were closed) in Chicago, popularized the basic style and served as a training school for the next generation: Jelly Roll Morton and His Red Hot Peppers, Louis Armstrong with his Hot 5 and Hot 7, and so on. Armstrong's groups relied strongly on the composition and piano work of Lil (Lillian) Hardin, and they later married and subsequently divorced.

The habit was, and is, for the better bands to recruit promising young players and give them a start; then the ones with sufficient talent and following would break away after their years of apprenticeship to form their own bands. This is not so different from the way Diaghilev's dancers left him to go and seek their own fortunes, or the way string quartets regenerate. But probably the strongest factor in the proliferation of jazz was its connection with the new radio and recording industries. People knew Scott Joplin from the published sheet music and the odd piano roll, but they knew the work of the great jazz players, like Armstrong, from records and coast-to-coast network broadcasts.

Dixieland music is the sound of the Roaring Twenties, America's period of uncontained indulgence. F. Scott Fitzgerald called it the Jazz Age. The exuberant heterophony of the New Orleans sound, and its splendid rhythmic vitality, are in some ways synonymous with the unconditional optimism in the country at large—the optimism that was shattered by the stock market crash in 1929 and the Great Depression that followed.

THE BIG BANDS.   One element of jazz we've overlooked so far is its ubiquitous *swing.* Music that isn't tied to written notation is naturally freer to indulge in rhythmic nonprecisions, even to encourage them and make of them high art. The swing era of the 1930s and 1940s cultivated softer, suaver beat patterns than the Dixieland style, and blues tempos were a good deal more common than the strident up-tempos of Dixieland. The cooler movement was met with the thicker sounds of the *big band* and its full sections of reeds and brasses. This represents a formidable shift in sonority. (And racial mix: There were famous white bands, famous black bands, and some tentative crossings over.) The master of the style was Fletcher Henderson (1897–1952), who had wanted to be a professor of chemistry but instead saw his band headlining, from 1923, at the famous Roseland Ballroom in New York. Henderson's disciples, notably the clarinetist Benny Goodman (1909–86) and the trombonist Glenn Miller (1904–44; he was killed in a plane crash) fashioned the big bands of the 1930s and 1940s. Henderson later became staff arranger for Goodman's band.

Big bands aren't that big: 20 people or less, perhaps three or four trumpets, two to four trombones, three to five reed players who mostly play saxophone but can double clarinets and occasionally flute, and a rhythm section of piano, bass, and drums. Such a group lends itself less to the breezy free-for-all you hear in Dixieland than to call-and-response relationships between the big-name soloist and the backup band, or antiphonal effects between, say, saxes and brass. And the larger the performing group, the more some version of notated music is required. Increasingly one hears strings of variations where some passages are composed and notated in the old style and some improvised. Big-band players talk about *riffs* (marking time over the chord changes), *vamps,* and *chatter.*

The seminal composer in this idiom was Duke Ellington, to whose work we turn momentarily. Other major figures of the swing era are Harry James and Tommy Dorsey (who introduced Frank Sinatra), Guy Lombardo and His Royal Canadians, Paul Whiteman and his orchestra (who encouraged Gershwin), Chick Webb (who introduced Ella Fitzgerald)—all based in New York. In Kansas City and Chicago, there was Count Basie; in California, Artie Shaw and later Stan Kenton, who introduced the notion of progressive jazz. Another club band you may know already is Ricky Ricardo's band at the Tropicana in *I Love Lucy.* There are hints of parody in much of what they do, and the emphasis is naturally on Caribbean rhythms, but at the same time it's typical good club music. The big Havana dance scene in the American musical comedy *Guys and Dolls* (1950) is to much the same effect.

Do not underestimate the power of the feelings this music arouses in people born after World War I: the generation of your grandparents. They did not remember the Roaring Twenties but instead the pendulum swing to the horrors of the Depression and going off to war again. This is the music they heard on their radio sets and Victrolas: the music that was all too frequently interrupted with the news flashes of air raids and death. It was music for the New Year festivities in Times Square, music to keep the spirits up. But the big-band slow dances were for many, many couples the music they remembered most vividly of all: dancing to it cheek to cheek, bidding each other tearful and fearful farewells, and wondering if they would ever see each other again.

Duke Ellington
and his big band

ELLINGTON: *NEW EAST ST. LOUIS TOODLE-O* (1937)

Duke Ellington's band was part of the scene in Washington, D.C., until the end of World War I. They moved to New York in the early 1920s, and from 1927 to 1932 were the main attraction at the Cotton Club in Harlem. Ellington was primarily a composer/conductor, his works strongly based on the musical personality of his players but at the same time becoming more and more extended, notated compositions. In his early "jungle" period, he developed his trademark nocturnal sound, with growling interjections from brass and reeds and understated but pervasive support of low drumbeat and pizzicato bass; later, he investigated jazz colors, not just blue but in one famous case *Black, Brown and Beige* (1943).

The *New East St. Louis Toodle-O* is a 1937 remake of a song first recorded in 1927 by Ellington and his trumpet player Bubber Miley. "Toddle-Oo" in the original title is a reference to an ancient citizen of East St. Louis whose walk was as low as a toad's. This 1937 version is simpler and a good deal suaver than the first, and the brilliant solo work is by Cootie Williams. (Don't listen for Duke Ellington playing the piano here; although he's listed in the credits, his participation is imperceptible.) The form consists of two strophes based on a 32-bar song, A-A-B-A, that grows out of an original and quite characteristic chord progression:

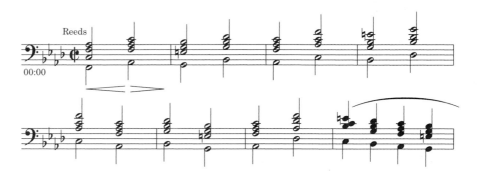

Admire the very slick, dark sounds of this most celebrated of the big bands. In the eight-bar introduction alone, notice the perfect understatement of the saxophones, the evocative chime, and the foreshadowing of the solo trumpet with wah-wah mute—a vestige of the jungle sound; and in the trombone response lies a very good example of what is meant by swing. As you enjoy the solo work for the muted trumpet, count off the four phrases of the first strophe, noting the shift to a strut rhythm for the B part, with reeds and plunger-mute trumpet responses. The second strophe features trombones, soon overtaken by the clarinetist (Barney Bigard), who begins to come through in the second A and dominates the bridge, bending pitches left and right. The ending reminds you of another image prominent in Ellington's work, that of a ponderous steam locomotive. Here the piece seems to roll heavily to a steam-letting-off conclusion.

Listening Chart

 CD 4, TR 7

Duke Ellington (1899–1974)
New East St. Louis Toodle-O (1937)

For: big band: 2 trumpets, cornet, 4 trombones (including a valve trombone), 4 reed players (clarinets, saxophones), guitar, 2 basses, drums, chimes, piano

Type: Based on 32-bar song
Meter: ¢
Key: F minor
Duration: 02:59

This remake of a decade-old work, recorded 5 March 1937, is an excellent example of the sophisticated sound world discovered by Ellington and perhaps the best of the big bands. The introduction presents, unadorned, the underlying chord progression.

00:00	**Introduction**	8 bars. The chimes, low register, and minor key suggest a dark, nocturnal atmosphere—Ellington's specialty. Trumpet solo and brass enter.
	Chorus 1	Features Cootie Williams with wah-wah-muted trumpet.
00:20	a	Trumpet solo cultivates a vocal quality, like a gravel-throated singer.
00:40	a	Chord progression and accomp. virtually identical; trpt. solo develops.
00:58	b	The break launches into a strut, with major-mode inflections.
01:19	a	Suave, smooth sound of the sax section is an Ellington trademark.
	Chorus 2	The full big band, by sections, still low and mysterious.
01:38	a	Brasses; bass rhythms speed up; saxophone punctuations.
01:58	a	Clarinet soloist (Barney Bigard) breaks out from the brass work.
02:16	b	Clarinet dominates the break; chime returns.
02:37	a	Trumpet returns, sax countermelody; locomotive-stop conclusion.

Duke Ellington (1899–1974) and his Famous Orchestra went on to make a major European tour just before World War II, at the height of their fame. The orchestra declined during the war owing to changes in personnel. After the war Ellington concentrated on recording his big pieces—unprecedented marvels of texture, tempo, and sophistication—in the new LP format. From the 1930s on, jazz is a story of ceaseless world travel, radio, film, and above all phonograph recordings. The phonograph record allowed music to circulate to a public of theretofore unimagined size, and it captured one-time compositional modes well. Jazz became big business and a major American export. Jazz festivals in England, France, and Holland rivaled the homegrown versions. Together, jazz and popular music began to overtake classical music in economic clout.

BEBOP. The big bands and dance orchestras with their arrangements and notated compositions had by the 1940s successfully popularized one kind of jazz-based music. But the result was an increasingly far cry from the original principles of the New Orleans style. Black musicians in smaller combos returned to the aggressively personal style of improvisation, adding much more complex rhythms and chords. *Bebop,* or just *bop,* was the name given to this new jazz style that emerged in New York in the 1940s; the word itself (drawn from scat singing) expresses the kinds of accents the musicians preferred.

www.prenhall.com/masterworks
composer profiles
Parker

Bebop was largely the creation of the South Carolinian trumpet player Dizzy Gillespie (of puffed out cheeks and weirdly built trumpet, 1917–93), and **Charlie Parker (1920–55),** called Bird and Yardbird—an alto sax player. Both were products of Earl (Fatha') Hines's big band. Their new style was worked out in jam sessions during a two-year strike of the American Federation of Musicians, then introduced after the recording ban was over in a series of 1945 recordings: *Groovin' High, Salt Peanuts,* and *Hot House.* Bebop is much faster than swing, both in tempo and prevailing note values; it thrives on seventh chords and even more complicated sonorities and sometimes investigates alternative scales.

PARKER: *LADY BE GOOD* (1946)

Lady Be Good, based on the title song from a stage play by George and Ira Gershwin (1924), comes from the end of Parker's first period, when he and Dizzy Gillespie went to Los Angeles for a nightclub engagement and recording sessions. Parker's particular expertise was in improvising new melodies over a small repertoire of borrowed harmonic progressions, adapting the old songs to the busier new rhetoric and, not coincidentally, avoiding royalties. Parker's roots in Kansas City blues and traditional jazz are always obvious, but his melodic innovation is altogether new.

Listen closely to the beginning, just after the applause subsides, for you can hear one of the musicians ask, "Lady Be Good?" The pianist (Arnold Ross) molds the miscellaneous four-bar introduction into a second four bars of true lead-in, and for a moment you recognize the unmistakable beginning of the Gershwin song.

But the piano skattelybops immediately away from the original, touching on the tune again only at the beginnings of the phrases. Again the form is a 32-bar A-A-B-A; the atmosphere seems to be that of the old-fashioned swing band, but the threads of improvisation are undeniably those of bebop. Count off the form to yourself at least once, for it's important to have it in mind: 8-bar intro (4 + 4), then three 32-bar choruses (8 bars × 4).

Parker himself enters for the second chorus, and now only his first four notes are those of the Gershwin song. At first he dwells on relatively simple syncopated figures in eighth and quarter notes; he already knows he will be in for two choruses and is carefully pacing his composition. It begins to pick up steam with the first bridge (the B of A-A-B-A); then, in Parker's next chorus (with a new background riff in the trumpet and saxophone), you get a superb example of his melodic inventiveness as the solo line forms a series of arched phrases out of 16th-note passagework, long on chromaticism and with elegant references to what has come before. The recording fades out after the second saxophone chorus.

In June 1946 (*Lady Be Good* is from January), Parker's drug and alcohol addictions led to a nervous breakdown, and he was confined in a California mental institution. From 1947 to 1951 he worked again in New York and abroad, developing the Afro-Cuban and Afro-American styles; the New York nightclub Birdland was named after him. Banned from club appearances by the narcotics squad, Parker plummeted into suicide attempts and a stay at Bellevue Hospital before dying of physical and mental depletion in the New York apartment of the Rothschild family.

Listening Chart

  CD 4, TR 8

Charlie Parker (1920–55)
***Lady Be Good* (1946)**

For: jazz combo featuring Charlie Parker, alto saxophone: 2 alto saxophones, tenor saxophone, piano, bass, drums

Based on the song of the same name by George and Ira Gershwin

Type: Based on 32-bar song
Meter: $\frac{4}{4}$
Key: G major
Duration: 03:10

Gershwin's original is the title song from a stage play of 1924. Parker's rendition was recorded during a concert performance on 28 January 1946 in Los Angeles.

00:00	**Introduction**	Traditional opening vamp (4 bars x 2). A voice says "Lady Be Good?"
	Chorus 1	(32 bars, 8 x 4.) Piano, bass, drum set; features Arnold Ross, piano.
00:17	a	The Gershwin melody at first, improvisatory thereafter. The chord
00:30	a	progression of the song is maintained throughout: the listener's
00:43	b	mind provides the melody, as the pianist (and later, Parker) weaves
00:57	a	the cool, complex bebop: thus something old, something new.
	Chorus 2	Parker's first chorus (32 bars). The sax somewhat wheezy.
01:11	a	Only the first four notes are recognizable as Gershwin's melody. In
01:25	a	his first chorus he generally proceeds from syncopated figures in eighth
01:39	b	and quarter notes. Parker has the content of both 32-bars choruses in
01:52	a	mind from the start. One of the players mutters approval (01:25).
	Chorus 3	Parker's second chorus (32 bars). New background figure in trpt., sax.
02:06	a	In bar 5 (02:14) he sets out in a flurry of arching 16th-note phrases
02:20	a	with the phrase contours and content closely related to each
02:34	b	other. The closing motives refer to Parker's opening gambit in
02:48	a	chorus 2.
03:03	(appl.)	(The other players go on to do their choruses.)

One of the several reactions to bebop was the cool jazz of the 1950s, pioneered by the trumpet player Miles Davis (1926–91). Davis moved from St. Louis to New York in 1944 to apprentice himself to Charlie Parker, and was shortly playing in big bands. The ensemble with which he made his epochal recordings of 1949–50 (later issued as *Birth of the Cool*) was a nonet, a big band stripped down to its essentials. Davis plays without vibrato; the rhythms are slower and more curvaceous, emphasizing lyric expression over Parker's fast passagework.

A key figure in the birth of the cool was the arranger Gil Evans (1912–88), who had worked on Parker's *Anthropology* and *Yardbird Suite*. Evans's contribution to the nonet recordings included the famous *Boplicity;* later he arranged for the Davis albums *Miles Ahead* (1957), *Porgy and Bess* (1959), and *Sketches of Spain* (1960). The other famous Miles Davis recording of this period is *Kind of Blue* (1959).

Large ensemble work is typical of festival performances and big-label recordings. In the more ordinary world of the clubs and recital halls, cool jazz of the 1950s and 1960s was dominated by smaller groups, notably the Modern Jazz Quartet, the Dave Brubeck Quartet, and the Bill Evans Trio (piano, bass, drums). Intimate cool became, in one manifestation, West Coast jazz, the after-hours music of the LA studio musicians. Davis, meanwhile, went on to work with electronic instruments, microtones, rock accompaniments, and the like, as represented by the influential recording of 1969, *Bitches Brew,* a monument of the movement typically called jazz rock or fusion.

Jazz, even more than opera, is the story of individual stars. The list of major figures I have passed quietly over—Chick Corea, John Coltrane, the singers Billie Holliday and Ella Fitzgerald, Charles Mingus, Thelonius Monk come immediately to mind—is much longer than the dozen or so artists you've just read about. When two gifted individuals, like Fatha' Hines and Louis Armstrong in 1928 or Gillespie and Parker in the mid-1940s, entered the same constellation, or when other extraordinary artists came together at the Newport Jazz Festival, something wonderful and unique would nearly always transpire—much as the Spring-September constellation of Rudolf Nureyev and Margot Fonteyn was a one-time episode in the annals of ballet.

There's a dark side, too, to jazz, as there is in rock music of a later time: Jazz—taking place, as it did largely in nightclubs—is also an institution with a marked propensity for alcohol and drug dependency. Too many of these fine artists, from Joplin and Bessie Smith to Charlie Parker, Billie Holliday, and Bill Evans, fried themselves over the years. It seems a terrible price to pay for genius.

 MERICAN CLASSICAL MUSIC

In classical music composition, the search for a compositional voice where American values held their own with the European styles was not easy. The customary course of schooling for the promising American composer or performer was to regard Europe as a finishing school, perhaps to aspire to study with a teacher like Liszt. However, in the American Northeast, notably the Boston–New York corridor, there was serious music teaching and music composition by such engaging personalities as the organist-composer Dudley Buck (1839–1909), who had trained at the Leipzig Conservatory and later taught at the New England School of Music, and Horatio Parker (1863–1919), professor and dean (from 1904) of the School of Music at Yale. The best of the American Romanticists were Edward MacDowell, trained at the Paris Conservatoire and in Germany, and Mrs. H. H. A. Beach.

Amy Beach (1867–1944) was the first major woman composer from the United States. A musician of tremendous abilities, she negotiated the demands of career, marriage, and fame with enviable aplomb—the sort of grace that often characterized women of the American upper class in her day. Like most well-bred girls of the era, Amy Marcy Cheney was introduced to the piano by her mother. When the family moved to Boston she had the opportunity of studying with excellent local teachers of piano and harmony, and in 1883 made her local debut as soloist in a piano concerto. In 1885, at the age of 18, she married the Boston physician Henry Harris Aubrey Beach, twenty-five years her senior. Thereafter she styled herself, in tribute to that happy arrangement, Mrs. H. H. A. Beach.

www.prenhall.com/masterworks
composer profiles
Beach

In the 25 years of her marriage until her husband's death in 1910, Beach tried to limit her public appearances to an annual piano recital and the premieres of her own works. Meanwhile she profited from her leisure to absorb the vast repertoire of the European late-Romantic period, putting to work what she had taught herself in compositions of ever increasing ambition and sophistication. This was the period of her best large-scale work: the Gaelic Symphony (1894), Violin Sonata (1896), and Piano Concerto (1899). The Boston Symphony Orchestra gave the first performances of the symphony and, with Beach as piano soloist, the concerto. Quite apart from the intrinsic merit of the works, which is substantial, both premieres were historic in the annals of women in music.

Amy Beach
(c. 1900)

BEACH: FROM VIOLIN SONATA IN A MINOR, OP. 34 (1896)

II. SCHERZO

The American art music repertoire drew at first primarily on the European heritage. The stylistic vocabulary of this sonata is not so different from that of Brahms or Dvořák, with more than a few suggestions of the Hungarian or Slavonic dance and merry gypsy-like fiddling. With the title "scherzo," Beach suggests the lighthearted cleverness and dance-and-trio formal organization of the European model, though choosing duple instead of triple meter. For its *time,* then, the movement is quite traditional.

But for its *place,* New England, the movement is special indeed, evidence of the substantial ownership American composers had begun to claim in classical music. Beach

exerts a tight control over her chosen materials, with nearly every gesture referring one way or another to the neighbor-note motive (*x* in the example) of the opening phrase. The slow homophonic trio, for instance, plays out over a long-held low G punctuated with the motive, first in the violin and then in the left hand of the piano. The harmonic design is eyebrow-raising, as ordinary harmonic goals are reached via darting excursions to distant key areas. Beach's natural lyricism shines through; the bold contours of the phrases, and their considerable length, are quite attractive. One senses a highly refined intellect at work—no rough-hewn pioneer simplicity here.

The scherzo comes from an expansive 30-minute sonata in four movements first performed by Franz Kneisel, violin, and the composer in January 1897, during a concert by the Kneisel String Quartet. By the early 1930s, after decades of performing the work, Beach was in the habit of making judicious cuts in the sonata and advised other artists to do the same. But she played the scherzo as written, though sometimes omitting the repeat.

The performers on the recording—Joseph Silverstein, violin, and Gilbert Kalisch, piano—are both American artists noted for their commitment to the New England repertoire. Silverstein, longtime concertmaster of the Boston Symphony Orchestra, later

Listening Chart

 CD 4, TR 9

Amy Beach (1867–1944)
Violin Sonata in A Minor, op. 34 (1896)
II. Scherzo

For: violin and piano

Type: scherzo and trio
Meter: $\frac{2}{4}$, ¢
Key: G major
Duration: 04:10

The merry spirit and dance-and-trio formal organization are that of a scherzo in the European tradition. Much of the language devolves from the melodic motive heard at the outset.

	Scherzo		
00:00	a		G major, molto vivace. The sprightly fiddle tune and interweaving piano
00:28	a rep.		leave the tonic key after a dozen bars (00:13), soon reaching the dominant, D major.
00:56	b		D major, darting through distant keys to return to G.
	Trio		
01:33	part 1		G minor, più lento. Two broad homophonic phrases in the piano over a low-G drone in the violin; rich chromaticism.
02:25	part 2		Vn. joins the lugubrious homophony, with the drone in the piano l. h. Motive *x* increasingly prominent.
03:08		transition	The head motive and accelerando effect the return to:
	Scherzo		G major, tempo I. After a dozen bars of strict repeat, cuts ahead to
03:16	a		material from the b section, then accelerates into a coda with violin trills
03:46	coda		and a cadence on the low G.

became conductor of the Utah Symphony. Kalisch is a principal member of the Boston Symphony Chamber Players and teaches music at the State University of New York at Stony Brook.

After being widowed, Mrs. Beach traveled in Europe for three years, appearing in the major German capitals as Amy Beach. She returned to the United States at the outbreak of war in 1914 to live in New York, where she maintained her careers in performance and composition while playing a significant role in the organization of the Music Teachers National Association (MTNA) and the Music Educators National Conference (MENC), both still active today. In this and many other ways her work constitutes a fine example of how women's involvement in the arts shaped our national identity.

Just before his death, Liszt gave Edward MacDowell (1860–1908) a strong boost with public endorsements, and MacDowell returned home from Europe with successful tone poems, piano concertos, and orchestral suites to his credit. The document nominating MacDowell as the first professor of music at Columbia University, in 1896, calls him "the greatest musical genius America has produced." The demands of university administration—and the commercial market—caused him to curtail his interest in big works, with the result that his most characteristic American composition is the set of ten *Woodland Sketches* for piano, including "To a Wild Rose" (1896). MacDowell had the excellent idea of leaving his home in Peterborough, New Hampshire, to be used as an artists' colony. This is the famous MacDowell Colony, still very much alive and well. Amy Beach, who outlasted MacDowell by 35 years, enjoyed annual visits to the MacDowell Colony and in her will left it the royalties from sales of her works to help ensure its continuation.

Meanwhile, Charles Griffes (1884–1920) came close to developing an American Impressionism. A student of Englebert Humperdinck in Berlin, he spent his career teaching at a prep school in upstate New York, where he composed stage and orchestral works (notably the familiar Poem for Flute and Orchestra, 1918), chamber music, songs, and solo piano compositions. At the end of his life he was approaching an atonal style commensurate with European developments a decade earlier.

It's interesting to speculate on the reasons why the work of these classical American composers has faded from the repertoire, whereas Sousa marches, Joplin rags, and the great parlor songs and blues have made an enduring place for themselves. Would Griffes have rivaled Debussy if he had been exposed to a more vibrant concert life? Were MacDowell and Mrs. Beach barking up the wrong tree? To this day there is an ongoing tension in indigenous American music between popular styles and the more elevated traditions of European art music. Generally speaking, the former have been better understood by the American public at large and certainly more successful at the bank, while the latter enjoy greater esteem among intellectuals and academics. Of course the same tension existed between popular music and art music in Europe, but it is a particularly American phenomenon that both styles have been regarded as equal partners in our national heritage and that they so commonly intersect and interact. The one is no less American than the other. For a parallel phenomenon in the world of architecture, think of Disneyland and Frank Lloyd Wright's Guggenheim Museum in New York, each built in the 1950s; both are wonders of American design.

These very concerns preoccupied an important trio of twentieth-century American classical composers: Charles Ives (1874–1954), George Gershwin (1898–1937), and Aaron Copland (1900–90).

www.prenhall.com/masterworks
composer profiles
Ives

IVES, GERSHWIN, COPLAND.   They are an unlikely trio: Ives a Yankee businessman and patriot, who composed music in his spare time; Gershwin, a Brooklyn Jew and first-generation American, whose genius as a songsmith made him rich and famous despite his almost neurotic self-doubts about his technical preparation; and Copland, who was trained abroad and fancied himself a member of the European-American musical élite but ended up beloved as a composer of patriotic works that are played in America as often as Elgar's marches are in England. Together they managed, without particularly intending it, to give definition to a national style for classical music. And their work coincides with America's ascendance in the world as a political superpower.

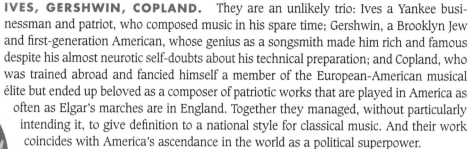

Ives

Ives's father, George Ives, had been a bandmaster during the Civil War and continued in the profession in Danbury, Connecticut. Danbury was a typical New England town, fond of patriotic songs, holiday picnics on the town green, and baseball—and, of course, there was church on Sunday, with organ playing and the grand old hymns with which American Protestantism is so richly endowed. There was something of Leopold Mozart in George Ives; he honed his children's aural and dextral skills by having them play hymns at the piano, but with the left and right hands in different keys. Experiences such as these conditioned Charles Ives with an unusual sensitivity to the sounds around him: how in a parade, for example, you hear not just one band passing in review but the others before and after. In real life, and especially outdoors, music can be a happy cacophony, a kind of noise in which Ives took special joy. He mastered church organ playing and tried hard at baseball; at Yale he was an uninspired student but for his music tutelage at the hands of the master composer Horatio Parker.

All these experiences found their way into Ives's music, at which he worked most assiduously in the years between the beginning of the century and World War I. Composition for Ives had little to do with the public: He did not seek to have his works performed, and published only a few, the better to be able to give them away to friends. These included a collection of *114 Songs* and a piano sonata called *Concord, Massachusetts,* where each movement is named after one of the town's celebrated literary figures: Emerson, Hawthorne, The Alcotts, Thoreau. There is also a published collection, *Essays Before a Sonata* (1920).

Ives's great instrumental works—quartets, symphonies, and other compositions grouped into what he called orchestral sets—remained in manuscript. Mrs. Ives (*née* Harmony Twichell, who figures programmatically in a number of works) thought her husband's interest in composition rather daft and insisted on putting the manuscripts in boxes in the garage. The result is that Ives's work, given in its near entirety to Yale at his death, was in utter disarray. Scholars have spent a full generation sorting all the paper and redoing the scores, and orchestras now have a fair chance of bringing Ives's big works to life. For instance *Three Places in New England,* composed around 1912 and made familiar in a reduced scoring premiered in 1931, has only been available in restored full score since 1976.

IVES: "PUTNAM'S CAMP," FROM *THREE PLACES IN NEW ENGLAND* (1912)

Ives has a memorable, sometimes outlandish grasp of texture and performing force, where blocks of players and their musical material do not necessarily relate to each other and sometimes clash violently. That is the case in this orchestral triptych evoking patriots, settings, and events dear to the hearts of New Englanders: the slow footfall of Colonel Robert Gould Shaw's "Colored Regiment" in the Civil War, as suggested in the famous statue in Boston Common; a Fourth of July picnic; a Sunday morning walk along the Housatonic River in Connecticut.

The second of the *Three Places in New England* is a park near Redding, Connecticut, on the site of General Israel Putnam's encampment in the winter 1778–79. A child wanders away from the holiday picnic (sponsored, says Ives, by the First Church and the Vil-

Listening Chart

 CD 4, TR 10

Charles Ives (1874–1954)
***Three Places in New England* (1912)**
Putnam's Camp, Redding, Connecticut

Type: symphonic scene
Meter: $\frac{4}{4}$
Key: B♭ major, etc.
Duration: 05:51

For: piccolo, 2 flutes, 2 oboes, English horn, 2 clarinets, 2 bassoons, contrabassoon; 4 horns, 2 trumpets, 2 trombones, tuba; timpani, bass drum, snare drum, cymbals, gong; piano, celesta, organ; 2 harps; strings.

Resist the temptation to try to identify every tune. What's intriguing here is Ives's sense of music as omnipresent life, where tidbits of favorite melodies are apt to strike the ear without warning, then evaporate.

00:00	Introduction	An orchestral "roll-off" with a jazzy twist.
00:10	**March**	The march begins gently and ordinarily, then disintegrates. At 00:26 (in ww.) fragments of *The British Grenadiers*, a Revolutionary marching song. The tumble continues, then the music regroups for a fanfare.
00:51	restatement	A bolder statement of the march, with trombone counterpoint (cites the trio of Sousa's *Semper fidelis*); a bit of the *Battle Cry of Freedom* and *Yankee Doodle*.
01:10	episode	A carefree little cadence and long dissolve: the children at play.
02:15	**Dream sequence**	The point where Liberty appears. A drum cadence begins, irregularly. Wispy motives from the quoted tunes.
03:05	accelerando	The figure in the bass develops into a vamp. The soldiers march out of camp.
03:24	episode	Putnam appears. The fanfare introduces treatment of *The British Grenadiers* and *Hail, Columbia!* (03:51), gathering into:
03:59	encounter	Everyone cheers, as though colliding.
04:13	episode	The cadence from 01:10, followed by a jazzy lick (04:25). The child awakes, hears the children at play, and returns to the picnic.
04:35	**March**	The march regroups in confusion; more collision at 04:42.
04:49		*The British Grenadiers* in solo trumpet.
05:09	restatement	
05:18	chaos	. . . the percussion suggesting fireworks, . . .
05:43	"cadence"	and a bit of *The Star-Spangled Banner*.

lage Cornet Band). He falls asleep and dreams of a tall woman, perhaps Liberty (02:15). The Revolutionary soldiers march out of camp to a popular tune, *The British Grenadiers,* that was sung in Putnam's regiment (03:05). Suddenly Putnam himself walks over the hill and the soldiers cheer. The boy wakes, hears the children's games (04:13), and runs back to listen to the band and join in the holiday merrymaking.

Ives's offbeat humor, as sensed here, is often in play elsewhere: In the Fourth Symphony, for example, he calls for a chorus, preferably without voices. This kind of thing reminds you that Ives's creative world had little to do with the daily hurly-burly of securing performances or paying for the groceries. It's a mark of his originality that no other composer of his time or afterward sounds remotely like Ives's.

www.prenhall.com/masterworks
composer profiles
Gershwin

Gershwin, unlike Ives, delighted in pleasing the public, and can certainly be counted one of America's great success stories. His early drudge work in Tin Pan Alley, New York's music publishing district, found him sitting on the sidewalk outside Remick's playing the pieces that were for sale inside, an experience that doubtlessly contributed to his great facility as a composer of pop songs. Had pop and commercial music been his only work, he would nevertheless be remembered as a major figure in American music. His song "Swanee" was an all-time hit of the era, and to this day everybody knows songs

George Gershwin

he wrote for Broadway or the movies. But most importantly, Gershwin found a viable connection between the concert hall and the pleasure palace; he "legitimized" jazz.

This chapter in Gershwin's life began when the great American bandleader Paul Whiteman arranged, for both political and business reasons, to give a Lincoln's Birthday concert of American music at Carnegie Hall. Gershwin began his contribution somewhat reluctantly but ended up setting the world on fire with *Rhapsody in Blue* (1924), for piano and orchestra. (The clarinet glissando right at the beginning came out of a rehearsal, as have many lasting performance traditions. It was written into the published score.) *Rhapsody in Blue* left the world clamoring for more, and Gershwin was deluged with invitations to repeat the success. To these he responded with the great Piano Concerto in F (1925) and the ballet *An American in Paris* (1928) for a Chicago company called the Ballet Caravan. All of these works are for a big orchestra and have reasonably classical forms, yet they are tuneful and direct in harmony, long on swing and heavily blue. They also promoted the voguish dance steps of the era, notably the Charleston. One of the extraordinary features of Gershwin's music is how comfortably its extravagant rhythms and chords are notated, so the performer has a good chance of approximating the desired effect at first reading. With the jazz-based forms, this is a real talent.

Gershwin's *Porgy and Bess* (1935), his most ambitious undertaking, continues to investigate the intersection of popular and classical styles. The source was *Porgy,* a stage play by the African American writer DuBose Heyward, and Gershwin's original idea was to fashion a Broadway musical from it. He went at the task with great diligence, embarking on a long correspondence with Heyward and then, more interestingly, visiting Charleston, South Carolina, to study the folkways of the black people there. The locale was a good one, for the sand islands off the South Carolina and Georgia coast were insulated enough that a rich and undiluted local musical practice had grown up there. Gershwin grasped not just the forms and melodies but the passion of the culture that had created them.

His decision to use recitative and a continuous musical texture in *Porgy and Bess* lent gravity to the undertaking by turning a stage show into a kind of folk opera; by the same token it rather upped the ante with the public and the critics. Projects like these run the danger of seeming condescending, especially with the passage of years, but Gershwin's dignified and affectionate solution has stood the test of time well and is even more popular today than it was in 1935.

 GERSHWIN: "SUMMERTIME," FROM *PORGY AND BESS* (1935)

Listening again to "Summertime," you'll remember its structure easily enough: two strophes of 16 bars (not a blues, although there are several similarities) with instrumental breaks between the vocal phrases. The points of intersection with the many American songs you have now encountered are clear. "Summertime" comes in the long tradition of singing Americans. Think, now that you've got considerable listening experience under your belt, about the bluesy effects in the melody and the rich chromaticism in the accompaniment. The story of *Porgy and Bess* is both sad and beautiful. Porgy is a cripple who lives in a corner shanty and pushes himself around on a wheeled cart; Bess, a woman of ill repute, Crown's girl. When Crown, the high-rolling stevedore, kills Robbins in a brawl over a dice game, Bess gives him money to get out of town. Sportin' Life, a slimy peddler of "happy dust," offers to take her to New York, but instead Bess takes shelter with Porgy. After a hurricane, Crown reappears to take Bess away and Porgy knifes him, then chokes him to death: "Bess, you got a man now, you got Porgy." Bess succumbs to the happy dust and goes north with Sportin' Life. Discovering this, Porgy harnesses his goat cart to go find her.

The principal subject matter, as Gershwin sees it, is the neighborhood of Catfish Row. With the wonderful scene at the wake for Robbins ("He's gone, gone, gone" / "Fill up the saucer" [with money to pay for the burial] / "My man's gone"), the cameo street scenes (a strawberry woman and a crab man sing of their wares), the church picnic on Kittiwah Island ("It Ain't Necessarily So")—and, of course, in "Summertime"—Gershwin creates an authentically American local color that was, and in many respects remains, without parallel on the opera stage.

Not surprisingly, the initial run of *Porgy and Bess* was neither long nor greatly successful, as well-meaning but wrongheaded journalists complained that the genre of the work was confused. Gershwin and the promoters were concerned about its length and ended up cutting a half dozen major numbers. Before a new production could be organized and put on the road, Gershwin was diagnosed with the brain tumor to which he succumbed a few months later. But the revival of 1952, with Leontyne Price as Bess, William Warfield as Porgy, and Cab Calloway as Sportin' Life, was a triumph, leading to an international road show that played to packed houses from Milan to Vienna, Berlin to London, and at length reached the Soviet Union. (Truman Capote covered this Russian

Listening Chart

George Gershwin (1898–1937)
Porgy and Bess (1935)
 "Summertime"

For: Clara (sopr.), chorus, orchestra

Text: By Ira Gershwin (1896–1983), after a novel by DuBose Heyward
 (1885–1940)

 **CD 1, TR 1**

Type: Opera aria, strophic
Meter: ¢
Key: B minor
Duration: 02:17

Catfish Row, Charleston, South Carolina. A woman named Clara sings her baby a lullaby. Two strophes, with dreamy orchestral introduction, interlude, and closure; the wordless chorus enters for the second strophe.

00:00	Introduction	Horn and bassoon, then languid clarinet.
00:05		Undulating figure begins in clarinet, then halves in speed (bells).
	Strophe 1	
00:14	a	Rocking motion continues in accompaniment.
00:27	b	. . . Elision in English horn, strings.
00:41	a	Same as before + English horn elision.
01:53	c	Reaches closure, with flute solo to conclude.
01:07	Interlude	Like the introduction.
	Strophe 2	
01:11	a	Adds chorus "oohs" and violin countermelody.
01:24	b	Richer accompaniment continues; note that the
01:37	a	melody is now doubled in woodwinds.
01:49	c	
02:00	Cadenza	Singer lifts to a high point, then floats downward.
02:11	Orch. close	Reminiscence of melody in low strings.
		(The scene continues.)

trip in a 100-page article for the *New Yorker* magazine, "The Muses Are Heard," a verité piece that just preceded *In Cold Blood*.) By the 1980s *Porgy and Bess* was being regularly produced and recorded, and today every American singer of note knows the parts—although the Gershwin estate still insists that all the singers be black, and a full score remains very hard to come by.

Like Stravinsky (with *The Firebird, Petrushka,* and *The Rite of Spring*), Aaron Copland achieved fame on the strength of three ballets, each in its own way a turning point in the history of dance. Like Stravinsky, too, Copland and his choreographers drew upon subjects and dance forms from their own heritage. *Billy the Kid* and *Rodeo* are, obviously, based on scenarios of the American West; in *Rodeo* American choreographer Agnes de Mille established a horsey style of dancing that had many successors, notably in ballet scenes from Rodgers and Hammerstein's *Oklahoma!,* which she also choreographed.

Copland garnered the commission for *Billy the Kid* and *Rodeo* not long after returning home from three years of study in France with Nadia Boulanger. His French connections were critical to his early American successes. Boulanger commissioned an organ symphony from him for her U.S. debut, and Serge Koussevitzky, recently arrived from Paris to conduct the Boston Symphony Orchestra, fostered and premiered other early works.

One has the sense, then, that Copland came almost by accident into his strong affection for the American pioneer spirit. But by the time he was approached for a ballet about a young pioneer husband and wife establishing a new house in the mountains of Pennsylvania, his ideas about what he called "plain music" were the dominant force in his musical thinking. The new ballet was *Appalachian Spring,* a creation of the choreographer Martha Graham (1893–1990). She had found the title in a poem by Hart Crane, where it refers to running water, not the springtime renewal that came to dominate the vision of both the composer and the choreographer.

RECOMMENDED LISTENING:

Copland: Appalachian Spring *(1944)*

www.prenhall.com/masterworks
recommended listening

After *Appalachian Spring,* Copland was never less than a hero of American music, and it was in this capacity that he was invited to write movie scores (Steinbeck's *Of Mice and Men,* Wilder's *Our Town*) and attracted the lifelong devotion of such artists as the young American conductor Leonard Bernstein. Copland's *Outdoor Overture* and *A Lincoln Portrait* gave Americans new patriotic music to be proud of during World War II.

Copland's life spanned nine-tenths of the twentieth century. But while Copland's lectures and writings on the contemporary scene were the contributions of a senior statesman, he never again regained the ratio of wins to losses that characterizes the very best composers. One might perhaps argue that America, having discovered her dominion over the world after the Second World War, had matured past Copland's own simple gifts.

Indeed, after the war the United States became the major player in the most sophisticated modes of composition. Copland led the way in establishing this atmosphere for serious new music in the United States, having cosponsored an important series of contemporary music concerts in the 1930s with his colleague Roger Sessions (1896–1985). It was at roughly this juncture that the major American universities and conservatories began to become powerhouses of new music and the key patrons of mid-century. Sessions was long affiliated with Princeton and later the Juilliard School of Music in New York. The Boston composer Walter Piston was on the faculty at Harvard. Howard Hansen was president of the Eastman School of Music in Rochester, New York; Samuel Barber, of Juilliard. The American universities played a significant part in welcoming European refugees of the 1930s and 1940s, revolutionizing America's role in international music affairs. This is one of the subjects of our final chapter.

Copland

BROADWAY

European light opera and operetta of late Romanticism found receptive audiences in the United States. Gilbert and Sullivan's masterpieces (*H.M.S. Pinafore,* 1878; *The Pirates of Penzance,* 1879; *The Mikado,* 1885) reached New York a few weeks after their London openings. In one of the G&S plays the principals get right to the heart of things:

This particularly rapid unintelligible patter
Isn't generally heard and if it is it doesn't matter
Matter matter matter matter matter matter . . .

In *The Mikado,* three Japanese maidens, Yum-Yum, Pitti-Sing, and Peep-Bo, come home from boarding school in a rickshaw, giggling mightily and twirling parasols as they go. These people have nothing to do with Japan, of course, but are English at their maximum Englishness, playing at dressing up and quietly mocking other civilizations. The music is a dance-hall rondo.

It was all good fun and made serious money, and Americans were naturally eager to imitate the style. The American cellist Victor Herbert (1859–1924) composed more than two dozen successful operettas (*Babes in Toyland,* 1903; *Naughty Marietta,* 1910). The Hungarian-American composer Sigmund Romberg (1887–1951) was well positioned, by his Austro-Hungarian heritage, to follow suit with 70 more (*The Student Prince,* 1924; *The Desert Song,* 1926; *New Moon,* 1928). Even Sousa had composed operetta (*El Capitan,* 1895).

But these were European-based forms, and indigenous American music theater descended in equal measure from the minstrelsies and vaudevilles. It was the songsmiths Irving Berlin, Jerome Kern, Cole Porter, and George Gerswhin who began the process of converting the revues and follies into the "book" musicals that coalesced in the 1920s. Kern was the first pioneer, in a series of musicals for the tiny Princess Theater in New York (*Nobody Home* and *Very Good Eddie,* 1915). After World War I new entries came in hot pursuit: Gershwin's *Lady Be Good* (1924), *No, No, Nanette* (Vincent Youmans, 1925), and *The Girl Friend* (Richard Rodgers, 1926). With Jerome Kern's *Show Boat* (1927), the first wildly successful musical, the gifted librettist Oscar Hammerstein II came to the fore. The Broadway musical had been born.

Next to jazz, no musical art form has been so distinctly American, or so commercially successful, as the Broadway musical. Characterized by fast-moving stories where the songs and dances are integrated into the drama to advance both the plot and the characterizations, and with subject matter drawn from across the fabric of American society, the musical comedy had immense appeal to the American middle class. Broadway is a rough-and-tumble world, where fortunes are made and lost overnight, but hit musicals enjoyed unimaginably long runs that made the promised riches worth the gamble.

www.prenhall.com/masterworks
composer profiles
Rodgers and Hammerstein

Rodgers and Hammerstein became a team just before World War II and went on to dominate the genre during the 1940s and 1950s with a series of smash hits:

The Broadway Musicals of Richard Rodgers (1902–79) and Oscar Hammerstein II (1895–1960) (selected list)

Oklahoma! (1943; film 1955): title song, "Oh, What a Beautiful Mornin'",
  "People Will Say We're In Love"
Carousel (1945; film 1956): "Carousel Waltz," "You'll Never Walk Alone,"
  "Real Nice Clambake"
South Pacific (1949; film 1958): "Some Enchanted Evening,""Dites-moi,"
  "Gonna Wash That Man Right Outa My Hair"
The King and I (1951; film 1956): "Getting to Know You," "Hello Young
  Lovers," "Shall We Dance?"
Flower Drum Song (1958; film 1961)
The Sound of Music (1959; film 1964): title song, "Do-Re-Mi," "Climb
  Ev'ry Mountain," "Edelweiss"

The two artists were an ideal match. Like Gilbert and Sullivan, they nourished each other's strengths and covered their weaknesses. Usually the libretto, based on a pre-existing play or book, came first and the composer responded, but with both pairs it sometimes happened that the composer would write a song and the librettist would then fashion words to it. It's the teamwork that counts. In the first verse of the first song of *Oklahoma!,* Hammerstein comes up with this unwieldy image:

> The corn is as high as an elephant's eye
> An' it looks like it's climbin' clear up to the sky.

Rodgers sets it effortlessly as the harmonic lead-in to the famous refrain "Oh, What a Beautiful Mornin'", and the result works just fine. Hammerstein's lines can be very droll, as in this example from later in the same play:

> Pore Jud is daid,
> A candle lights his haid!
> He's lookin' oh, so purty and so nice.
> He looks like he's asleep,
> It's a shame that he won't keep,
> But it's summer and we're runnin' out of ice.

Rodgers writes a comic funeral dirge to go with it, all the funnier in that the villain Jud isn't actually dead yet, but is in fact singing along.

Rodgers and Hammerstein had a particular knack for coming up with one of the fundamental necessities for hit theater, a memorable setting. *Carousel,* set on the clambaking coast of Maine, brims with color from the moment the curtain rises to reveal a huge merry-go-round. So does *Oklahoma!,* with its fringe-topped surrey and cowboy dances. The wartime hit *South Pacific,* based on James Michener's novel *Tales of the South Pacific,* features a chorus of seabees and nurses on a Polynesian island, the betel-nut chewing Bloody Mary, and the love of the all-American Nellie Forbush for the cultivated Frenchman Émile de Becque.

RODGERS AND HAMMERSTEIN: "SOME ENCHANTED EVENING,"
FROM *SOUTH PACIFIC* (1949)

In French Polynesia during World War II, Ensign Nellie Forbush, a young nurse from Little Rock, falls quietly in love with an older man, the French planter Émile de Becque, only to learn of his two mixed-race children from a Polynesian wife who has died. Meanwhile the peddler Bloody Mary uses her tropical pleasure island, Bali H'ai, to lure the handsome Lieutenant Cable into marriage with her niece Liat. *South Pacific* is about life and love in wartime, and in some measure about overcoming naiveté and racial prejudice as the world grows inexorably smaller.

With the roles of Nellie Forbush in *South Pacific* and later the airborne *Peter Pan* (1954) and Maria in *The Sound of Music* (1959), Mary Martin (1913–90) was Broadway's reigning musical star. Émile De Becque was played by Ezio Pinza (1892–1957), a celebrated bass just then concluding a long affiliation with the Metropolitan Opera. "Some Enchanted Evening" is an excellent example of the sentimental romantic solo aria by the male or female star. The form is that of a 32-bar song, A-A-B-A, as in the Duke Ellington and Charlie Parker selections. The recording is from the original cast album.

Listening Chart

 CD 4, TR 11

Richard Rodgers (1902–79) and Oscar Hammerstein II (1895–1960)
***South Pacific* (1949)**
"Some Enchanted Evening"

Type: 32-bar song
Meter: c
Key: C major
Duration: 03:01

For: Émile de Becque, a French plantation owner (bass: Ezio Pinza); theater orchestra

Text: by Oscar Hammerstein II

A sentimental romantic aria by the male star. Other good examples are "If I Loved You" from *Carousel* and "Hello Young Lovers" from *The King and I*.

00:00	Introduction	Sentimental violins: the language of love.
00:21	a	A simple 32-bar song, a-a-b-a. Emile, the suave Frenchman, serenades Nellie. Ezio Pinza's operatic voice makes this the definitive performance.
00:59	a	Romantic violin answers the voice.
01:37	b	The "break": a moment of introspection. Big orchestral swell (01:47) to:
01:52	a	With full, lush orchestration. Pinza's falsetto lift (02:24) at the end of the phrase sets up his famous close in the coda phrase.
02:33	Coda	Derived from b. At the close, note the artistry of the vocal technique.

Pinza's use of falsetto at the end comes from necessity (when a pitch is too high to sing softly in full voice), but the effect was so memorable that it became widely imitated.

With its big production numbers ("There is Nothing Like a Dame," "Honey Bun"), ingenuous songs ("Dites-moi," "Happy Talk"), and serious soliloquies, *South Pacific* typifies the genius of the Rodgers-and- Hammerstein "book" musical, where nearly every song was a hit. There's always a memorable ballade for the contralto, here "Bali Ha'i"; in *Carousel* "You'll Never Walk Alone," in *The King and I* "Something Wonderful," in *The Sound of Music* "Climb Ev'ry Mountain." The superb overtures and orchestration are those of Robert Russell Bennett (1894–1981). Everybody in show business relies on disciples to help in the inevitable pinch as opening night approaches, since neither the overture nor the final orchestration can be done until the last rewrites are finished. Gershwin, Bernstein, and Sondheim all left the orchestration to others, at least in part.

RECOMMENDED LISTENING:

Rodgers and Hammerstein: other excerpts from South Pacific *(1949)*

www.prenhall.com/masterworks
recommended listening

The only real competitors to Rodgers and Hammerstein were Alan Jay Lerner and Frederick Loewe (*Brigadoon,* 1947; *My Fair Lady,* 1956; *Camelot,* 1960), and Frank Loesser (*Guys and Dolls,* 1950; *How to Succeed in Business Without Really Trying,* 1961). With the 1960s, as you know, came all manner of challenges to the social relevance of art, and the Broadway stage mutated accordingly. Hollywood, where soundtrack technology was rapidly being perfected, meanwhile gobbled up the Broadway hits. Beware, however: That technology also overdubs nonsinging stars with studio singers. The songs of Deborah Kerr in *The King and I,* Natalie Wood in *West Side Story* (1961), and Audrey Hepburn in the lavishly costumed *My Fair Lady* (1964) were all dubbed by the California soprano Marni Nixon.

LEONARD BERNSTEIN (1918–90). The glamour and possible financial rewards of Broadway could not have failed to lure Leonard Bernstein, America's phenomenon of the mid-century. Bernstein, on the surface at least, excelled at everything he did: He was a brilliant pianist, conductor, composer, television personality, and model for the jet-setting Beautiful People. In 1958 he was named first American-born conductor of the New York Philharmonic. He had had major stage successes with the ballet *Fancy Free* (1944), the musicals *On the Town* (1944) and *Wonderful Town,* based on the stage hit *My Sister Eileen* (1953), and a splendid musical on Voltaire's *Candide* (1956; revised 1973, 1982, 1988). In the mid-1950s Bernstein was joined by the young composer/librettist Stephen Sondheim, a student of Oscar Hammerstein and the American composer Milton Babbitt, hired to provide the lyrics for a show to feature choreography by Jerome Robbins. This was, of course, *West Side Story* (1957), mid-century's answer to *Porgy and Bess.*

Oklahoma!: "Oh, What a Beautiful Mornin'" (Gordon McRae in the film version, 1955)

 BERNSTEIN: "SOMEWHERE," FROM *WEST SIDE STORY* (1957)

www.prenhall.com/masterworks
composer profiles
Bernstein

The story is a *Romeo and Juliet* of the backlots of Manhattan. The Anglo Jets and Puerto Rican Sharks, always on the verge of a rumble, bait each other unmercifully.

West Side Story: the rumble (film version, 1961)

Tony, an aging Jet, falls for Maria, sister of the Sharks' leader, Bernardo. A rumble at the end of Act I results in the first killings, and by the final curtain Tony has been shot to death in the aftermath.

Like Gershwin, Bernstein and his collaborators stopped to rethink the elements of the Broadway theatrical. *West Side Story* was among the first of the mega-dance musicals, with modern jeans-and-sneakers dance steps from the overture to the closing. (The orchestral showpiece "Symphonic Dances from *West Side Story*" strings together the ballet music.) There were superb songs ("I Feel Pretty," "Maria," "Somewhere") and every rhythmic trick in the book. Like *Porgy and Bess, West Side Story* came to be regarded as native American theater at its best.

Bernstein lived and breathed the great masterworks every day of his life. He thought of music as a long sequence of references forward and back. "Let's go to the Prokofiev section," he might say while rehearsing Beethoven. One result is that his music alludes in countless ways to the kinds of repertoire we have studied in this course, titles he conducted hundreds of times during his life. The final tableau in *West Side Story,* for example, is not merely that of Maria cradling Tony's lifeless head in her arms, but an obvious reminiscence of the similar scene at the close of *Tristan und Isolde.* In the big "Tonight" sequence, themes are woven together in counterpoint, rather like the Berlioz's *réunion des thèmes* from the *Fantastique.* In "Somewhere," the allusion is to a theme from Beethoven's "Emperor" Concerto (no. 5), movement II:

Sondheim's lyrics are strong throughout. Here they verge on a universal sentiment, understood by everyone who has known a love that circumstance cannot allow:

> We'll find a new way of living
> We'll find a way of forgiving
> Somewhere . . .
>
> Somehow, Someday, Somewhere!

Listening Chart

 CD 4, TR 12

Leonard Bernstein (1918–90)
West Side Story (1957)
"Somewhere"

For: a girl; theater orchestra

Text: Stephen Sondheim (b. 1930)

Type: 32-bar song
Meter: $\frac{4}{8}$
Key: E major
Duration: 02:15

Tony, an Anglo, has fallen in love with the Puerto Rican Maria. In the finale of act I, Tony has killed the leader of the Sharks, a Puerto Rican gang, in a rumble. The famous song "Somewhere" comes during the act II ballet where the lovers dream of finding escape from their impossible circumstance. The voice, heard from the shadows, is that of an unidentified girl.

00:00	Horn cue	A 32-bar song, like "Some Enchanted Evening."
00:04	a	Solo cello and violin dialogue on the opening interval.
00:32	a	Fl. continues the imitative figure; rich chords in cello trio. Vns. swell into:
01:00	b	As though a refrain, with tender responses in vc., hn., low ww.
01:31	a	Full strings, with another swell into:
01:58	b for close	"Somewhere" refrain for close.
		(The dream ballet continues, turning into a nightmare.)

Bernstein tried hard to equal the success of *West Side Story* with another Broadway triumph, but his bicentennial musical called *1600 Pennsylvania Avenue* failed, and his opera *A Quiet Place* (1983) received few performances. By contrast, both the Chichester Psalms (1965) and Mass (1971), a multimedia extravaganza commissioned by Jacqueline Kennedy Onassis for the opening of the Kennedy Center in Washington, D.C., found comfortable places in the repertoire. Meanwhile, Bernstein had become arguably the most interesting conductor of his era. His tenure with the New York Philharmonic coincided with majestic accomplishments in stereo recording and television, the opening of a fine new hall, and improved working conditions for his musicians. After retiring from New York he went from orchestra to orchestra in a series of passionate artistic love affairs: Beethoven with the Vienna Philharmonic, Berlioz in France, Mahler in Amsterdam.

In his last years a book sensationalizing his bisexuality had the effect of making him seem human after all, and his subsequent public image was not enhanced much by his smoking himself to death. Yet no one ever did more for American music, in all its manifestations, than this man everybody called Lenny. And no one incited more young people to go ahead and dive into the profession he so loved—myself included.

Sondheim, for his part, has since become the grand master of serious Broadway musical theater. With *A Little Night Music* (1973), *Sunday in the Park with George* (1984), and *Into the Woods* (1987; based on children's fairy tales) he gave thinking audiences much to ponder, a welcome foil to the intellectually disinteresting work of Andrew Lloyd Webber. *Sunday* is particularly fine, bringing to life the characters in Seurat's famous pointillistic painting (the girl, amusingly, is named Dot) of Parisians strolling on a Sunday afternoon. The painting is in the Chicago Art Institute.

SEARCHING FOR OUR IDENTITY.   For the last several dozen pages you've been reading about many different kinds of musics, all of which can lay good claim to being proper American music. Never mind that Chicago and San Francisco have different tastes than New York, or that academics pursued one direction while flappers danced off in another. Never mind, for that matter, that you might not have heard of any of it until now. Take in the choice available to you the next time you visit a record store, and ask yourself which of it is true American music. (In the next chapter, we touch on rock and the increasing fusion of classical and popular idioms.) Don't jump to a conclusion just yet.

Nowadays, too, our collective ethnic identity is constantly changing, and we're rightly curious about musics we know still less about: those of Native Americans, say, or our ancestors in India, Africa, Arabia, Japan, and China. Scholarship and composition and performance in America are incorporating these styles as well.

Now that the search for what is viable in American music passes on to you, spend some time thinking about the family tree. One branch goes from Joplin and King Oliver to Louis Armstrong and Bessie Smith and thence forward; another from Gershwin to Copland to Bernstein and Sondheim; another from the conservatories of Europe to the universities of America. Our musical identity is, and always has been, a collective one. That is its principal strength. So find your own identity first of all; then figure out how it relates to the whole, quite lovely picture. Then go on to contribute to American culture what you alone can give it.

Chapter 9

But today, the Rock cries out to us, clearly, forcefully,
Come, you may stand upon my
Back and face your distant destiny,
But seek no haven in my shadow,
I will give you no hiding place down here.

—Maya Angelou (b. 1928),
in *On the Pulse of Morning* (1993)

Getting Hip and Staying That Way

*E*uropean history in the twentieth century has been a constant process of redrawing the map, as events of the recent past in central and northern Europe have pointedly reminded all of us. If you add to the devastation of the two world wars the political and economic terror that preceded and followed both of them, you can see a social disruption very nearly the equal of the Black Plague. Only since 1950 has there been any semblance of stability in Europe, and even that is comparative, limited at best to certain privileged pockets of the continent. Survival by adaptation was as necessary for musicians as for any other segment of society. Opera houses, symphony orchestras, artists, and composers all changed. Many of the venerable institutions of music survived by reorganizing; a few died out. Music had to learn to function with the labor unions, the recording industry, and broadcasting; it had to adapt to intrusive governmental controls and then its utter dependence on state subsidy. European music had to deal with increased competition from the Americas and Asia. And everybody eventually had to come to terms with rock.

*S*CHOENBERG, BERG, WEBERN

We left the Old World, at the end of Chapter 7, with the *Rite of Spring* in Paris on the eve of World War I, and then we took a quick look at its aftermath in France. In Vienna, beginning with late Mahler, the aesthetic goal was one of progress from late Romanticism's music of our routine daily feelings toward a much deeper expression of the elemental truths that lurk in our innermost selves. This was *Expressionism,* given not a little of its impetus by the work of the Viennese psychologist Siegmund Freud (1856–1939), with his liberating but terrifying notions that there are controlling forces within us that we can be powerless to will away. Parallel developments included the abstract paintings of Gustav Klimt (1862–1918) and Wasilly Kandinsky (1866–1944), with whom Schoenberg had a long correspondence, and German-language Expressionist drama, long on violent monologues, rape, and murder. Expressionism dealt in psychological extremes: confusion, nightmares, the scream.

Arnold Schoenberg (1874–1951) began to develop expressionist leanings in a search for what he later called the "emancipation of dissonance." In the beautiful string sextet *Verklärte Nacht* ("Transfigured Night," 1899), he uses a very thick and unstable

Schoenberg and his
self-portraits

tonality, strongly Wagnerian in counterpoint and ornament, to evoke a poem in which
lovers with a secret converse in the frozen night. In *Erwartung* ("Waiting," 1909), for
soprano and orchestra, he writes a long, terrified monologue of a woman waiting for her
lover in the dark, culminating in her scream as she trips over a body.

More radical still is Schoenberg's 1912 treatment of the 21 poems called *Pierrot
lunaire* ("Moonstruck Pierrot"). Pierrot is the clown of the Commedia dell'Arte, memori-
alized in the song "Au clair de la lune"; you've also met him in Schumann's *Carnaval.*
The original poems, in French, were by a Belgian poet named Albert Giraud; their rewriting into the version Schoenberg uses is by Otto Erich Hartleben.

SCHOENBERG: FROM *PIERROT LUNAIRE* (1912)

(1) MONDESTRUNKEN—(5) VALSE DE CHOPIN

Pierrot does not speak in the poems, but is described and sometimes spoken to in a series
of weird, surrealistic images. He is a solitary figure, besotted and bedazzled by a cold, forbidding moon; the cycle is, generally speaking, nightmarish. As the melodramas
progress, his character transforms itself from a distant, remote figure to a slightly more
humanized one.

The structural scheme of each poem is the same: 13 lines arranged in stanzas—4 + 4
+ 5—with lines 7 and 8 repeating 1 and 2, and line 13 a repeat of line 1:

1. Mondestrunken
Den Wein, den man mit Augen trinkt,
Gießt Nachts der Mond in Wogen nieder,
Und eine Springflut überschwemmt
Den stillen Horizont.

1. Moon-Drunk
The wine that through the eyes is drunk,
at night the moon pours down in torrents,
and a spring-flood overflows
the silent horizon.

Geluste, schauerlich und süß,	Desires, shuddering and sweet,
Durchschwimmen ohne Zahl die Fluten!	swim unnumbered through the floods!
Den Wein, den man mit Augen trinkt,	The wine that through the eyes is drunk
Gießt Nachts der Mond in Wogen nieder.	at night the moon pours down in torrents.
Der Dichter, den die Andacht treibt	The poet, whom devotion drives,
Berauscht sich an dem heilgen Tranke,	grows tipsy on the sacred drink,
Gen Himmel wendet er verzückt	and toward heaven turns, enraptured,
Das Haupt und taumelnd saugt und schlürft er	his head: and, reeling, sucks and slurps up
Den Wein, den man mit Augen trinkt.	the wine that through the eyes is drunk.

The French call this stanza form a *rondeau.* There are interesting musical implications in such an arrangement, with its recapitulatory lines in the middle, the opportunity for a new thought thereafter, and the coda-like reiteration at the close. Schoenberg does not regard the rhyme scheme as dictating a constraining form, but instead as the opportunity to discover a variety of recapitulatory tactics.

The first feature that may strike you about this memorable work is the unusual treatment of the solo voice. The reciter declaims her part in general contours instead of specific pitches. The effect is called speech song, or *Sprechstimme,* and is notated with little x's in the stem of the note:

The idea is to touch on the given pitch and proceed on through it to the next. Sprechstimme, despite the name, is not really an attempt to make singing more like speech. On the contrary, the net effect is to underscore a poetry of simple craziness and the effects of strong drink. *Pierrot,* properly delivered, can make you almost seasick.

The basic instrumental force consists of a pianist, a flutist doubling piccolo, a clarinetist doubling bass clarinet, a violinist doubling viola, and a cellist. Permutations in the scoring give each of the songs a unique instrumental combination. *Mondestrunken,* for example, is for flute, violin, and piano, with the cellist entering after the midpoint; the Chopin Waltz is for flute, clarinet, and piano with the clarinet changing to bass clarinet at the same juncture. No two movements begin with exactly the same instrumentation. The "Pierrot ensemble" proves so malleable under Schoenberg's sure control that it has become a standard core of contemporary chamber ensembles.

Mondestrunken centers on the opening piano ostinato, which seems to outline two third-based chords:

The motive flavors nearly every bar of the accompaniment. Meanwhile, there is subtle but obvious text painting, as in the flurry at the springtide overflow and the rhythmic slowing just afterward, for the still horizon. At the inner text repetition of "Den Wein, den man mit Augen trinkt," the singer falls drolly to her low point, as though in dazed half memory of the proposition, and the instrumental interlude ritards almost to a halt. The start of the poet's strophe is cocky and arrogant, although the motto continues in the flute and, at half speed, in the violin. After the *molto ritardando,* the music tumbles away, cadencing in a complex sonority that manages to capture all 12 pitches in the last bar, 11 of the 12 in the last two chords.

In *Valse de Chopin* the poet lies sleepless with desire, haunted by a melancholy nocturnal waltz. In an off-putting (albeit utterly Expressionistic) image, both the waltz and the desire cling to the poet "like a spit-tinged drop of blood colors the lips of a consumptive." The poetic reference to Chopin's tuberculosis is clear, as are the musical references made by the arabesque-laden texture. It's a little more difficult to hear contours of a waltz, though on repeated listenings you can construct a hint of oom-pah in the very first bar and a lyric waltz tune out of the clarinet line. After the internal text repeat comes an instant of recapitulating the first bar. At the end the oom-pah-pah accompaniment, which has consistently lacked the oom, dissolves into a single pitch. The short-short-long rhythm so prominent at the end emerged toward the midpoint as a kind of instrumental chuckle. Here it seems almost Beethovenian.

Schoenberg is equally sensitive to the overall contour of these "thrice seven" poems. Part I is high and willowy, emphasizing moon-drenched images; in part II the night is featured, and low registers begin to exert control, those of cello, bass clarinet, and the piano left hand. The imagery is darker, too, a poetry of crime and punishment, with references to hanging. Pierrot longs for the past and his unseen homeland, and part III is about thoughts of this homeward journey, emphasizing the full ensemble—although with one quite ravishing serenade for cello and voice.

Pierrot lunaire is, finally, *atonal:* It is not based primarily on major and minor scales and expectations of harmonic cadence, departure, and return. That does not make it, by any means, lacking in form or even tune. The opening bars of *Mondestrunken,* for example, are quite tuneful, based on familiar intervals and relationships.

Atonality, what results from the "emancipation of dissonance," takes many forms. In *Pierrot lunaire* and the less tonal parts of *The Rite of Spring,* freedom from key is achieved largely by piling up familiar sonorities in unfamiliar ways: A close look at any

Listening Chart

 CD 4, TR 13–14

Arnold Schoenberg (1874–1951)
Pierrot lunaire (1912)
   (1) **Mondestrunken** — (5) **Valse de Chopin**

For: reciter (Sprechstimme), flute (+ piccolo), clarinet (+ bass clarinet), violin (+ viola), cello, piano

Text: by Albert Giraud in the German translation of Otto Erich Hartleben (1864–1905)

Type: Song cycle, rondeau texts
Meter: $\frac{2}{4}$ and $\frac{3}{4}$; $\frac{3}{4}$
Key: NA, free atonality
Duration: 01:38, 01:16

Pierrot lunaire achieves its astonishing sound first by use of speech-contours called *Sprechstimme*, second by vastly imaginative treatment of the five instrumentalists, such that no two of the 21 total songs begin with the same instrumental force. Pierrot, the poet, comes from the Commedia dell'Arte tradition; the settings are strongly Expressionistic and symbolic, focusing on cold, white moonlight—tinged in the Chopin waltz by a drop of blood—and drunkenness.

1. *Mondestrunken* ("Moon-Drunk")

00:00	**Stanza I**	The main motive in the piano, with violin pizzicato.
00:03	li. 1–2	Flute assumes prominent dialogue with piano.
00:13	li. 3–4	*Forte:* the springtime floods. A moment of stillness.
00:22	interlude	Flute with main motive, then a cadenza-like passage; motive again.
	Stanza II	
00:39	li. 5–6	"Aching lusts." The violin, arco, now prominent.
00:48	li. 7–8 (=1–2)	Light, twinkling textures return with the text reprise.
00:57	interlude	The twinkles zero in on:
	Stanza III	
01:02	li. 9–10	Harsh piano chords: the poet gets drunk.
01:12	li. 11–12 . . .	"Toward Heaven tilts back his head." Climax.
01:19	. . . li. 13 (=1)	"And laps and swills the wine . . ." Folds back into cadence.
01:30	close	The opening motive to close.

5. *Valse de Chopin*

00:00	**Stanza I**	The image is of spat blood on disease-white lips.
00:05	li. 1–2	Flute, clarinet, piano: gracious and elegant at first: the arabesques and
00:11	li. 3–4	the "spat blood" refer to Chopin.
00:17	interlude	Bold chords erupt in the piano.
	Stanza II	
00:19	li. 5–6	"Wild, lust-filled chords splatter despairing dreams . . ."
00:25	li. 7–8 (=1–2)	". . . like spat blood on the lips." A new chuckling motive.
00:30	interlude	Crescendo of the instruments.
	Stanza III	(Clarinetist switches to bass clarinet.)
00:35	li. 9–10	The melancholy night-waltz nags at the
00:45	li. 11–12	sleepless poet, cleaving to the brain
00:50	li. 13 (=1)	like spat blood on the lips.
00:57	close	Hints of the main motive from no. 1—also Beethoven V?

one simultaneity will usually show a reasonably traditional chord or chords, while the ordering of the events emphasizes disjunctures, inconclusiveness, puzzles, and clashes—the same concepts at issue in, say, a cubist painting. The next phase of the movement toward atonality, in Vienna at least, was devoted to achieving a more philosophically valid nontonality. But in the early stages, and in some idioms popular today, the distinctions between post-Wagnerian tonality, pantonality, and atonality are very faint; many of the harshest and most dissonant works from the early decades of the twentieth century are in point of fact prevailingly tonal. Take care not to associate atonal modes of composition with disorganization.

Schoenberg attracted into his intellectual circle two very gifted colleagues, **Alban Berg (1885–1935)** and **Anton Webern (1883–1945)**. Together they reasoned through the implications and first possibilities of their theories of atonality. Not the least interesting aspect of this so-called *Second Viennese School* is how very differently the two composers went about it. Berg, for example, composed big, bold, stark works, notably the operas *Wozzeck* and *Lulu*. Both are on severe modernist subject matter: *Wozzeck* concerning the plight of a poor foot soldier in the German army who eventually cuts the throat of his live-in, Marie; *Lulu* about a high-class prostitute who is eventually murdered by Jack the Ripper. Webern, by contrast, thought in microcosmic terms, trying to distill to its essence every musical concept that preoccupied him. His works are very brief: Webern's whole output fits on three CDs.

Berg and Webern

Listen, now, to a quite remarkable movement from one of Webern's most influential works. But before you do, stop to reassemble in your mind the themes-and-variations we've encountered so far: those from the Haydn Quartet and Beethoven's Fifth and the Brahms Haydn Variations. Reflect for a moment on how they worked.

 WEBERN: FROM SYMPHONY, OP. 21 (1928)

II. THEME AND VARIATIONS

Pierrot lunaire will have familiarized you with the basic sound of this movement: its intimate orchestration (clarinet, bass clarinet, a pair of horns, harp, and strings) and a melodic style that prefers wide leaps and disjunctures to stepwise, scalar tunes. These contours highlight the many issues of space that occupy Webern here: the horizontal space between the melodic pitches, the wide vertical spaces of most of the "chords"—or, better, simultaneities—and the dramatic use of moments of complete silence. There's also a novel sense of space in how the instruments interrelate, for themes pass freely from one instrument or instrument group to the next and thus seem always to be darting through the space. Indeed, the music flies by, over in less than two minutes. You need to keep your wits about you and follow the listening chart several times to begin to sense the various compositional processes at work here.

The theme is followed by variations I–VII and a coda, each of the 9 sections lasting exactly 11 measures, for a total of 99 bars. As usual, vivid changes of texture and speed indicate the dividing points. Even on first listening you may begin to sense another kind of contour: the way the second half of each segment seems somehow to reflect the first. At the center of each 11-bar unit (bar 6, that is) there's some point of emphasis—a pause, or a change of tempo, or a climax of sorts—followed by shapes familiar as having just been heard.

In fact, the system here is deucedly clever, for the theme and each of its variations actually turns on the center and mirrors itself in a kind of musical *palindrome.* (A verbal palindrome reads the same backward as forward, as in "Madam, I'm Adam.") There are some parallels elsewhere in the history of music, notably a palindromic motet by Machaut (the medieval French composer) appropriately called "My End Is My Beginning." The theme of Webern's movement,* then, looks like this:

Each variation proceeds to do the same thing, as does the coda. Moreover, variation IV at the center serves as a big pivot point. Aspects of variation V are paired with III, VI with II, VII with I, and the coda with the theme. The option of subjecting musical arrangement to this sort of retrograde treatment—called *cancrizans,* or "crabwise," in earlier times— is a principal attraction of atonal music.

*Music on pp. 325, 327–29 copyright 1929 by Universal Edition.

Listening Chart

 CD 4, TR 15

Anton Webern (1883–1945)
Symphony, op. 21 (1928)
Movement II: Theme and Variations

For: clarinet, bass clarinet, 2 horns, harp, strings (no double bass)

Type: Theme and variations, palindromic
Meter: ¢
Key: NA: atonal, serial
Duration: 02:54

The second movement of Webern's Symphony, op. 21, shows his passion for distilling musical materials to their essence. Each of the 9 sections (theme + 7 variations + coda) consists of exactly 11 measures. Each, moreover, progresses to a midpoint at bar 6, then turns and mirrors itself in a musical palindrome. The basic series (or row) is constructed so that it looks backward on itself. The symmetricalities, then, are all-pervasive.

00:00	**Theme**	Melody in clarinet; responses in harp, horns. Mirrors where the quarter notes change briefly to eighths (00:09).
00:16	**Var. I**	Lively, polka-like figuration for the strings.
00:30	**Var. II**	Horn 8ths; dialogue of clarinets; pizzicato strings and harp.
00:43	**Var. III**	Willowy clarinet, scampering strings, loud exclamations in horn. Pivots around harp and horn ritard.
01:05	**Var. IV**	Slower, more tranquil, the implied triple meter lending a waltzy feel. Mirrors at the undulating ritard in horns, winds, harp.
01:33	**Var. V**	Insistent chords in strings, with crescendos; leaping harp. The big crescendo leads into:
01:48	**Var. VI**	Clarinets and horns, vigorous dynamics, the rhythms now quite complex. Merges into:
02:08	**Var. VII**	Tutti. Lyric swells frame the pizzicato and staccato work. End seems to overlap start of:
02:29	**Coda**	Loud 2-note exclamation; pause, then soft rebound. The solo violin lyric mirrors back to the exclamation as closure.

Listen again to this movement, this time for the shift from variation to variation and for the pivot point and palindrome in each. Once you know it's there, it's easy to hear. The whole is a stunning stride forward in musical sound, belying the often heard lament of the moderns that there's nothing new left to do.

SERIAL MUSIC. But what of the pitch content of Webern's Symphony, so different in look and sound from anything you've heard before? The palindrome is just one of the effects made workable by an all-new way of composing music. The Symphony, op. 21, is a relatively early example of the technique of *serial* composition (at first called *twelve-*

tone composition) as it had been formulated by Schoenberg and his school. The idea here is that the composer preselects a *series* of the twelve pitches, arranging them in a row with the contours and relationships he seeks to explore in his composition. One typically strives for a row that embraces multiple pitch symmetries. In the Symphony, op. 21, the row is as follows:

As part of the precompositional stage of planning, the composer then constructs from the basic row a matrix, or set, of its 12 transpositions, each up a half step. These are labeled with a **P** (for Primary) and the numbers 0, 1, 2, 3, 4, 5, 6, 7, 8, 9, 10, 11. Since the rows will also be used in reverse, or retrograde, the chart also shows **R** indications in the right margin. This particular row has very interesting characteristics: Because it centers on the tritone (F–B, notes 6 and 7) and mirrors itself (intervals 7–12 are the same as 6–1), the **R** 6 form equals **P** 0, from which point the matrix, too, mirrors itself. (See the right margin of the example.)

Moreover, the row also functions by inversion. One thus constructs yet another matrix by inverting (reversing) the intervals contained in the primary form of the set. In this case, the row starts on A, falls a minor third to an F♯, rises a half step to G, then rises another half step to A♭, and so on. The inversion thus starts on A, rises the minor third to C, falls a half step to B♮, falls another half step to B♭, and so on. The matrix below thus shows the **I** forms and the **RI** forms.

The idea is that the composer doesn't use a particular pitch until all the others are used up: horizontally, vertically, or in some combination of the two; then he or she moves to another version of the row. The theme of Webern's second movement, for example, uses **I** 8 (inversion on F) in the clarinet and **I** 2 (on B) in the harp and horns. The treatment is exact:

Thema

Now look more closely at the properties of the matrix on p. 328. Note how the primary row is palindromic around the *tritone* (F–B) at the center: Pitches 7–12 mirror 6–1. The interval between the first pitch and the last (A–E♭) is also a tritone. Finally, this symmetricality means that the interval content of the row—and thus its shape and its sound—is the same read left to right or right to left (i.e., in retrograde); thus **RI** 6 is identical to **I** 0, and so forth. The total number of possible permutations of the row is reduced by half.

Consider once more the opening of the Theme and Variations. It is not merely that the one line uses **I** 8 and the other **I** 2, but each form of the row is the retrograde of the other. In terms of pitch content, the clarinet line read right to left will produce the harp and French horn line read left to right. Thus the music pivots in a number of fashions around bar 6: It is by no means an accident, for example, that the A–E♭ in the clarinet at the turning point comes above E♭–A in the harp, for the symmetry here is bilateral.

You won't hear all these relationships at once, at least not until after you have studied the published score and worked all this through for yourself. But you can't miss getting a sense of the various kinds of cross references; and the strongly emphasized identity of the tritone intervals colors what the piece sounds like whether or not you can identify this particular interval by ear.

Serial composers, then, use this large spectrum of opportunities at their disposal in a variety of ways. A strict treatment would make no exceptions to the rule; a freer treatment might include sections that make little reference to the rows. The net effect is a music of big leaps and broad spaces and a curious kind of twinkling. Themes and cadences become less discernable or nonexistent: You listen for textural effects and, particularly, for certain kinds of intervals as they achieve a structural significance.

Most people can't tell just by listening whether an atonal work is serial or not. Nor should seriality be of prime importance to the listener. What serial practice does is to give the composer a coherent, intellectually (and mathematically) pleasing set of materials to use in building a composition. The new world of sound that serialism opened up for composers was a thoroughly welcome step forward in the eternal quest for revealing new ways of expressing one's artistic instincts. And it was not long before they began to experiment with serializing other parameters of music: dynamic level, mode of attack, and instrumental grouping.

If you are a typical first-time listener, you may complain that serial music is mathematical and not musical, that it lacks tunes and makes you uncomfortable. Possibly you will consider taking a stand against "academic" or "professorial" music—a fairly standard essay by first-year newspaper critics. (The Viennese serialists gave their first performances at chamber music concerts to which the press was not invited.) Yes, mathematics is at issue here, and the music is quite sophisticated and structurally complex; it tends to assume you have developed a quick ear and a good mind for music. But Bach fugues are mathematically sophisticated, too, and you've already accustomed yourself to other sorts of difficulties in music composition. Here at your first exposure to this new sound world you must listen again and again until the shapes and sounds become familiar to you. Then you will discover the music's true delights: Atonality is unfamiliar by comparison with tonal music, which you hear every day. Spending some time with it is the best way to make atonality familiar.

Art music has been strongly influenced by serialism. Many of the most serious composers since Schoenberg and his school have strongly embraced it, and virtually all have tried their hand at it. The thought that lies behind serialism is the same analytical reasoning that brought the great advances in computing, linguistic theory, and so forth: all of them difficult, yet all of them very much of our time.

Schoenberg's serial period began in 1923. Following the death of his wife Mathilde that October, he married Gertrud Kolisch, sister of the violinist Rudolf Kolisch, his pupil and founder of a celebrated string quartet that specialized in Bartók and the music of the Second Viennese School. (The Schoenbergs' daughter Nuria later married the Italian serialist Luigi Nono.) In 1933, as it became increasingly clear that the Viennese Jews were in danger of their lives, the Schoenbergs emigrated to the United States and settled in Los Angeles, where Schoenberg taught at UCLA and the University of Southern California. Berg died in 1935, just after completing the Violin Concerto, leaving his opera *Lulu* unfinished; his widow kept the work from completion and publication, but after her death it was finished and triumphantly produced in 1979. Webern was an active conductor and radio commentator in the late 1920s and the 1930s. Losing his radio post after the Nazi annexation of Austria (the Anschluss), he passed the war years in seclusion at his home in the Vienna suburbs, then during a visit to his daughter near Salzburg was shot to death by an American military policeman for violating a curfew.

THE EMIGRATION

Schoenberg was among the first in the wave of European artists and scholars to seek refuge in the United States from Nazi persecution. More even than Stravinsky, who came in 1939, he affected American compositional thinking, since unlike Stravinsky he was a gifted and committed teacher (see the photograph on p. 361). *Style and Idea* (1950) was written in Los Angeles, and his seminars of advanced young composers included several of the important figures alive today. After both Schoenberg and Stravinsky were established permanently here, it might well be said that the focus of serious music composition had shifted from Europe to American shores.

Beginning with reliable steamship travel in the nineteenth century, European composers and performing artists had looked forward to visiting the United States in their quests for wealth and fame. The most celebrated composers actually to make the trip were Offenbach, Johann Strauss II, Dvořák, and Mahler; but Berlioz, Wagner, and Tchaikovsky had all intended to come. Dvořák's New World Symphony and Tchaikovsky's Piano Concerto were premiered in the United States. Nijinsky and the Ballets Russes came in 1916; the Paris Conservatory Orchestra made a propaganda tour in late 1918 to celebrate Franco-American wartime unity, which turned into a victory tour when news of the armistice reached them at their concert in Richmond, Virginia.

The Russian Revolution of 1917 left Prokofiev, Rachmaninov, and Stravinsky footloose and homeless. Prokofiev lived primarily in France from 1918, but he sojourned in the United States in 1921 to produce his opera *The Love for Three Oranges.* He returned to live reasonably comfortably under the Soviet regime in 1932, visiting Hollywood once more in 1938 to study techniques of film scoring. Sergei Rachmaninov (1873–1943) left Russia for the first time in 1906, then permanently in 1917. He resided in Switzerland and from 1935 in New York and Los Angeles. His famous Rhapsody on a Theme of Paganini for Piano and Orchestra (1934) was premiered by the Philadelphia Orchestra, with Leopold Stokowski (a British-Polish-American) conducting, with Rachmaninov at the piano. The conductor Serge Koussevitzky (1874–1951) left Russia for Paris, where he gave wildly popular concerts—including the premiere of the *Pictures at an Exhibition*—before coming to the United States to conduct the Boston Symphony Orchestra (1924–49). Koussevitzky was succeeded in Boston by the Alsatian Charles Münch, whose Franco-German ancestry had enabled him to guide the Paris Conservatory Orchestra successfully through the years of the Nazi occupation.

The shocking realization that the Nazi empire had conceived a final solution to the Jewish question dawned on civilized people only gradually as the 1930s advanced. As late as September 1938 Neville Chamberlain, the prime minister of England, imagined that he and the French had purchased "peace with honour" by acquiescing to the Nazi rape of the Czech Sudentenland. "Peace for our time," he proclaimed from No. 10 Downing Street. . . . "Go home and get a nice quiet sleep." A few months later it was clear that Paris, London, and Moscow were also in Hitler's sights.

Ordinary citizens could only watch helplessly as their world collapsed once again, while yet another generation of their young men was called up to active duty. Musicians were privileged in that they were travelers by profession and equipped to survive away from home. Paul Hindemith (1895–1963) fled Berlin in 1938, after four years of harassment for "Bolshevist" leanings, having a Jewish wife, and playing in a string quartet with Jewish musicians. At Yale he led the early music ensemble and taught composition. In 1950–51 he delivered the prestigious Charles Eliot Norton Lectures at Harvard (published as *A Composer's World,* 1952); other composers who have given the Norton Lectures include Stravinsky, Copland, and Bernstein. The French composer Darius Milhaud (1892–1974), a Jew, came to Mills College in Oakland and after the war alternated that position with residency at the Paris Conservatoire.

The most famous conductor in the world, Arturo Toscanini (1867–1957), had been a fixture in New York since 1908 but had since become the darling of Bayreuth and the Salzburg Festival. He broke his Bayreuth contract in 1933 over the Nazi proclamation forbidding Jewish musicians at what was rapidly becoming a temple to the Master Race, then canceled his Salzburg appearances of February 1938, the month of the Austrian Anschluss. Instead, he conducted the Palestine (i.e., Jewish) Symphony Orchestra, which he had helped establish, and a refugee orchestra at the Lucerne Festival. The Greek conductor Dimitri Mitropoulos, closely associated with the Berlin Philharmonic, came to the United States in 1936 at Koussevitzky's invitation and stayed to conduct the Minneapolis Orchestra and the New York Philharmonic. George Szell, who had been first conductor of the Berlin State Opera (1924–29), happened to be in the United States when the war broke out. German-speaking university professors, bringing musicology with them, joined faculties from Berkeley to Harvard.

Americans can be proud of the welcome their nation accorded European refugees and the speed with which their contributions were assimilated into the fabric of music making here. The emigration also brought a huge influx of talent and ideas. The Europeans fanned the flames of the American musical scene into a wildfire. They built, or helped build, the institutions that came to define American preeminence in the musical world: the New York Philharmonic, the Boston Symphony Orchestra and Tanglewood, the Metropolitan Opera, Juilliard, musical life in Cleveland, Detroit, Houston, Denver, Los Angeles, and San Francisco. Not all the emigrants were happy here, of course, and several succumbed to medical and psychological problems. Bartók, whose time in the United States was short and prevailingly unhappy, nevertheless composed his best major works here.

Bartók

Béla Bartók (1881–1945) and his wife came to New York in October 1940. He was Hungary's most distinguished musician, having been professor of piano at the Budapest Academy of Music from 1907 and since the 1920s a celebrated composer of stage works, quartets (the best since Beethoven), piano works (*Mikrokosmos,* six volumes of progressive difficulty), and orchestral music. Additionally he was an important ethnomusicologist of the many national practices to be found in Hungary. His collection of Hungarian popular song had earned the imprimatur of the Hungarian Academy of Sciences. The Concerto for

Orchestra is the only work he completed in the United States; it was commissioned by the Koussevitzky Music Foundation for the Boston Symphony Orchestra. Bartók's fee was $1,000.

The concept of Bartók's concerto is simple yet essentially unprecedented: The orchestra is its own soloist, and the constituent sections are each given virtuoso solo work along the way. Thus the work pays homage to the capabilities of the BSO under Koussevitzky, and it has since become a favorite showpiece for orchestras everywhere. By mid-century standards the Bartók Concerto for Orchestra was very Old World. Today, 1943 seems almost as long ago as 1913, and the sense of anachronism is much less jolting.

www.prenhall.com/masterworks
recommended listening

RECOMMENDED LISTENING:

Bartók: Concerto for Orchestra (1943)

"And so," to apply a line from *Peter and the Wolf* to music at mid-century, "here is how things stood." Schoenberg was dead, or very nearly so. His American period had been fertile and diverse, reflected in important advances in serialism (Fourth Quartet, 1936) on the one hand and a renewed interest in Expressionism (*A Survivor from Warsaw,* 1947) and religious themes on the other. Stravinsky, having married again and settled in Hollywood, was thriving. His American ballets with George Balanchine—a veteran of the Ballets Russes—included *Orpheus* (1948) and *Agon* (1957), the latter announcing his turn to serialism; additionally there were many important large-ensemble instrumental compositions. Stravinsky's major work of the middle period is the opera *The Rake's Progress* (1951), to a text by W. H. Auden and Chester Kallman, first performed in Venice. The compositions of the 1950s and 1960s are largely cantatas and works commemorating the dead (Dylan Thomas, John F. Kennedy). From 1948 onward Stravinsky's ideas and daily life were strongly influenced by his amanuensis, Robert Craft, with whom he published recollections and reminiscences that act as sequels to his autobiography of 1935.

Old Sibelius, in Finland, had declined into a quiet alcoholism after writing the tone poem *Tapiola* (1926), but his seven symphonies and many fine orchestra compositions (the *Karelia* and *Lemminkäinen* suites, the symphonic poems *Finlandia* and *Pohjola's Daughter,* and a Violin Concerto) had made him a venerated artist both at home and abroad.

In England, Benjamin Britten (1913–76) fostered a rebirth of new English opera with *Peter Grimes* (1945), *Billy Budd* (1951), *Death in Venice* (1973), and a cycle of smaller church theatricals, or "parables," in the mid-1960s: *Curlew River, The Burning Fiery Furnace,* and *The Prodigal Son.* Additionally, there is the superb *War Requiem* (1961), its conciliatory purpose recognized in the choice of the Soviet soprano Galina Vishnevskaya (wife of the cellist Rostropovich), the English tenor Peter Pears, and the German baritone Dietrich Fischer-Dieskau as soloists. Britten's contemporary Michael Tippett (b. 1905) came to fame with his oratorio on Nazi atrocities, *A Child of Our Time* (1941), where American spirituals are used like the chorales in a Bach cantata as morals to the musical story. Tippett blossomed somewhat more slowly than Britten, but his steady output of major work can now be seen as at least the equal of Britten's: four symphonies, fantasias on themes of Handel and Corelli, and the operas *The Midsummer Marriage* (1955), *The Knot Garden* (1970), and *New Year* (1989).

In the Soviet Union, Prokofiev remained a major voice throughout the war, producing seven symphonies, the ballet *Romeo and Juliet,* some of the most interesting piano and violin concertos after Brahms, and movie music for *Alexander Nevsky* and *Ivan the Terrible.* He died on the same day as Stalin, 5 March 1953. His prolific successor was the Soviet master Dmitri Shostakovich (1906–75), composer of 15 symphonies, 15 quartets, and the major opera *Lady Macbeth of Mtsensk* (1934).

In Paris, where the matter of royal lineage is always at issue, Ravel's mantle had passed to the aging members of the prewar affinity group that the surrealist filmmaker Jean Cocteau had called Les Six, notably Milhaud, Francis Poulenc (1899–63), and Arthur Honegger (1892–1955). But the most interesting music being produced in France was that of a descendant of the French Organ School, Olivier Messiaen (1908–92), a professor at the Conservatoire and organist at the Church of the Trinité. Adapting the church modes and a nonmetered rhythmic idiom into an advanced modernist style, he had by 1950 produced the marvelous organ cycle *La Nativité du Seigneur* (1935), *Quatuor pour la fin du temps* (1941), and the virtuoso piano work *Vingt regards sur l'enfant Jésus* (1944). His work in the 1950s focused on musical imitations of the birdsongs he collected as an avocation. Meanwhile, the American ultramodernist John Cage was collecting mushrooms with equal vigor.

THE AVANT-GARDE.   "Schoenberg is dead," wrote the *enfant terrible* of the avant-garde, Pierre Boulez (b. 1925), in an early 1950s manifesto reminding the younger generation that serialism was still in its infancy. Boulez's particular objective was to apply rigorous serialism to rhythm, volume, and timbre, retaining a studied neutrality of emotion; his string of major works in the late 1940s and early 1950s culminated in *Structures* for two pianos (1952) and *Le Marteau sans maître* (1954), a cycle to abstract poetry of René Char for contralto, alto flute, viola, guitar, and percussion. At Darmstadt, the European center for new music, Boulez and the German composer Karlheinz Stockhausen discovered their affinities, and they went on to lead the European branch of the post–World War II *avant-garde:* the "forward guard," or vanguard of new music.

The avant-garde thrived, interestingly, in Poland in the shadow of Witold Lutos awski (1913–94). In part, this was a political activism in response to the Soviet regime; in large measure, it was the work of Krzysztof Penderecki (b. 1933), whose violent *Threnody for the Victims of Hiroshima* (1960), with its screaming tone clusters, represented on the page in unconventional graphic notation, became a celebrated example of artistic response to the nuclear threat. Progressive music continues to be heard in Poland at the annual autumn festivals of contemporary music in Warsaw.

An important American contribution to the avant-garde was the *chance music* of John Cage (1912–92). Chance music is deliberately indeterminate in both composition and performance. From Zen philosophy Cage developed the idea of musical experiences generated by random choices, as in throwing coins or dice to select the materials for a happening (*Music of Changes,* 1951). In *4'33"* (1952) there is no sound at all, other than the ambient noise of the venue. Chance music was a strong influence on American art in the 1950s and 1960s.

THE ELECTRONIC AGE

In 1937, David Sarnoff, the president of the National Broadcasting Corporation and the Radio Corporation of America (NBC and RCA), succeeded in convincing the legendary Toscanini to return from his short-lived retirement in Italy to conduct a new symphony orchestra assembled just for him: the NBC Symphony. The first performance under Toscanini—a Vivaldi concerto grosso, Mozart's 40th, the Brahms First Symphony—was on Christmas night 1937 before an exclusive audience who held programs printed on silk, the better not to rustle over the air. The broadcast lasted from 10:00 to 11:30 P.M., Eastern time. Fifty million Americans, one-third the population, are said to have listened to the Toscanini broadcasts.

The NBC Symphony under Toscanini was in some respects the high-water mark of the golden age of broadcasting, the beginning of the electronic age. The fidelity of broadcast live performances was substantially greater than that of records at the time, and technologically speaking radio was far more advanced than the mechanics of the gramophone and Victrola. In Europe, the air belonged to the governments: The BBC, established in 1922, rapidly became the largest and most influential employer of musicians in Britain, and the BBC Symphony, established in 1930, became one of the world's great orchestras. The French, Italian, and German radio orchestras have parallel histories, with the South German and Bavarian Radio Orchestras (those of the Suddeutscher and Bayerischer Rundfunk) achieving particular prominence. In the United States, the air theoretically belongs to the people and practically speaking belonged to competing capitalist enterprises. The networks consisted of local stations linked by the rival wire services of Western Union Telegraph and Bell Telephone. NBC and its record company, RCA Victor, competed with CBS (the Columbia Broadcasting System) and its Columbia records. Major national corporations sponsored the cultural programming. There was a famous *Bell Telephone Hour* and *Voice of Firestone* series; Texaco sponsored (and still sponsors) the Saturday afternoon broadcasts of the Metropolitan Opera. General Electric and General Motors bought commercials even during wartime, when they had nothing to sell to the public.

However capitalistic its primary motivation, the vision of the early radio and television barons was formidable. They dreamed of the educational and social force of broadcasting, and acted on their dreams. Good commentators spoke as well about music as Edward R. Murrow did about current affairs, and the generation of Americans whose listening habits were conditioned by radio in the 1940s and early 1950s knows more art music, and more about it, than any generation before or since. They were glued to the Toscanini broadcasts, and could discuss a Brahms symphony or the Verdi Requiem with enthusiasm.

Art music survived on network television for only a very short time. Gian Carlo Menotti's *Amahl and the Night Visitors* (1951) was a Christmas Eve tradition in America during the black-and-white era; Leonard Bernstein's popular Young People's Concerts of the 1960s were the last serious commitment of network broadcasting to live music. Art music shifted in the 1970s to PBS, and it is enjoying a partial resurgence now on the cable channels. The difference is that virtually all the modern broadcasts are tapes of performances that would have happened anyway; the musicians are not employees of the network. Nowadays the only live musicians employed by the networks are the late-night bands.

The high point of the NBC Symphony Orchestra coincided with the development of the LP recording and a war between RCA, proponents of the 45 rpm recording, and Columbia records, proponents of the 33 rpm recording and 12-inch discs. RCA won only for pop singles, while Columbia far outdistanced RCA on classical music recordings in the 1950s. The LP microgroove format expanded the contents of a side from 4½ minutes to over 20, and high-fidelity engineering improved its quality substantially. Stereophonic sound followed in 1958.

ELECTRONIC COMPOSITION.   During the war, tape recording had been developed from primitive efforts using coils of wire. In this process analog signals are recorded electromagnetically on a plastic tape to which an emulsion of metal particles has been applied. (Scotch tape, too, was a wartime product.) Tape segments can be easily spliced, so a technically flawless performance is engineered by patching in retakes. Tape can also track simultaneous channels, offering the possibility of later overdubbing. Tape revolutionized everything about music commerce, from the recording session to the movie soundtrack.

It was the combination of tape recording with artificial sound synthesis that opened the eyes of progressive composers to the possibilities of electronic music. If a tape could be spliced at all, it could be spliced upside down, or backward—mechanical equivalents of inversions and retrogrades. It could also be fashioned in loops. The motives for compositional working out could come from any sound source, even a simple sound effect. The principles of this *musique concrète* were worked out in the late 1940s at the French radio laboratories.

Of the early electronic instruments, the most attractive to composers were the *ondes Martenot* and the *Theremin,* both named after their inventors. Martenot's machine generated sound with an oscillator and loudspeaker, the right hand playing a keyboard and the left controlling knobs for tone color and volume. The Theremin, or etherphone, was built in 1920 by the Soviet engineer Léon Theremin (Lev Termen) and is played by moving the hands between two radio antennas positioned at right angles to one another: one controlling pitch and the other volume. The effect is of watching a magician waving his hands in the air to produce weird and wonderful surrealistic sounds.

The Franco-American composer Edgard Varèse (1883–1965) had moved to New York in 1915, and during the 1920s he promoted avant-garde ideas of rhythm, pitch, and tone quality, notably in works with prominent percussion. An early proponent of harnessing electronics for music composition, he composed an *Ecuatorial* for bass voice, winds, percussion, and two Theremins or *ondes Martenot* to a sacred Mayan text (1934), then turned his attention to planning a broadcast happening from radio stations all over the world. He snapped up the tape recorder and became a pioneer of true electronic music, notably with his *Poème électronique* for the Philips Pavilion at the Brussels World's Fair of 1958. The Philips building had been designed by Le Corbusier and was meant to suggest a circus tent from the outside and a cow's stomach within. Varèse composed a multimedia abstraction where a tape loop in three channels was played endlessly over 400 speakers in the building as images were projected onto the walls.

Electronic studios, in which it was possible to generate sounds from electronic sources and then manipulate and preserve them through the medium of magnetic tape, grew up around the European state radio stations and the American universities. At mid-century the principal attractions of electronic music for composers were three: the all-new sounds at the composer's disposal, the potential for precise serial control of the non-pitch elements of sound (and its opposite: the potential for true random sound arrays), and the freedom from the vagaries of music's middle man—the performer. Hypothetically, anyway, the composer could exert total control of the artwork; once recorded it would exist unchanged for all time, like a Michelangelo sculpture. Technologically and mathematically oriented composers could also see electronic/tape technologies rapidly converging with those of the brave new world of computers.

SYNTHESIZED SOUND.   Electronic organs descended from those developed by Hammond and Wurlitzer in the 1930s were the first widely adopted post-acoustic musical instruments, attractive in large measure because they were so much less expensive than conventional pipe organs. In 1955 RCA developed the first synthesizer of serious use to composers: the RCA Mark II. This was a room-sized contraption of vacuum tubes, switches, tape decks, and keyboards that at least in theory had the capability of approximating the wave form of any musical sound. Following a dispute with the American Federation of Musicians, who feared (rightly, as it turned out) the encroachment of electronic media on employment opportunities for live musicians, the machine was reassembled at Columbia University, where it became the Columbia-Princeton Electronic Music Center. The RCA Synthesizer was the staging ground for American response to the influential *Gesang der Jünglinge* ("Song of the Young Boys," 1956), for voice and synthesized sounds on tape, by the composer Karlheinz Stockhausen. The Princeton composer Milton Babbitt, whose interest in electronic music extends back to 1959, completed his first Composition for Synthesizer in 1961. There followed *Vision and Prayer* for soprano and tape (1961) to a text by Dylan Thomas, *Ensembles for Synthesizer* (1964), and *Philomel.*

Milton Babbitt and the RCA Mark II Synthesizer

BABBITT: FROM *PHILOMEL* (1964)

The combination of a live performer with a taped "accompaniment" allows the composer objective control of most of the elements of the performance along with the presence and spontaneity that only a living artist can supply. (The matter of whether or not to applaud the loudspeakers at a tape-only concert performance, when the composer isn't there—is one of modern life's little embarrassments; electronic-only music should be listened to in private.) Babbitt's superb 19-minute work, *Philomel,* brings together the work of a fine poet of the era, John Hollander; one of the great singers of modern music, Bethany Beardslee; and a tape prepared at the Princeton-Columbia studio. The myth at issue is that of Philomel and Tereus.

Philomel has been violated by Tereus and her tongue cut out so she cannot tell her story. She takes her revenge by weaving a tapestry that shows his crime, then serving up his son to him for dinner. Fleeing Tereus into the forest of Thrace, Philomel is transformed into a nightingale, "the ruined bird whose song pours out of the darkness with a voice restored from incoherence." Hollander summarized his project:

> The voices could represent variously what she heard in the woods, what she thought she heard there, what she fancied she heard inside her head, and so forth. A pivotal dramatic moment would involve her own discovery of her renewed voice, albeit as a bird; I wanted a final strophic aria on the subject of music and pain, also. In addition, I wanted to try to make full use of the amazingly flexible acoustical resources of the sound synthesizer.

The tape component consists both of synthesized pitches and, in *musique concrète* fashion, manipulation of bits and pieces of "recorded soprano," that is, Beardslee's own voice. (Thus even when another soprano sings the work, it's Beardslee's voice on the tape.) She appears on stage in her traveling cloak, and begins to sing with the surround sound from a two-channel tape and four loudspeakers. After the metamorphosis she removes the cloak to reveal a brilliant garment. On the CD you are hearing a recording of the live performance and the tape.

The work has three sections. The first (the excerpt on your CD) has to do with Philomel rediscovering her voice: growing from the vowel sound "ee," then the words "feel" and "tree," and on to other plays on the sounds contained in the names Philomel and Tereus: "feel a million," "filaments and tears," and so on. At length she finds phrases and stanzas—and a new voice.

> What is that sound?
> A voice found? . . .
> What is this humming?
> I am becoming
> My own song.

Altogether there are five phrase-groups for the soprano, separated by brief tape interludes.

The music of the first section emphasizes wide leaps over the full extent of the soprano's range, while from the tape come equally wide arpeggios and many-voiced chords created by stacking up the constituent intervals from the twelve-tone series.

Listening Chart

 CD 4, TR 16

Milton Babbitt (b. 1916)
Philomel (1964)
   Part I

For: soprano, recorded soprano (voice of Bethany Beardslee), and synthesized
   sound

Text: by John Hollander (b. 1929)

Type: Lyric scene,
   sectional
Meter: $\frac{3}{4}$
Key: NA: atonal,
   serial
Duration: 05:02

Fleeing Tereus into the forest of Thrace, Philomel is transformed into a nightingale, "the ruined bird whose song pours out of the darkness with a voiced restored from incoherence." The tape component consists both of synthesized pitches and manipulations of the voice of Bethany Beardslee, who offered the 1964 premiere at Amherst College in Massachusetts.

00:00	Introduction	(vocalise)	Tape. Synthesized sounds plus soprano vocalise on "eeeee."
00:22	**Phrase 1**	Ee-ee-ee	Live soprano. Philomel tries to find a voice. "ee" becomes
01:07		I feel a million trees	"feel" and "trees"—she begins to find words.
01:25	Interlude	Not true tears . . .	Tape. Wordplay on "tr" sounds: *true, tears, trees, Tereus.*
01:35	**Phrase 2**	Is it Tereus I feel?	Question and answer between taped and live voices.
01:49		. . . filaments	Wordplay on "f" sounds: *feel, filaments, Philomel.*
02:13	Interlude		Tape. "Tereus" distorted.
02:26	**Phrase 3**	Trees in my hair . . .	Lost in the forest, lost in the night, lost in silence.
03:06	Interlude	Pillowing melody	Tape. Echoes the most rhythmic words.
03:11	**Phrase 4**	Lost, lost	Her story continues, ending with the great line
03:39		Philomel stilled . . .	"Feeling killed, Philomel stilled, her honey unfulfilled."
03:50	Interlude		Tape. Echoes that line.
03:53	**Phrase 5**	A voice found.	Her voice found: *sound, found, bound, astound.*
04:28	Duo	I am becoming	Tape and live soprano join in a duo:
		My own song.	She has become a songbird.
04:41	Interlude	(vocalise)	Tape. Return of opening gesture, many voiced.

The pitch content is derived from a series that allows figures like the ones in this example to fall out naturally. The series also gives rise to the very particular interval configurations that begin to attract the acute ear: pairs of consecutive or simultaneous half steps. These dawn on you gradually if at all; primarily the ear is attracted to dozens of new sounds deployed through a strikingly novel configuration of space as created by the *register* of the pitches themselves, the various forms of antiphony involved in the speaker/tape setup, and the complexities of the rhythmic character.

   A live performance of *Philomel* or one of its relatives is thrilling on several fronts, not least of which is the sense of witnessing the birth of the electronic age. What could be more sensible than a singer carrying her accompaniment around on tape? But the technology is a good deal older than even yesterday's Macintosh. The master tape of

Philomel, now nearly four decades old, is beginning to decompose, and Babbitt says he has no plans to remaster it.

www.prenhall.com/masterworks
composer profiles
Babbitt

Milton Babbitt (b. 1916) was a true pioneer in musical thinking of our time. Born in Philadelphia and raised in Jackson, Mississippi. Babbitt enjoys, when the occasion suits it, claiming to be a southerner. He was a composition student of Roger Sessions, whom he joined on the Princeton faculty in 1961; but from the first his interests were what we would now call interdisciplinary, involving an equally impressive command of logic and mathematics that prepared him to concentrate on the mathematical principles of sets and set theory. Babbitt's natural orientation to musical thinking is thus one of scientific scrupulousness, and his contributions to the theory of music have been, accordingly, quite substantial. In an effort to achieve serial ordering of all the parameters of music, for example, he postulated a five-dimensional musical space, where every musical event is characterized by its pitch name, register, dynamic level, timbre, and duration. From there he developed precisions of duration and distance between sound events into true serial rhythms. Babbitt coined much of the vocabulary of modern serial music in both theory and practice: pitch class, interval class, combinatoriality, partitions, time points. His dense and difficult prose outlines a system where the numerical equivalent of the row also generates the time points and other parameters of each sound event. Babbitt is aware that his theoretical constructs make demands on the outer limits of the listener's perceptual abilities, even if he is sometimes frustrated by the "resentment and denunciation" his work can provoke. At the same time he has a marked sense of humor, affixing coy titles to such complex serial works as *All Set* and *Whirled Series,* the latter reflecting his avid interest in baseball. He has also composed sentimental cabaret songs.

Babbitt's combination of rapier-like analytical thinking, humanizing good humor, and total absorption in whatever issue is at hand have made him one of the most influential teachers of his time. Students have flocked his way, from Stephen Sondheim to computer composers, serialists, and theorists practicing today all over the world.

No serialist can ignore Babbitt's work, but advanced serialism means different things to different composers. Among the leading serialists today are Donald Martino (b. 1931) and Charles Wuorinen (b. 1938), both of whom excel in big orchestral music, and George Perle (b. 1915), who has pursued a simpler and more concordant system he calls "twelve-tone modality." Perhaps the most distinguished living American composer, Elliott Carter (b. 1908) favors free atonality that grows (like serial music) from cells and intervals selected to control the work. These are treated in very complex formal structures where strands of musical material mutate in shape and time independently of other strands in the same web.

George Crumb (b. 1929), meanwhile, ignores much of this in his search for other kinds of new sounds. Controlling pitches by numerology and form by the zodiac, he assembles a veritable encyclopedia of unconventional sound sources. He might have a pianist pluck the piano strings or strike them with blunt objects or even bow them with fishing line; his impressive vocabulary of vocal pyrotechnics includes tongue clicking, shrieking, hissing, and whispering. In the famous *Ancient Voices of Children* (1970) the soprano sings into a grand piano to the accompaniment of (among other things) Tibetan prayer stones, a saw, and a toy piano.

In Europe, György Ligeti (b. 1923) worked in electronic music in the late 1950s and then turned to atmospheric works based on slowly moving tone clusters in a system he calls micropolyphony. You may know his *Lux aeterna* for chorus as the weird screamy music from *2001: A Space Odyssey.* Pierre Boulez continues to investigate a freer serialism than Babbitt's, one that incorporates chance elements and open-ended permutations of materials—so a great deal of his later work remains in progress. Wooing Boulez from the New York Philharmonic back to France was a central objective of the Pompidou administration's arts policy. To that end in the early 1970s, one of the most advanced computer music studios in the world was built for Boulez beneath the Centre Georges Pompidou in Paris: IRCAM, the Institut de Recherche et Coordination Acoustique/Musique.

Miniaturization, first made possible with the transistor and printed circuits, soon rendered the RCA synthesizer obsolete. Modular tabletop components were in the works by the time *Philomel* was becoming widely known. The next generation was dominated by the synthesizers of Robert Moog (introduced in 1964) and Donald Buchla, one of the designers of IRCAM. Synthesizers were incorporated into every aspect of music making, from the academy to the rock band (Pink Floyd) to the TV studio (Paul Schaeffer on David Letterman's show). The 1968 record *Switched-On Bach,* prepared on a Moog by Walter (now Wendy) Carlos, enjoyed an immense popularity, and a 25th-anniversary CD was released in 1992. Virtually all commercial music began to rely heavily on synthesizers. John Adams's opera *The Death of Klinghoffer* (1991) uses several electronic instruments in the orchestra pit.

Mass-produced, mid-market electronic keyboards like the Yamaha DX-7 of the mid-1980s put rudimentary sound synthesis into the hands of anybody who cared about it enough to spend a few hundred dollars. The electronic keyboard was easily adaptable as a component of a computer system. You doubtless know someone with a Yamaha-type synthesizer; it's probably plugged into a computer setup.

Digital synthesis, where sound waveforms are related to number patterns (and vice versa), began to be perfected in the late 1970s, concurrent with the advent of the office computer. An early commercial success was the floppy-disk digital synthesizer called the Synclavier, widely used for performance as well as composition; very shortly thereafter components like the Sound-Blaster card could put the same capability into a desktop computer. The critical link—today we call it *interface*—between electronic systems is the digital-to-analogue conversion necessary between computers, which deal in numerical representation, and loudspeakers, which are ultimately driven by an electric signal analogous to a sound wave. The process of *sampling* quantifies sound waves in digital representation. In the MIDI protocol (Musical Information Digital Interface), for example, a virtually unlimited number of tracks of music can be quantified in real-time sequences and saved as digital files. A show-tune composer of my acquaintance now composes at the electric keyboard, saves his work as MIDI files, invokes a quantizing and notation program, and waits a few seconds while his work is turned into notated musical score and individual parts for the performers. (All the musical examples in this book and on the autotutorial screens were produced from files that can also be played back as sound.)

While digital technology has revolutionized the recording industry through the CD and now the DAT, or digital audiotape, computing and sound synthesis have opened music composition to all. These new composition tools have changed the way we think about music in much the same way that word-processing programs and laser printers changed the way we think about printing and typography. The advantages of these high-tech tools are obvious. The composer can tinker with the music until it exactly meets his or her specifications, adjusting all the parameters of the music to undreamed-of tolerances. There's no possibility for performer error. You have the orchestra, so to speak, in your pocket.

ROCK AND POP. The revolution in electronics affected popular music at least as much as it did art music. Modern rock music is almost by definition electrified. The electric guitar was introduced in the generation just following microphones and loudspeakers with the stand-on-the-floor Hawaiian guitar built by the Californian Leo Fender (1937), then designs based on the look and feel of the acoustic guitar. The Les Paul model built by Gibson guitars in the 1940s and later is still the instrument of choice for

many rock bands: the one with the solid body and classic cutaway design, equipped with treble and bass pickups and control knobs for the volume and tone of each. Most of the later elements of the electronic revolution, including synthesizers, are found in the rock band of today, but it was the electric guitar—and, of course, the beat—that established rock style to begin with.

Rock music emerged in the 1960s from the rock 'n' roll of the 1950s, a white adaptation of the complex of black commercial idioms in vogue at the time, primarily rhythm and blues (or R&B, i.e., blues with a beat and often a do-wop chorus) but also its relatives, the boogie-woogie and urban blues. The name comes from the song "Rock Around the Clock" (1955) by Bill Haley and His Comets, one of the most popular representatives of an idiom catering to white middle-class dance parties of suburban teenagers. Most of the music descends from the 12-bar blues forms and the 32-bar A-A-B-As you already know about. The dancing was either too frenzied or too close, and the sexuality of the texts became more overt with each passing month. There was much parental wringing of hands over rock 'n' roll. The record companies responded with "clean" pop (Connie Francis, Pat Boone); black musicians responded with a fusion of R&B, gospel, and pop, brought to prominence by the Detroit label Motown Records (Diana Ross and the Supremes, Little Stevie Wonder, the

Elvis

Temptations), and later soul and funk. And there was Elvis (1935–77). Presley's co-opting of the rock 'n' roll sound for what was basically country-and-western singing—

rockabilly—was scarcely noticed as a stylistic mutation; his sexual wiggling, however, couldn't be ignored by anybody.

In retrospect, the pop music of the 1950s seems relatively pristine. Rock emerged in the San Francisco Bay Area of the mid-1960s, chiefly with the Grateful Dead and with Jefferson Airplane and Grace Slick—the Bay Area in those days having become a kind of nirvana of alternative lifestyle, with strong emphasis on radical politics, drugs, and sex. These were the topics of rock music; its sound, dominated by electric guitars and violently amplified—some six or seven times louder than rock 'n' roll—just as abrasive as its lyrics. Rock showed some promise of breaking out of the 12-bar blues and A-A-B-A forms that gripped many of the other popular styles, and there was real performance interest to be found in rock's emphasis on virtuoso improvisation by the guitarists. Rock appealed to educated white young people of the middle class, idealistic and frightened by the world around them.

The Supremes

THE BEATLES (1961–70).   Meanwhile, from England, the Beatles were conquering the world. They had everything going for them: good looks, good management, good luck, and some real musical genius. And to top it all off, they quit while they were ahead, so that they became a myth, and their records, in turn, became collectors' items.

The four young men—John Lennon, George Harrison, Paul McCartney, and Ringo Starr (guitar, lead guitar, electric bass, drums, respectively)—coalesced from earlier groups during 1961. They rose to fame at home in Liverpool and in Hamburg; by 1963 Beatlemania had swept England and they had their first gold record ("She Loves You"). Beatlemania preceded their arrival in the United States in February 1964, where they made their historic appearance on the Ed Sullivan Show. The audience of mostly teenagers screamed uncontrollably over these enthusiastic boys in matched collar-less jackets and mop-top haircuts. "I Want to Hold Your Hand" soared to the top of the charts and stayed there for weeks, as the Beatles and their entourage (production folk, groupies, and the scheming moneymen Lennon called "the suits") progressed to Washington and Miami and back to a tumultuous welcome in England. This was the start of the biggest, and most lucrative, business the music world had ever seen. The Beatles were a genuine cultural phenomenon.

The fabulous success, public adulation, and all that money went on to take their all-too-predictable toll. The Beatles careened through marriages, addictions (the manager who created the phenomenon, Brian Epstein, drank and drugged himself to death), and ultimately Eastern spiritualism with the guru Maharishi Mahesh Yogi, who in decidedly nonspiritual fashion went on to capitalize on the relationship. They invented many of the modern practices of studio production and postproduction marketing: the promotional film (now the rock video), the spinoff movie (*Yellow Submarine*), television appearances,

The Beatles

and product tie-ins. They owned their own conglomerate (Apple Corps, Ltd., parent company of Apple Electronics, Apple Music Publishing, Apple Records, Apple Films, Apple Television, Apple Wholesale, and Apple Retail—but not Apple Computers) and their corporate souvenir shop, Apple Boutique. Gradually the Beatles drew apart, recording together less and less until their association was legally dissolved in 1970.

In all, the Beatles released 13 albums and 22 singles, plus spinoffs, in seven years. Their entire output fits on 15 CDs. It was not just commercial savvy that made the Beatles great, however, or even that they were incomparably seductive performers. It was that McCartney and Lennon were gifted and fertile lyricist/composers. Their poetry was ripe for its age and always rhythmic and clever; the lyrics and music appear often to have come simultaneously, with an integrity of expression that only genesis can provide. The Beatles also understood how to adapt the electronic age to their artistic purposes. Their records are engineered to the max with multitracking, electronic sounds, and imaginative use of stereophonic effects.

RECOMMENDED LISTENING:

The Beatles: "Hey Jude" (1968)

Composed and recorded in July–August 1968, "Hey Jude" topped the charts in a few weeks, earned its first gold record in September, and went on to sell over 2 million copies by the end of the year. In a significant precursor of rock video, the song was not only filmed but also premiered on David Frost's television talk show.

There's a story behind the composition. John Lennon's romance with Yoko Ono had led him to abandon his wife Cynthia, a favorite of the other Beatles, and his 5-year-old son Julian. McCartney visited Cynthia, bringing a rose for her and a song for her son. He had written it in the car: "Hey Julian, it's not so bad. / Take a sad song, / and make it better." The other text allusions are less clear: McCartney at the same time was breaking off his engagement with Jane Archer and perhaps was interested in Cynthia Lennon. John Lennon, meanwhile, saw the text ("You were made to / Go out and get her") as approving his affair with Yoko Ono. "I took it very personally," he said.

The recording sessions were correspondingly emotional, as the 40-piece backup band began to sing along in the "na-na" refrains. The studio audience sang along at the David Frost Show as well, and you are very coldhearted if you don't find yourself humming to the CD. That is one measure of the Beatles' magic: The exhortation to take a sad song and make it better underscores the humane side of 1960s rebelliousness, and the stirring turn from the wistfulness of the beginning to the resolve that so prolongs the piece said something else equally important about the times.

The Beatles' last tour in 1966 came on the heels of John Lennon's public announcement that "The Beatles are more popular than Jesus Christ." This was met in the United States and elsewhere by municipal and radio station proclamations banning their music, record burnings, and in Memphis, picketing by the Ku Klux Klan. Their August 29 appearance at Candlestick Park in San Francisco was the last live concert of the Beatles. After that they kept to the studios.

Beatlemania and the rock revolution culminated in the happening at Woodstock in August 1969, the great camp meeting of a generation ready to tune in, turn on, and drop out—a generation now less violently angry at the events of 1968 (the assassinations of Robert Kennedy and Martin Luther King, Kent State, the Democratic Convention in Chicago, and above all Vietnam) than dazed beyond comprehension. Afterward there was no longer much distinction between rock and any other form of pop. The vocabulary of subclassification gets complicated, although possibly it is better learned in the street than from a textbook. To summarize, there were the English invasion (the Rolling Stones, the Who), heavy metal (Led Zeppelin), acid rock (Jimi Hendrix, Janis Joplin), punk (the Sex Pistols), rock opera (*Hair, Jesus Christ Superstar*), disco and club rock (*Saturday Night Fever*), new wave, salsa (a Puerto Rican/Cuban idiom), reggae, and now rap and hip-hop. As you listen to these musics, keep your ears open for how the words are being used, how the music sounds, and how it is mutating.

The rock concert of today is a full-fledged media event, with sound synthesis, carefully engineered amplification and mixing, light shows, not to mention T-shirts. Parallel developments in marketing and public relations are harnessed so that the concert tour, rock video, and so forth are all channeled toward the sale of studio recordings. The rock revolution is well named.

 USING THE ELEMENTS

The term *fusion* was originally applied to the 1970s music that combined jazz and rock, but it's a good word to keep in mind as you trace the trends of music in the last 20 years. Nowhere is there a rule of art that says artists must try to reconcile conflicting styles or bridge the gulf between classical and popular, yet that process seems to be very important to many musicians practicing today. Whether you call such movement fusion or eclecticism or synthesis is immaterial; you may not even be convinced that it's happening at all. But it's hard not to see the riot of musical styles afoot today as responses that have in common a need to control the proliferation of sound sources now all about us. Already in the late 1950s Gunther Schuller had coined the term *third-stream music* to characterize eclectic composition that tries to assimilate classical art-music designs (the first stream) and the improvisatory discoveries of jazz (the second stream).

Working through these issues has taken place less in symphony halls and opera houses than at the American university, where, insulated in some measure from the whims of the public and the precarious balance sheets of the big orchestras, composers have found time and encouragement for their work—not to mention the stimulating company of their colleagues and students. Of the American composers cited a few pages ago, Babbitt taught at Princeton, Martino at Brandeis and Harvard, Wuorinen at Columbia, Crumb at Pennsylvania, and Perle at the University of California, Davis and Queens College. Few music departments are without at least a couple of interesting composers on the faculty. The economics of their situations—lots of talent and interest, not much money—have fostered a large and important body of contemporary chamber music, most of which has premiered on college campuses. Sometimes it is written for or commissioned by new music ensembles at the university or particular members of the performance faculties. Since the 1970s many wonderful new works have been composed for the professional chamber groups devoted to contemporary music that have blossomed in metropolitan areas: the Da Capo Players of New York and EarPlay of San Francisco, and many others.

The Da Capo Chamber Players, founded in 1970 by the violinist Joel Lester and a "Pierrot ensemble" (that is, the cohort of instrumentalists required for Schoenberg's *Pierrot lunaire*), quickly established a reputation for high virtuosity in the repertoire and garnered financial backing from virtually all the funds and foundations supporting serious music in the United States. (The name of the ensemble comes from their practice of offering featured works twice in one concert, before and after the intermission.) They have premiered nearly 100 new works composed expressly for them and accrued a large discography. Additionally, their residencies at colleges and universities across the country have influenced the present generation of young composers by demonstrating the beauteous music that can be achieved by committed musicians of the highest quality and professional standards. A fine example of their work, and of the contemporary chamber idiom, is their disc devoted to the music of the University of Chicago composer Shulamit Ran (Bridge Records, 1995).

 SHULAMIT RAN: *PRIVATE GAME* (1979)

Private Game was composed for the tenth anniversary concert of the Da Capo Players in March 1980. It is a duo for two superb musicians: the clarinetist Laura Flax and the cellist André Emilianoff. (Both are still affiliated with the group.) The commission specified that the composer should incorporate the group's name into the musical design in any way she desired. Initially, Ran says, she was tempted to interpret the instruction loosely: "*da capo,* today?" Then she became intrigued by the notion of using strict repetitions in a particular scheme: "They are essential, for they give the piece coherence, but they may or may not be consciously perceived as repetitions on first hearing. They are my private game."

The three repeated cells—the *da capos*—fall in the sequence 1–2–1–3–2–3, a *rondeau*-like arrangement not so distant from the scheme that intrigued Schoenberg in *Pierrot lunaire*.

Cell 1

Cell 2

Cell 3

Cells 1 and 2 are major structural organizers, a kind of first ("impassioned, as though in a great rush") and second ("gentle, Schubertian") theme; cell 3 figures as a merry connective interlude. The feature that perhaps most attracts the ear is the strong tendency of prominent moments to involve rising half steps, as bracketed in cell 1 of the example. Notice, for instance, how the long-held notes in the clarinet (00:23, 01:40) incorporate the same chromatic intervals.

But revel above all in the remarkable array of musical combinations created by only two players, as the composer peppers her score with instructions for the private game: "like an explosion," "each attack as though by surprise," "rush a bit," "mocking, gross," "sing out," "rhapsodic, with bravura." At 01:31 you hear the clarinetist repeat the same pitch again and again using alternate fingerings to achieve maximum timbral differentiation. Meanwhile the duo operates in terms of ordinary musical gestures you have come to recognize in works from Mozart to Schoenberg. The players sometimes vie for preeminence, occasionally join in moments of concord and homophony, veer into cadenza passages, and at length settle—via a positively Romantic reminiscence of the "Schubertian" cell—into a quite traditional closure.

Listening Chart

 CD 4, TR 17

Shulamit Ran (b. 1949)
Private Game (1979)

Type: Chamber work in one movement
Meter: Free; quarter-note pulse
Key: NA, free polytonality
Duration: 04:04

For: clarinet and cello

The composer writes, "There are three brief *da capo* sections interlaced into the piece in a 1-2-1-3-2-3 sequence: 1 and 2 appear at key points structurally; 3 is more transitory and ornamental. They are essential, for they give the piece coherence, but they may or may not be consciously perceived as repetitions on first hearing. They are my private game. Enough said."

00:00	**Beginning**	A rounded unit defined by the 1-2-1 *da capo* arrangement.
	cell 1	Wide leaps, "impassioned, as though in a great rush," two similar phrases.
00:09	cont'd.	Clarinet plunges settle on long notes over cello pizz., with motivic close (00:23).
00:33	cell 2	The "gentle, Schubertian" figure hints at $\frac{6}{8}$.
00:46	cont'd.	Transitional material: birdlike clarinet with more thumping cello.
00:52	cell 1	*Da capo* of cell 1.
01:01	**Middle**	Dominated by clarinet.
	cont'd.	Big arpeggios and leaps in both instruments, disjointedly.
01:08	cell 3	A sudden, jazzy scamper in close harmony, then cascades down.
01:16	cont'd.	A moment of conjoint motion leads to a clarinet climax.
01:24		The mocking-bird effects now obvious; cadenza ends in motivic close (01:40).
01:53	cell 2	*Da capo* of cell 2. The "gentle, Schubertian" figure now effects transition.
02:07	**End**	Dominated by legato cello.
	cont'd.	Long, broad cadenza, with clarinet echoes and response.
02:50	cell 3	*Da capo* of cell 3.
03:00	closure	The motive heard at 02:07 begins a quiet close, with reminiscence of cell 2 (03:27).

Shulamit Ran (b. 1949) was born and educated in Israel, where her prodigious gifts were recognized by her piano teacher and family friends who took her to play the piano for Pablo Casals and Artur Rubinstein. At age 14, she won scholarships to study piano and composition (with Norman Dello Joio) at the Mannes College of Music in New York, where she moved in 1963 with her mother. Launched into a strenuous career as concert pianist by an appearance on one of Leonard Bernstein's televised Young People's Concerts, she nevertheless continued to develop a strong compositional voice. She premiered her 1971 Concert Piece for piano and orchestra with Zubin Mehta and the Israel Philharmonic.

Meanwhile, a recording of *O the Chimneys* (1969), setting Holocaust poetry by the Nobel Prize winner Nelly Sachs, attracted the attention of the American composer and University of Chicago professor Ralph Shapey. He arranged for Ran to be invited to join the composition faculty, although she had never been to Chicago and knew no one there. Her interview was "an instantaneous meeting of minds. . . . It was a leap of faith for them, and a strange coincidence for me."

Since 1973, Ran has been professor of composition at the University of Chicago. The meteoric progress of her career was suddenly interrupted by the diagnosis of a brain tumor and surgery to remove it; her recovery took a year. "No one could emerge from such an experience without realizing the fragility and preciousness of life. . . . I realize more than ever how much I love life." She has won all the prestigious composers' awards, including election to the American Academy and Institute of Arts and Letters (1989) and the 1991 Pulitzer Prize for her First Symphony. Since 1990 she has halved her faculty appointment in order to serve as the Chicago Symphony's composer in residence. Ran's opera *Between Two Worlds: The Dybbuk* (1997) was premiered by the Chicago Lyric Opera. Her fanfare *Chicago Skyline* (1991), commissioned for the 40th anniversary of Chicago's classical music station, WFMT, was recorded by the Chicago Symphony and has become a municipal trademark.

Ran

Ran makes you want to claim citizenship in the contemporary music scene, perhaps even write some music yourself.

> I somehow have a deep trust that if, after all the struggle that I go through in writing something, I finally am able to say, "O.K., this is really what I wanted to say," that it will speak to others, too. I don't think that I'm detached from humanity. I think that I live on the same planet and have the same general, big concerns that all people do. I think there is a lot more that binds us together as a species than separates us. That, sometimes, is forgotten.

MINIMALISM. Beyond the academy, another response to the stresses and strains of the 1960s was the American movement called *minimalism,* which emerged in California in the 1970s and was being widely noticed in the 1980s. The defining characteristic is repetition. The composer chooses naive metric patterns and melodic cells and repeats them incessantly over very long periods of time, so a kind of pulsing hypnotic quality emerges, not dissimilar from certain aspects of North Indian music. Typically some very gradual shift of focus will be put into play, perhaps a key mutation or transfer of performing force; the ostinato cycles phase in and out. The marketplace liked minimalism because it made few demands on the ear; academics tended to hate it.

An important precursor of minimalist works was *In C,* composed by Terry Riley (b. 1935) in 1964—the same year as *Philomel.* The entire score fits on one printed page; it is a chance piece, where any number of instrumentalists play the 53 melodic cells in order and at a pulse established by a pianist drumming out octave Cs. The decision to move on to the next motive rests with the individual musician, and it isn't over until everybody is finished with the 53rd cell; the work usually lasts about 45 minutes. The example shows 14 of the cells. The implied harmonies are limited to those around I, IV, and V chords in C.

RECOMMENDED LISTENING:

Riley: In C *(1964)*

Other minimalists include Steve Reich (b. 1936), high priest of percussion (*Drumming,* 1971) after the African and Indonesian models, and Philip Glass (b. 1937), a theater composer strongly influenced by Indian music, jazz, and rock (*Einstein on the Beach,* 1976). It's true that a little minimalism goes a long way, but its basic approach has major implications for other forms of art music. Not the least of these is the successful bridging of ethnic differences that comes from embracing elements of non-Western music.

The most successful fusion of minimalism and the traditional forms has been in the music of **John Adams (b. 1947)**, a Berkeley-based composer. He studied at Harvard, and then while teaching at the San Francisco Conservatory embraced in turn electronic media and minimalism (*Shaker Loops,* 1978; *Grand Pianola Music,* 1982). In 1987, to extraordinary fanfare for a classical composer, his opera *Nixon in China* premiered in Houston and was followed by PBS broadcasts, a world tour, LPs, CDs, and a videotape.

The choice of subject matter, Richard Nixon's state visit to Mao Tse-tung in 1972, was both provocative and shrewd. The situation was rich with the promise of stage spectacle—a huge portrait of Chairman Mao, Chinese theater and dance, and above all the landing of Air Force One—and the faces and characters were still alive in the minds of people everywhere. Nearly everybody who saw the opera had been glued to their TV sets as the events being depicted on stage had actually taken place; the principals themselves—Richard and Pat Nixon, Henry Kissinger, Chou En-lai—could have come to Houston to see themselves on stage. (They didn't.) Moreover, *Nixon* was good psychodrama, since the characters reveal to us their innermost thoughts as they participate in the momentous events. The minimalist musical fabric is at times long-winded, and often takes second place to the production and the libretto, but the net effect was arguably as successful as any in American opera. Music for the ballet sequence "The Chairman Dances" has since become standard concert fare.

Adams

Nixon was a collaboration of Adams, the British librettist Alice Goodman, and the progressive stage director Peter Sellars. This same trio created their second opera, *The Death of Klinghoffer,* in 1991. Many of the singers had been in *Nixon in China,* representatives of the new breed of American artist who sings everything from Bach to Ives to the present with equanimity.

The subject matter, as in *Nixon,* came from headline news, although in this case it was decidedly unsettling. In October 1985 the Italian cruise ship *Achille Lauro* was hijacked by Arab terrorists while at anchor in Port Said, Egypt. Many of the passengers had gone that day to visit the pyramids. Those who stayed behind were taken hostage, among them a Jewish couple from New Jersey, Marilyn and Leon Klinghoffer. Klinghoffer, confined to a wheelchair, was eventually machine-gunned and tossed overboard. The body later washed up on a distant beach. (The aftermath of the story, not recounted in the opera, is equally dramatic: The U.S. Air Force diverted the plane carrying the terrorists from Libya to Italy, and the *Achille Lauro* terrorists were identified by Mrs. Klinghoffer and held for trial in Italy; but the much-sought-after Abu Nidal, on the same plane, was allowed to leave.) The opera's apparent theme is the agonizing American experience in the Middle East. But, in fact, *Klinghoffer* is less about Americans than about Arabs and Jews, less about an isolated incident of violence than about a millennium of cruel racial conflict.

The theatrical concept of *The Death of Klinghoffer* is a cross between conventional number opera and multimedia pageantry. The authors promoted a parallel, perhaps somewhat strained, with the Bach passions. There are eight singers, one with multiple roles, and the main characters are often represented on stage both by a singer and a dancer.

RECOMMENDED LISTENING:

Adams: excerpt from **The Death of Klinghoffer** *(1991)*

www.prenhall.com/masterworks
recommended listening

The Death of Klinghoffer: Stephanie Friedman in Omar's act II aria

A chorus and dance troupe provide other commentary, sometimes in choruses of astonishing impact (as in the prologue choruses of Exiled Palestinians and Exiled Jews), at other times in vivid ballet, as when the dancer Klinghoffer drags his own lifeless body offstage. Synthesized sound components fit naturally into the orchestral score.

Since Klinghoffer, Adams has composed the Chamber Symphony (1992) and the Violin Concerto (1993) for Jorja Fleezanis, concertmaster of the Minnesota Orchestra. His new symphony, *Naive and Sentimental Music,* was jointly commissioned by four orchestras and first performed in February 1999 by the Los Angeles Philharmonic.

SERIOUS MUSIC TODAY. The economic climate has sharply threatened the very existence of America's big orchestra and theater companies. Good composers who resolutely choose to ignore market forces in their quest for artistic integrity have a hard time finding performances and listeners and a publisher. It's tough to watch commonplace entertainment take the lion's share of the resources, leaving the elevated art forms high and dry.

But there are several encouraging signs. One is the growingly comfortable coexistence and cross-influencing of the styles we have been treating; another is what appears to be the increasing willingness of cultured people to be involved in the big picture of serious art. And unexpected phenomena in classical music—the John Adams operas, for example—keep on occurring.

Take the case of Górecki's Third. Symphony No. 3 by the Polish composer Henryk Mikolaj Górecki (b. 1933) is a work for soprano and orchestra on old Polish folk texts, composed in 1976. Since then it had resided on the back burners of the orchestral repertoire until its 1992 recording on the Nonesuch label by the Baltimore conductor David Zinman, the young American soprano Dawn Upshaw, and the London Sinfonietta. Promoted through intensive airplay over the British New Classic FM station, it became an artifact of pop culture, topping the classical charts (a first for a living composer) and placing number 6 in pop, ahead of Madonna.

American classical composers are doing fine, too. John Corigliano (b. 1938) is a neo-Romantic, tonal composer, author of the "electric rock opera" *The Naked Carmen* (1970). His Symphony No. 1 (1990), composed "as a memorial to friends and colleagues of the composer who had died in the AIDS epidemic," won a Pulitzer Prize and is being played all over the country. Eileen Taaffe Zwilich (b. 1939), a student of Sessions and Carter, emerged in the 1980s as a powerful voice in instrumental composition. Her Symphony No. 1 (1983) likewise won a Pulitzer Prize, and since then she has turned out concertos, symphonies, and chamber music of great distinction. Zwilich has become something of a national role model for women composers, and continues to compose fine music in abundance.

The Japanese composer Toru Takemitsu (1930–96) became well known and well loved in the United States. His is a thoroughly personal music of timbre and space, having much in common with Japanese tradition but freely using Western elements as well. Takemitsu's work has made the sounds of *biwa,* the Japanese lute, and *shakuhachi,* the bamboo flute, familiar to American concert audiences; performances of his big orchestral works are anticipated with pleasure.

Tan Dun (b. 1957) continues to build aesthetic bridges between Asia and the West. Born in the Hunan province of China, he planted rice for two years during the Cultural Revolution of the 1970s, then worked in a Beijing opera troupe. Inspired by a live performance of Beethoven's Fifth Symphony, he found his way to the Beijing Conservatory to study composition, and from there to Columbia University for doctoral studies in music. While his base of operations remains New York, the multicultural nature of Tan's work has given him a global exposure. The strength of its reception has earned him exclusive contracts with Sony Classical for his recordings and G. Schirmer for his music publications. His opera *Marco Polo,* premiered in Munich in 1996, was thought in many circles to be the high point of the season.

www.prenhall.com/masterworks
composer profiles
Tan

TAN: "OPERA IN TEMPLE STREET," FROM *SYMPHONY 1997*

Tan's *Symphony 1997: Heaven—Earth—Mankind* is a massive work commemorating the reunification of Hong Kong with China on 1 July 1997. What may at first strike the ear as a somewhat miscellaneous collage is in fact a studied commingling of seeming opposites: past and present, East and West, strictly notated concert music and improvisatory theater—an expression, surely, of the *yin* and *yang* of Chinese cosmology. "Maybe there really is no distinction between the past and future," remarks the com-

Tan Dun with *bianzhong* bells.

poser; "everything is a circle." The general organization as well as specific allusions make it is clear that the composer has aspired to create a kind of Beethoven's Ninth for the '90s: a symphony of world brother- and sisterhood.

Central to the work is the sound (and look) of the *bianzhong:* tuned bells hanging from a frame, a kind of instrument found in many ancient Asian cultures. (The most familiar is the Indonesian *gamelan.*) This particular set of 65 bells is some 2,400 years old, unearthed in 1978 along with more than a hundred other musical instruments from the tomb of the nobleman Yi of the kingdom of Zeng. The instrument would have been played by a team of perhaps five musicians, three striking the small bells with a pair of wooden mallets and two more with long sticks to strike the large bells. Doubtless these were young women, for the coffins of twenty-one girls lie alongside Yi and his musical instruments, probably buried alive with their prince.

Part I, Heaven, uses the solo cello as kind of narrator, and a choir of children's voices to establish the purity of past and future. A love song, "Jasmine Flower" (also used in Puccini's *Turandot*), is heard, then an evocation of street celebrations at Chinese New Year: Dragon Dance–Phoenix–Jubilation (with motives from Beethoven's Ninth). The excerpt chosen for your CD, an encounter with a street opera in Hong Kong, is the transition from part I to part II. Part II, Earth, is a concerto for cello solo, bianzhong, and orchestra, developed from pre existing work to demonstrate the *Yi-Ching's* teaching of continual change. The sub-movements Water–Fire–Metal continue the treatment of equilibrium of natural elements. Part III, Mankind, opens with a vignette adapted from a film score honoring victims of war, becomes a Lullaby, and then culminates in a jubilant Song of Peace, adapted from a text of the great Chinese poet Li Po (701–62) with overtones of Schiller's "Ode to Joy," the poem set by Beethoven in the Ninth Symphony.

The performers were Yo-Yo Ma as solo cellist, the Hong Kong Philharmonic Orchestra, Yip's Children's Choir, and the Imperial Bells Ensemble of China, conducted by the composer.

Listening Chart

 CD 4, TR 18

Tan Dun (b. 1957)
Symphony 1997: Heaven–Earth–Mankind (1997)
"Opera in Temple Street"

For: Taped material played on a CD by the cello soloist; *bianzhong* bells, cellos, and basses

Type: mixed-media collage
Meter: NA
Key: NA
Duration: 06:02

Recorded sounds of a traditional street opera company in Hong Kong are engulfed by the orchestral players who then yield to the *bianzhong*—an instrument buried 2,400 years ago but now alive again. An allegory of past and present that serves to introduce part II: Earth.

00:00	**Street scene**	(Tape.) Clapping, cymbals, drum call attention to the players.
00:10	the players	The actors—two men, one woman—introduce themselves with poetry ("shiny pearls of light on flowers" / "gentlemen and ladies accompany the bridegroom").
00:16	(drone)	A low-C drone emerges from the live players: cellos, basses.
00:32	song	The actors dance and sing, improvising on an old love-song in the bowed and plucked string instruments with percussion. The live drone begins to oscillate with ornamental wobbles and threatens to engulf the song (01:20), as the present has engulfed the past. But the song, like the past, continues.
02:10	**Bianzhong**	(Live.) The *bianzhong* overlaps the fadeout of the song.
02:34	cell 1	Lower bells drawing on the main interval of the song; accelerando.
03:12	cell 2	A fast rhythmic pattern with prominent triplets coalesces in the higher bells, played with brushes.
03:58		Melodic motives emerge as the players take harder sticks, enhancing the polyphony.
05:00	cell 3	The lowest bells add an ostinato-like bass pattern, strongly duple. Fadeout.

Take, too, the cases of dozens of young American composers born in the 1950s. Steven Mackey (b. 1956), one of Babbitt's successors at Princeton, leads a dizzying life of commissions and first performances. He has his publications and recordings (*Lost & Found,* 1996), and struggles, like the rest of his generation, to find the intersections of artistic merit and popular appeal.

Composers born in the 1960s and 1970s are now establishing themselves. Music composition is a popular course of graduate study in the United States: Every day, all

Mr. Mackey and
the Kronos
Quartet, 1992

over the country, young people are working on their serial and post-serial techniques, their orchestration, their electronic and computer music skills—even their counterpoint and fugue. All of them are hustling performances and recordings of their music, and it doesn't take much looking around to find vibrant concerts of new music by student composers where you can gauge their interests and concerns and go home with a sense of What's Happening—today.

Add to that the thousands of young people employed one way or another in the commercial music industry—it takes a real composer with solid technique and good aesthetics to write for a computer game or a television commercial—and you have genuine cultural phenomena, in abundance, to ponder. From this evidence, anyway, it would appear that people worry too much about the decline of serious music.

Epilogue

What Next?

$\mathcal{W}$hat's different about living in a present surrounded by active artists is that you have to make up your own mind about their art. The advantage to gazing back at somebody else's era is that there has been the opportunity to achieve some critical distance. As you know—from your own life—it often takes the passage of time to lend perspective to the course of events. Perspective separates the meaningful from the meaningless, sorts fact from fiction, and often allows us to distinguish more of the real truth.

In the present, on the other hand, you get to be part of the hurly-burly. Our time, you should not be surprised to discover, has many parallels with times past. There is much good music and even more bad music. The relationship between art and money is uneasy at best. The press, on which we ought to be able to rely for guidance, seems content to dwell on the comings and goings of the dozen stars of the season. Art sometimes leaves the public behind.

And civilized, thinking individuals continue to disagree violently about the values of true art, while less civilized people continue to enjoy categorizing what they don't like—or don't understand—as trash. The invective is every bit as virulent as in the great polemics of the past ("What a good thing it isn't music," someone remarked of the *Fantastique*), and the public hysteria sometimes the modern equivalent of the welcome accorded *The Rite of Spring*. Meanwhile, artists continue to push at the outer limits of our perception as hard as they know how.

Consider an obvious case in point, the controversial photographs of Robert Mapplethorpe, which eventually involved the U.S. government and several of the most august institutions in America's art world. How you react to this issue of our particular epoch is your own business, but remember that truly cultured people base their response on thoughtful analysis of and sympathy with the mission of art—and that this process is often a struggle.

Certainly one of the central problems of new music has always been the distance between the concerns of the artist and those of the public. Many, possibly most, important new compositions are difficult to listen to. The mind is apt to equate the unfamiliar with the offensive. It really *is* hard to make sense of new works on one hearing—you wouldn't even think of doing it with a Beethoven sonata—and harder still for a composer to get the kinds of multiple performances and recordings that would allow you to study a new work through repeated listenings. But that doesn't absolve us intelligent listeners from the obligation to encourage new music by giving it our attention. Begin with the assumption that the composer wouldn't be presenting it if he or she didn't think it was good. Then allow simple curiosity to run its course. Ask yourself the usual questions: What's happening? Where does this piece come from, and where is it going? How does it work? How do I fit in?

Clearly, our electronic age offers a vast new array of opportunities for composers, musicians, and listeners. Ours is a civilization of leisure time and disposable income. We are hooked on entertainment and have ended up spending a great deal more on music than ever before in the history of the world. And we're bombarded with the digitized, miniature products of a system of engineering, manufacture, and distribution so sophisticated that only dreamers could have imagined it a decade ago.

Such a conspicuous revolution inevitably lays waste. Our symphony orchestras, deemed less relevant to entertainment than professional sports, have for decades been struggling financially. Even though most professional musicians earn only modest salaries, the numbers required for the symphonic repertoire make the orchestra an unwieldy and inefficient institution by modern standards of management. Few orchestras can afford to take chances with the repertoire, and the symphony hall risks becoming a museum for the old masters. Government funding, while a very welcome development, constitutes a drop in the budgetary bucket, and patrons and patronesses may be on the decline.

The key to surviving revolution has always been the ability to adapt. Leonard Bernstein tapped the imagination of his era by his creative use of television. Many of the best performing artists now cross over between classical and pop music with equanimity. The violin virtuoso Nigel Kennedy is as comfortable in a Rock-a-Mania concert as at Carnegie Hall, for example, and virtually all the modern opera stars have done crossover recordings (*West Side Story* with Kiri Te Kanawa, Marilyn Horne, and José Carreras; *Kismet* and *Man of La Mancha* with Samuel Ramey). Some of the most interesting classical music being produced today is by musicians who understand the power of the CD to make a highly specialized repertoire financially viable, since the medium reaches a much larger public than would come to any one performance venue. We have begun to imagine a time when virtually the whole of notated music will be available at a good sound library.

And then there is multimedia. MTV and its relatives are one case in point. The quick assimilation of the rock video into modern culture is not entirely unwelcome, and the mingling of media is such an obvious opportunity that you wonder why it didn't crop up sooner. (Actually it did: Ernie Kovacs, in the early days of black-and-white TV, did some remarkable things with music and the screen.) The aesthetic problem is the confusion of images: MTV too often draws you away from the music and text, diffusing instead of focusing your thoughts.

Anybody with a computer now has astonishing possibilities of sound production at his or her fingertips, and the thousand-channel interactive cable network is just around the corner. It's difficult to imagine a more exciting time to be a music lover.

Or, for that matter, to be alive. Ours remains a world of great dreams and greater dreamers. Many of the dreams for a better world of Eleanor Roosevelt and Jawaharlal

Schoenberg and
his pupils

Nehru and Golda Meier have come true; the humanizing visions of Presidents Kennedy and Carter—both of whom loved fine music—continue to linger in our collective spirit. Pablo Casals and Yehudi Menuhin and countless other great musicians have been among the dreamers of our time who used music, as Orpheus did, to tame the furies of the atomic age. Adopting Beethoven's utopian vision, the "Ode to Joy," as the anthem of the European Community is altogether apt for our time. Never forget the power of music to determine a greater humanity for us all.

So the future of music now falls to you. The possibilities are limited only by your imagination. Usually the music appreciation series continues with "great composer" courses (Music of Mozart, Music of Stravinsky) or genre courses (Opera, Choral Music). There are also entry-level courses in harmony and musicianship, which should be pursued by those interested in composing their own songs. Many departments allow students to minor in music, and most music minors of my acquaintance have not regretted the extra effort.

While you're in college, take the opportunity to explore the related disciplines: painting (consider the juxtaposition of Stravinsky and Picasso), literature in its original language (Goethe's *Faust,* the work of Molière or Mallarmé, anything by Shakespeare, and all lyric poetry), theater, history, electronics, mathematics, and computing.

Those of you who have been inspired by your discovery of art music may be considering majors in music. The major curriculum at most colleges and universities consists of coursework, in approximately equal measure, in performance, history, and theory and composition. (At conservatories the curriculum is by definition strongly oriented toward performance.) In the upper division one gradually refines one's path in the direction of one's chosen career, focusing on composition, historical research and writing, philosophies and techniques of teaching, or a variety of technical skills. It's true that music is a highly competitive world, but so, too, are most enterprises entered by college graduates. Earning a living as a performer of classical music is tough, but it can be done, and done with great satisfaction. Moreover, there are countless positions that mingle music study

The author and his conducting students, University of California, Davis.

and performance. Chief among these is teaching, which is not only pleasurable but highly valued in our society. Everybody knows that civilization will die without good teachers. And I do not know better forums than the classroom or the concert hall to convey your joy in art music to others.

Whatever your major, the pursuit of fine music is a lifetime activity. Keep up with the world of art music by making frequent trips to a good music store, reading one of the major metropolitan newspapers, subscribing to at least one literately-inclined magazine, and going to as many live concerts as time and your pocketbook will allow. Art, properly done, will sustain you, challenge you, comfort you. And it may show you a path. Listen to it.

Glossary

a (Ital.): for. The indications *a*2 or *a*3 mean the line is to be played by both or all three members of the section.

a cappella (Ital., "in chapel fashion"): Without instrumental accompaniment; applied to choral music, particularly of the Renaissance.

a tempo (Ital.): Return to the original tempo.

absolute music: Instrumental music without illustrative or programmatic intent.

accelerando (Ital.): Growing faster; accelerating.

accent: Emphasis of a musical event, typically by increased volume or sharper attack.

accidental: Notational symbol used to raise or lower a pitch.

accompagnato (Ital.): Accompanied; as in recitativo accompagnato (recitative with orchestral accompaniment).

acoustics: Science of sound and its perception.

ad libitum (Lat.): At will, or at the pleasure of the performer; typically an optional part that may be left out.

adagio (Ital.): Slow. Also used generically to describe a slow movement.

Agnus Dei (Lat., "Lamb of God"): Last movement of a choral mass.

Alberti bass: Accompanimental figure for the left hand in keyboard music, named after the composer Domenico Alberti (c. 1710–40), where the triads are broken into patterns of short note values.

alla breve (Ital.): Time signature indicating progress by half note.

allargando (Ital.): A broadening (and often slowing and swelling), usually at the end of a movement.

allegretto (Ital.): Somewhat slower than allegro, and by extension somewhat lighter.

allegro (Ital.): Fast. Allegro assai = quite fast. Allegro con brio = fast and bright. Allegro ma non troppo = not too fast. Allegro moderato = moderately fast. Allegro molto = quite fast. Allegro vivace = fast and spirited.

alto (Ital.): (1) The second highest of the four customary voice parts, below the soprano and above the tenor. (2) Singer with that vocal range. (3) [in scores] Viola. The term *alto* is also used to describe models of the flute and clarinet lower than the usual one.

andante (Ital., "walking"): At moderate speed.

andantino (Ital.): Term that has come to mean a little faster than andante, but which once meant a little slower than andante.

animato (Ital.): Animated; typically suggesting getting faster.

answer: Response in a new voice to the subject of a fugue, usually a fifth above it.

antecedent: That which precedes the consequent: thus the first half of a two-part phrase, where the second seems to be an appropriate outcome of the first.

anthem: English sacred choral composition for the Anglican service, often accompanied by organ; also, any solemn hymn.

antiphony (adj. antiphonal): Referring to music by multiple performing groups separated by space.

arabesque: Florid turn of melody.

arco (Ital., "bow"): Cancels the instruction "pizzicato" ("pizz.").

aria (Ital.): Composition for solo voice, usually a movement of a larger work.

arioso (Ital.): Lyrical manner midway in style between recitative and aria, especially in operatic solo scenes.

arpeggio (Ital., "harplike"): Chord where the pitches are played in succession rather than simultaneously.

assai (Ital.): Very; as in Allegro assai (very fast).

atonality: Having no allegiance to tonality; not having a key.

attacca (Ital.): Attack; that is, go on to the next movement without pause.

augmentation: Stating familiar melodic materials in longer-than-ordinary note values.

augmented interval: Intervals a half step wider than the corresponding major or perfect interval.

avant-garde (Fr., "forward guard"): Term that describes the most progressive or radical element of an artistic movement.

baguette (Fr.): Drumstick; usually part of a direction to the timpanist or bass drum player to use an alternative kind of stick. Baguettes d'éponge = sponge-headed drumsticks. Baguettes de bois = wooden drumsticks.

ballad: Self-contained narrative (i.e., storytelling) song. Also, any singable or popular tune.

ballade (Fr., pronounced "bah-*lahd*"): Title given by Chopin to four major one-movement works for piano solo. Later composers, notably Brahms, also used the title.

bar: The basic unit of meter; same as measure.

bar line: Vertical line separating measures (or bars) of music in a score.

baritone: (1) Voice part midway between tenor and bass. (2) Brass instrument having the appearance of a small tuba. (3) Member of an instrument family between tenor and bass; as in baritone saxophone.

bass: (1) Lowest-sounding voice part. (2) Double bass viol, lowest of the orchestral string instruments. (3) Lowest-sounding line in a score, or the lowest pitch in a chord. (4) Lowest-sounding member of a family of instruments, as in bass clarinet.

basso continuo (Ital.): In Baroque music, a continuously sounding bass part over which the rest of the composition is built.

beat: Prevailing metrical pulse.

bebop: Jazz style that emerged in the 1940s, an alternative developed by black musicians to the white big bands.

bel canto (Ital., "beautiful singing"): Prevailing vocal ideal in solo vocal music from the Baroque forward.

binary form: Musical form in two sections (graphed as A and B), very often repeated (A-A-B-B).

bitonality: Use of two keys at once.

blue note: Flattened inflection of scale degrees 3 and/or 7 in a major key.

blues: Musical style at the heart of the music of black Americans and permeating jazz and popular forms.

boogie-woogie: Fast jazz style that developed in the 1930s, featuring a driving ostinato bass.

bop: See *bebop.*

bourrée (Fr.): Lively Baroque dance movement in duple meter, usually with prominent upbeat.

bridge: (1) In sonata form, passage in the exposition that takes the harmony away from tonic and to dominant, arriving at the second group. Used interchangeably with, but more often than, the term *transition.* (2) Component of string instruments that raises the strings off the belly.

BWV: *Bach-Werke-Verzeichnis,* or index of Bach's works, organized by genre.

cadence: (1) Arrival at harmonic rest. (2) In parade music, the drumbeat.

cadenza: Passage of improvisatory display for the soloist, especially in a concerto.

canon: Musical procedure where a second voice is generated by following a rule (or "canon").

cantabile (Ital.): Singingly; in lyric fashion.

cantata (Ital., "sung work"): Genre of vocal composition originating in the Baroque, sacred or secular, for soloist or chorus.

cantus firmus (Lat.): Melody borrowed from some other work to serve as the basis for a new polyphonic composition.

cantus firmus mass: See *cantus firmus.* A Renaissance mass in which all the movements are based on the same cantus firmus is termed a cyclic mass (see *cyclicism*).

capriccio (Ital.): A caprice, usually a light, fanciful, and imaginative solo work that darts about from segment to segment.

celesta: Keyboard instrument of the orchestral percussion section where metal plates are struck by hammers; invented in the late nineteenth century.

chaconne (Fr.): Work built on an ostinato bass (or ground bass). See also *passacaglia.*

chamber music: Originally, music not intended for the church, theater, or concert hall. Now the term implies a performing group of small size.

chanson (Fr.): Song.

chant: Monophonic liturgical repertoire of the Catholic church. See also *plainchant, Gregorian chant.*

character piece: Descriptive miniature composition of the Romantic period, usually for piano.

chorale: Congregational hymn of the Lutheran church.

chorale prelude: Work for organ based on a Protestant chorale and serving to introduce its singing.

chord: Group of pitches sounding simultaneously; often a triad (three notes) or seventh chord (four notes).

chromatic scale: Scale that includes all 12 pitches.

chromaticism: Style of composition that makes pointed use of chromatic melodies and harmonies. See also *semitone.*

circle of fifths: Diagram in which the 12 pitches and associated keys are set around a circle where each member is a fifth higher than the one before it.

clavier: Keyboard; often used as generic term to describe any keyboard instrument.

clef: Sign that associates a line on a staff with a particular pitch and thus serves as a "key" to the system.

closing theme: Theme that concludes the exposition in sonata form.

coda (Ital., "tail"): Closing section of a movement.

col legno (Ital., "with the wood" of the bow): Hitting the strings with the wood, instead of the hair, of the bow.

collegium musicum (Lat.): Society of musicians performing for their own pleasure.

coloratura (Ital.): Florid embellishment of a vocal line, especially for soprano in the high register; also, a soprano who specializes in such parts.

compound meter: Meter containing triple (instead of duple) subdivisions of the beat (e.g., $\frac{6}{8}$, $\frac{9}{8}$, and $\frac{12}{8}$).

con brio (Ital.): With spirit, lively; as in Allegro con brio.

con fuoco (Ital.): With fury, furiously; as in Allegro con fuoco.

con moto (Ital.): With motion; as in Allegro con moto.

con sordino (Ital.): With mute, muted. Cancelled by the indication "senza" (without).

concert overture: Overture intended to stand alone in a concert, not to go before a theater piece.

concertante (Fr.): Concerto-like composition for more than one solo instrument and orchestra, popular in France in the eighteenth century.

concertino: Soloists in a concerto grosso (often two violins). See also *ripieno*.

concertmaster: Principal first violinist in an orchestra.

concerto: Work for soloist(s) and orchestra.

concerto grosso: Instrumental ritornello form from the Baroque, where a small group of solo players (the concertino) alternates with the large orchestra (ripieno).

consequent: Musical material that follows the antecedent and gives it balance and closure.

consonance: Musical stability as perceived in certain intervals and chords; the opposite is dissonance.

continuo: Bass line of a Baroque work with instruments, and the instruments that play it; same as thoroughbass. Provides the underpinning for Baroque composition. See also *figured bass*.

contralto: Lowest female voice.

contrapuntal: Adjectival form of *counterpoint*.

counterpoint: Manner in which two or more melodic lines are combined and juxtaposed to produce pleasing and technically correct intermingling.

countersubject: In fugue, the melodic material that accompanies statements of the subject.

crescendo (Ital.): Growing louder; the opposite is decrescendo.

cyclicism: Use of a theme in more than one movement.

da camera (Ital., "of the chamber"): Type of Baroque sonata or concerto more secular than its counterpart, the sonata or concerto da chiesa.

da capo (Ital., "from the top [head]"): On reaching this instruction (or its abbreviation, D.C.) in the score, the performers go back to the beginning of the movement and play until the word *fine* ("end").

da chiesa (Ital., "of the church"): Type of Baroque sonata or concerto somewhat more rigorous than its counterpart, the sonata or concerto da camera, in that it emphasizes fugal counterpoint.

decrescendo (Ital.): Growing softer.

development: Section in sonata form between the exposition and the recapitulation that investigates the possibilities inherent in the material stated thus far.

diatonic: (1) Succession of whole tones and half steps that make up a major or minor scale. (2) Interval drawn from that succession.

Dies irae: Gregorian plainchant for the dead; the sequence from the Requiem Mass.

diminished interval: Interval a half step narrower than the corresponding minor or perfect interval.

diminuendo (Ital.): Growing softer; same as *decrescendo*. Abbr. dim.

diminution: Technique generally accomplished by stating familiar melodic materials in shorter-than-ordinary note values. See also *augmentation*.

dissonance: Unpleasantness or instability perceived in certain intervals and chords; the opposite is consonance. In classical Western music dissonant intervals require resolution to consonance before closure.

divertimento (Ital.): A light work for chamber ensemble, popular as entertainment music in the Viennese Classical period.

divisi (Ital.): Indication in an instrumental part that the section is to divide the lines. Abbr. div.

Dixieland: New Orleans–style jazz for small combo; favored by white musicians.

dolce (Ital.): Sweet.

dominant: Fifth scale degree and/or the triad or seventh chord built on it.

double fugue: (1) Fugue where the subject and countersubject are of equal importance, thus suggesting simultaneous subjects. (2) Fugue where two subjects are treated independently, then together.

double stop: Playing two strings at once on a stringed instrument.

downbeat: The initial and strongest beat in a measure. See also *upbeat*.

drone: Line of constant pitch, or the instrument that plays it.

dynamics: Degrees of loudness.

embouchure: Shape and position of the mouth at the mouthpiece of a wind instrument.

entr'acte (Fr.; Ital.: *intermezzo*): Piece performed between the acts of an opera or play.

episode: Subsidiary passage other than the main thematic material.

equal temperament: Technique of adjusting tunings that divides the octave into 12 equal half steps.

espressivo (Ital.): Expressive; expressively.

ethnomusicology: Branch of study that treats musics of the world, particularly emphasizing music and culture, and music and oral transmission.

étude (Fr., "study"): Composition meant to investigate a particular problem of technique.

euphonium: Tenor brass instrument, lying in a range between the trumpet and the tuba.

exposition: (1) In sonata form, the first section, where the main thematic material is presented, always with a modulation to a second key area. (2) In fugue, the stating of the subject (or answer) in each of the voices, especially the opening statement.

Expressionism: Term (borrowed from literature and art) used rather loosely to describe the music of Schoenberg and his school. The artist portrays not simply an object but his or her internal reactions; what results is (in art) exaggerated, distorted, internalized.

falsetto: Abnormally high register of the male voice, in the range of the female voice.

fantasia: Free-form composition, a flight of fancy.

fermata (Ital.): Held out. At the fermata sign, the perfomer holds the pitch or chord at will (or at the will of the conductor).

figured bass: Baroque notational practice where numbers below the bass line indicate chords to be played by the continuo keyboard artist.

finale (Ital.): Typically the last scene in an act of an opera.

fine (Ital., "end"): Marking in a score that shows where to stop after having made a da capo or dal segno repeat.

Five, the: The Russian Five, or Mighty Handful (*moguchaya kuchka*).

forte (Ital.): Loud.

fortissimo (Ital.): Very loud.

fragmentation: Common way of treating thematic material, especially in the development.

French overture: Baroque form favored by the French composers and their imitators; the kind of movement that begins stage works and instrumental suites of the period.

fret: On certain kinds of string intruments (guitar, lute, viols), a raised position on the fingerboard that shows where to stop the string in order to produce the appropriate pitch.

frog: The hair-tightening mechanism on a bow; the portion of the bow the player holds in the hand.

fugato: Imitative, fugue-like passage in a non-fugal movement.

fugue: One-movement work in imitative counterpoint, where the theme is stated in each voice as a series of subjects and answers.

G. P. (Ger.): Abbr. in orchestral scores for *General-pause:* Everybody pauses.

gavotte (Fr.): Baroque dance in moderate duple meter with prominent upbeat.

genre (Fr., "gender"): Kind, type. Genre in music terminology is typically related to performing force.

Gesamtkunstwerk (Ger., "total artwork"): Wagner's theory of opera wherein all branches of art, including poetry, narrative, design, and architecture, are harnessed in a global art form, opera.

Gewandhaus: Building in Leipzig, the cloth merchant's guild hall. A celebrated series of concerts began in 1781; eventually the Leipzig orchestra took the name of the hall.

glissando (Ital.): Slide across the specified range of the instrument.

Gloria: Second movement of a choral mass.

grace note: Ornamental pitch, usually the upper neighbor, played rapidly and without fixed rhythmic value.

grave (Ital.): Slow, solemn.

grazioso (Ital.): Graceful, gracious.

Gregorian chant: Name commonly given to the plainsong of the Catholic church, setting the Latin liturgy. Its connection with Pope Gregory the Great (r. 590–604) is uncertain.

ground bass: Repeating bass pattern over which there is continuous variation in the upper parts; same as basso ostinato.

harmonic: (1) High, fluty sound produced on a string instrument by touching the string gently rather than fully stopping it, forcing it to vibrate at a higher position in the harmonic series. (2) Position in the harmonic series.

harmony: Technique of organizing pitch simultaneities (chords) and its study. Generally speaking, harmony concerns vertical sonority, and melody concerns the horizontal.

hemiola: Rhythmic/metric device where two bars in triple meter are made to sound like three bars in duple, usually just before the cadence in Baroque dance music.

homophony: Musical texture in which all the parts move simultaneously with simple chord progressions.

hymn: Strophic religious composition, generally for the congregation to sing.

idée fixe: Berlioz used this term to describe the motto theme of his *Symphonie fantastique* (1830), and said in the printed program that it had to do with the artist's vision of his beloved.

imitation: Compositional practice where motives and melodies, once stated, are taken up by the other voices successively, while originating voices go on in counterpoint.

imitative counterpoint, imitative polyphony: Polyphonic practice based on imitation.

Impressionism: Term used primarily to describe the work of the painters Monet, Renoir, etc., where loosely articulated images are fashioned from blotches of color; the goal was a particularly powerful brilliance. The term is used by extension in music to describe the work of the French masters Debussy and Ravel.

improvisation: Free, live invention of music, usually without notated parts.

incidental music: Music for use with a play, consisting of an overture, entr'acte pieces, music for pageantry (e.g., a wedding march), or songs sung by the actors.

intermezzo (Ital.): Orginally, music or light music theater to go between the acts of a serious theater piece. In the nineteenth century the term was used, notably by Brahms, as the title of free piano compositions.

interval: Distance between two pitches.

inversion: Vertical reversing of a musical relationship, either by switching a pair of voices or by turning a theme in the opposite direction.

isorhythm: Use of a single, unvarying rhythmic module throughout a voice part, usually the tenor; principle of construction in the fourteenth and early fifteenth-century motet.

K. numbers: Numbers attached to Mozart's works refer to a thematic catalog for Mozart written by Ludwig von Köchel (1862; rev. through 1964).

Kapellmeister (Ger.; Ital.: *maestro di cappella*): Chapelmaster: a court composer/conductor who composed music for and led the palace opera company, orchestra, and church services.

key: Tonal center of a piece of music, toward which the music seems to gravitate. It is defined by a particular tonic pitch and its quality of major or minor. There are 12 major and 12 minor keys.

keyboard: White-and-black key mechanism that activates a piano, organ, or similar instrument.

Kyrie: First movement of a choral mass.

La Scala: The opera house in Milan, built 1778, which took its name from the church, Santa Maria della Scala, originally on the site.

langsam (Ger.): Slow.

larghetto (Ital.): Somewhat faster than largo.

largo (Ital.): Quite slow. The slowest commonly specified tempo.

ledger lines: Short lines that extend the staff.

legato (Ital.): Smoothly, without space between the pitches.

Leitmotiv: German for "leading motive," a compositional device developed by Wagner.

lento (Ital.): Slow, although not quite as slow as largo.

libretto: Text of an opera.

Lied (Ger., pl. *Lieder*): Term for a solo song, especially to a Romantic text of the late eighteenth or nineteenth century.

Liederkreis (Ger., "song cycle"): First applied to Beethoven's *An die ferne Geliebte,* then, in particular, to Schumann (*Dichterliebe*).

l'istesso tempo (Ital.): The same tempo; keep the beat the same.

liturgy: Formalized order of church services. The Catholic liturgy, divided into Mass (Eucharist: celebration of the Last Supper) and Divine Office (Matins, Vespers, etc.), specifies certain texts common to each service type (the Ordinary), as well as texts specific to the feast day (the Proper).

ma (Ital.): But; as in Allegro ma non troppo.

madrigal: Most commonly, a Renaissance setting of a secular poem to unaccompanied vocal polyphony.

maestoso (Ital.): Majestic.

maestro di cappella (Ital.): Chapel master.

major: In tonality, the brighter and more open of the two modes of scales, characterized by half steps between scale degrees 3 and 4 and 7 and 8.

Mannheim School: Name given to a school of composers who wrote for the virtuoso orchestra of Duke Carl Theodor in the mid-1740s and are thought to be one of the most significant forerunners of Viennese Classicism.

marcato (Ital.): Marked; emphatically.

mass (Ital./Lat., *missa;* Fr., *messe;* Ger., *Messe*): Central public service of the Catholic liturgy, a celebration of the Last Supper; same as Eucharist. Mass is sung by a cantor and the choir. For musical purposes, the most important parts are the choral components of the Ordinary: Kyrie eleison, Gloria, Credo, Sanctus, Agnus Dei.

mazurka: Polish country dance in triple meter, often with accentuation of the second beat.

measure: Basic unit of meter (i.e., one complete metric unit), delineated by the bar line; same as measure.

melisma: Group of several pitches sung to a single syllable.

melody: Coherent, pleasing horizontal succession of pitches; a tune.

meno (Ital.): Less; as in meno mosso.

meter: Organization of rhythmic pulses or beats into hierarchies of weak and strong.

mezzo (Ital.): Half; used to modify the basic dynamic levels (e.g., *mezzo forte, mezzo piano*) and for the voice part mezzo soprano.

Mighty Handful, the (Rus., *moguchaya kuchka*): Term first used by a Russian critic to describe an affinity group of five nationalist Russian composers: Balakirev, Borodin, Cui, Mussorgsky, and Rimsky-Korsakov.

miniatures: Little pieces; commonly in the Romantic piano and song literature.

minor: In tonality, the darker and more enigmatic of the two modes of scales, characterized particularly by the half step between scale degrees 2 and 3.

minuet: Dance form in $\frac{3}{4}$ common in the Baroque and Classical periods.

M.M.: Abbreviation for Metronome de Maelzel.

mode (adj. *modal*): (1) One of the two subdivisions of tonal scales: major or minor. (2) One of the white-note scales, or church modes, of the Middle Ages and Renaissance. (3) One of the medieval rhythmic modes.

moderato (Ital.): Moderately.

modulation: Process of moving from one key area to another.

moll (Ger.): Minor.

molto (Ital.): Very; as in Molto allegro.

monody: Term describing Italian accompanied solo song of the early seventeenth century.

monophonic: Having a single voice.

monothematic: Having a single theme.

mosso (Ital.): Moving, lively; as in più mosso.

motet: In its most general sense, texted vocal polyphony. The term describes highly significant genres from the Middle Ages through the high Baroque.

motive: Melodic or sometimes rhythmic cell that retains its character and identity throughout a movement or multimovement composition.

movement: Self-contained component of a larger work.

music drama: Term applied to Wagnerian opera and related works that suggests a different and by implication more serious treatment of character and plot than that found in traditional opera.

musicology: Scholarly study of music, particularly the history of music.

musique concrète (Fr.): Term applied to an early technique of electronic music where segments of magnetic tape were manipulated (pitch modification by speed change), cut (loops, etc.) and respliced, and then stored to be used for compositional effect.

mute: Device used to reduce the volume of an instrument, almost invariably damping its tone quality as well. See also *sordino.*

neumatic: Describing groups of several notes per syllable of chanted text.

nocturne (Ital.: *notturno*): Night music, especially a short Romantic piano piece.

non troppo (Ital.): Not too much; as in Allegro non troppo.

obbligato (Ital.): A part that must not be left out.

octave: Interval between a pitch and another of twice the frequency: middle C to the C above it, for example.

opera: Work of music theater (music, drama, spectacle) where much or all of the text is sung and music plays the most significant part.

opus (Lat., "work," abbrev. op.): Used with a number, typically assigned by the publisher, to identify a work in a composer's output.

oratorio: Multimovement setting of a sacred text, usually with emphasis on choral movements.

orchestration: The way music is scored for the orchestra.

Ordinary: Portion of the liturgy (Mass and Office) that remains the same from day to day.

ossia (Ital.): Alternative version of a reading, usually simpler.

ostinato (Ital., "obstinate"): Repetition of a pattern many times to constitute the structural underpinning of a piece.

passacaglia (Ital.): Work built on an ostinato bass (or ground bass), often a descending chromatic bass.

Passion: Extended vocal and instrumental setting of the Crucifixion story from one of the Gospels.

pastorale: Movement that expresses a rural atmosphere or describes country characters and scenes.

pedal point: Sustained pitch usually in the bass (often the dominant, sometimes the tonic) over which the music continues to move. It is usually a component of final closure.

pentatonic: Scale or mode of five pitches, common in folk musics.

pesante (Ital.): Heavily.

phrase: Basic unit of musical structure, typically eight measures, that represents a more or less complete musical idea.

pianissimo (Ital.): Very soft.

piano (Ital.): Soft.

piece: Musical work, implying a complete musical work (with all its movements).

pitch: Discrete, identifiable musical sound of a fixed number of vibrations per second.

più (Ital.): More; as in *più forte* or *più allegro*.

pizzicato: Effect produced by plucking, rather than bowing, the string.

plainchant: Term used for the monophonic liturgical repertoire of the Catholic church. Used interchangeably with *chant, plainsong,* and *Gregorian chant.*

plainsong: See *plainchant.*

poco (Ital.): Somewhat, a little; as in *poco a poco.*

point of imitation: See *imitative counterpoint, imitative polyphony.*

polka: A couple dance to skipping steps in lively duple meter.

polonaise: Aristocratic Polish dance in triple time.

polyphonic: Having more than one voice.

polyrhythm: Superposition of different rhythms and/or meters.

polytonality: Use of several keys at once.

ponticello (Ital.): Bridge of a stringed instrument. *Sul ponticello* = at the bridge, a thin, nasal, or whiny sound.

portamento (Ital.): Gentle sliding up into a pitch.

prelude: Instrumental opening movement, often improvisational in character, that precedes a fugue or, sometimes, a group of movements.

presto (Ital.): Quite fast.

program: Literary context of a descriptive ("programmatic") piece, especially in the nineteenth century.

progressive jazz: Jazz from the 1940s and 1950s where the goal was to renew and expand the orchestral jazz tradition.

Proper: Portion of the liturgy (Mass and Office) that contains texts specific to the feast day or occasion.

quartertone: Pitch halfway between consecutive semitones.

ragtime: American musical style of great popularity at the turn of the twentieth century, characterized by strongly syncopated (ragged) rhythms; the usual form is like that of the American march, involving two strains and a trio.

rallentando (Ital.): Growing slower. Abbr. rall.

range: Compass of a musical instrument or voice part, from its lowest note to its highest. See also *register.*

recapitulation: In sonata form, the third main section (after exposition and development), where the main thematic material is presented as it was in the exposition, although with the second group remaining in the tonic key. More generally, any large-scale structural return to the major thematic material.

recitative (Ital.: *recitativo;* Fr.: *récit*): In opera and related genres, a vocal passage imitating the rhythms and inflections of speech; often a recitative is followed by an aria. When crisply delivered and accompanied by simple chords in the continuo, the recitative is considered *secco* (dry); with orchestra, it is *accompagnato.*

register: Division of the range of a voice or musical instrument (e.g., high, middle, low). Roughly synonymous with *tessitura.*

Requiem: The Mass for the dead of the Roman Catholic church.

retrograde: In reverse order, common procedure in certain kinds of counterpoint and in twentieth-century serial music.

réunion des thèmes, grande: Berlioz's term for the simultaneous combining of themes first heard consecutively.

rhapsody: Free-form instrumental work, generally carefree and episodic.

rhythm: Subdivision of time, principally by establishing length of notes.

ripieno (Ital.): Orchestral ensemble in a concerto grosso, in textural opposition to the concertino.

ritard (Ital.): Lessening in speed; gradual slowing down. Abbr. rit.

ritenuto (Ital.): Held back, implicitly more abruptly than ritard or for shorter duration. Abbr. riten.

ritornello: Recurring passage.

rococo: Term used to describe the style in art during the reign of Louis XV of France (1715–74) and by extension any gracefully ornamented music.

Romanticism: Emphasis on the spiritual or passionate (as opposed to the intellectual) in literature, art, and music. Used particularly to describe music written from c. 1830 to the end of the century.

romanza: Songful or ballad-like movement, often the second in a solo concerto.

rondo: Musical form in which the main section recurs between subsidiary episodes, often in an overall sonata pattern (the sonata-rondo).

round: Strict canon (at the unison), usually for three voices, which can continue perpetually.

row: Pitches, usually all 12, ordered in a succession that serves as the basis of a composition. See also *series.*

rubato (Ital.): Literally, "robbed time" (*tempo rubato*): the improvisatory adjustment of strict meter.

scale: Ascending or descending series of notes that define a mode or tonality, usually by the terminal pitch.

scena (Ital.): Operatic scene for one character, generally embracing a recitative, aria, and finale close.

scherzando (Ital.): Playful. Abbr. scherz.

scherzetto (Ital.): Short movement or passage in the manner of a scherzo.

scherzo (Ital., "joke"): Movement type directly descended from the minuet and trio and, like the minuet, usually appearing as the third movement of a four-movement instrumental work.

score: Notation for an ensemble where a staff is given to each part or section.

secco (Ital.): Dry. Recitativo secco is recitative delivered rapidly in speech rhythms and accompanied by the continuo force or a keyboard instrument.

secular: Worldly; not having to do with the church.

segue (Ital.): Go on, usually to the next movement.

semitone: Distance between two adjacent notes on a keyboard; same as half step.

semplice (Ital.): Simply.

sempre (Ital.): Always, ever, as in *sempre più allegro*.

senza (Ital.): Without; typically cancels *con sordino* (with mute) indications, thus meaning "remove the mute."

sequence: (1) Series of motives restated at ascending or descending pitch levels. (2) The medieval sequence is an important category of Gregorian chant where a series of text couplets, eventually rhymed poetry, was set syllabically.

serial: Compositional technique in which elements have been prearranged in a fixed series.

series: Ordering of elements of pitch, rhythm, dynamics, etc., that serve as the basis of a composition. Music so constructed is called serial.

seventh: Interval between a pitch and another six diatonic steps apart. A semitone less than an octave is a major seventh; a semitone less than that is a minor seventh. Both are strongly dissonant intervals, the major seventh pulling to resolve upward, the minor seventh to resolve down. See also *seventh chord.*

seventh chord: Common enhancement to triadic harmony wherein a fourth pitch is added to the triad, up another third, thus: root + 3rd + 5th + 7th.

sforzando, sforzato (Ital.): Suddenly forceful or emphasized. Abbr. sfz., sf.

sonata: Instrumental composition, usually for soloist or soloist and keyboard. Originally the term sonata (played music) was used as opposed to cantata (sung music) and toccata (keyboard music).

song cycle (Ger.: *Liederkreis*): Group of songs, generally with texts by the same poet, unified by a story line or literary theme.

soprano (Ital.): Highest voice part.

sordino (Ital.): Mute. Abbr. sord. *Con sordino* = with mute. *Senza sordino* = without mute.

sostenuto (Ital.): Sustained; as in Andante sostenuto. Often a slower-than-usual tempo is implied. The right pedal on a piano is the sostenuto pedal, allowing the strings to vibrate until the pedal is released and lowers the dampers.

sotto voce (Ital.): In an undertone; barely heard.

spiritoso (Ital.): Spirited.

Sprechstimme (Ger.): Speaking voice. Abbr. Sprechst; notated with *X*'s through the note stems.

staccato (Ital.): Separated; short and sharp.

stretto (Ital.): Concluding episode at increased speed; in fugue, overlapping statements of the subject near the end of the work.

stringendo (Ital.): Quickening; sometimes a lurch forward.

strophic: Having the same music for all the units (or strophes) of the text, as in a hymn.

Sturm und Drang (Ger., "storm and stress"): Literary movement in eighteenth-century Germany and Austria, applied to stormy, emotional, minor-keyed symphonies of the Classical period.

subito (Ital.): Suddenly, as in *subito forte.* Abbr. sub.

subject: Melodic idea or theme on which a composition is based. The theme of a fugue is called its subject.

suite: (1) Group of dances in various national styles, usually preceded by an extended prelude or overture, common in the Baroque period. (2) Series of movements extracted from a larger work (often a ballet) to make an effective concert work.

suspension: Pitch held over from a previous chord, becoming dissonant in the new chord, and resolving downward.

symphonic poem: One-movement work for orchestra with narrative or descriptive intent. Same as tone poem.

symphony: Extended work for orchestra, usually in four movements (fast, slow, dance form, fast); the principal form of orchestral composition.

syncopation: Placing the accent on the ordinarily weak beats of a measure.

tempo (Ital., "time"): Speed or rate of speed. Tempo is indicated by a (rather approximate) direction in Italian (e.g., Allegro non troppo), a metronome marking (M.M.), or both. Tempo primo (Tempo I) = at the original tempo.

tenor: The higher of the male voices.

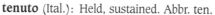

tenuto (Ital.): Held, sustained. Abbr. ten.

tessitura: Prevailing range, or ambitus, of a part—high, middle, low—in relation to the overall compass of that part.

texture: Term used to describe the vertical character of a musical passage, especially how the voices interact. One speaks, for example, of monophonic, homophonic, and polyphonic textures.

thematic transformation: The recomposition of a theme as it is reused so that gradually its character becomes radically different.

theme: A principal melody, a basic point of melodic reference in a movement.

theme and variations: Movement type where the given theme is modified in a series of variations.

through composed: Music composed from beginning to end without internal repetitions. In general, the opposite of strophic.

tie: Notational device used to continue a rhythm across a bar line.

timbre (Fr.): Tone color that distinguishes the character of an instrumental or vocal sound.

toccata: Improvisatory showpiece for organ, often an introductory movement preceding a fugue. Originally the term toccata (keyboard music, "touched" with the fingers) was used as opposed to cantata (sung music) and sonata (instrumental music).

tonality (adj. *tonal*): System of music composition that establishes relationships through use of a tonal center (the tonic) and a major or minor key built from it.

tone poem: One-movement work for orchestra with narrative or descriptive intent. Same as symphonic poem.

tonic: Initial scale degree or the triad built on it; thus the most important member of the scale or chord.

tranquillo (Ital.): Calmly, tranquilly.

transposition: Moving of a passage of music from one pitch level to another. Composers also notate parts for transposing instruments (B♭ clarinet, horn in F) such that when the player plays the notated pitches the appropriate-sounding pitches come out; such a part is called a transposed part.

tremolando (Ital.): With tremolo.

tremolo (Ital.): Effect with string instruments where very quick up-and-down bowings produce an unsettled effect. Also a similar alternation between two pitches, possible (unlike string tremolo) on other instruments including keyboards.

triad: Chord built of three pitches in intervals of the third.

trill: Fast alternating between a main pitch and the diatonic pitch above it.

trio: (1) Music for three performers; in music that descends from Baroque practice, this implies two treble instruments and basso continuo. (2) The center section of form in the minuet and trio family, generally in somewhat reduced orchestration or more passive setting.

"Tristan" chord: First chord in Wagner's *Tristan und Isolde,* poignant and inconclusive when first heard, then later becoming identified with unfulfilled desire and, at length, its fateful resolution.

troppo (Ital.): Too much; as in Allegro non troppo (not too fast).

tutti (Ital.): All; everybody.

twelve tone: Name given by Schoenberg to his system of composition using a row or series as the basis of a composition.

unison: Interval (or rather, non-interval) that exists between two notes of identical pitch. A chorus of equal voices might sing a hymn in unison; choral chant is sung in unison. Abbr. unis.

upbeat: Beat that precedes the downbeat.

vibrato: Effect used by woodwind and string players and by singers to enhance tone quality. The musician cycles just above and below the desired pitch, using pulsations of the diaphragm (for winds and voices) or a back-and-forth motion of the left hand on the fingerboard (for the strings).

vivace (Ital.): Vivacious, bright.

vivo (Ital.): Alive, vigorous.

voce (Ital.): Voice.

waltz: Dance in $\frac{3}{4}$ time that developed in the late eighteenth century and became the ballroom rage of the nineteenth.

whole-tone scale: Scale that progresses only in whole steps instead of the patterns of half steps and whole steps that define major and minor scales.

Anthology of Musical Scores

Kyrie eleison (*Kyrie cunctipotens genitor*)
(10th century)

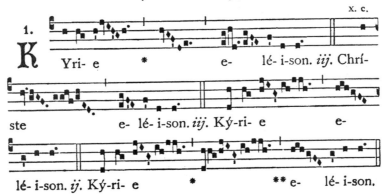

1. Kyrie * eleison. iij. Christe eleison. iij. Kyrie eleison. ij. Kyrie * ** eleison.

Hymn: *Pange lingua* (c. 1264)

Hymn. 3. Pange lingua gloriósi Córporis mystérium,

Sanguinísque preti-ó-si, Quem in múndi pré-ti-um Frúctus véntris gene-ró-si Rex effúdit génti-um. 6. Geni-tó-ri,

Geni-tóque Laus et jubi-lá-ti-o, Sá-lus, hónor, vírtus quoque Sit et benedícti-o : Procedénti ab utróque

Cómpar sit laudá-ti-o. Amen.

Henry Purcell
"When I am Laid in Earth" (Dido's Lament)
from *Dido and Aeneas* (1689)

J. S. Bach
Fugue in C Minor
from *The Well-Tempered Clavier,* book I (1722)

Wolfgang Amadeus Mozart
from *Eine kleine Nachtmusik,* K. 525 (1787)

I.

III.

MENUETTO.
Allegretto.

Trio.

Menuetto da capo

Robert Schumann
from *Carnaval* (1835)

Arlequin.

Valse noble.

Fryderyk Chopin
Mazurka in A Minor, op. 17, no. 4 (1834)

William Billings
David's Lamentation (1778)

Dav - id, the king, was grieved and moved, He went to his chamber, his chamber, and wept; And as he went he wept, and said:

"O my son, O my son, Would to God I had died, Would," etc. "Would," etc. "For thee, O Ab-sa-lom, my son, my son!"

Scott Joplin
Maple Leaf Rag (1899)

Tempo di marcia.

M. L. R.

Recommended Listening

The disks recommended below are chosen largely from the archive of Sony Classical and Columbia Masterworks recordings and are all likely to be found in your local record library. Most are still in print and for sale in the $10 price range.

32 Prokofiev: *Peter and the Wolf* (1936)

Prokofiev – Peter & the Wolf – Bernstein. New York Philharmonic / Bernstein. (Columbia) CBS MYK 37765 (Great Performances).

32 Britten: *The Young Person's Guide to the Orchestra* (1948)

Variations and Fugue on a Theme of Purcell, op. 34. New York Philharmonic / Bernstein. Sony Classical 47541 (the Royal Edition).

110 Monteverdi: excerpt from *Orfeo* (1609)

L'Orfeo – Claudio Monteverdi. Monteverdi Choir / English Baroque Soloists / Gardiner. Archiv 419 250-2.

115 Pachelbel: Canon in D (c. 1700)

Pachelbel's Canon – Baroque Favorites. English Chamber Orchestra / Leppard. (Columbia) CBS 38482 (Great Performances).

117 Mouret: Rondeau, from First Symphonic Suite (c. 1729)

Pachelbel's Canon – Baroque Favorites. English Chamber Orchestra / Leppard. (Columbia) CBS 38482 (Great Performances).

133 Handel: Music for the Royal Fireworks (1749)

Handel – Water Music / Music for the Royal Fireworks. La Grand Écurite et la Chambre du Roy / Malgoire. Sony Classical SBK 48285 (Essential Classics).

172 Mozart: Piano Concerto in C Major, K. 503, movts. II–III

Beethoven – Piano Concerto No. 4 [etc.]. Fleisher / Cleveland Orchestra / Szell. (Columbia) CBS MYK 37762 (Great Performances).

174 Mozart: Symphony No. 40 in G Minor, K. 550 (1788), movts. II–IV
Mozart: Symphony No. 41 in C Major, K. 551 ("Jupiter," 1788)

Mozart – Symphonies No. 35, 40, 41. Cleveland Orchestra / Szell. Sony Classical SBK 46333 (Essential Classics).

175 Mozart: Overtures to *The Marriage of Figaro*, K. 492 (1786) and *The Magic Flute*, K. 620 (1791)

Mozart – Eine kleine Nachtmusik [etc.] – Walter. Columbia Symphony Orchestra / Walter. (Columbia) CBS MYK 37774 (Great Performances).

175 Mozart: arias from *The Marriage of Figaro* and *Don Giovanni*, K. 527 (1787)

Opera Arias: Donizetti – Bellini – Verdi – Puccini – Mozart. Cotrubas / Te Kanawa / Scotto / Domingo. Sony Classical SBK 46548 (Essential Classics).

182 Beethoven: Sonata No. 8 in C Minor, op. 13 ("Pathétique," 1799)

Beethoven – Sonatas – Serkin. Rudolf Serkin. (Columbia) CBS MYK 37129 (Great Performances).

182 Beethoven: Sonata No. 14 in C♯ Minor, op. 27, no. 2 ("Moonlight," 1801)

Beethoven – Sonatas – Serkin. Rudolf Serkin. (Columbia) CBS MYK 37129 (Great Performances).

184 Beethoven: Sonata No. 23 in F Minor, op. 57 ("Appassionata," 1804 – 1805)

Beethoven – Sonatas – Serkin. Rudolf Serkin. (Columbia) CBS MYK 37129 (Great Performances).

184 Beethoven: Piano Concerto No. 4 in G Major, op. 58 (1806)

Beethoven – Piano Concerto No. 4 [etc.]. Fleisher / Cleveland Orchestra / Szell. (Columbia) CBS MYK 37762 (Great Performances).

190 Beethoven: Symphony No. 9 in D Minor, op. 125 (1824)

Beethoven – Symphony No. 9 – Ormandy. Philadelphia Orchestra / Ormandy. (Columbia) CBS MYK 37241 (Great Performances).

195 Schubert: Symphony No. 8 in B Minor ("Unfinished," 1822)

Schubert – Unfinished Symphony. Cleveland Orchestra / Szell. Sony Classical SBK 48268 (Essential Classics).

207 Berlioz: *Symphonie fantastique,* movts. I–IV (1830)

Berlioz – Symphonie Fantastique – Overtures – Bernstein. New York Philharmonic / Bernstein. Sony Classical SMK 47525 (the Royal Edition).

212 Liszt: Hungarian Rhapsody No. 2 in C♯ Minor (1847)

Liszt – Brendel. Alfred Brendel. Vanguard Classics OVC 4024.

218 Schumann: Piano Concerto in A Minor, op. 54 (1845)

Schumann – Piano Concerto – Serkin – Ormandy. Serkin / Philadelphia Orchestra / Ormandy. (Columbia) CBS MYK 37256 (Great Performances).

218 Mendelssohn: Violin Concerto in E Minor, op. 64 (1844)

Mendelssohn – Tchaikovsky – Stern. Stern / Philadelphia Orchestra / Ormandy. (Columbia) CBS MYK 36724 (Great Performances).

247 Brahms: Symphony No. 3 in F Major, op. 90 (1883)

Brahms – Symphonies Nos. 2 & 3. Cleveland Orchestra / Szell. Sony Classical SBK 47652 (Essential Classics).

248 Mahler: Symphony No. 1 in D Major (1888)

Mahler – Symphony No. 1 – Bernstein. New York Philharmonic / Bernstein. (Columbia) CBS Masterworks MK 42194.

252 Smetana: *The Moldau* (1874)

Mendelssohn – A Midsummer Night's Dream – Smetana – Bizet. Cleveland Orchestra / Szell. Sony Classical SBK 48264 (Essential Classics).

256 Tchaikovsky: Violin Concerto in D Major, op. 35 (1878)

Mendelssohn – Tchaikovsky – Stern. Stern / Philadelphia Orchestra / Ormandy. (Columbia) CBS MYK 36724 (Great Performances).

258 Puccini: excerpts from *Madama Butterfly* (1904)

Opera Arias: Donizetti – Bellini – Verdi – Puccini – Mozart. Cotrubas / Te Kanawa / Scotto / Domingo. Sony Classical SBK 46548 (Essential Classics).

265 Ravel: *Daphnis and Chloe,* Suite No. 2 (1912)

Ravel – Bolero, La Valse [etc.] – Bernstein. New York Philharmonic / Bernstein. (Columbia) CBS Masterworks MYK 36714 (Great Performances).

272 Ravel: *La Valse* (1920), *Boléro* (1928)

Ravel – Bolero, La Valse [etc.] – Bernstein. New York Philharmonic / Bernstein. (Columbia) CBS Masterworks MYK 36714 (Great Performances).

310 Copland: *Appalachian Spring* (1944)

Copland – Appalachian Spring – Bernstein. New York Philharmonic / Bernstein. (Columbia) CBS MYK 37257 (Great Performances).

314 Rodgers and Hammerstein: excerpts from *South Pacific* (1949)

South Pacific. Original Broadway Cast. Sony Broadway SK 53327.

333 Bartók: Concerto for Orchestra (1943)

Bartók – Concerto for Orchestra [etc.]. New York Philharmonic / Bernstein. Sony Classical SMK 47510 (the Royal Edition).

345 The Beatles: "Hey Jude" (1968)

The Beatles – Past Masters – Volume Two. EMI CDP 7 90044 2.

351 Riley: *In C* (1964)

Terry Riley – In C. (Columbia) CBS MK 7178.

352 Adams: excerpt from *The Death of Klinghoffer* (1991)

John Adams – The Death of Klinghoffer. Lyon Opera / Nagano. Elektra Nonesuch 9 79281-2.

Credits

Washington, c. 1612/1620, oil on canvas, 1.435 × 1.288 (56½ × 50⅝).
44 Steve J. Sherman.
45 Liason Agency, Inc./Roger-Viollet.
47 Department of the Air Force, United States Air Force Band of the Golden West
49 Art Resource, N.Y.
51 Arnold Eagle.
53 Stone.
58 Corbis.
59 Staatliches Museum Schwerin/Schwerin.

Chapter 3
64 AKG London Ltd.
74 Library of Congress.
78 Culver Pictures, Inc.
82 Art Resource, N.Y./Giraudon.
83 Corbis.
88 AKG London Ltd.
89 Foto Leutner Fachlabor.
93 San Antonio di Padua Mission/John Robinson.
97 Liason Agency, Inc./Hulton Getty.
101 Library of Congress.

Chapter 4
106 Art Resource, N.Y./Alinari.
107 Italian Government Tourist Board.
108 Art Resource, N.Y./Foto Marburg.
112 Art Resource, N.Y./A.D. Gabbiani.
116 Walter H. Scott.
119 The Granger Collection.
120 Corbis-Bettmann.
122 Art Resource, N.Y./Bildarchiv Foto Marburg.
134 Bildarchiv Preussischer Kulturbesitz.

Chapter 5
144 Art Resource, N.Y./Erich Lessing.
146 Royal College of Music.
147 The Granger Collection.
158 Hulton Getty/Liason Agency, Inc.
159 Johann Nepomuk della Croce, The Mozart Family, 1790–1791, oil on canvas, 140 × 186 cm, Mozart House, Salzburg, Austria. © Photograph by Erich Lessing, Art Resource, N.Y.
160 Photo Researchers, Inc.
176 Art Resource, N.Y./Erich Lessing.

Chapter 6
180 (top and bottom) Art Resource, N.Y./Giraudon.
181 Beethoven-Archive.
192 Corbis.
199 Reunion des Musees Nationaux.
202 (left) Culver Pictures, Inc.; (right) Art Resource, N.Y./Giraudon.
205 D.K. Hoffman.
209 (top) Cliché Bibliotheque Nationale de France – Paris; (bottom) Art Resource, N.Y./Giraudon.
210 (left) Bibliotheque Nationale de France; (right) The Granger Collection.
213 Corbis.

Chapter 7
228 Brown Brothers.
233 Corbis.
234 The Lundorff Collection.
242 Liason Agency, Inc./Hulton Getty.
249 Doubleday Direct, Inc.
250 Smetana Museum, Prague.
255 Archivo Iconografico/Corbis.
256 Liason Agency, Inc.
260 AKG London Ltd.

264 (left) AKG London Ltd./A. Biert; (right) AKG London Ltd.
269 (top left) Art Resource, N.Y./Giraudon; (top right) Picasso and Stravinsky in a sketch by Jean Cocteau. The Spanish artist designed the decors for Pulcinella (1920)/© 1998 Estate of Pablo Picasso/Artists Rights Society (ARS), New York; (bottom left) Courtesy of the Library of Congress; (bottom right) Liason Agency, Inc./Hulton Getty.

Chapter 8
276 Corbis.
281 Corbis.
282 Corbis.
284 Integrity Press.
288 Music Division. The New York Public Library for the Performing Arts. Astor, Lenox and Tilden Foundation.
293 Frank Driggs Collection/Archive Photos.
296 Corbis.
302 University of New Hampshire, Milne Special Collections and Archives.
305 (top) Sony Classical; (bottom) American Society of Composers, Authors, and Publishers.
310 Art Resource, N.Y./National Portrait Gallery, Washington, D.C.
314 Culver Pictures, Inc.
315 Culver Pictures, Inc.

Chapter 9
320 Copyright 1981 Richard Fish, Photographer.
324 Universal Edition A.G.
332 Liason Agency, Inc./Hulton Getty.
337 Princeton University, Department of Music.
343 Corbis.
344 Corbis/UPI.
345 Frank Driggs Collection.
350 Stuart Rogers Photography/Scott Reilly.
352 San Francisco Examiner.
353 Hermann J. Baus, Cologne, Germany.
355 Sony Classical/Gil Gilbert.
357 Walter H. Scott.

Epilogue
361 Copyright 1981 Richard Fish, Photographer.
362 Neil Michel/Axion

Anthology of Musical Scores
372 *The Liber Usualis: with Introduction and Rubrics in English*, Desclée Company, Tournai, Belgium, 1961, pp. 25; 957–959.
373-75 Purcell, *Dido and Aeneas in Full Score*, Dover Publications, Inc., New York, 1995, pp. 84–86.
376–77 Johann Sebastian Bach, *The Well-Tempered Clavier: Books I and II, Complete*, Dover Publications, Inc., New York, 1982, pp. 8–9.
378–82 Wolfgang Amadeus Mozart, *Complete Serenades in Full Score, Series II*, from the Breitkopf & Härtel Complete Works Edition, Dover Publications, Inc., New York, 1990, pp. 225–228; pp. 231–232.
383–84 *Piano Music of Robert Schumann*, Edited by Clara Schumann, Series I, Dover Publications, Inc., New York, 1972, pp. 88–89.
385–87 Frederic Chopin, *56 Mazurkas, from the First, Critically Revised, Complete Edition*, Edwin F. Kalmus, Publisher of Music, New York, pp. 24–26.
388 *The B. F. White Sacred Harp: As Revised and Improved by W. M. Cooper and Others*, Sacred Harp Book Co., Inc., Troy, Alabama, p. 239.
389-91 *The Collected Works of Scott Joplin*, edited by Vera Brodsky Lawrence, The New York Public Library, Astor, Lenox and Tilden Foundations, 1971, pp. 26–28.

Index

Italic page numeration indicates the main entry for the indexed item. The abbreviation I (e.g., 231I) indicates an illustration; LC, a listening chart; S, a score.

A

Abelard, Peter, 62
Abu Nidal, 352
Adams, John, *351–53*, 352I
  Death of Klinghoffer, The, 342,
    352–53, 353I
Aeneid, The (Virgil), 112, 209
African, African American music,
  281–83, 290–95, 290–301
Agoult, Marie, Countess d', 199, 210
Albéniz, Isaac, 254, 261
Alberti, Domenico, 145
Alberti bass, 145,*165,* 166
Alcotts, the, 276, 305
Amadeus (film), 176
Amati family (violin makers), 116
"Amazing Grace," 279
American classical music, *301–10*
American Federation of Musicians,
  299, 337
American music, *275–317*
Anderson, Marian, 283
Angelou, Maya, 318
"Angels We Have Heard on High,"
  27–29, 28S
Aquinas, St. Thomas, 71–72
Ariosto, Ludovico, 95
Armstrong, Louis, 290, *293–94,*
  293I, 295, 301, 317
atonality, 322–24, 330. *See also*
  serial music
"Au clair de la lune," 320
Auden, W. H., 333
Auric, Georges, 58, 58I

B

Babbitt, Milton, 42, 314, 337I,
  338–41, 328I, 347, 356
  Philomel, 338–41, 340LC, 351
Bach, Carl Philip Emmanuel, 146
Bach, Hans, 119

Bach, Johann Christoph, 116, 119,
  164
Bach, Johann Sebastian, 3, 5, 11,
  29, 33, 42, 43, 46, 48, 49, 53,
  106, 111, 115, 117, 118,
  119–21, 120I, 122, 123–26,
  127–32, 133, 134–38, 139,
  140, 145, 163, 164, 201, 202,
  216, 218, 244, 277, 280, 352
  Art of Fugue, The, 7, 120, 123,
    128–29, 131
  Badinerie, from Orchestral Suite
    No. 2 in B Minor, 57, 132, *133,*
    133LC, 148, 149
  Double Concerto in D Minor, BWV
    1043, 53, *123–25,* 126LC
  Feste Burg ist unser Gott, Ein'
    (cantata 80), *134–37,* 137LC
  Fugue in C Minor. *See Well-*
    Tempered Clavier, The
  Well-Tempered Clavier, The, 127,
    128, 129, 130–31, 149, 213;
    Fugue in C Minor from Book I,
    20, *130–31,* 131LC, 376–77S
Bach-Werke-Verzeichnis
  (Schmieder), 53, 121
Badinerie. *See* Bach, J. S.
Balakirev, Mili, 255
Balanchine, George, 51, 268, 333
Ballet Caravan, 307
Ballets Russes, 259, *263–68,* 331
Balzac, Honoré de, 202
Barber, Samuel, 310
Bardac, Emma, 260
Barenboim, Daniel, 125
Barnum, P. T., 224
Baroque, the, 29, 32, 33, 42, 45,
  47, 50, *105–41,* 148, 149
Baroque concerto, 45, *122–27*
Bartered Bride, The. See Smetana
Bartók, Béla, 4, 8, 47, 164, 168,
  254, 330, 332–333, 332I
Basie, Count, 296

basso continuo, 111–12
Battle, Kathleen, 9, 283
Baudelaire, Charles, 260
Bay Psalm Book, The, 276
Bayreuth, 197, 209, 235, 237–38,
  322
BBC, BBC Symphony, 335
Beach, H. H. A., 302
Beach, Mrs. H. H. A. (Amy),
  302–04, 302I
  Scherzo, from Violin Sonata in A
    Minor, op. 34, *302–03,* 303LC
Beardslee, Bethany, 338, 340
Beatles, The, 344–46, 345I
bebop, 298–301
Beethoven, Johann (brother), 182
Beethoven, Karl (brother), 182
Beethoven, Ludwig van, 1, 7, 8, 9,
  11, 33, 42, 43, 44, 45, 46,
  145, 151, 157, 158, 164, 165,
  168, 177, 179, *181–92,* 181I,
  192, 195, 200, 202, 203, 216,
  243, 247, 248, 259, 315
  piano concertos, 168, 184, 315
  piano sonatas, 53, 147, 181, 182,
    184, 189
  string quartets, 46, 147, 164,
    166, 181, 184, 199
  symphonies, 8, 53, 143, 182,
    183–84, 187, 189–91, 192,
    195, 203, 207, 209, 355, 361
  Symphony No. 5 in C Minor,
    op. 67, 1 40, 52, 54, 56, 149,
    150, *184–87,* 188–91LC, 324,
    354
Beggar's Opera, The, 138
Beijing Conservatory, 354
Belasco, David, 258
Bell, Joshua, 9
Bellini, Vincenzo, 50, 220, *221–24,*
  225
  "Casta diva" (*Norma*), *221–24,*
    223LC

Bell Telephone, Bell Telephone Hour, 335
Bennett, Robert Russell, 314
Berg, Alban, 58, 319, 324, 324ı, 330
Berg, Helene, 330
Berlin, Irving, 48, 311
Berlin Philharmonic, 332
Berlin State Opera, 332
Berlioz, Hector, 3, 6, 42, 45, 140, 160, 168, 195, 199, 201, *202–09,* 202ı, 209ı, 212, 213, 217, 218, 234, 240, 247, 253, 259, 315, 331
   Symphonie fantastique, 8, 43, *203–08,* 208ʟᴄ, 209, 259, 315, 359
Bernini, Gianlorenzo, 106
Bernstein, Leonard, 9, 11–12, 12ı, 35, 52, 249, 259, *314–17,* 332, 335, 350, 360
   West Side Story, 52, 315ı; "Somewhere," from, *314–16,* 316ʟᴄ.
   Young People's Concerts, 335, 350, 360
bianzhong, 355, 355ı
Bigard, Barney, 297, 298
big bands, *295–98,* 296ı
Billings, William, 276, *277–81*
   David's Lamentation, 278, 278ʟᴄ, *279–80,* 280ʟᴄ, 388s
binary form, *57,* 132, 156
Binchois, Gilles, 82, 82ı, 85
Bizet, Georges, 221, 242–43, 259, 261
Bliss, Mr. and Mrs. Robert Woods, 8
blues, *290–94,* 304, 308, 343
Boccherini, Luigi, 161
Boito, Arrigo, 229, 230, 232
Bonaparte, Napoleon. *See* Napoleon
Boone, Pat, 343
Borodin, Alexander, 255, 263
Boston Symphony Orchestra, 302, 303–304, 310, 331, 333
Boulanger, Ernest, 369
Boulanger, Lili, *269–72,* 269ı
   Psalm 24, *270–71,* 271ʟᴄ
Boulanger, Nadia, 4, 269, 269ı, 271, 272, 310
Boulez, Pierre, 12, 241, 334, 342
Brahms, Johannes, 11, 42, 43, 44, 48, 164, 168, 192, 207, 210, 216, 217, *243–47,* 243ı, 253, 259, 282, 335
   Variations on a Theme by Haydn, op. 56a, *244–47,* 246ʟᴄ, 334

Brandeis University, 347
Breitkopf und Härtel, 216
Brill, Mark, 93
British Grenadiers, The, 306, 307
Britten, Benjamin, 31–32, 254, 258, 333
broadcasting, 295, 335–36
Broadway, 17, 52, 307, *311–17*
Brubeck, Dave, Quartet, 301
Bruckner, Anton, 192, 242
Brumel, Antoine, 85
Brunelleschi, Filippo, 85
Bryant Minstrels, 283
Buchla, Donald, 342
Buck, Dudley, 301–02
Bull, John, 99
Buxtehude, Dietrich, 119–20
BWV. *See Bach-Werke-Verzeichnis*
Byrd, William, 44, *90–92,* 99
   Mass in 4 Parts, 29, 84; *Agnus Dei* from, *90–92,* 92ʟᴄ, 97, 103, 114, 125

Caccini, Francesca, 108
Caccini, Giulio, 108, 109
cadence, modulation, *38–39*
Cage, John, 334
Callas, Maria, 224
Calloway, Cab, 308
Cambrai cathedral, 58, 82
camerata (Florence), 108
Campion, Thomas, 100
Canterbury cathedral, 78
Capote, Truman, 308–09
Carlos, Walter (Wendy), 342
Carnaval. See Schumann, Robert
Carnegie Hall, 307
Carreras, José, 360
Carter, Elliott, 341, 354
Carter, Jimmy, 361
Casals, Pablo, 11, 33ı, 350, 361
"Casta Diva" (*Norma*). *See* Bellini
Castiglione, Baldassare, 89, 99
Catherine the Great, empress of Russia, 144
Cavaillé-Coll, Aristide, 259
CBS, 335
Chaliapin, Fyodor, 263
Chamberlain, Neville, 331
chamber music, 44, 47–48. *See also* string quartet
Champollion, Jean-François, 202
chanson de geste, 74
chant. *See* plainchant
Char, René, 334

Charlemagne, 2, 42, 63–64, 74, 179
Charles I, king of England, 112
Charles the Bold, duke of Burgundy, 82
Chaucer, Geoffrey, 80
Cheney, Amy Marcy. *See* Beach, Mrs. H. H. A.
Chéreau, Patrice, 241
Cherubini, Luigi, 181
Chicago Art Institute, 317
Chicago Lyric Opera, 350
Chicago Symphony Orchestra, 125, 350
Chopin, Fryderyk, 3, 42, 168, 196, 198, 201, 207, *213–15,* 213ı, 217, 259, 264, 288, 322
   Mazurka in A Minor, op. 27, no. 4, 20, *213–15,* 215ʟᴄ, *385–87*s
Chou En-lai, 352
Chrétien de Troyes, 74
Civil War (American), 275, 284, 305
Classical style, 42, 43, 46, 55, *143–77,* 195, 220
Cleveland Orchestra, 11
Cliburn, Van, 9
Cocteau, Jean, 58, 58ı, 269, 334
Colloredo, Archbishop, 160
Coltrane, John, 301
Columbia-Princeton Electronic Music Center, 337, 338
Columbia Records, 11–12, 335–36
Columbia University, 304, 337, 347, 254
Columbus, Christopher, 2, 42, 63, 81
Compère, Loyset, 85
Concertgebouw Orchestra (Amsterdam), 227, 249, 316
concerto, 42, 44
   in the Classical period, 44, 151, *166–72*
   See also Baroque concerto
concerto grosso, 123
concert overture, 42, 44–45
contemporary music. *See* 20th-century music
continuo. *See* basso continuo
Coolidge, Elizabeth Sprague, 8
Copernicus, Nicolas, 81
Copland, Aaron, 4, 51, 275, 305, *309–10,* 310ı, 317, 332
   Appalachian Spring, 8, 51, 51ı, 310
Corea, Chick, 301
Corelli, Arcangelo, 42, 105, 116, 121

Corigliano, John, 354
Cornelius, Peter, 212
Cotton Club (New York), 297
counterpoint, 27–29
Couperin, François, 118
Craft, Robert, 333
Crane, Hart, 310
Cristofori, Bartolomeo, 164
Crumb, George, 341, 347
Cui, César, 255

D

Da Capo Chamber Players, 347
Dante Alighieri, 80
da Ponte, Lorenzo, 174
David, Jacques Louis, 180
David's Lamentation. See Billings
Davis, Miles, 301
Death of Klinghoffer, The. See
    Adams
Debussy, Claude, 1, 42, 164, 212,
    256, 259, *260–65*, 260ı, 287
    Prélude à L'Après-midi d'un
        faune, 260–61, 264, 264ı
    Soirée dans Grenade, La, 261–63,
        *263*ʟᴄ, 266
Debussy, Claude-Emma (Chou-
    Chou), 260
Declaration of Independence
    (American), 3, 42, 142,
    143–44
Degas, Edgar, 51, 260
Delacroix, Eugène, 202
Dello Joio, Norman, 350
de Mille, Agnes, 309
Déploration sur la mort de Johannes
    Ockeghem. See Desprez
Desprez, Josquin, 42, 71, 82, *85–90,*
    88ı, 93, 133
    Déploration sur la mort de
        Johannes Ockeghem, 85–88,
        88ʟᴄ, 93, 103, 111
    Missa Pange lingua, 84, 89ı
Diabelli, Anton, 164
Diaghilev, Sergei, 107, 263–65, 268
Diderot, Denis, 143
Dido and Aeneas. See Purcell
Dies irae, 49, 73, 205–07, 208
digital sound, 10, 342–43
diminished seventh chord, 200, 205,
    236
D'Indy, Vincent, 259
Disney, Walt, 32
Dittersdorf, Carl Ditters von, 158
"Dixie," 283
Dixieland, 295

Donizetti, Gaetano, 50, 220, 221,
    224, 225
Dorsey, Tommy, 296
Dowland, John, 42, *100–03*
    Flow My Tears, 21, *101–03,* 101ı,
        102ʟᴄ
Dryden, John, 14
Dufay, Guillaume, 42, 82–83, 82ı,
    85
Dukas, Paul, 259
Dumas *fils,* Alexandre, 229
Dun, Tan. *See* Tan Dun
Dunstable, John, 82
Durey, Louis, 58, 58ı
Dutoit, Charles, 9
Dvořák, Antonín, 11, 53, 247,
    252–53, 282, 331

E

Eastman School of Music, 310
Easy Instructor, The, 279
Ein' feste Burg ist unser Gott
    (cantata). *See* Bach, J. S.
Eine kleine Nachtmusik. See Mozart,
    Wolfgang Amadeus
Eleanor of Aquitaine, 75
electronics, electronic music, 10, 12,
    34, *335–43,* 345
Elgar, Edward, 247, 254, 301
Elizabeth I, queen of England, 90,
    100
Ellington, Duke, *296–98,* 296ı
    New East St. Louis Toodle-O,
        297–98, 296ʟᴄ
Emerson, Ralph Waldo, 276, 305
Emilianoff, André, 347
Encyclopédie, 143
Enlightenment, the, 143–44,
    147–48
Ensemble Clément Janequin, 87
Epstein, Brian, 344
Este, Ercole d', duke of Ferrara, 89
Este, Leonora d', 95
Esterháza, 157–58, 176ı
Esterhazy, Nikolaus and Paul Anton,
    Princes, 155–58, 159, 162,
    172, 176
Evans, Bill, Trio, 301
Evans, Gil, 301
Expressionism, 319

F

Falla, Manuel de, 254, 261, 264
fasola. *See* shape-note notation
Fauré, Gabriel, 46, 164, 260

Fender, Leo, 343
figured bass, 111
Fischer-Dieskau, Dietrich, 333
Fisk Jubilee Singers, 282, 282ı
Fitzgerald, Ella, 296, 301
Fitzgerald, F. Scott, 1, 295
Fitzwilliam Virginal Book, 99
Five, the Russian. *See* Mighty
    Handful
Flagstad, Kirsten, 250
Flax, Laura, 347
Fleezanis, Jorja, 353
Florentine camerata. *See* camerata
Flow My Tears. See Dowland
Fonteyn, Margot, 301
form, *54–57*
Forster, E. M., 40
Foster, Stephen, 283
Francis, Connie, 343
Francis I, emperor of Austria, 162,
    179
Franck, César, 46, 242, 259, 260
Franklin, Benjamin, 143
Frederick the Great, king of Prussia,
    120, 122ı, 144, 146
Freemasonry, 58, 160
French Organ School, 259, 334
French overture, 48, 132–33, 139
French Revolution, 3, 42, 43, 143,
    179–81, 180ı, 199
Frescobaldi, Girolamo, 112
Freud, Siegmund, 248, 319
Friedman, Stephanie, 353ı
Froberger, Johann Jakob, 112
Frost, David, 345–46
fugue, 29, 31, 42, 123–24, *127–32,*
    206
function, key, *36–38*
"Furiant." *See* Smetana: *Bartered*
    Bride, The
Furtwängler, Wilhelm, 250

G

Gabrieli, Andrea, 107
Gabrieli, Giovanni, 107, 112
Galilei, Galileo, 105, 108
Galilei, Vincenzo, 108
gamelan, 355
Gates, William, 93
genre, *44–52*
Genzinger, Maria Anna von, 165
George I, king of England (George,
    elector of Hanover), 121
George III, king of England, 144,
    159
Géricault, Théodore, 202

Gershwin, George, 15–17, 48, 52, 275, 287, 296, 299–300, 305, 307ɪ, *307–09,* 311, 314, 315, 317
   Lady Be Good (musical), 311. *See also* Parker, Charlie
   Porgy and Bess, "Summertime," 15–17, 15ɪ, 17ʟᴄ, 39, 48, 52, *308–09,* 309ʟᴄ, 315
Gershwin, Ira, 17, 299, 300, 309
Gesualdo, Carlo, 95
Gewandhaus Orchestra (Leipzig), 216, 218
Gibbons, Orlando, 99
Gilbert and Sullivan, 311, 312
Gillespie, Dizzy, 299, 301
Ginsberg, Allen, 44ɪ
Giotto, 80
Giraud, Albert, 320, 323
Glass, Philip, 354
Glinka, Mikhail, 255, 261
Gluck, Christoph Willibald von, 110, 146, 146ɪ, 202
Goethe, Johann Wolfgang von, 46, 145, 193, 194, 199
   Faust, 193, 194, 199, 202, 209, 361. *See also* Berlioz, Liszt
Goldberg, Johann, 120
Goodman, Alice, 352
Goodman, Benny, 295
Górecki, Henryk Mikolaj, 354
gospel songs, singing, 280–81, 281ɪ, 283
Götterdämmerung. See Wagner, Richard
Gould, Glenn, 11, 165
Gounod, Charles, 259
Graham, Martha, 51, 51ɪ, 310
Grateful Dead, 344
Gregorian chant. *See* plainchant
Gregory the Great, pope, 63, 64, 64ɪ
Gretchen am Spinnrade. See Schubert
Grieg, Edvard, 46, 213, 242, 253–54
Griffes, Charles, 304
Grisi, Giulia and Giuditta, 223–24
Guarneri family (violin makers), 116
Guarini, G. B., 95, 98
Gutenberg, Johannes, 81

H

Haley, Bill, and His Comets, 343
Hamlisch, Marvin, 288
Hammerstein II, Oscar, 311, 314. *See also* Rodgers and Hammerstein

Handel, George Frideric, 5, 42, 46, 50, 105, 106, 107, 112, 118, 119, *121–22,* 127, 132, 133, 138–40, 146, 176, 202
   Messiah, 10, 30, 50, 54, 122, *138–40,* 141ʟᴄ, 145, 148
Handy, W. C., *291–93*
   St. Louis Blues, 261, *292–94,* 294ʟᴄ
Hansen, Howard, 310
Hardin, Lil (Lillian), 293ɪ, 295
harmony. *See* melody and harmony
Harrison, George. *See* Beatles, The
Hartleben, Otto Erich, 320, 323
Harvard College, University, 276, 310, 332, 347, 351
Hawthorne, Nathaniel, 305
Haydn, Franz Joseph, 5, 42, 44, 46, 49, 50, 52, 58, 140, 145, 151, *157–59,* 158ɪ, 160, 161–64, 164–66, 172, 175–77, 181, 192, 193, 202, 243, 244
   Piano Sonata No. 59 in E♭ Major, *165–65,* 165ʟᴄ
   String Quartet in C Major, op. 76, no. 3 ("Emperor"), *161–63,* 163ʟᴄ, 324
   string quartets, 46, 147, 161
   symphonies, 25–26, 41, 156, 172, 176
Haydn, Michael, 157
Haydn Variations. *See* Brahms
Heiligenstadt Testament, 182–83
Heine, Heinrich, 178, 179
Hello, Dolly (film), 294
Henderson, Fletcher, 294, 295
Hendrix, Jimi, 346
Henry II, king of England, 75
Henry IV, king of France, 109
Henry VIII, king of England, 85
Hepburn, Audrey, 314
Herbert, Victor, 311
Heyward, DuBose, 17, 307, 309
Hildegard of Bingen, *69–71*
   Kyrie eleison, 69–71, 71ʟᴄ
Hilliard Ensemble, 9
Hillier, Paul, 12
Hindemith, Paul, 4, 332
Hines, Earl (Fatha'), 299, 301
Hitler, Adolf, 331
Hoboken, Anthony van, 165
Hollander, John, 338, 340
Holliday, Billie, 301
Holoman, D. Kern, 362ɪ
Holst, Gustav, 33, 254

Honegger, Arthur, 58, 58ɪ, 334
Hong Kong Philharmonic, 356
Horigome, Yuzuko, 116ɪ
Horne, Marilyn, 360
Hot 5, Hot 7 (Armstrong bands), 293ɪ, 294, 295
Houdon, Jean-Antoine, 146
Hugo, Victor, 202
Humperdinck, Englebert, 304
Hus, Jan, 250

I

Ibsen, Henrik, 46, 254
I Love Lucy (television), 296
incidental music, 46
InQuire, 12, 93
instruments. *See* musical instruments
Io mi son giovinetta. See Monteverdi
IRCAM, 342
Isaac, Heinrich, 83, 89
Israel Philharmonic, 350. *See also* Palestine Symphony Orchestra
Ives, Charles, 275, *305–07,* 305ɪ, 352
   "Putnam's Camp," from *Three Places in New England, 306–07,* 306ʟᴄ
Ives, George, 305
Ives, Harmony (*née* Twichell), 305

J

James II, king of England, 112
James, Harry, 296
Janáček, Leoš, 253
jazz, 4, 12, 41, 283, *290–301,* 307, 311
Jefferson, Thomas, 142
Jefferson Airplane, 344
Jennens, Charles, 141
Joachim, Joseph, 243
Joffrey, Robert, 51–52
John, king of Bohemia and duke of Luxembourg, 80
John, king of England, 75
Joplin, Janis, 346
Joplin, Scott, 1, *287–89,* 288ɪ, 295, 301, 317
   Maple Leaf Rag, 20, *287–88,* 289ʟᴄ, 389–91s
Joplin, Scott, Opera Company (New York), 288
Joseph II, emperor of Austria, 144
Josquin. *See* Desprez, Josquin
Joyce, James, 236
Juilliard School of Music, 310, 332

K

K. numbers. *See* Köchel
Kalisch, Gilbert, 303
Kallman, Chester, 333
Kandinsky, Wasilly, 319
Karr, Gary, 12
Keats, John, 59
Kennedy, John F., 3, 42, 333, 361
Kennedy, Nigel, 9, 360
Kennedy, Robert, 346
Kenton, Stan, 296
Kentucky Harmony, The, 279
Kerman, Joseph, 258
Kern, Jerome, 311
Kerr, Deborah, 314
key. *See* function, key
Khan, Ghengis, 81
King, Martin Luther, 283, 346
King James Bible, 3, 42
Kissinger, Henry, 352
Klimt, Gustav, 319
Klinghoffer, Leon and Marilyn, 352
Kneisel, Franz; Kneisel String
    Quartet, 303
Köchel, Ludwig von, 53, 160
Kodály, Zoltán, 254
Kolisch, Rudolf, 330
Koussevitzky, Serge, 8, 310, 331,
    333
Kovacs, Ernie, 360
Kreutzer, Rodolphe, 166
Kronos Quartet, 44ɪ, 357ɪ
*Kyrie eleison (Kyrie Cunctipotens
    genitor)* (plainchant), *67–69,*
    68ʟᴄ, 75–76, 372ꜱ

L

Lady Be Good (arr. from Gershwin).
    See Parker, Charlie
La Guerre, Elisabeth Jacquet de, 118
Landini, Francesco, 80
La Rue, Pierre de, 85
La Scala (Milan), 220, 229
Lasso, Orlando di, 90
Lawrence, Vera Brodsky, 288
Le Corbusier, 336
Led Zeppelin, 346
Leipzig Conservatory, 216, 301
Leitmotiv, 236–37
Lennon, Cynthia, 345–46
Lennon, John. *See* Beatles, The
Lennon, Julian, 345
Leonin, 42, 76
Lerner, Alan Jay. *See* Lerner and
    Loewe

Lerner and Loewe, 314
Lester, Joel, 347
Lester, Lottie May and Melvin,
    280–81
Letterman, David, 342
Li Po, 355
Lied, Lieder, 50, 192–94
Liederkreis. *See* song cycle
Ligeti, György, 342
Lind, Jenny, 224
Liszt, Cosima. *See* Wagner, Cosima
Liszt, Franz, 3, 42, 46, 160, 168,
    195, 199, 201, 207, *209–13,*
    210ɪ, 218, 242, 243, 253, 254,
    259, 304
liturgy (Roman), 64–66, 134
Loesser, Frank, 314
Loewe, Frederick. *See* Lerner and
    Loewe
Lomax, Alan, 279, 280
Lombardo, Guy, and His Royal
    Canadians, 296
London Sinfonietta, 354
Longfellow, Henry Wadsworth,
    253
Longshaw, Fred, 293
Lorenzo the Magnificent. *See* Medici,
    Lorenzo de'
Los Angeles Philharmonic, 353
Louis XII, king of France, 89
Louis XIV, king of France, 104, 106,
    106ɪ, 118
Louis XV, king of France, 118, 159
Louis XVI, king of France, 144, 179
Louis-Philippe, king of France, 201
LP (long-playing) records, 298,
    336
Lucerne Festival, 332
Ludwig II, king of Bavaria, 241
Lully, Jean-Baptiste, 105, 118
Luther, Martin, 89, 133–34, 137
Lutos awski, Witold, 334

M

Ma, Yo-Yo, 9ɪ, 356
MacDowell, Edward, 4, 302, 304
MacDowell Colony, 304
Machaut, Guillaume de, 42, 80, 82,
    325
Mackey, Steven, 2ɪ, 356, 357ɪ
Madonna (singer), 354
madrigal, 42, 48–49, 58, 83,
    94–99, 100
Maelzel, Johann Nepomuk, 23
Maeterlinck, Maurice, 46, 261
Mahler, Alma (Schindler), 248

Mahler, Gustav, 7, 33, 44, 48, 168,
    191, 192, 227, 243, *247–49,*
    249ɪ, 256, 259, 267, 287, 316,
    319, 331
Malibran, Maria, 224
Mallarmé, Stéphane, 260, 261, 361
Mannes College of Music, 350
Mannheim orchestra, 146
Manzoni, Alessandro, 229
Mao Tse-tung, 352
Maple Leaf Rag. See Joplin, Scott
Mapplethorpe, Robert, 359
Marais, Marin, 118
Marcabru of Gascoigne, 74
Maria Theresa, empress of Austria,
    144, 147, 159
Marie Antoinette, queen of France,
    144
Marie-Louise, empress of France,
    179
Martenot, Maurice, 336
Martin, Mary, 313
Martinez, Andréz, *93–94*
    Agnus Dei, from "Zapotec" Mass,
    93–94, 94ʟᴄ
Martino, Donald, 341, 347
Mary II, queen of England, 112
Masons. *See* Freemasonry
mass, 42, 49, *65–66,* 83–84
Massine, Léonide, 264
Mather, Cotton, 276
Matheson, Johann, 120
Mathías, Juan, 93
Mazurka in A Minor. *See* Chopin
McCartney, Paul. *See* Beatles, The
McRae, Gordon, 314ɪ
Meck, Nadezhda von, 256, 260
Medici, Lorenzo de' (Lorenzo the
    Magnificent), 83
Medici, Marie de', 109
medieval music. *See* Middle Ages
Mehta, Zubin, 125, 350
Meier, Golda, 361
melody and harmony, *25–27*
Mendelssohn, Felix, 5, 42, 45, 46,
    50, 56, 140, 160, 168, 195,
    201, 207, 216, 217, *218,* 252,
    254
Mendelssohn, Moses, 218
Mengelberg, Willem, 249
Menotti, Gian Carlo, 335
Menuhin, Yehudi, 9, 361
Messiaen, Olivier, 334
Messiah. See Handel
meter. *See* rhythm and meter
Metropolitan Opera (New York),
    248, 258, 332, 335

Meyerbeer, Giacomo, 207, 225
Michelangelo, 1, 105–06
Michener, James, 312
Middle Ages, 5, 41, 42, 52, 58, *63–81*
Midori, 9
Mighty Handful, the, 58, 254–55
Miley, Bubber, 297
Milhaud, Darius, 53, 53i, 58, 58i, 290, 332, 334
Miller, Glenn, 295
Mills College, 53, 332
Mingus, Charles, 301
minimalism, 350–51
Minneapolis Orchestra, Minnesota Orchestra, 332, 353
minuet-and-trio, 57, 156–575
Missouri Harmony, The, 279
Mitropoulos, Dimitri, 332
Modern Jazz Quartet, 301
modern music. *See* 20th-century music
modes, church, 69
modulation. *See* cadence, modulation
moguchaya kuchka. See Mighty Handful
Molière, 105, 118, 175, 361
Molinet, Jean, 85, 88
Monet, Claude, 260
Monk, Thelonius, 301
Montesquieu, Charles-Louis, Baron de, 143
Monteverdi, Claudio, 33, 42, *95–99,* 97i, 106, 107–08, 109–10, 268, 272
   Io mi son giovinetta, 95–97, 98LC, 103, 125
Montpensier, Mademoiselle de, 118
Montreal Symphony, 9
Moog, Robert, 342
Morley, Thomas, 100
Morton, Jelly Roll, and His Red Hot Peppers, 295
motet, 42, 49, 77–78, 82, 83, 84–85
Motown Records, 343
Mouret, Jean-Joseph, 117–18
Mozart, Constanze (*née* Weber), 160, 161
Mozart, Leopold, 146, 159, 159i, 305
Mozart, Maria Anna (Nannerl), 159, 159i
Mozart, Wolfgang Amadeus, 7, 8, 9, 10, 11, 12, 42, 45, 46, 50, 58, 59, 105, 107, 143, 145, 146, 151–57, *159–61,* 159i, 160i,

163, 166, 166–72, 172–74, 174–75, 175–76, 181, 183, 192, 193, 202, 216, 217, 243, 248, 249, 259, 349, 361
  chamber music, 46, 161, 164
  kleine Nachtmusik, Eine, K. 525, 20, 21i, 39, 57, 148, 149, 151, *152–57,* 155LC (movt. I), 156LC (movt. III), 161, 378–81s (movt. I), 382s (movt. III)
  operas, 51, 143, 155, 160, 164, 174–75
  Piano Concerto in C Major, K. 503, 162, *168–72,* 171LC
  symphonies, 53, 160, 172, 186, 335
  Symphony No. 40 in G Minor, K. 550, movt. I, 56, *172–74,* 173LC
Münch, Charles, 331
Murrow, Edward R., 335
musical instruments, *31–35*
Music Educators National Conference (MENC), 304
Music Teachers National Association (MTNA), 304
musique concrète, 336
Mussorgsky, Modest, 581, 255, 255i, 263
Mutter, Anne-Sophie, 9

N

Napoleon Bonaparte, emperor of France, 3, 42, 53, 144i, 145, 162, 177, *179–81,* 180i, 183, 199, 200
National Conservatory of Music, New York, 253
nationalism, 200–01, 207, 210, 229, *250–54*
NBC, NBC Symphony, 335–36
Negro spiritual. *See* spiritual
Nehru, Jawaharlal, 360–61
Neue Leipziger Zeitschrift für Musik, 217
New East St. Louis Toodle-O. See Ellington
New England singing schools, 276, 277
New England School (Conservatory) of Music, 302
Newport Jazz Festival, 301
Newton, Isaac, 104
New York City Ballet, 268
New York Philharmonic, 11–12, 125, 248, 314, 316, 332, 342

Nietzsche, Friedrich, 236
Nijinska, Bronislava, 264
Nijinsky, Vaslav, 263–64, 264i, 268, 331
Nixon, Marni, 314
Nixon, Patricia, 352
Nixon, Richard, 352
Nonesuch Records, 288, 354
Nono, Luigi, 330
Norma. See Bellini
Norman, Jessye, 8, 9i, 283
Norman Conquest, 2, 42
Norrington, Roger, 9
Notker the Stammerer, 73
Notre Dame School (Paris), 41, 58, 76–77
nuance, 30
Nuper rosarum flores (Dufay), 85
Nureyev, Rudolf, 295

O

Oath of the Tennis Court, 179, 180i
Obrecht, Jacob, 83, 89
Ockeghem, Johannes, 42, 82, 82i, 83, 85–86, 88
Offenbach, Jacques, 286, 331
Oliver, King, 294, 295, 317
Onassis, Jacqueline Kennedy, 316
Ono, Yoko, 345–46
opera, 42, 50–51, 108–10, 113–14, 174–75, 220–25, 228–43
opera buffa, 121, 174
"Opera in Temple Street." *See* Tan Dun
opera seria, 110, 121, 146, 174, 175, 221
operetta, light opera, 311
oratorio, 42, 50, 133, 138–341
organum, 75–77
Ormandy, Eugene, 11
Otello. See Verdi
Ozawa, Seiji, 8i, 9

P

Pachelbel, Johann, 115–16
Paganini, Nicolo, 196, 199, 209, 209i
Palestine Symphony Orchestra, 332
Palestrina, Giovanni da, 90
Pange lingua (plainchant), 71–72, 72LC, 372s
Paris Conservatoire, 53, 202, 206, 260, 269, 302, 332
Paris Conservatory Orchestra, 45i, 203, 218, 331

Parker, Charlie, *299–301*
  Lady Be Good, 299–300, 300LC
Parker, Horatio, 302, 305
passacaglia, 113, 114, 115, 245, 246
passion, 137–38
Pasta, Giuditta, 223
Patti, Adelina, 224
Pavarotti, Luciano, 8, 258
Pavlova, Anna, 268
Pears, Peter, 258, 333
PBS, 335
Penderecki, Krzysztof, 334
Perahia, Murray, 12, 170
Perceval, 74
Pergolesi, Giovanni Battista, 138, 146
Peri, Jacopo, 108–09, 108I, 111
Perle, George, 341, 347
Perlman, Itzhak, 125
Perotin, 42, 76–77
Petrucci, Ottaviano, 88
"Petrushka" chord, 265
Philadelphia Orchestra, 11, 331
Philip the Good, duke of Burgundy, 82
Philomel. See Babbitt
piano sonata, 159, 164–66
Picasso, Pablo, 264, 269, 269I, 361
Pierrot lunaire. See Schoenberg, Arnold
Pink Floyd, 342
Pinza, Ezio, 313
Pippin, Donald, 51
Piston, Walter, 310
pitch, *19–20*
plainchant, 20, 42, *64–74*
Play of Robin and Marion, The, 52
Polo, Marco, 81, 107
polyphony. *See also* texture
  development of, 75–80
  imitative, 29, 83–84
pop. *See* rock and pop
Porgy and Bess. See Gershwin, George
Porter, Cole, 48, 311
Poulenc, Francis, 58, 58I, 334
Prague Conservatory, 253
Prague National Theater, 250
Presley, Elvis, 343–44, 343I
Price, Leontyne, 283, 308
Princess Theater (New York), 311
Princeton University, 310, 341, 347, 356
Private Game. See Ran
program music, 203, 212, 248

Prokofiev, Sergei, 31–32, 46, 168, 315, 331, 334
  Peter and the Wolf, 12, 31–32, 39, 52, 333
Proust, Marcel, 46
Psalm 24. *See* Boulanger, Lili
Puccini, Giacomo, 220, 224, 233, 256, 258
Pulitzer Prize, 288, 350, 354
Purcell, Henry, 8, 31, 42, *112–13*
  Dido and Aeneas, "Dido's Lament," 8, 111, *113–15,* 114LC, 373–75S
"Putnam's Camp." *See* Ives, Charles
Putnam, Israel, 306, 307

𝒬

Quantz, Johann Joachim, 146
Queens College, 347
Querelle des Buffons, 146

ℛ

R&B, 343
Rabelais, François, 89
Rachmaninov, Sergei, 263, 331
radio, radio orchestras. *See* broadcasting
ragtime, 283, 287–89, 292, 293, 304
Rainey, Ma, 293
Rameau, Jean-Philippe, 118
Ramey, Samuel, 360
Ran, Shulamit, 42, *347–50,* 349I
  Private Game, 347–49, 349LC
Raphael (Raffaello Sanzio), 1
Ravel, Maurice, 59, 164, 226, 227, 259, 262, 264–65, 272
Razumovsky, Count Andreas, 164, 181, 184
RCA, RCA Victor, 335, 336, 337
RCA Mark II synthesizer. *See* synthesized sound, synthesizer
Reading abbey, 78
Reich, Steve, 354
Reicha, Anton, 206
Renaissance, the, 3, 5, 6, 29, 32, 42, 49, 52, *81–103*
Requiem Mass, 49, 73, 85–86
Revere, Paul, 276
Revolution, Revolutionary War (American), 143, 275
Revue wagnerienne, 242
rhythm and blues. *See* R&B
rhythm and meter, *22–25*

Richard I (the Lion-Hearted), king of England, 75
Ricordi, 220
Rifkin, Joshua, 288
Riley, Terry, 351
Rimbaud, Arthur, 260
Rimsky-Korsakov, Nicolai, 31, 58, 207, 255, 261, 263, 265
Rinuccini, Ottavio, 109
Rite of Spring, The. See Stravinsky
Robbins, Jerome, 314
Robeson, Paul, 283
Robison, Paula, 12
rock and pop, 301, 319, *343–48*
Rodgers, Richard. *See* Rodgers and Hammerstein
Rodgers and Hammerstein, 52, 309, *311–14*
  "Some Enchanted Evening," from *South Pacific, 312–14,* 313LC
Rodrigo, Joaquin, 254
Roller, Alfred, 248
Rolling Stones, The, 346
Romani, Felice, 223, 224
Romanticism, 42, 43, *179–225*
  late Romanticism, *227–72*
Romberg, Sigmund, 311
rondeau, rondo, 117–18, 320–21, 348
Roosevelt, Eleanor, 360
Rosen, Charles, 144
Ross, Arnold, 299
Ross, Diana, 343
Rossini, Gioachino, 7, 45, 50, 107, 220, 221, 225
Rostropovich, Mstislav, 333
Rousseau, Jean-Jacques, 143
Rubinstein, Artur, 350
Rubinstein, Nicolai, 254
Rückaufová, Terezie, 250I
Ruckers family (harpsichord makers), 117
Rückert, Friedrich, 249
Rudolph, archduke of Austria, 164
Russian Revolution, 331

𝒮

Sachs, Nelly, 350
Sacred Harp, The; Sacred Harp singing, 279–81
Sacre du printemps, Le. See Stravinsky: *Rite of Spring*
St. Gall (monastery of), 73
St. James of Compostela, cathedral of, 73, 75

St. Louis Blues. See Handy
St. Mark's basilica (Venice), 58, 107, 107ɪ
St. Martial of Limoges (monastery of), 73
St. Peter's basilica (Rome), 105–06
St. Stephen's cathedral (Vienna), 157, 192
Saint-Saëns, Camille, 9, 12, 46, 213, 242, 259–60
Salieri, Antonio, 175–76, 177
Salomon, Johann Peter, 176
Salzburg Festival, 332
San Antonia di Padua, Mission, 93ɪ
Sand, George, 215
San Francisco Conservatory, 351
Sarnoff, David, 335
Sayn-Wittgenstein, Carolyne, Princess, 210, 212
scales, *35–36*
Scarlatti, Alessandro, 126, 145
Scarlatti, Domenico, 107, 145
Schaeffer, Paul, 342
Schikaneder, Emanuel, 174
Schiller, Friedrich von, 221, 355
Schindler, Alma. *See* Mahler, Alma
Schindler, Anton, 187–88
Schmieder, Wolfgang, 53
Schnitger, Arp, 117
Schoenberg, Arnold, 42, 58, 247–48, *319–24,* 320ɪ, 327, 331, 333, 347, 349, 361ɪ
   Pierrot lunaire, 61, *320–24,* 323ʟᴄ, 347
Schoenberg, Gertrud (*née* Kolisch), 330
Schoenberg, Mathilde, 330
Schoenberg, Nuria, 330
schools, *58–59*
Schubert, Franz Peter, 42, 43, 48, 53, 168, 179, *192–95,* 192ɪ, 216, 243
   Gretchen am Spinnrade, 193–94, 194ʟᴄ
   songs, 48, 192–94
   symphonies, 53, 192, 194
Schuller, Gunther, 347
Schumann, Clara (*née* Wieck), 59, 196, 197, 198, 199ɪ, 216–17, 243
Schumann, Robert, 42, 48, 59, *195–99,* 199ɪ, 201, 207, 209, 212, 215, *216–18,* 243, 247, 254, 259
   Carnaval, 196–98, 198ʟᴄ, 320, 383–84s

Piano Concerto in A Minor, op. 54, 59, 168, 217–18
Schütz, Heinrich, 105, 112, 244
Scotto, Renata, 224
Scribe, Eugène, 224, 225
Second Viennese School, 58, 324, 327, 330
Sellars, Peter, 352
Semper fidelis. See Sousa
serial music, 42, *326–30,* 338–40
Serkin, Rudolf, 11
Sessions, Roger, 310, 341, 354
Seurat, Georges, 260, 317
seventh chord, 37–38 *See also* diminished seventh chord
Sex Pistols, The, 346
Sforza, Cardinal Ascanio, 88–89
Shakespeare, William, 46, 50, 56–57, 175, 193, 202–03, 218, 229–32, 361
Shankar, Ravi, 351
shape-note notation, 279–80, 388s
Shapey, Ralph, 350
Shaw, Artie, 296
Shaw, Robert Gould, 306
Shostakovich, Dmitri, 7ɪ, 44, 334
Sibelius, Jan, 44, 46, 201, 254, 333
Sills, Beverly, 224
Siloti, Alexander, 210ɪ
Silverstein, Joseph, 303
"Simple Gifts," 274
Sinatra, Frank, 296
Singspiel, 174
Six, Les, 58, 58ɪ, 334
Slick, Grace, 344
Smetana, Bedřich, 46, 201, *250–52*
   Bartered Bride, The, "Furiant," *250–52,* 250ɪ, 252ʟᴄ
   Moldau, The, 46, 251–52
Smith, Adam, 144
Smith, Bessie, 293, 294, 301, 317
Smith, George, College for Negroes, 288
Smithson, Harriet, 202–03, 202ɪ, 207
Société des Concerts du Conservatoire. *See* Paris Conservatory Orchestra
Société Nationale de Musique, 260
Soirée dans Grenade, La. See Debussy, Claude
Solti, Georg, 4
"Some Enchanted Evening." *See* Rodgers and Hammerstein
"Somewhere." *See* Bernstein, Leonard

sonata da camera, da chiesa, 47, 117
sonata form, 42, *55–57, 151–55,* 158, 160, 219–20
Sondheim, Stephen, 314, 316, 317, 341
song cycle, 42, 48, 188, 194, 195
Song of Roland, The, 74
Sony, 11, 12
Sophocles, 175
Soumet, Alexandre, 223
Sousa, John Philip, 23, *284–87,* 284ɪ, 288, 289, 304, 311
   Semper fidelis, 284–86, 286ʟᴄ
South Pacific. See Rodgers and Hammerstein
spiritual, 253, 282–83
Spontini, Gaspare, 202
Sprechstimme, 321
staff notation, *20–22*
Stalin, Joseph, 334
Starr, Ringo. *See* Beatles, The
"Star-Spangled Banner, The," 18, 49, 306
Stasov, Vladimir, 58, 254, 255
State University of New York at Stony Brook, 304
Steinbeck, John, 310
Stendhal, 202
stereophonic recording, 316, 336, 345
Stern, Isaac, 11, 125
Stockhausen, Karlheinz, 334
Stokowski, Leopold, 331
Stradivari family (violin makers), 116
Strauss, Johann, II, 243, 286, 331
Strauss, Pauline, 250
Strauss, Richard, 10, 31, 48, 227, 243, 249–50, 258, 259
Stravinsky, Igor, 4, 11, 42, 43, 107, 168, 259, 260ɪ, 264, *265–68,* 269ɪ, 272, 290, 309, 331, 332, 334, 361
   ballets, 51, 264, 265, 309, 333
   Rite of Spring, The, 12, 51, 228, 264, *265–68,* 268ʟᴄ, 309, 319, 322, 359
   Sacre du printemps, Le. See Rite of Spring, The
Strepponi, Giuseppina, 229
Striggio, Alessandro, 109
string quartet, 42, 44ɪ, 46, 148, 151, 161–64, 357ɪ
Sturm und Drang, 144
suite of dances (Baroque), 42, 45, 132–33

Sullivan, Ed, 344
Sumer is icumen in, 78–80, 78i, 80lc, 115
"Summertime." *See* Gershwin, George: *Porgy and Bess*
Supremes, The, 282, 343, 344i
Sutherland, Joan, 244
Sweelinck, Jan Pietrszoon, 112
swing. *See* big band
symphonic poem. *See* tone poem
Symphonie fantastique. See Berlioz
symphony, 42, 44, 151, 172–74.
    See also Beethoven, Berlioz, etc.
Symphony Hall (Boston), 227
synthesized sound, synthesizer, 34, 34i, *337–43,* 337i, 353
Szell, George, 4, 11, 332

T

Tailleferre, Germaine, 58, 58i
Takemitsu, Toru, 354
Tallis, Thomas, 90
Tan Dun, *354–56,* 355i
    "Opera in Temple Street," from *Symphony 1997, 354–56,* 356lc
Tanglewood Music Festival, 332
Taskin, Pascal, 117
Tasso, Torquato, 95
Tate, Nahum, 113, 114
Tchaikovsky, Piotr, 3, 24, 42, 44, 56, 168, 242, 247, 249, 252, *256–58,* 256i, 331
    ballets, 46, 51, 256
    operas, 256
    Romeo and Juliet, overture-fantasy, 56–57, *256–57,* 257lc
    symphonies, 24, 256, 258
Te Kanawa, Kiri, 360
Telemann, Georg Philip, 119–20
television, 316, 335–36, 360
Texaco, 335
texture, 27–29
Théâtre des Champs-Élysées (Paris), 267
Theremin, Léon, 336
Thomas, Dylan, 333, 337
Thomas à Becket, 78
Thomas de la Hale, 78
Thomas, Michael Tilson, 9
Thoreau, Henry David, 276, 305
Three Places in New England. See Ives, Charles
TimeWarner, 12
Tippett, Michael, 333

titles, *52–54*
tonality, 26, 35–39, 69, 103, 106
tone poem, 42, 46
Toscanini, Arturo, 332, 335
trio sonata, 47, 117
Tristan und Isolde (Anglo-Norman romance), 74
"Tristan" chord, 240–41
Triumphes of Orianna, The, 100
troubadours, trouvères, 74–75
Turina, Joaquin, 254
twelve-tone composition. *See* serial music
20th-century music, 43–44, *319–57*
Tyler, Anne, 1

U

United States Marine Band, 284, 288
University of California, Berkeley, 332
University of California, Davis, 347, 362
University of California, Los Angeles (UCLA), 330
University of Chicago, 347, 350
University of Pennsylvania, 347
University of Southern California (USC), 330
Updike, John, 1
Upshaw, Dawn, 9, 354
Utah Symphony, 304

V

Vanhal, J. B., 158, 161
Varèse, Edgard, 336
Variations on a Theme by Haydn. *See* Brahms
Vasnier, Madame, 260
Vaughan Williams, Ralph, 254
Verdelot, Philippe, 85
Verdi, Giuseppe, 42, 43, 50, 107, 168, 201, 220, 221, 222, 224, 225, *228–33,* 228i, 243, 249, 253, 258, 259, 335
    Otello, 51, *229–33,* 232lc
Verrett, Shirley, 283
Versailles, 106, 133, 179
Viardot, Pauline, 224
Victoria, queen of England, 218, 282
Victoria, Tomás Luis de, 90, 93
Vidal, Peire, 74
Vienna Opera, 248
Vienna Philharmonic, 248, 316

Vinci, Leonardo da, 1, 89
Viñes, Ricardo, 261
Virgil, 112, 209
Vishnevskaya, Galina, 333
Vivaldi, Antonio, 9, 42, 105, 106, 118–19, 119i, 126–27, 335
vocal music, 47–50
Vogl, Johann Michael, 192
Voice of Firestone (radio series), 335
voices and instruments, *30–35*
Voltaire, 143, 314
von Bülow, Hans, 199
Vyšehrad castle, 251

W

Wagner, Cosima (*née* Liszt, von Bülow), 199, 213, 241, 242
Wagner, Richard, 7, 42 43, 50, 54, 107, 168, 199, 207, 209, 212, 213, 216, 222, 223, 225, 227, 228, *233–43,* 233i, 247, 248, 254, 258, 259, 260, 331
    "Brunnhilde's Immolation." *See Götterdämmerung*
    Götterdämmerung, 226, 235, *237–40,* 239lc, 242
    Ring of the Nibelung, The, 234–40, 235i, 241
    Tristan und Isolde, 234, 240–41, 31
Wagner, Wieland, 242
Walter, Bruno, 249
Warfield, William, 308
Webb, Chick, 296
Webber, Andrew Lloyd, 317
Weber, Aloysia, 160
Weber, Carl Maria von, 200, 201, 205, 236, 252, 259
Weber, Josepha, 160
Weber, Sophie, 160
Webern, Anton, 42, 58, *324–31,* 324i
    Symphony, op. 21, *324–30,* 326lc
Weelkes, Thomas, 100
Well-Tempered Clavier, The. See Bach, J. S.
Wesendonk, Mathilde, 240
Wesley, Charles, 280
Western Union Telegraph Co., 335
West Side Story. See Bernstein, Leonard
White, Benjamin Franklin, 279
White, George L., 282

Whiteman, Paul, 296, 307
Who, The, 346
Widor, Charles-Marie, 259
Wieck, Clara. *See* Schumann, Clara
Wieck, Friedrich, 218
Wielhorsky, Michel and Mateusz, Counts, 181
Wilbye, John, 100
Wilde, Oscar, 1, 258
Wilder, Thornton, 310
William III, king of England, 112
Williams, Cootie, 297, 298

Willson, Meredith, 287
Winchester Cathedral Choir, 93
Wipo of Burgundy, 73
Wonder, Stevie, 343
Wood, Natalie, 314
World War I, 3, 9, 42, 43, 227, 228, 262, 286, 296, 297, 305, 311, 319
World War II, 3, 42, 43, 249, 296, 298, 310, 311, 313, 319
Wright, Frank Lloyd, 304
Wuorinen, Charles, 341, 347

Yale University, 302, 305, 332
Yi of Zeng (nobleman), 355
Youmans, Vincent, 311

Z

"Zapotec" Mass. *See* Martinez, Andréz
Zinman, David, 354
Zwilich, Eileen Taaffe, 354